# Scream Queens

# Scream Queens

## HEROINES OF THE HORRORS

## Calvin Thomas Beck

*Robert Stewart, Associate Editor*

COLLIER BOOKS
A Division of Macmillan Publishing Co., Inc.
New York

COLLIER MACMILLAN PUBLISHERS
London

# A Note of Acknowledgment

We would like to express our gratitude to the many fine hands that have made our tasks all the more pleasurable and easy during the long period of time that it has taken to produce *Scream Queens*. Walt Lee's encyclopedic *Reference Guide to Fantastic Films* proved to be of immense value. This three-volume set (available from Chelsea-Lee Books, Box 66273, Los Angeles, California 90066) should be on the shelf of any reader/filmgoer with the slightest interest in this area of film. Correspondence re *Scream Queens*, along with any additions or corrections that the reader would care to offer, will be more than gratefully accepted. This invitation also extends to *Heroes of the Horrors*, the companion volume to *Scream Queens*. Many thanks to those individuals who have aided in this project: Brooke Wilding, for her finely honed translations of necessary foreign-printed materials; Geoffrey Mahfuz, who turned up with previously unlocatable film pressbooks; Richard "Reginie" Einiger, for his valuable insights into the exhibitor's point of view; Chris Steinbrunner, for a wealth of cinematic lore, and a special tribute to Chris's mother, the late Maria Steinbrunner; the late Bert Gray; John Cocchi, adept at answering the trickiest research questions; Paul Roen, for his critical perceptions; Drew Simels, for invaluable research and editorial assistance; Lorraine Steurer, for copyediting that leads one safely through the Typographic Jungle. Also: Ed Reicher, Leigh Hanlon, Bob Schaeffer, Mrs. Emory Lewis, Tim Johnson, Sol Goldstein, Donald C. Willis, Don Glut, William Griffin, Don Longobucco, Kay Wanous, Larry Ivie, Joe Dante, Jr., Jon Davison, Ellen Couch, Cherry Weiner, Alex Soma, Joe Franklin, Michel Parry, Marc Ricci, J. R. T. Hopper, Vic Ghidalia, Keith Hall, Jr., Stanley Wanagiel, and Rita Altemara. We are especially grateful to Simone Blaché for making available rare photographs from her family collection.

—C.T.B.

Macmillan Publishing Co., Inc.
866 Third Avenue, New York, N.Y. 10022.
Collier Macmillan Canada, Ltd.

Library of Congress Cataloging in Publication Data
Beck, Calvin Thomas.
  Scream queens.
  Bibliography: p.
  Includes index.
  1. Moving-picture actors and actresses—Biography. 2. Horror films—Biography. I. Title.
PN1998.A2B383  791.43′028′0922 [B]  78–15336
ISBN 0–02–508170–5
ISBN 0–02–012140–7 pbk.

First Collier Books Edition 1978

*Scream Queens* is also published in a hardcover edition by Macmillan Publishing Co., Inc.

Printed in the United States of America

# Scream Queens

Barry Brown, 1951–1978

# *Dedication*

Probably the highest pleasure derived from having a lifetime love affair with SFantasy-horror is to discover a few kindred souls with whom I've been able to share my thoughts and infatuations. Before long, one shares one's pains, happiness, dreams, and aspirations with certain people who are sensitive enough to transcend the superficial routine of everyday existence and go searching with you for diamonds in the dust. My very dear friend, Barry Brown, was this kind of sensitive soul—perhaps too sensitive. He died, age twenty-seven, on June 25, 1978. This book is dedicated to his memory.

—C.T.B.

# Preface

Back in the 1940s, when we were all remarkably young, small, and impressionable and went to the movies, the action on the screen often came to a dismal, grinding halt during romantic girl-meets-boy interludes. This was tantamount to waving a red flag in front of a bull, especially during kiddie matinees: It would signal virtually all the youngsters to jeer, toss popcorn and spitballs around, or to run up and down the aisles for a candy bar or just to prove who was the loudest and most daring in a cathedral of flickering dreams and escapism.

When we grew older and were greeted by a far greater abundance of SFantasy films in the 1950s, theatre management still had the devil to pay with demanding kiddie audiences if screen fare bore any resemblance to the formula-bound, antiseptic productions popularized by Debbie Reynolds and Doris Day in their salad days. They were part of Hollywood's monolithic concept of the *female personality*. Whether in the 1940s or in the 1950s, youngsters were canny enough to avoid such claptrap by escaping to comic books, listening to dramas like "Suspense," "The Shadow," "I Love a Mystery," and "Jack Armstrong: The All American Boy" on the radio; and, on TV, there was "Lights Out!" "Captain Video," "Space Cadet," "Captain Midnight," "Tales of Tomorrow," and other preferred shows. And, of course, those great theatre matinees loaded with serial chapters, suspense-actioners, SFantasy features, and myriad cartoons.

As for the adults—coming from another era, jaded and weary—they lapped up everything that theatres would dish out at a time when admissions averaged between 50¢ and $1.00, before TV replaced one "adult-slanted" vacuum with another.

Being actually the best and most perceptive patrons of the arts, before social conditioning can program them into confused adults, youngsters have an innate understanding for the good, the bad, and the ugly, and loathe boredom with unbridled passion—especially mundane fakery and pretentiousness. While it may seem paradoxical that SFantasy has provided many of the gutsiest and most dynamic films, youngsters always have loved and comprehended the genre long before learning how to read. Today, adult audiences, recalling fondly their great hours of escape in the 1940s and 1950s, also support and encourage SFantasy to the degree that it is now a major industry on various media levels.

At a time when some production companies were still floundering in a myopic morass, dealing with built-in bombs like *At Long Last Love*, *A Matter of Time*, and the 1978 version of *Valentino* (all three may have been successful thirty-five years ago), more astute filmmakers knew their audiences better and created financially spectacular hits such as *The Exorcist*, *Young Frankenstein*, *Jaws*, and *The Omen*.

By combining some originality with major elements borrowed from *Flash Gordon*, *The Dam Busters*, *The Forbidden Planet*, *This Island Earth* (and its direct descendant, *Star Trek*), with some of the ambience of *The Wizard of Oz*, George Lucas, a genre buff since boyhood, used his talents ingeniously and brought in *Star Wars*, the most profitable production in film history. If not as profitable, Steven Spielberg's *Close Encounters of the Third Kind* now ranks among the five biggest box-office hits.

Outside of a few stars such as Greta Garbo, Bette Davis, and Joan Crawford, who personified some of the most flamboyant, if not liberated, screen characterizations throughout the thirties and forties, SFantasy acted as a great catalyst to counteract one-and-a-half dimensional stereotypes à la Day and Reynolds, only surpassed in monotony by Jeanette MacDonald, Esther Williams, and many other talented victims of the old studio system. When the cornball vehicles that stigmatized them died out overnight, MacDonald, Williams, and many others didn't endure for long.

Not all of SFantasy is above reproach. The genre has also developed some of its own bombs. Who can wax very wistful over Bert I. Gordon's filmic torture, *Village of the Giants*, and, more recently, *The Food of the Gods*? And how many are there who can look back with much fondness on two Jekylls no one could Hyde: *Son of Dr. Jekyll* and poor Edgar Ulmer's *Daughter of Dr. Jekyll*? And yet, though the list of unintentional filmic horrors could be longer, many preserve a mysterious fascination by remaining, at the very least, noteworthy and even timeless when measured against most non-genre failures.

Even when SFantasy films seemed to scrape bottom, its women may have been treated irreverently but rarely uninterestingly and irrelevantly. The number of ladies who have been carried off by fiends and monsters are by now legion; but where would all the creatures and heavies be without Scream Queens to complement their madness and depravity? Younger buffs and wide-eyed neo-fans may well marvel over Sissy Spacek coping with telekinetic horror in *Carrie*, Melinda Dillon in awe of UFOs (and maybe even of rambunctious Richard Dreyfuss) in *Close Encounters*, and Carrie Fisher giving Darth Vader his comeuppance in *Star Wars*. But none should forget their glorious antecedents and respective counterparts who range back over the years: Gail Russell in *The Uninvited*, Patricia Neal in *The Day the Earth Stood Still*, and Jean Rogers witnessing Ming the Merciless getting *his* comeuppance in *Flash Gordon*.

*Scream Queens'* mission is to put women's great contribution to SFantasy-horror films in proper perspective for the first time in book form. The opening chapter, "From Fort Lee with Fear," presents a historical overview, encompassing the genre since before the turn of this century and continuing on to the present. The following chapters are in chronological order, permitting you to time-travel through the film galaxy.

—Calvin Thomas Beck

# From Fort Lee with Fear

*L*ate in 1976, the image of the threatened, badgered, and embattled screen Scream Queen was radically altered with the blood-covered Sissy Spacek in Brian DePalma's highly popular *Carrie*, symbolizing all the world's tormented females taking a militant stance. High school misfit Carrie, turning on her enemies, unleashed a telekinetic mind-power blast of apocalyptic intensity in what was virtually a metaphysical display of the feminine collective unconscious achieving its ultimate revenge. The following year, Sissy Spacek assumed even more mythic dimensions as the avenging harpy of Robert Altman's *3 Women*. Spacek's progression from a *Prime Cut* (1972) white-slave victim to a mass-murder accomplice in *Badlands* (1973) to roles of superior female vengeance can be viewed as an exact encapsulation of the evolution of women in fantasy films from the beginning of film history. Both films and audience-awareness have matured from the days when secret rooms with sliding panels and actors in gorilla suits epitomized horror and suspense, when white-slavers lurked in

every alley, when the scream of a hapless and helpless heroine was a cue for the top-billed male performer to save the day.

There were, of course, early films in which women had control—not only as part of the filmic story plots but also as producers, writers, and directors (Alice Guy-Blaché, Lois Weber, June Mathis). All-but-forgotten today is *The Last Man on Earth* (1924), a film that seems to pick up where Altman's *3 Women* allegory ends. Mordaunt Hall reviewed it in *The New York Times*: "A boisterous and frivolous fantasy, concerned with a world of women and the sudden discovery of a solitary man. . . . It is the year 1960, when, through some curious plague, all males over fourteen become victims and die. The women do not seem grief-stricken as they go about their respective duties with bright faces and weird costumes. The fashions are given to transparent hoop skirts and pantaloons or the simpler mode of the one-piece bathing suit. The Presidentess of the United States has permitted the White House to become a ruin, with towering weeds and high grass

1

The terrified and enraged Carrie White (Sissy Spacek) stands drenched with blood and calls forth her telekinetic powers for purposes of destruction in Brian DePalma's *Carrie* (1976).

on the hitherto beautiful lawns." When Elmer (Earle Fox) is discovered, he is valued at $10 million and sent to the White House to witness a prizefight between the "Senatoress" from Massachusetts and the "Senatoress" from California. Elmer is the prize. "An entertainment for the brain-weary" was Hall's summation. Donald W. Lee's screenplay was based on a story by John D. Swain, and Jack G. Blystone directed for Fox. With tinted sequences, the film also starred Derelys Perdue and Grace Cunard.

In 1933 *The Last Man on Earth* was remade by Fox as a sound film titled *It's Great to Be Alive* (with simultaneous shooting of a Spanish-language version, *El Ultimo Varón Sobre la Tierra*). *The Last Man on Earth* may have been prompted by the publication in 1923 of John Long's novel, *When Woman Rules!*, something of a precursor to the 1958 *World Without Men* by Charles Eric Maine (pseudonym for David McIlwain). Alice Guy-Blaché's Solax Company brought the matriarchy theme to film even earlier than *The Last Man on Earth*

when she produced *In the Year 2000* (1912), a satire soon followed by the Joker Company's *In the Year 2014* (1914).

The Solax Company was located in Fort Lee, New Jersey—where the Scream Queens began. Only they weren't called Scream Queens back then. Instead, they were known as Serial Queens, and Fort Lee was picked as the site of these early cliff-hangers because the Jersey Palisades provided one hell of a cliff to hang from. Overlooking the banks of the Hudson River, Fort Lee was first settled around 1700. Built to command the Hudson, the Fort was abandoned by General Greene on November 20, 1776, after Fort Washington, across the river, was taken by the British. Incorporated as a municipality in 1904, Fort Lee became an early focal point of filmmaking activity partially because it was convenient to Manhattan.

As recently as 1960 there were still a few barnlike remnants of what was once a vast array of studios when Hollywood was on the Hudson. Of the few that survived, several had already succumbed to decay from neglect or abandonment. Others had been converted to warehouses. One remained, for many years, the property of Mrs. Elmo Lincoln, widow of the original screen Tarzan seen in *Tarzan of the Apes* (1918). The filmmakers had long departed, and the building served its final years as an embroidery mill, later standing as an empty hulk. Inside, it still retained the high overhead catwalks and beams originally constructed to hoist spots and backdrops. A MidLantic Bank occupies the lot today, obliterating all memories of this studio.

Situated on Bergen Boulevard in Ridgefield, New Jersey (bordering on Fort Lee), it was only one of the many film-making centers that spread out from Fort Lee, down to North Bergen, Union City, and Jersey City. The untrammeled countryside that once existed on the Palisades from North Bergen to the land north of Fort Lee was conducive to the making of Westerns, thrillers, chillers, and serial adventures. By 1950, the creeping menace of suburbanization had arrived. Over the next few years

ABOVE: An early "screening" (c. 1880s) before regular movie projection became a reality.

BELOW: Writer-director Lois Weber collaborated with Fred Miller on the screenplay of the first *Tarzan of the Apes* (1918). *Left to right*: Colin Kenney, Thomas Jefferson, George French, Elmo Lincoln (as Tarzan), Enid Markey (as Jane), and Bessie Toner. Scott Sidney directed. Edgar Rice Burroughs had many complaints, but the film was an instant success.

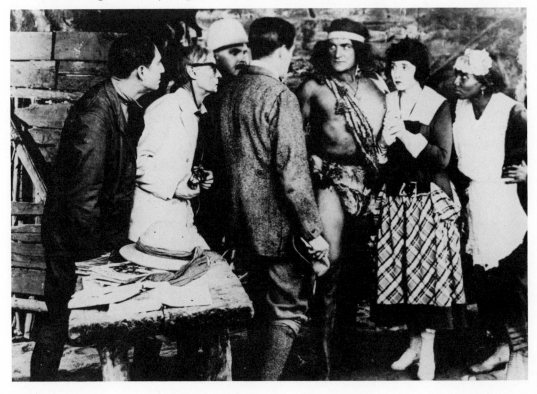

these nostalgic lanes of film memories would diminish and all but vanish. By the seventies they were buried under vast high-rise monoliths that now bestride the Palisades like imperial guardian colossi, sentinels for what remains—a patch of land known as North Hudson Park, across the street from where this is being written.

When the condominium owners and apartment dwellers descend from their aeries, they find few reminders of the area's moviemaking roots. There is a striking post-office mural depicting Fort Lee's film heritage. There are occasional library and museum exhibits of old production stills, and sometimes the New Jersey newspapers carry film-nostalgia features. There is Bonded Film Storage, a large edifice filled with film vaults, serving as a mausoleum for the movies. But, for the most part, the citizens go about their daily business, hardly giving a thought to the fact that they are walking the streets where Scream Queens were first transmogrified into flickering shadows, long, long ago.

In those days, casts and crews traveled to Fort Lee by ferry. Arriving at the 125th Street ferryhouse in Manhattan, the actors, while waiting for the ferry to arrive, sometimes grabbed a quick breakfast at Murphy's, a saloon and restaurant located near the ferryhouse. Once the ferry was underway, those without transportation might pass among the cars on the ferryboat to hitch a ride. The trip took about an hour.

On the Jersey side, one arrived at Edgewater at the foot of the cliffs—about three miles from Fort Lee. A drive beneath the trees along the river road led up steep grades that climbed to the top of the Palisades, bringing the merry filmmakers to Fort Lee's trolley-track-covered Main Street. Another four blocks brought them to a turn at Fourth Street (now Lemoyne Avenue). The drive continued through the woods to the dirt roads of Coytesville, about two miles from the Palisades. Here, on First Street, everyone gathered at Rambo's, a two-story hotel and tavern that was the central meeting place for film companies. One reason for the gathering was that Western saloon scenes were shot in front of Rambo's; another was that dressing rooms were available upstairs. Alongside the hotel was a grape arbor where everyone met for lunch, although nothing was ever served but ham, eggs, bread and butter, coffee, and apple pie. For a different menu, they sometimes ate at Pete Cella's hotel, a quarter-mile walk from Fort Lee's Main Street. If automobiles were needed for certain photoplays, they were rented from Mereo's Garage on Hudson Boulevard. One of the roads through the woods used for filming ran parallel to what is Anderson Avenue today. Heading for the cliffs, the actors would stage risky fight scenes. On the way up the Hudson to Englewood a number of homes, such as the Browning and Morror estates, were available for location use, when needed.

Mark Dintenfass, who headed the Champion Company, was the first to build a film studio in the Coytesville-Fort Lee area, in 1909. It was a building that remained standing for many years, occupied by the Hansford Brown Company. After audiences took delight in the New Jersey outdoor scenes of Edison's *The Great Train Robbery* (1903), directed by Edwin S. Porter (1869–1941), New Jersey was considered ideal for exteriors by the New York-based Vitagraph, Edison, and Biograph companies. The World-Peerless Studio was

1909: Al Christie doing a "Western"—in Bayonne, New Jersey.

built on Main Street in Fort Lee in 1914; Carl Laemmle's Universal Film Manufacturing Company had an important Fort Lee branch, and the Goldwyn Studios were in Fort Lee. In 1912 the French film director Alice Guy-Blaché built her $100,000 studio on Lemoyne Avenue, slightly west of what is today the Fort Lee Bridge Plaza; it was "the best-equipped moving-picture plant in the world." The Eclair Company also had its studio in Fort Lee, located on Linwood Avenue. Directing for Eclair was Etienne Arnaud (1879–1955), a former associate of Alice Guy-Blaché's at Gaumont in France, where he had directed from 1906 to 1911, beginning with *Attrapez mon Chapeau!* (1906). It was the first screenplay work of Louis Feuillade, later famed for his *Fantomas* serials.

This Hollywood East expanded to the surrounding areas: Pathé was situated at the corner of Webster Avenue and Congress Street in Jersey City Heights, and Louis Gasnier's Astra Film Company filmed out of this studio, releasing its films through Pathé beginning in 1915. A small film lab was located in Cliffside, New Jersey, and, in Bayonne, New Jersey, in 1908, Dave Horsley launched the Centaur Company, which changed its name to Nestor within the year.

Fort Lee's Main Street was dusty and unpaved. The trolley track had sidings that allowed the trolley to pull over to the side so that a trolley going in the opposite direction could pass. Two times a day, a horse pulled a wagon, with rear water sprinklers, down Main Street to lay the dust. One young actor who walked down Fort Lee's dusty Main Street was Milton Berle. In his autobiography, he reminisces about how his fabulous mother got him his first film

"May not actresses, who realize how fleeting youth is, preserve themselves in their prime?" asked the *Boston Herald* in 1896, when Benjamin F. Keith began showing Vitascope films at his Boston vaudeville house. Later, RKO was formed when Boston banker Joseph Kennedy entered the management of the Film Booking Office, and there followed a merger of FBO, the Keith-Albee-Orpheum vaudeville theatre circuit, and RCA to create "Radio-Keith-Orpheum." Next door to Keith's vaudeville palace is the Adams House, still in operation today as one of Boston's more pleasant eating establishments.

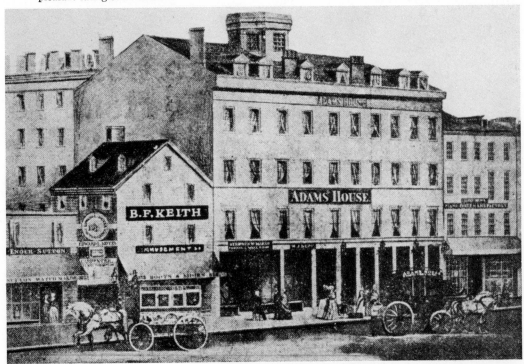

Replacing Alice Guy-Blaché at Gaumont in France was Louis Feuillade, who carried on the thriller tradition Alice had launched. In this scene from Feuillade's *Juve vs. Fantomas* (1917), Inspector Juve prepares for Fantomas's trickery by donning special spiked guards around his midriff—feeble defense against the snake entering through the window.

assignment. Pathé was making a Pearl White serial with Paul Panzer and Crane Wilbur. Milton's mother shrewdly bypassed Pathé's main offices in Jersey City Heights and went directly to where the film was going to be shot—in the countrylike surroundings of the Fort Lee–Coytesville area atop the Palisades.

"It meant my cutting school for a day," he says, "and Mama playing sick from the department store, but she didn't think twice about that. She had me up at the crack of dawn, and we set off for the Fort Lee ferry at 125th Street.

Despite never having been in this New Jersey area before, she instinctively seemed to know how to zero in on her goal, with little Milton by her side. The ferry arrived at the Edgewater dock under the towering Palisades cliffs, situated several miles from where production was going on.

"Mama and I got off, and she moved with all the sureness of Queen Victoria stepping down on native soil. Before I could look around, she had hitched us a ride with a farmer going in the right direction. He let us off right at Rambo's."

At last Milton's mother located the Pathé crew in the process of setting up scenes for *The Perils of Pauline*. Milton was now on the first lap of his film career. "I was so young that I really didn't know what was going on. . . . Of course, I didn't know the first thing about putting on makeup—in those days, every actor did his own—but a nice, pretty lady came over to me and said, 'Let me help you, sonny.' All I remember about her is that she was friendly and that she had blonde hair with a headband across her forehead. I kept looking around hoping to see a 'star.' I wanted someone who really shone, and all the time I never knew it was Pearl White who was putting my makeup on me. I found out who she was only when we got over to the car of the railroad train on which we would be filming."

The Edison Company launched the Patents War in an effort to protect its camera, eventually resulting in the 1908 formation of the Motion Picture Patents Company (comprised of Edison, Biograph, Vitagraph, Essanay, Lubin, Selig, Kalem, Méliès, and Pathé), which sought to monopolize distribution, control film stock, maintain anonymity of actors, and freeze film lengths at one reel. Obviously, such backward-looking practices could not last long. Audiences insisted that the two reels of D. W. Griffith's *Enoch Arden* (1911) be shown together. Bootleg cameras were in use throughout the New York and New Jersey area, and detectives hired by the Patents Company to squelch this speakeasy filming were such a nuisance that this became one factor in the desertion of Fort Lee for other film locations. One detective who prowled the Fort Lee forests, like some misguided serial hero, was the relentless sleuth Al "Slim" McCoy. Fictionalized, McCoy and the other patents detectives figure prominently in the plot of Peter Bogdanovich's *Nickelodeon* (1977) comedy, a film that succeeds in capturing the spirit of the period by extrapolating the facts and anecdotes of film history.

Fred J. Balshofer, coauthor of the Fort Lee memoir, *One Reel a Week*, directed for the New York Motion Picture Company (also known as the Bison Company), and he remembered that "McCoy and his cohorts appeared every place we went to photograph around Coytesville. Someone in our company would spot one of the spies approaching and give me the signal. I folded the legs of the tripod, put the camera over my shoulder, and took off down the road or into the woods. When the detective reached Al Richard, who always remained behind, he usually suffered a change of heart and started back to where he came from. . . . When Jules Brulatour brought a camera built especially for the independents by Lumière in France, there seemed to be a ray of hope. The camera did not infringe on any of the Edison Patents."

But the camera didn't work, leaving Balshofer still subject to McCoy's harassments. "The towns of Fort Lee and Coytesville were so small it was a cinch for McCoy and his added assistants to hound

TOP: 1912: *The Suffragette* (Edison), hardly a social-consciousness epic, slapsticked feminist problems to the hilt.

BELOW: Dorothy Dunbar and Bill Shilling appeared in this Fort Lee-produced film, *Galatea*. This sequence shows the statue coming to life.

us. Now that the French camera was a bust, they bore down harder than ever. That forced us to do something about it, so in the summer of 1909 we sneaked out of New York City up to the small town of Neversink in the Catskill Mountains." But the problems continued, and by November of 1909, Balshofer and his Bison Company actors headed for the West Coast.

The interest in the West Coast as a more suitable site for filming began as early as 1907, and the real exodus westward got underway three years later after Colonel William Selig of Chicago's Selig Polyscope Company decided to build a $75,000 studio at Edendale, California. While Alice Guy-Blaché was directing her East Coast thrillers, Colonel Selig was envisioning a whole new angle—thriller stories in serial form. This idea was so potent that it was to remain a part of the motion-picture industry through many changing trends and fashions up until 1956, and it's not stretching a point to note that movies such as the James Bond series and TV shows such as *The Bionic Woman* continue the form.

In 1912 the Edison Company developed a tie-in with *McClure's Ladies World* magazine. While Edison released monthly one-reelers (each a complete story) under the overall title of *What Happened to Mary?*, *McClure's* printed each in the series as a short story, progressively detailing the misadventures of eighteen-year-old Mary (Mary Fuller) in New York after her escape from her foster father in a small town. Selig went to the *Chicago Tribune* and proposed a similar tie-in with a more exciting and romantic tale, *The Adventures of Kathlyn* (1913), starring the attractive blonde Kathlyn Williams. It was a calculated maneuver to aid the *Tribune* in its bitter and competitive circulation rivalry with six other papers. The resulting increase in circulation spurred later publication of the complete novel as a Bobbs-Merrill book.

*The Adventures of Kathlyn* had both wild animals and an Indian setting, and the serials that followed were constructed to showcase actresses threatened by any con-

ceivable kind of danger. Often the dangers were quite real. After *Who Will Mary Marry?* (1913), Edison actress Mary Fuller, who did all her own stunts, starred in *The Active Life of Dolly of the Dailies* (1914). Many of her filmed feats, such as racing a motorboat, were foolishly executed stunts she had never before attempted. In a climb down a rope made of bedsheets hanging from a seven-story window, she survived a fall, narrowly missing a sharp iron picket fence.

In 1914, a total of 11 serials began exhibition, including Pathé's *The Exploits of Elaine* with Pearl White; Kalem's 119-chapter *The Hazards of Helen* with Helen Holmes (who went to Universal and was replaced in mid-chapters by rodeo rider Helen Gibson); Universal's *Lucille Love, Girl of Mystery* with Grace Cunard of Paris (who was actually Harriet Mildred Jeffries of Columbus, Ohio); and Thanhouser's *The Million Dollar Mystery* with Florence La-Badie, Marguerite Snow, and James Cruze. This trio, the year previous, had appeared together in *Dr. Jekyll and Mr. Hyde*, also from the New Rochelle-based Thanhouser Company that had converted the New Rochelle Skating Rink into a film studio in 1910. Blonde and blue-eyed Florence La-Badie was born in Montreal in 1894, and began her film career with Biograph in 1912, but her film career—and her life—were destined to last only another five years. In the fall of 1917, the brakes of her automobile refused to work during a trip through the Adirondacks, and she died in an Ossining, New York, hospital. (Many years later, the life of another film personality was saved at the Ossining hospital when ten-year-old Peter Fonda, near death, was rushed there after a gun accident.)

The 23 chapters of *The Million Dollar Mystery* were filmed at a cost of $125,000, with $10,000 being won by secretary Ida Damon of St. Louis, Missouri, for the best 100-word solution to the mystery. The story concerned the hounding of Florence Hargreave (LaBadie) by a strange organization, the Black 100, seeking $1,000,000 from her father. While the chapters were grossing $1,500,000, playing in 7000 theaters, the *Chicago Tribune* serialized the Harold Mac-Grath novel. The success brought about a sequel serial that same year, *Zudora—The Twenty Million Dollar Mystery.*

Yet another tie-in, between Pathé and the Hearst chain, led to what is curiously the best-remembered of all the silent serials —*The Perils of Pauline* (1914). Why "curiously"? Because one only has to sit through a few scenes to realize that *The Perils of Pauline*, with its contrived situations, slapdash photography and farcical acting, was woefully inferior to the other serials of the day. A 1914 review in the *New York Dramatic Mirror*, commenting on the twelfth of the twenty episodes, read as follows: "Near the opening of this picture, several ingeniously arranged dissolves show a peril that Pauline (Pearl White) avoided in the previous installment. While she reads a newspaper account of the escape of lions at the wedding, which fate and Harry (Crane Wilbur) prevented her attending, the scene changed into the actual enactment of the startling events described in the paper. Of course, dissolves of this nature are not original with the Pathé director, but those used here seem particularly appropriate and well contrived. The twelfth chapter of *Pauline* lacks the thrills of some of its predecessors, although there is a fair amount of melodrama introducing the usual characters, supplemented by a band of gypsies. Owen (Paul Panzer) engages the leader of the band to kidnap Pauline and hold her pri-

TOP: Pauline Frederick (1883–1938) began in films in 1915 as a Famous Players actress. She was so acclaimed in the role of *Madame X* (1920) that it became her nickname. Her fiftieth film was *Her Honor, the Governor* (1926), with Boris Karloff. Her last was the 1937 *Thank You, Mr. Moto*, with Peter Lorre as Moto; Pauline played the mother of a Chinese prince.

CENTER: A 1915 production, filmed in Fort Lee, of *Joan of Arc*.

BOTTOM: Pearl Fay White (1889 – 1938), the "Queen of the Silent Serials." One of her more horrific serials was *The House of Hate* (1918), in which "The Terror" threatened.

soner in a sequestered camp. The plan works smoothly up to the point where the jealousy of a gypsy woman in love with the leader is aroused. As usual, Harry is scouring the country in search of his sweetheart. He meets the jealous woman, is advised of the whereabouts of Pauline, and downs her captor in a rough fight. Then the gypsy woman seems to repent her kindness, for she finds a huge snake, conceals it in a basket of flowers, and sends the offering to the 'pretty lady with the blonde hair.' Pauline buries her nose among the blossoms, and there the film ends, which is something like breaking off a story in the middle of a sentence. Settings for the picture are all that the incidents require. Acting is kept in the key of exaggerated melodrama."

The story had fantasy elements of reincarnation and mummies but mainly concerned the efforts of Owen to get his hands on the inheritance left to Pauline. A much more critical review of the sixth episode appeared in *The Moving Picture World*: "We can not truthfully say that this *Pauline* series is holding up very well. It started off finely, but is poor this week. This number carries the action on without getting it, in any true sense, along any. Rough incidents, in which the players are or seem to be in great peril, are not real action; they are film users and need to be a bit better done than in this two-reel offering to be thrilling. The photography is poor."

The paradox of the legend that has grown around this crude serial can partially be explained by the reuse of the title throughout the years. After Marie Dressler's 1918 burlesque, *The Agonies of Agnes*, there was a 1933 sound serial titled *The Perils of Pauline*, in which Pauline Hargrave (Evalyn Knapp), in Indochina, battles the nefarious Dr. Bashan (John Davidson) in the quest for a deadly-gas formula engraved on an ivory disc. Betty Hutton portrayed Pearl White in a rambunctious

Pearl White filming in Fort Lee on the Palisades rocky cliffs. Note ropes attached to both camera and performers as safety precaution.

biographical film, Paramount's *The Perils of Pauline* (1947), leading to announcements that Hutton would also appear in films based on the lives of Clara Bow, Sophie Tucker, and Theda Bara; these movies were never made. Clips of Pearl White in the 1961 *Days of Thrills and Laughter* compilation survey and the sixties TV series *Silents Please!* were followed by Universal's 1967 made-for-TV movie, *The Perils of Pauline*, an updated version in which the Russians try to put Pauline (Pamela Austin) into orbit. The 1967 film continues to play in current syndicated television bookings.

Another factor in the persistence of the odd legend that *Perils of Pauline* was the only important silent serial is simply that Pearl Fay White, who was born in 1889, *was* very popular in her time, being one of that first group of actresses whose names were promoted in print. She was billed as "Thrilling, Terrifying, Titanic, Terrific, The Death Defying Sensation, Pearl White" and "The Lady Daredevil of the Fillums," so the advertisements alone were enough to give one pause. The ad copy was very much allied to the circus-poster tradition. Despite the presence of an autobiography, *Just Me*, one has difficulty in separating the real Pearl White from the Pearl White of various promotional stunts. Nevertheless, it seems that a filmed riot scene in a Chinese restaurant was a genuine riot, the result of the restaurant management's deciding that it would rather not cooperate in the filming, and she really did ride a steel girder to the twentieth story of a building under construction on 42nd Street as part of an April 1917 recruiting campaign.

During the filming of one scene for *The Perils of Pauline*, a balloon was anchored about seventy-five feet in the air off the rocky cliffs near Coytesville. Closeups were being shot of Pearl White while the balloon's owner, Leo Stevens, hid out of sight in the basket of the balloon. The rocks suddenly shifted, and the balloon began an unscheduled flight across the Hudson toward New York. The balloon was not equipped for flight, having no rip cord to open the valve for a descent. By climbing the shrouds, Stevens was able to open the valve, and they made a rough but safe landing near Philadelphia later that day. This incident was also incorporated by Bogdanovich into his *Nickelodeon* homage. (Similar real-life folderol persists to the present day: A 1977 runaway balloon over Manhattan made the front page of the *Daily News*, but the newspapers seemed unaware that this was actually a staged event for a documentary film.)

In a 1922 stage performance in Paris, having just finished flying a suspended airplane over the heads of the audience, Pearl White was almost killed when she came in for a landing just as a fifty-pound weight plummeted to the stage, ripping one entire wing completely off the plane.

When the Grim Reaper finally did make an entrance, he beckoned not at Pearl but at her stunt man. Nothing in *Plunder* (1923), the story of buried treasure beneath a Manhattan skyscraper, had as much human drama as the grisly, hushed-up August 11, 1922, event that transpired during the filming. Dressed and bewigged as Pearl White, thirty-eight-year-old stunt man John Stevenson attempted a leap from a moving bus to the steel girder of a bridge. His hands slipped in the dust atop the gir-

*Plunder* (1923)—Pearl having the upper hand.

der, and he fell twenty-five feet, dying a short time later in Roosevelt Hospital from a concussion and skull fractures. Many bystanders believed that the victim of the accident was Pearl White herself, and, in the midst of this tragedy, Pathé added to the confusion by adhering to familiar publicity statements that Pearl White always did her own stunts. Pearl White made no comment on either Stevenson's death or the publicity lie. *Plunder* was her last serial. She vanished from the theatre screens and died in 1938.

Rivaling Pearl White in popularity was Ruth Roland, who was acclaimed the "Queen of the Thriller Serials." She had been born August 26, 1892, in San Francisco, and at the age of two had been billed as "Baby Ruth" in vaudeville. Returning to the stage at 16, she began at $35 a week with the Kalem Company in Santa Monica in 1911, appearing during the next few years in more than 200 one-reelers, climaxed by Kalem's *Girl Detectives* series. Her first serial was Pathe's *The Red Circle* (1915). By this time, the cliffhanger gimmick, leaving an episode unresolved as a method of inveigling patrons back for the next episode, had been fully established.

Other serials that began running in 1915 included Universal's *The Broken Coin* with Grace Cunard; North American Film Corporation's *The Diamond from the Sky* with Mary Pickford's sister Lottie; *The Fates and Flora Fourflush—The Ten Million Dollar Vitagraph Mystery Serial* (a three-chapter parody of *The Million Dollar Mystery*) with Clara Kimball Young; Signal's *The Girl and the Game* with Helen Holmes; Vitagraph's *The Goddess* (with Anita Stewart as Celestia, a lovely young woman who has been raised by millionaires to believe that she comes from heaven and must reform the world); Pearl White in *The New Exploits of Elaine* and *The Romance of Elaine*; Norma Phillips and Margaret Loveridge in Reliance's *Runaway June*; and Marguerite Courtot in Kalem's *The Ventures of Marguerite*.

The early serial trend of highlighting the heroine in the title continued into 1916

with Universal's *The Adventures of Peg O' the Ring* (starring Grace Cunard in the dual role of a woman scratched by a lion during pregnancy and her daughter who improbably shows werecat tendencies as a result); International Film Service's *Beatrice Fairfax* with Grace Darling; Kleine's *Gloria's Romance* with Billie Burke (who had married Florenz Ziegfeld the previous year, and who was portrayed by Myrna Loy in the 1936 *Great Ziegfeld*); Signal's *Lass of the Lumberlands* with Helen Holmes; Universal's *Liberty, A Daughter of the U.S.A.* with Marie Walcamp; Pathé's *Pearl of the Army* with Pearl White; Niagara's *Perils of Our Girl Reporters* with Helen Green; and Essanay's *The Strange Case of Mary Page* with Edna Mayo.

Wharton Studios' fifteen-chapter *The Mysteries of Myra* (1916), written by Charles W. Goddard and British psychical researcher Hereward Carrington, not only had Harry Houdini as technical adviser but also used two-color sequences along with atmospheric lighting and camerawork in what was the first American serial to explore parapsychology. Theodore and Leo Wharton directed. The story featured scenes of "thought monsters," plants emitting poison gas and elementals, as it told of

*Patria* (1916)—Irene Castle clutched.

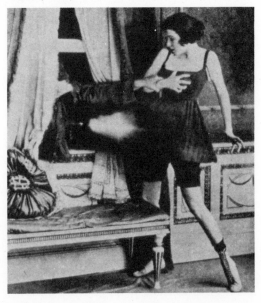

the threat to Myra (Jean Sothern) by a mystical organization, the Black Order. Before his death, her father had willed his fortune to the Black Order, specifying that they would receive the money only if all three of his daughters happened to die before the age of eighteen. Two of the girls have already committed suicide when occult investigator Dr. Payson Alden (Howard Estabrook) steps in to protect Myra. His occult investigation consists mainly of placing photographic plates against Myra's forehead to obtain "thought images." Art Varney (Allen Murnane) is torn between his love for Myra and his orders from the Black Order to hasten her death. Others in the cast were M. W. Rale and Bessie Wharton. The chapter titles reveal some of the other aspects of this serial: "Witchcraft," "The Elixir of Youth," "Levitation," "The Mystic Mirrors" and "Suspended Animation."

By this time the beckoning rays of California sunshine were illuminating the horizon. One of the earliest documented moves to California was in the fall of 1907 when Colonel Selig sent Thomas Parsons, director Francis Boggs, and some actors to Los Angeles, where they worked out of a former Chinese laundry on Eighth and Olive Streets, building sets on the roof for such films as *Carmen*. Selig, a former magician who had formed his company in 1897, had originally gone to California just to spend a winter there. The studio he later built on Alessandro Street in Edendale, covering a city block, was behind a vine-covered wall with ornate, Spanish-design, wrought-iron gates. Biograph moved to California in January 1910, taking over an abandoned carbarn at Pico and Georgia Streets. The Imp Company moved to California around 1911, starting a studio in Boyle Heights in East Los Angeles. In 1911 Dave Horsley moved his Nestor Company from Bayonne to California, where he constructed the first West Coast studio, across from a tavern at the corner of Gower Street and Sunset Boulevard. This was the Blondeau Tavern, headquarters of the Al Christie Westerns. The neighborhood later be-

came known as Gower Gulch, and its later history is dramatized in the 1975 feature *Hearts of the West*.

The Patents War, heavy taxes in the East, the April 6, 1917, American intervention in World War I, and a bitter 1917–18 winter with rationed coal and electricity couldn't compare with the diversity of locales surrounding Los Angeles, the California labor laws, low taxes, and a climate that provided at least three hundred days a year suitable for filming. For some it was paradise. Actor Nat C. Goodwin, in his 1914 autobiography, rhapsodized, "What a royal country is California! . . . As I stand under the trees at sunset, I contemplate a scene not equaled even in the beautiful Austrian Tyrol! . . . I see the bovine and the hog bow as the Angelus is heard. The lilac and the rose hold converse and whisper to the sun to shed less light that they may embrace and sink into the night. . . . All is hushed, the fowls bidden hence by the watchman, Chanticleer, to their respective homes, Mistress Hen to quench the fires and prepare for dawn. The stately Eucalyptus nods his head signifying that time is done. The sun apologetically starts away to make his daily run. The vegetables prepare themselves for the noonday meal, the barley and the oats keep tune to the zephyr's lullaby as they sink gracefully into slumberland. . . . My home is by the sea. My lot is one hundred feet wide. Its height is interminable. It is a thousand fathoms deep! My

1911: Dave Horsley's studio during Hollywood's earliest period.

front yard extends to the Antipodes. Am I not to be envied?"

Meanwhile, back in Fort Lee, the end was near. Apollo Pictures took over the Solax Studio in 1917, and, in June 1918, the Astra Company made its move to California, where it began filming out of the Universal Studios. Fewer and fewer actors made the trek from Manhattan to Fort Lee. The motion-picture photographer Arthur Miller, who lived in Fort Lee in the early twenties, noted, ". . . By this time Fort Lee had seen about the last of motion-picture studio production, and the migration to California was beginning to take its toll of the few studios in New York."

As the film industry made its quantum westward leap, there were evident changes in filmmaking styles and tempo, but they still lagged behind some European centers, especially Germany, where sophisticated idea patterns were developing more rapidly, stylistically as well as thematically. Outstanding artists of the macabre—such as Paul Wegener, Conrad Veidt, Emil Jannings, Rudolf Klein-Rogge, Lil Dagover, and Brigitte Helm—were all working in a plethora of artistically and intellectually superior productions during a time when more esoteric themes were anathema in most American studios.

Germany and other European silent-film hubs were delving into Expressionistic concepts anent the psychic, as in *Destiny* (1921), or capturing the Gothicism of actual *histoire noir* as in *Nosferatu* (1922) and *Der Student von Prag* (1926). German stars, writers, and directors were ascending Valhalla, reaching for the moon, prowling the labyrinthine cul-de-sacs of dimly lit Poesque alleyways of the imagination. American studios were content with clutching claws emerging from trapdoors manipulated by Simon Legree types or other hooded nemeses. Deep-set provincialism would continue to affect the quality of a large share of American films throughout the twenties. Silent suspense-horror films in the United States were hung on pegs suspended near Lon Chaney's makeup kit. His several best films are acclaimed classics only because they emulated European technique down to every last possible detail, i.e., *Phantom of the Opera* (1925) and *The Hunchback of Notre Dame* (1923). Then, of course, there was the Chaney presence—

The 1918 *Blue Bird*, filmed in Fort Lee. Directed by Maurice Tourneur, the six-reeler had tinted sequences.

Jules Raicourt and Marguerite Clark in *Prunella* (1919), filmed in Fort Lee for release through Paramount.

German actress Lil Dagover as she looked four years after her arrival in Hollywood in the early 1920s.

ABOVE: The Universal trademark symbol of a twirling globe was employed in this quaint Halloween publicity shot featuring Universal actress June Marlowe.

BELOW: Ad art: *The Unholy Three.*

15

shrewdly calculated histrionics created by a makeup master who died for his art at an early age (see *Heroes of the Horrors*, the first book in this series).

But this was all a far-distant scream from the quasi-Valhallian spectrum attempted on the German screen via the scripts of Thea von Harbou (Mrs. Fritz Lang): *Siegfried* (1923), *Metropolis* (1926), and *Destiny*. There also were the great creative contributions of Henrik Galeen—*The Golem* (1920) and *Alraune* (1928); Paul Leni, the director of *Waxworks* (1924) and *The Cat and the Canary* (1927); G. W. Pabst, who directed Brigitte Helm in *The Loves of Jeanne Ney* (1927) and L'Atlantide (1932); and writer-director Paul Wegener, who also starred in such classics as *The Golem* and *Svengali* (1927). The list of great German talent during the twenties seemed inexhaustible. In a more realistic vein, the Russians were recreating moments of history with a dramatic sense for power, darkness, and dawn as had rarely been seen outside of the immortal historical work of D. W. Griffith, *Birth of a Nation* (1915) and *Intolerance* (1916), and Abel Gance's monumental *Napoleon* (1926). Eisenstein with *Potemkin* (1925) and *Oktober* (1927), Pudovkin with *Mother* (1926) and *The Deserter* (1933), and Dovzhenko with *Arsenal* (1929) and *Earth* (1930) were the front-rank Russian directors who, along with the Germans, helped influence and change the whole face of filmmaking.

It was inevitable that, as filmmaking began to reach for higher realms of expression in various parts of Europe, the image of man and woman on the screen would also change. Even American styles began to undergo a drastic alteration. The uncouth, straw-in-the-hair, bumpkin look, epitomized by films like *Tol'able David* (1921) and Charles Ray's unruly cowlick image of country boy with cheeks so bare, gave way to the sophisticated, if not more intelligent, approach of such actors as Valentino, John Gilbert and Ronald Colman.

The Pollyannish, sometimes shrinking violet, usually sweet innocence archetype personified by Mary Pickford and her goldilocks for two decades was supplanted by less cornfed symbols of womanhood—Clara Bow, the ever-popular Mae Busch, and the teenage Joan Crawford. The hokey *femme fatale*—Nita Naldi, Nazimova, Theda Bara —confronted general audience disbelief. (How could someone whose name was an anagram for "Arab Death" be for real?) They were soon replaced by the illustrious grandeur and dramatic artistry of Greta Garbo, Gloria Swanson, and the natural gentility of Dolores Costello. Even though women in European films often appeared more vivd and true to life than their cutout paper-doll sisters in the American cinema, at least a handful of great Scream Queen portrayals in American films of the twenties still impress, notably Lucille La Verne's fanatical malevolence in Griffith's *Orphans of the Storm* (1922) and ZaSu Pitts' monstrous avarice in Erich von Stroheim's *Greed* (1923).

The filmic cliché of the Scream Queen heroine-in-distress, with an ever-present villain or "menace" in one guise or another always in pursuit, persisted well into the thirties. Whether it was Mae Clarke in *Frankenstein* (1931), Helen Chandler in *Dracula* (1931), or some now-forgotten handwringer, the Poor Helpless Darling would stand around powerlessly awaiting her fate. This approach is being used even today, although modern directors attempt more sophisticated filmic manipulations. Following the abductions by the Frankenstein Monster and Count Dracula, Mae and Helen naturally satisfied their early thirties fans by being saved at the last minute by their respective heroes.

Four years later, *Frankenstein* director James Whale decided he would liberate Scream Queendom by having Elsa Lanchester appear as Mary Shelley to narrate the opening of *The Bride of Frankenstein* (1935). Mary Shelley was the daughter of pioneer feminist Mary Wollstonecraft, who not only championed free love in the late eighteenth century but also wrote the controversial sociological milestone, *Vindication of the Rights of Women* (1791). Mary

TOP: William Holden, Gloria Swanson, and Erich von Stroheim in Billy Wilder's *Sunset Boulevard* (1950), which succeeded in turning Hollywood's past into cynical *film noir*.

BOTTOM LEFT: Greta Garbo in George Fitzmaurice's *Mata Hari* (1931).

BOTTOM RIGHT: After *King Kong* (1933), Merian C. Cooper produced *She* (1935), one of the seven different screen adaptations of H. Rider Haggard's supernatural romance. It still towers over all the other films based on this novel. Directed by Irving Pichel and Lansing C. Holden, spectacular sets and costumes surrounded actors Randolph Scott, Nigel Bruce, and Helen Gahagan. Gahagan later married Melvyn Douglas and became a congresswoman. She was deposed by Richard M. Nixon after a bitter, insidious campaign in which he used "dirty tricks" to convince voters that she was a Communist.

A vampiric-lesbian relationship was hinted at in this *Dracula's Daughter* (1936) scene between Nan Grey (*left*) and vampire Gloria Holden. One set used in the film was Ming's laboratory from *Flash Gordon*.

Bela Lugosi and Helen Chandler in *Dracula* (1931).

Wollstonecraft died as a result of complications in giving birth to Mary. Nineteen years later, Mary Shelley created *Frankenstein or the Modern Prometheus*, generally considered the first true novel of science fiction. After her scene as Mary Shelley (discussing Frankenstein with Lord Byron and Percy Shelley), Elsa Lanchester finally shows up in the last reel of *Bride of Frankenstein* as The Lady Monster—the most imaginative fright femme since Brigitte Helm's robot Maria in *Metropolis*. (See page 51.) The *dominant* female film monster had at last emerged on American screens.

By 1935, the pattern of women-in-distress was broken. The film industry now offered the public an alternative—characterizations of females who could *create* dis-

tress. Thus it was quite natural for Universal to follow *Bride of Frankenstein* with *Dracula's Daughter* (1936) in which vampirical Gloria Holden pretends to abhor her dad's heritage (at one point even trying to be a normal human) but succumbs to the old bloodlust and threatens Otto Kruger. Fay Wray, the reigning empress of all Scream Queens, refined the deepest aspects of beast versus beauty into an art form that remained virtually unchallenged through one decade and well into the next. There was and still is a place for the Wray type, just as there is for its natural antithesis—the shrewdly designing, often diabolical woman loaded with enough self-destruction and/or malevolence to destroy family and neighborhood or to alter history. She would be depicted by various leading actresses in

18

ABOVE: Betty Furness helped uncover a spy ring in *North of Shanghai* (1939), made thirty-four other movies, and then began opening refrigerator doors.

TOP RIGHT: Ad art from the 1941 *Spider Returns* serial with Mary Ainslee.

BELOW RIGHT: Joyce Bryant is threatened by "The Claw" in Columbia's fifteen-chapter serial, *The Iron Claw* (1941).

the thirties and forties, but never better than by the immortal Bette Davis.

By the early forties, four major Scream Queen types were causing popcorn to be spilled on theatre floors across the country. There was the social, psychic vampire, personified by Bette Davis. There was the eternal damsel in distress. There was the gradual emergence of the physical female ogre, a tradition continued in 1941's *A Woman's Face*, fine *film noir* with a scar-faced Joan Crawford harboring various misanthropic and criminal tendencies until lover Melvyn Douglas uses plastic surgery to change both her face and disposition. There was the female, gorilla-feature creature, changed by a mad doctor into a siren but, alas, reverting to type, returning for encores in sequels plus numerous imitations

and offshoots in one monstrous form or another (as detailed in the Acquanetta chapter).

Enter 1944 with perhaps the best, if not first, clearly defined example of supernatural females—Dorothy Macardle's *The Uninvited*, an outstanding venture into terror with two female wraiths, one good and the other evil, haunting a mansion. Gail Russell is the potential victim of an evil spirit pretending to be her mother's ghost. Ghostbreaker Ray Milland intercedes just in time, aided by the unexpected presence of the good spirit. Though the haunted mansion was an old chestnut in the foyer that had lingered since Méliès' time, *Uninvited* was many notches above the bedsheet ghosties of the old school, introducing a profound, malignant, supernatural force

19

ABOVE: Kay Aldridge, Roy Barcroft, and Kane Richmond in Republic's fifteen-chapter serial, *Haunted Harbor* (1944). If the fans weren't satisfied with bondage scenes, the serial also offered sea monsters. Aldridge also portrayed the jungle heroine, Nyoka, in serials.

BELOW LEFT: Female mannequins are decapitated in the climax of Stanley Kubrick's *Killer's Kiss* (1955).

April Kent and Grant Williams in *The Incredible Shrinking Man* (1957), recently announced as a remake, with Lily Tomlin as *The Incredible Shrinking Woman*.

ABOVE: The influence of science fiction film costuming and SF illustration is seen in these 1961 creations by fashion design students of Chicago's Art Institute. *Left to right:* Flying-saucer dress can vanish just like an ordinary UFO because it's made with a disposable paper derivative; down-to-Earth contemporary two-piece suit; temperature-controlled interplanetary travel outfit, wired for outer space communications, also has weight compensation system—each panel of the balloon coat inflates separately, and hip-level belt has compartments for food, money, etc. Latter is "intended for short flights only," according to creator.

with an effective minimal budget. The Old Dark House type of drama got a new lease in *Psycho* (1960), when Alfred Hitchcock, following Robert Bloch's novel, killed off the heroine at midpoint, thereby assuring that she could never be rescued.

With these important basic fantasy-horror themes at their disposal, filmmakers would carry on for several decades—blending, shifting, and transposing characters and concepts to create execrable fare such as *Frankenstein's Daughter* (1958) and, worse yet, *Jesse James Meets Frankenstein's Daughter* (1966). In the seventies the main, femme horror themes were fused together in the following order: occult-religious scholarship; medical science shown in a rather infernal light; innocence and goodness at war with demon possession and the Devil; and monstrous transfiguration. Blend well and *voila!* You have *The Exorcist* (1973). Filmic exorcism and essays in the offbeat supernatural are, of course, not unique and have a genesis spanning several generations. The female almost always plays the most prominent role.

BELOW: Janet Leigh between takes on the *Psycho* motel room set.

ABOVE: Film studios often succeeded in influencing women's fads and fashions, but sometimes they went too far. Here's the original caption of these two photos, as churned out at the MGM publicity office: "Hairdo to Melt Men" . . . the Medusa Cut, new hair style for women created by famous hair stylist, Larry Mathews, is worn by Wendy Lou Taylor (*left*). It was 'inspired' by actor Tony Randall (*right*), seen here as he appears in a new motion picture fantasy, *The Seven Faces of Dr. Lao* (1964), in which the actor plays seven roles, including the snake-haired Medusa of Greek mythology. The 'snakes' in Miss Taylor's hair are fabric, with rhinestone 'eyes.' While Medusa could turn men to stone, Mr. Mathews says that his coiffure will melt men!"

CENTER LEFT: Annie Girardot as *The Ape Woman* (1964).

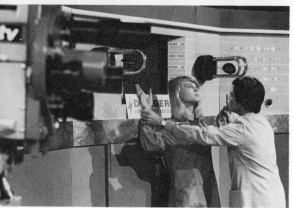

LOWER LEFT: Immediately after leaving drama school, Julie Christie went into this BBC-TV science fiction serial, *A for Andromeda* (1961) by Fred Hoyle and John Elliot. Played out against a remote stretch of coast in the West Indies, the story, set in the year 1970, tells of the impact of alien intelligence upon life on Earth. In this scene, Professor Dawnay (Mary Morris) questions Andromeda (Julie Christie) about her behavior.

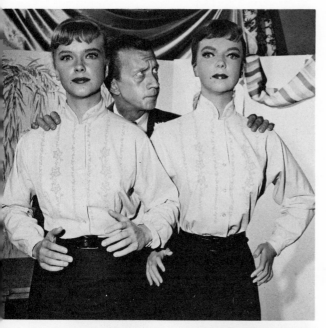

ABOVE: Eve (Joanne Woodward) in *The Three Faces of Eve* (1957). When Sally Field came up with not three, but fifteen multiple personalities in *Sybil* (1976), Joanne Woodward returned to this genre as Sally's psychiatrist. Another multiple-personality film from 1957 was Hugo Haas' *Lizzie* (with Eleanor Parker), adapted from Shirley Jackson's "The Bird's Nest."

TOP LEFT: In "The After Hours" tale on Rod Serling's TV series, *Twilight Zone*, Armbruster (James Mulhollin) is the picture of confusion as he tries to figure which one of the two ladies is actress Anne Francis and which one is her mannequin. In the story the two did not appear together; instead, the climax had Anne Francis *turning into* the mannequin (much like the end of the animated short, *Closed Mondays*). Set in a department store, "after hours," this half-hour drama owes a great deal to, and was obviously inspired by, John Collier's short-story classic, "Evening Primrose."

ABOVE: Mai Zetterling directs Ingrid Thulin in *Night Games* (1966), which concerns the efforts of a man to free himself from the memories of his childhood when his eccentric aunt and sexually extravagant mother (Thulin) had an abnormal influence on him.

Such stories have varied backgrounds, such as the ancient Greek tale of Proserpine, who was abducted into the nether regions by Pluto, Lord of the Underworld. Similarly, there is the tragedy of Orpheus, whose only love, Eurydice, dies and descends to Hades. The story received a poetic updating from Jean Cocteau in *Orpheus* (1949) with Jean Marais and Maria Casares, followed by a transposition to a contemporary Brazilian carnival setting in Marcel Camus' *Black Orpheus* (1959) with Breno Mello and Marpessa Dawn. Orpheus's unsuccessful attempt to reclaim Eurydice from Pluto's clutches is not unlike the efforts of Father Damien and Father Karas to exorcise the hell out of Regan in *The Exorcist*.

The same elements also exist in one form or another in several ethno-based classics. The cabalistic Yiddish psychic horrors of *The Dybbuk* have been adapted a number of times as play productions, as a 1937 Polish-made Yiddish-language film, as a TV drama (1958), and as a 1967 Israeli-West German film starring David Opatoshu (the film version of the S. Ansky play, *Between Two Worlds*). Satan or Mephistopheles recurs hundreds of times in European legend, as a basic classic by Marlowe (c. 1589) in his *Tragical History of Dr. Faustus*, as later monumentalized by Goethe's *Faust* (written and published in several phases between 1773 to 1831), and as Gounod's opera. The earliest film interpretations of 1897 and 1898 were followed by Alice Guy-Blaché's 1902 *Faust et Méphisto* and at least fifty other Faust films before the Richard Burton-Elizabeth Taylor starrer, *Doctor Faustus* (1967). Old Dr. Faustus regains his youth by promising his soul to the Devil but the innocent Margaret is in danger of having her own soul possessed by the Devil.

Satanic forces and their minions threatened the innocent in many films down through the years, but it took the innocence of a modern Margaret (Mia Farrow) and the selfish opportunism of a latter-day Faustus (John Cassavetes) to begin a new box-office bonanza trend with *Rosemary's Baby* (1968), faithfully adapted and directed by Roman Polanski from the Ira

TOP RIGHT: A precursor to George Lucas' *THX-1138* was this 1966 BBC-TV *Out of the Unknown* production of E. M. Forster's classic, *The Machine Stops*, in which a mother, Vashti (Yvonne Mitchell), and her son struggle to maintain their natural bond of love in an overcivilized world where human beings are tyrannized by machines.

CENTER RIGHT: Susan Denberg, the *Frankenstein-Created Woman* (1967), in a publicity photograph taken at the time of the film's release.

BOTTOM RIGHT: In *Dr. Faustus* (1967), Helen of Troy (Elizabeth Taylor) appears before Faustus (Richard Burton), tempting him to render his soul to Lucifer. The exotic wig creation of lightweight coiled tin was created by the Parisian hairstylist, Alexandre. Creator of the Marienbad hairstyle, the artichoke and the beehive, Alexandre also fashioned Tippi Hedren's coiffures in *Marnie* (1964). Women who have made their way to his atelier in the exclusive Rue Faubourg-Saint-Honoré include Garbo, Juliette Greco, Princess Grace, and Gloria Guinness, daughter of the Irish banker-brewer.

ABOVE: Few contemporary male writers are as gifted at capturing the essence of women as Tennessee Williams. His *Slapstick Tragedy* concerns a horrible and pathetically funny incident at the southernmost tip of the southernmost island in Key West. In the mid-sixties Broadway production at the Longacre Theatre are (*left to right*), James Olson, Zoe Caldwell, Margaret Leighton (standing), Kate Reid, and the Cocaloony Bird.

LEFT: Roman Polanski limned a terrifying intimate portrait of schizophrenia in *Repulsion* (1965) by filming the hallucinations of a young woman (Catherine Deneuve) as if they were stark realities. Earlier films about women and mental illness included *Home Before Dark* (1958), with Jean Simmons; and *The Snake Pit* (1948), with Olivia de Havilland.

ABOVE: Susan Strasberg in the STP freakout scene of *Psych-Out* (1968). Written by Betty Tusher and Betty Ulius, *Psych-Out* was one of the few convincing film portraits of the hallucinogenic sixties. Jennie (Strasberg), a seventeen-year-old runaway, wanders among the doper dropouts of Haight-Ashbury in search of her missing brother Steve (Bruce Dern).

BELOW: Victoria Vetri in *When Dinosaurs Ruled the Earth* (1969).

Levin novel. The roster of women in the cast included not only the helpless victim (Farrow) and instruments of the Devil (Ruth Gordon, Hope Summers) but also actress Victoria Vetri (of the 1969 *When Dinosaurs Ruled the Earth*) appearing under the name Angela Dorian. To top *Rosemary's Baby*, author Levin came up with *The Stepford Wives*, filmed in 1975, an exploitative effort to capitalize on the feminist movement with women being turned into "perfect wives" by their husbands, who have computer technology and Disney-style Animatronics at their disposal. An acceptable alternative to Levin's trendiness is the 1972 feminist fantasy, *Up the Sandbox*, based on the Anne Richardson Roiphe novel, with Barbra Streisand as a harassed housewife who opts for a rich fantasy life as an escape from her domain of domesticity. "The new tolerance," says Roiphe," should ultimately respect the lady who wants to make pies as well as the one who majors in higher mathematics."

26

LEFT: Scene from *Rosemary's Baby* (1968). In the laundry room of the Dakota Apartments (72nd Street and Central Park West), Rosemary (Mia Farrow) meets Terry (Angela Dorian), remarking that she resembles the actress Victoria Vetri. The dialogue was revealed as an inside joke by Roman Polanski: actress Angela Dorian and Victoria Vetri are the same person.

BELOW: A filmdom effort to turn the feminist movement into cold cash backfired when Betty Friedan and other feminist leaders walked out during a special promotional screening of *The Stepford Wives* (1975). Columbia Pictures also suggested that local theatres hold a "Perfect Wife" contest through disc jockeys by having husbands write "My wife is the perfect wife because . . ." entries, leading to "frequently funny on-air interviews." Lacking in suspense as it moved toward its obvious conclusion, the film ignored the feminist movement's meaningful aspects with a superficial and exploitive approach. The climax had women the complete victims of technology controlled by their husbands. *Left to right*, in a production still taken during the filming of the final scene: Toni Reid, Carol Mallory, Tina Louise, Katharine Ross, Paula Prentiss, Barbara Rucker, Nanette Newman, and Judith Baldwin.

Since *Rosemary's Baby*, nearly every major production team and studio has ventured into Scream Queen activity with unparalleled vitality—and much satanic proliferation. The talented Ken Russell directed the semihistorical medieval drama, *The Devils* (1971), adapted from the John Whiting play and Aldous Huxley's *The Devils of Loudon*, and featuring a magnificently diabolical protrayal of evil by Vanessa Redgrave as a hunchbacked nun who feigns demon possession that implicates and condemns heroic Oliver Reed to horrific torture and burning at the stake. In a more modern setting, *The Brotherhood of Satan* (1971) takes place in an inconspicuous American small town where no sexual discrimination exists in that nearly all the inhabitants coexist in Satanism.

In 1973, female Satanists were readily available to augment the ranks of Count Dracula (Christopher Lee) in *The Satanic Rites of Dracula*. After the 1973 apotheosis of all Scream Queen genres wrapped up in one brilliantly contrived commerical package, *The Exorcist*, with audiences retching and fainting because of the use of sound and image subliminals (see Wilson Bryan Key's 1976 book, *Media Sexploitation*), this film, inspired by *Rosemary's Baby*, spawned its own imitations. Juliet Mills (of the Mary Poppins School of Dramatic Arts) was very unPoppinslike in *Beyond the Door* (1975), a heavily promoted disappointment. And 1976 brought Lee Remick and Gregory Peck in the far more successful *The Omen*, but audiences were not unaware that in the Pecking order of imitations it was virtually a Lee Remake of *The Exorcist*.

In an inspired but dismally futile attempt to repeat *The Exorcist*'s enormous success, Warner Brothers brought back Linda Blair to appear in *Exorcist II: The Heretic*, in 1977, with director John Boorman attempting some esoteric experiments in color psychology and an elaboration on the philosophy of Teilhard de Chardin, while displaying some of the decade's best special-effects work. When audiences stayed away in droves, Boorman phoned in

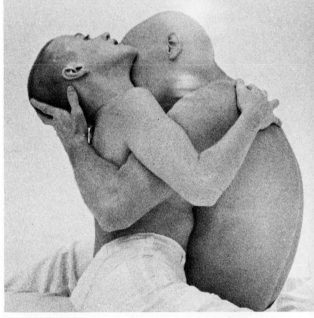

TOP: Carmilla (Ingrid Pitt) and Emma (Madeleine Smith) play the title roles in *The Vampire Lovers* (1970), based on J. Sheridan Le Fanu's classic *Carmilla*. The story of vampiric lesbianism was also filmed by Roger Vadim as *Blood and Roses* (1960).

ABOVE: Maggie McOmie and Robert Duvall make forbidden love in George Lucas' *THX-1138* (1971), a futuristic warning set in an oppressed underground society controlled by drugs and technology.

TOP: A Satanic rite from *The Satanic Rites of Dracula* (1973).

ABOVE: The comfortable world of Donald Sutherland and Julie Christie is shattered when their daughter drowns in this opening scene of Nicolas Roeg's *Don't Look Now* (1973), adapted from Daphne du Maurier's macabre tale of psychic horror. The film shows women very much in tune with intuition and the psychic world—which men reject or ignore. Sutherland's failure to acknowledge his own psychic gifts leads to his death.

ABOVE: Another *Rosemary's Baby* spinoff was *The Stranger Within* (1974), a made-for-TV movie from a Richard Matheson screenplay about a young wife (Barbara Eden) who becomes alienated from her husband (George Grizzard) when her unborn child begins controlling her life. Lee Phillips directed.

BELOW: The institutionalized sadism of *One Flew Over the Cuckoo's Nest* (1975). Louise Fletcher is second from the left in this production shot.

a new ending from Ireland, making a partial deletion of the intentional theatricality in the allegorical finale. New prints were shipped out with such haste that most filmgoers never knew they were not seeing the film as originally released. Meanwhile, a totally reedited third version was readied for release in the international marketplace. In addition to having two Linda Blairs (one good, one evil) and the return of Sharon, the secretary (Kitty Winn), the fourteen-million-dollar flop also featured Louise Fletcher as a psychiatrist, a role originally written for a male. Chris Sarandon, George Segal, and David Carradine were all considered for the part before the casting of Fletcher, best known for her Oscar-winning performance as the chillingly sadistic and wretched Nurse Ratched in Ken Kesey's *One Flew Over the Cuckoo's Nest* (1975). "I'm very much for the Equal Rights Amendment," said Louise Fletcher in June 1977. "I want to see it passed, and I've decided to do what I can to help it."

In the liberated cinema of the seventies, women are involved in all aspects of film production, gaining not only creative control but also power in executive positions. After thirty years of film editing, including *Jaws* (1975), Verna Fields became Executive Consultant at Universal. There are writers such as Joyce Hooper Corrington (the 1973 *Battle for the Planet of the Apes*); Shelley Duvall (who wrote eighty percent of her own dialogue for *3 Women*); Joan Torres (the 1972 *Blacula*); Jane Baker

(the 1969 *Captain Nemo and the Under-water City*); and newcomers such as Linda Karpel, who began her screenwriting career by choosing Fort Lee for the locale of her imaginative and faithful adaptation of Philip K. Dick's *Eye in the Sky* science-fiction novel (not yet on production schedules as of this writing). There are writer-producers such as Sylvia Anderson (the 1969 *Journey to the Far Side of the Sun*); agents such as Sue Mengers; and screenwriter-production designers such as Polly Platt (*Paper Moon*, *Pretty Baby*, and Orson Welles' as-yet-unreleased *Other Side of the Wind*). A new wave of female directors—Joan Darling, Stephanie Rothman, Elaine May, Jeanne Moreau, Roberta Findlay, Lee Grant, Dyan Cannon, Ellen Burstyn—follow in the footsteps of Alice Guy-Blaché, Cleo Madison, Dorothy Arzner, Ruth Ann Baldwin, Grace Cunard, Ida May Park, Ruth Stonehouse, Jeanie MacPherson, Lule Warrenton, Elsie Jane Wilson, Wanda Tuchock, Leontine Sagan, Elinor Glyn, Jacqueline Logan, Mary Field, Ida Lupino, Maya Deren, Barbara Loden, Agnes Varda, Mai Zetterling, and Lina Wertmuller. Few on this list, however, even approach the record held by Lois Weber, who, between 1908 and 1934, made four hundred films before her death in Hollywood on November 13, 1939. For a while Hollywood's leading spokeswoman on women's rights was Jane Fonda as she made the transition from *Barbarella* (1968) doll to the hard-edged Manhattan grit of *Klute* (1971), her choice of film roles reflecting her altered view of the world. But, in 1977, the world of the fantasy film suddenly projected the new 70mm stereo Scream Queen, accompanied by the fanfares of an enthralling John Williams score—a strong-willed woman who

TOP RIGHT: Sara (Jeanne Moreau) plays a scene in a film within the film *Lumière* (1976), directed by Jeanne Moreau.

RIGHT: Ida Lupino, seen here with John Clarke in "The 16 Millimeter Shrine" on *Twilight Zone*, directed many feature films and TV films during the fifties and early sixties. One of her strongest was the chilling *Hitch Hiker* (1953), about a psycho who threatens two businessmen on vacation.

made the term "equal rights" seem like nothing more than a conflict between primitives of a planet in another galaxy far, far away. Princess Leia Organa (Carrie Fisher) of George Lucas' *Star Wars* is the Senator from Aleraan, using her political position to secretly gather information against the Empire (in essence, a symbol of the same backward-thinking Establishment that Jane Fonda fought). The witty, intelligent Princess is a unifying force in bringing about the rebellion against the oppression of the powerful Empire, fighting alongside the male heroes. A far, far cry from Jean Rogers in *Flash Gordon* (1936), Princess Leia is the new Science-Fiction Woman of the Ages, supremely confident of her position in the universe, the stars like grains of sand in her hand. The cobwebbey trap doors of the twenties have slammed shut forever. A new era, a new ERA, a New Woman has begun.

—Cal Beck and Robert Stewart
*North Bergen, New Jersey*
*September 1977*

Jane Fonda was directed by husband Roger Vadim in *Barbarella* (1968).

Jean Rogers and Buster Crabbe in *Flash Gordon* (1936), one of the several inspirations for *Star Wars*.

# Alice Guy-Blaché

*T*he first woman filmmaker was Alice Guy-Blaché and the fantasy nature of many of her films places her prominently in any such survey as this book. With a career spanning 1896 to 1920, her exploratory work in film as a storytelling medium parallels that of Georges Méliès (1861–1938), generally credited not only as the first great film fantasist but also as the first to develop narrative techniques with such early titles as *Une Partie de Cartes* (1896), *The Bewitched Inn* (1897), *The Four Troublesome Heads* (1898), and *Cinderella* (1899).

Méliès' magic-trick films were imitated in England by G. A. Smith in 1898 and by the London maker of scientific instruments, Robert W. Paul, in 1899. Alice Guy, however, also began making fantasy films during this period, and she claimed that she had begun *before* Méliès. For many years the true extent of her pioneering work was lost to film history; many otherwise authoritative books on the birth of the cinema do not even mention her. One current work on women in films (written by a prominent "feminist" film reviewer) dismisses Blaché

with several others, utterly unaware of her presuffragette stance—almost as if film feminists hardly existed before the sixties.

Her daughter, Simone Blaché, recalls her as "a very dynamic and energetic person. Very self-reliant. She was somewhat shy but she overcame that very well. . . . In many respects she was a nineteenth-century person. She believed in the family. It was beyond her to understand life without the family structure. And yet she had strong feminist views. She was enthusiastic about everything she saw and heard that was feminist in any way." Alice Guy was born July 1, 1873, in Paris, and at the age of four was taken by her family to Chile. They left there two years later. The youngest of four daughters, she was educated at a Paris convent and decided to develop her secretarial skills after the death of her father, a book publisher. Through her mother's contacts on charity committees, she began working, at twenty-three as a secretary with Gaumont at a time when the company had just begun manufacturing cameras and projectors.

The first Lumière film, *La Sortie des Ouvriers de l'usine Lumière* (*Workers Leaving the Lumière Factory*) was made early in 1895. The first public exhibition of motion pictures for a paying audience (of thirty-three customers) was held December 28, 1895, by the Lumière brothers at the Salon Indien of the Grand Café in Paris, and Gaumont's equipment was marketed in the three years that followed. But Léon Gaumont lacked adequate films to demonstrate his machines, and this job fell on the shoulders of Mademoiselle Alice. She is credited with the first Gaumont narrative film employing sets, *Les Mesadventures d'une tête de veau* (1898). Using the garden alongside Gaumont's house on the grounds of the factory, she filmed *La Fee aux Choux* (*The Good Fairy in the Cabbage Patch* (1897), a fantasy about children sprouting up in a cabbage patch. Later it was retitled *Sage-femme de 1ere Classe*.

"I remember mother telling me that once some Turkish pasha came and ordered a solid gold camera, and it was made for him," recalled Simone. "Léon Gaumont himself had a very fertile and inventive mind, and he was interested in all sorts of inventions. He heard of the invention of the Lumière brothers, who had made a machine to make motion pictures, and he went to see how it worked. I don't think he got the Lumière camera. I think he made one of his own. Anyway, he and his associates began playing around with this instrument. They didn't know what to do with it. They just played around with it, taking pictures of moving things, such as trains, races, parades, and things like that. Mother was very interested in it. She was a secretary at Gaumont but also partly a saleslady. She was a little bit of everything in that company. One day while they were filming the arrival of a train at a station, she asked Gaumont if he would let her try something with the camera, and he said, 'What! What! What! All right, if you *want* to—it's a child's toy anyhow.' So that was the famous moment when she got together in a garden with some young friends of hers and put on

A scene from *La Fée aux choux* (*The Good Fairy in the Cabbage Patch*), made in 1897 by Alice Guy.

film the fairy tale of how children are born in cabbages."

Various circus performers began appearing in the Guy films that followed. "Mother got to know a very strange and interesting breed of people, lion tamers and all sorts of people like that," said Simone. With the exception of a few 1904 and 1905 titles, every one-reel film from Gaumont up to 1905 was directed by Alice Guy. She made special-effect trick films like *Le Fiancé Ensorcelé* and *Le Cake Walk de la Pendule* (*The Clock's Cakewalk*) along with fairy-tale-styled fantasies such as *La Momie* (*The Mummy*), *Lui, Faust et Mephisto*, *La Légende de Saint-Nicolas*, *La Fève Enchantée* and *Le Gourmand effraye* (*The Scared Glutton*). The O'ners, famous clowns, appeared in *Déméngement a la Cloche de Bois* (*Moving Out in the Night*). Other titles include the 1904 *Les Petits Couperus de Bois Vert* (*Little Thieves of Bois-Vert*), *Vendetta, L'Assassinat du Courrier de Lyon* (1904), *Hussards et Grisettes* (1901), *Le Voleur Sacrilege* (1903), *Le Crime de la Rue de Temple* (1904), and the longer *Rélubilitation* (1904).

*Esmeralda* (1905), an adaptation of Victor Hugo's *Hunchback of Notre Dame*, was followed by the even more ambitious *Vie du Christ* (1905), involving twenty-five sets and three hundred extras. Victorin Jasset (1862–1913) started at Gaumont as Alice Guy's assistant and production manager. He later directed several Gaumont films himself; particularly notable is the weird *Rêves d'un Fumeur d'Opium*. Journalist Louis Feuillade (1873–1925) joined the Gaumont team as a scriptwriter in 1905, when it was the largest studio in existence. Between 1905 and 1907 Guy directed more than one hundred short sound films (between one and two minutes each) using Gaumont's Chronophone wax-cylinder process. Another fantasy was *La Fée Printemps* (1906), filmed in color.

In 1906 she met Herbert Blaché-Bolton, an Englishman in charge of Gaumont's London office. During the filming of *Mireille* (1906) a few months later, he arrived to watch Guy and Feuillade at work. Not long after this month-long location trip, she married Blaché. In 1907 she temporarily abandoned directing to accompany her husband to Cleveland, where he attempted to supply Gaumont products to American exhibitors. Alice Guy's replacement at Gaumont in France was Feuillade, who later went on to perfect the thriller genre with his famed serials *Fantomas* (1913–14) and *Les Vampires* (1915–16). One 1913 Gaumont film was *In the Grip of the Vampire*, written by Léonce Perret.

When the Cleveland branch was not successful, the Blachés relocated in New York City. Simone Blaché, who was born at this time, stated in 1974, "She couldn't speak a word of English when she came here, but she overcame that. She was very generous and very warm. She had to love people and be loved by them."

She also had fallen in love with filmmaking and quickly found domestic life a bore. On September 7, 1910, she became president of the Solax Company at the corner of Fourth Avenue and 14th Street in Manhattan. Filming took place in Flushing, and the Solax Company released 325 films in the next four years; between thirty-five and fifty of those films were directed by Alice Guy-Blaché. After *A Child's Sacrifice* (1910) and *Falling Leaves* (1911), she filmed the operas *Mignon* (1912) and *Fra Diavolo* (1912). *Hotel Honeymoon* (1912) featured an animated moon smiling down on the live-action lovers.

Then, with 60,000 motion-picture theatres in the world, of which 15,000 were in the United States, Alice Guy began making thrillers. For *The Sewer* (1912), scripted by her set designer Henri Ménessier, a scene calling for an attack by sewer rats was filmed using real rats. Other titles in the same vein were *The Million Dollar Robbery* (1912) and *The Rogues of Paris* (1913). The Solax Company made a science-fiction film, *In the Year 2000* (1912), with a satirical story line in which women rule the world, but whether Alice Guy directed this militant feminist extrapolation has not been fully determined. Also in 1912,

*A Soul Adrift*, the life of an artist as seen by Alice Guy.

while Méliès was teetering on the brink of the disastrous closing of his Montreuil film studio, Alice Guy made plans to open a large new studio on Palisades Avenue in Fort Lee, New Jersey.

On February 12, 1912, Alice Guy heralded the rising of the Solax sun (her company's trademark) with a special Solax evening on Broadway, attended by many New York film personalities at Weber's Theatre. Her thrillers, coinciding with the birth of the serial, were executed with similar derring-do. For the crime drama *Mickey's Pal* (1912), she set fire to an automobile, and a production still from *The Beasts of the Jungle* (1913), filmed in the jungles of Fort Lee, New Jersey, shows her embracing a tiger. However, film and comic-strip historian Francis Lacassin reports that Herbert Blaché "strictly forbade her to use dynamite, which he considered too dangerous, and stood in for her as director on scenes of *The Yellow Traffic* [1914]." On a visit to Sing Sing, she was photographed sitting in the electric chair. "French prisons are much more comfortable, particularly the one at Fresnes," she announced to reporters.

Her fantasy films became more elaborate. In *The Shadows of the Moulin Rouge* (1913), a four-reeler that she wrote, produced, and directed, the plot involves the switching of live and dead bodies. The three-reel *Pit and the Pendulum*, adapted from Poe, had a cast of Darwin Karr, Blanche Cornwall, Fraunie Fraunholz, and Joseph Levering. Karr, Cornwall, Billy Quirk, and Claire Whitney were the regular stars of the "Solax Stock Company."

The three-reel *Dick Whittington and His Cat* (1913), based on the popular legends of the lord mayor of London, starred Vinnie Burns, who had just joined the Solax Stock Company, and Julia R. Hurley. Other Solax titles of 1913 were *Kelly from the Emerald Isle*, *A House Divided*, and *Ben Bolt*. The four-reel *Star of India* (1913) was a fantasy thriller in which ghastly deaths befall the various owners of a jewel taken from a Buddha's forehead. Directed by Alice Guy, it was the initial production of the new Blaché Features, Inc. (headed by Herbert Blaché), which replaced Solax and made fourteen films between November 1913, and November 1914, including *Fortune Hunters* (1913), *Fighting Death* (1914), and *Hook and Hand* (1914). However, Solax films from the previous year were also released in 1914—such as *The Monster and the Girl*, which Alice Guy directed, and *A Fight for Freedom or*

TOP RIGHT: Herbert, Alice, and Simone Blaché at the time of the 1912 construction of the $100,000 Solax studio in Fort Lee, New Jersey.

CENTER RIGHT: The interior of the Fort Lee Solax studio in 1913.

ABOVE: Alice Guy-Blaché with the tigress Sarah during the Fort Lee filming of *The Beasts of the Jungle* in 1914.

BELOW: Alice Guy-Blaché's adaptation of *The Pit and the Pendulum* (1913).

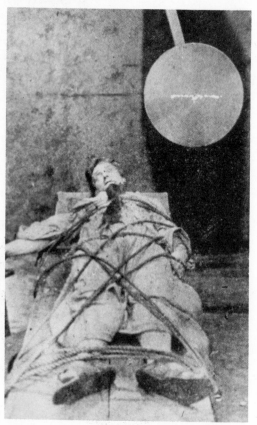

*Exiled to Siberia.* She wrote and directed *Woman of Mystery* (1914), a four-reel story about a soul that leaves its body, forcing the evil side of a detective's personality to surface with criminal acts. She produced and directed *The Dream Woman* (1914), a four-reeler based on the Wilkie Collins novel. Starring Fraunie Fraunholz and Claire Whitney, the film depicts a man threatened with death by a woman from his dreams, and this type of plot line persists to the present day with such films as Oliver Stone's *Seizure* (1974) and Charles Beaumont's *Perchance to Dream* on *Twilight Zone.* A total of nine films made by Blaché Features were directed by Alice Guy-Blaché.

In April 1914, Herbert Blaché became the founding president of the U.S. Amusement Corporation with Alice Guy-Blaché as vice president. The company was dedicated to literary and stage adaptations, but it still leaned toward thriller and fantasy material. He directed and acted in *The Chimes* (1914), a five-reeler based on the Charles Dickens Christmas tale. Tom Teiress, Fay Cusic, Alfred Hemming, Clarence Harvey, and Vinnie Burns appeared with Blaché in bizarre dream-world scenes showing a man receiving a guided tour from the spirit of the Christmas chimes. He also directed Langdon McCormack's *The Burglar and the Lady* and Dickens's *Mystery of Edwin Drood* (remade in 1935 with Claude Rains as the opium-smoking choirmaster).

Alice Guy-Blaché directed *The Empress, A Man and the Woman* (1917), adapted from Emile Zola's *Nana*, and Upton Sinclair's *The Adventurer*, adapted by Harry Chandlee and Lawrence McCloskey, all for the U.S. Amusement Corporation. The Blachés were also involved with the Popular Players and Plays company, where Herbert Blaché was director of production on such films as *Shadows of a Great City* (1915) and *The Girl with the Green Eyes* (1916). With this organization Alice Guy-Blaché directed titles such as *My Madonna* (1915), *The Ragged Earl* (1914), and *What Will People Say?* (1915), based on the story by Rupert Hughes. For *Spring of the Year* (1917), she went on location to the Florida Everglades.

*Who's Who in the Motion-Picture World*, in 1915, published the following: "Mme. Alice Blaché, president of the Solax Co., is probably the best-known woman executive and producer in the motion-picture world. She enjoys a unique distinction in the fact that she writes and directs practically all of her productions. She started the production of multiple reels in this country, and to her the credit is due for many of the best-known features produced in the early days of feature productions. Her recent and striking successes have been such well-known productions as *The Tigress, The Heart of a Painted Woman,* and *The Shooting of Dan McGrew.*"

Their decline began in 1917 when the Solax studio was rented to Apollo Pictures before eventually being sold and demolished around 1920. Independent producers had a hard time competing with the majors, but evidently Alice Guy had a if-you-can't-beat-'em-join-'em attitude; in 1918 she directed *The Great Adventure* with Bessie Love for Pathé from an Agnes Johnston scenario. Her last film was Pathé's *Tarnished Reputations* (1920), based on a Léonce Perret screenplay.

Despite Arthur Knight's assertion in *The Liveliest Art* that Fort Lee "was reduced to a ghost town" in 1918, Joe Brandt's Star Serial Corporation was located in Fort Lee for the 1922 filming of *Captain Kidd* with Eddie Polo and Katherine Myers at the Peerless Studios. With Fort Lee abandoned once again, just as it had been by Colonel Greene in 1776, the Blachés found it difficult to compete in the mushrooming motion-picture industry. "It is curious to note," wrote Francis Lacassin, "that it was the Blachés who helped Metro Pictures (which, after mergers, became Metro-Goldwyn-Mayer) to get off the ground, by entrusting them from their inception in March 1915, right up until 1918 with their various productions, thereby providing them, over a two-year period, with most of their output as distributors: a humble and unintentional contribution to the birth of a giant. But the Blachés' departure from their Fort Lee studio signified the end of an era."

In 1922 the Blachés were divorced. "When her marriage broke apart," said Simone, "I saw her almost on the point of committing suicide."

Alice Guy-Blaché retained the married name under which she had built her reputation. However, she found little film work other than synopsizing screenplays for magazine publication. Making a sudden impromptu return to France, with Simone and her son Reginald, but minus prints of her films, she was unable to reestablish herself in the French film industry, experiencing discrimination because she was middle-aged and a woman. Simone remembered, "Mother was really cherished in the United States. She used to say that people treated her so wonderfully here because she was a woman, because she was a woman in film. The situation in France was quite the reverse. She kept up her contacts with a number of people in the industry and went to see many pictures, but she was never able to get a film job again." Meanwhile, back in the United States, Herbert Blaché, having directed Ethel Barrymore in *The Hope* (1920) and Buster Keaton in *The Saphead* (1920), continued to work for Universal as a supervising production director throughout the twenties. He made no films after the arrival of talking pictures.

In 1925, in a magazine article, Alice Guy-Blaché reflected on her own career and the potential role of women in films. "It has long been a source of wonder to me that many women have not seized upon the wonderful opportunities offered to them by the motion-picture art to make their way to fame and fortune as directors of photodramas. Of all the arts there is probably none in which they can make such splendid use of talents so much more natural to a woman than to a man and so necessary to its perfection."

In 1927 she came back to the United States in hopes of acquiring her films. Simone Blaché recalled, "She had left everything here, and she had nothing to prove

Alice Guy-Blaché in 1959.

what she had done. She went to the Library of Congress and many other places where she thought her films might have been saved, but she could not find any of them."

When she was eighty years old, in 1953, the French government awarded her the Legion of Honor, but, according to Simone, "The only reason she is remembered at all now is that she made great efforts to stake her claim, to say 'I was the first person that ever did this. Now you've got to pay attention. You've got to take notice. I am the one who did it.' Finally, she was given the Legion of Honor for meritorious service. It was a very great day in her life, of course."

When Simone retired from the American diplomatic service in 1964, Alice Guy came to the United States for the last time —to live with Simone in Mahwah, New Jersey. There were no newspaper obituaries when she died in this country in 1968 at the age of ninety-five. Since that time six of her films have been located and preserved by the American Film Institute.

# May McAvoy

May McAvoy, who holds the distinction not only of appearing in the first talking feature film but also of starring in the first talking horror movie, was born in New York in 1901 in her family's brownstone at 41st Street and Park Avenue in New York City. The Waldorf-Astoria was built on the location where her grandfather and then her father owned a block-long livery stable.

"A lump of sugar," she said, "was responsible for my first break into motion pictures. Don't laugh! It's the truth. But let's start at the beginning. In 1914, after I was graduated from a New York public school, teaching fascinated me. Later, however, I was disappointed and abandoned the idea." Teaching was the profession her mother had in mind, and even when an agent made an offer, her mother was still opposed to the idea of May's going into acting.

She began doing modeling work, but her model friends—Helen Chadwick, Justine Johnston, Edna Murphy—were also involved in films and theatre. "Visiting them backstage one day, I was offered a part in a girl act. However, because of parental objection and stage fright, I did not accept. The owner of the act gave me a letter to an official of the Fox Film Company, but it took me so long to get up the courage to see him that when I did apply at the studios six months later he was no longer there. So I boldly presented myself at Metro's New York studios on 61st Street and told them that I'd like to go into the movies. I left some photographs, and luck must have been with me, for the casting director phoned and asked me to report at the studio at eight o'clock that very night. Hesitatingly, I made the wrong answer—of course. 'Oh! But I can't come tonight—won't you make it tomorrow?' I exclaimed. It was a classic. He replied, 'It's evident, Miss McAvoy, that you've had no motion-picture experience. Come tonight or not at all!' I went."

The job was a one-reel commercial for Domino Sugar. "The work must have pleased them, for I was asked to report next for extra work with Viola Dana in *Blue Jeans*. Spent six months doing extra work. Then I asked for small parts and got them.

May McAvoy, as Esther, embraced by Ramon Navarro, as Ben-Hur, in MGM's *Ben-Hur* (1926).

Lucky, wasn't I?" Dana remained one of her closest friends for decades to come.

May was seen in *Hate* (1917), *I'll Say So* (1918), and *To Hell with the Kaiser* (1918), which had a June Mathis screenplay. Then came the ingenue lead in *The Perfect Lady* (1918) with Madge Kennedy. "Miss Kennedy was wonderful to me, and I know that at times she actually turned her back on the camera to give me a chance!"

*The Devil's Garden* (1921), with a Violet Clark screenplay of W. B. Maxwell's story, led to her replacing Faire Binney in *Sentimental Tommy* (1921), which had a Josephine Lovett scenario based on Sir James M. Barrie's "Tommy" stories. It brought her stardom and led to a five-year Famous Players contract. "I worked with Famous Players for two years, and then broke the contract."

*A Private Scandal* (1921), with an Eve Unsell scenario, was followed by *The Top of New York* (1922), based on a story by Sonya Levien (who continued to work as a screenwriter for the next four decades). *Clarence* (1922) was adapted by Clara

Beranger from Booth Tarkington's play. *Kick In* (1922) was adapted by Ouida Bergere from Willard Mack's play. *Grumpy* (1923), also adapted by Beranger, was directed by Cecil B. de Mille's older brother, William, who also directed McAvoy in *Only 38* (1923). *Hollywood* (1923) was followed by *West of the Water Tower* (1924), adapted by Doris Schroeder from Homer Croy's novel, and *The Enchanted Cottage* (1924), adapted by Josephine Lovett from Sir Arthur Wing Pinero's play, with McAvoy rigged in a grotesque make-up. *The New York Times* reviewed:

Due to the modern magic of the camera, resourceful direction and thoroughly competent acting, Sir Arthur Wing Pinero's fantasy, *The Enchanted Cottage*, is much more satisfying on the screen than it was on the stage. The director, John S. Robertson, has filmed this singular digression from the author's well-known society plays with his customary restraint, availing himself of charming double exposure effects and most attractive settings.

In this weird effort, Richard Barthelmess gives a good performance in the difficult, gloomy rôle of a maimed, shell-shocked officer, perpetually conscious of his wrecked form and distorted face. This Oliver Bashforth seeks an abode away from his relatives so as to be as secluded as possible. Mr. Barthelmess is especially well supported by May McAvoy, whose make-up as the dependable, thoughtful governess of emphatically plain visage, is truly marvelous. The idea of this so-called fable can be summed up as lovers gazing upon each other through "blue spectacles." They are blind to physical shortcomings, seeing only the reflected beauty of the soul. Bashforth weds Laura Pennington, not because he loves her, but to deter his energetic sister from visiting him. Soon after the marriage, through discovering names of honeymooning couples of centuries ago, written with diamonds on the window panes of the enchanted cottage, a beautiful love dawns upon the couple, with the result that they see each other utterly transformed, and their conception is exhibited to the spectators. Bashforth straightens his body and a smile crosses his handsome face. The change in May McAvoy as Laura Pennington is far more striking. First she is seen with protruding teeth, tired eyes circled with wrinkles and a prominent nose.

There is nothing farcical about her countenance; she is merely unprepossessing. In a second or so the plain face fades out, its place being taken by one with even teeth, pretty lips and a modest and straight little nose. It is almost incredible that May McAvoy, an actress of undeniable beauty, could be so different with a set of false teeth and a bump on her nose.

After *The Bedroom Window* (1924) she acted for Ernst Lubitsch in *Three Women* (1924). *Tarnish* (1924) and *The Mad Whirl* (1925) were followed by another for Lubitsch, Oscar Wilde's *Lady Windermere's Fan* (1925).

She played the part of Esther in MGM's monumental *Ben Hur* (1926) made at a cost of $6,000,000 with 42 cameras filming the 250,000 chariot-race extras. She narrowly escaped injury on *Ben Hur* when a set burst into flame very close to her while she was standing engaged in conversation with F. Scott Fitzgerald. In First National's *The Savage* (1926), directed by Fred New-

BELOW: A prehistoric beast frightens a passenger and overturns a deck chair in this scene from *The Savage* (1926). May McAvoy and Ben Lyon starred in this First National film directed by Fred Newmeyer. Look close at the creature's neck and you can see the rope that was pulled to make his head move.

meyer, McAvoy and Ben Lyon confronted prehistoric beasts. *The Fire Brigade* (1926), with a Kate Corbaley story, was followed by *Matinee Ladies* (1927), the directorial debut of Byron Haskin, who later helmed many of the George Pal science-fiction films. She appeared in Warners' *Slightly Used* (1927) and negotiated a new contract with the company. "I'm awfully pleased because I played opposite Al Jolson in Warner's first Vitaphone feature picture, *The Jazz Singer* (1927). Following this I did more talking pictures, including *The Lion and the Mouse* (1928), *No Defense* (1929), *Stolen Kisses* (1929), and other equally interesting films. Between us, though, many a producer has told me that because I'm so little he had to put me in the foreground if he wanted me to be seen at all! Perhaps that's one reason I've been successful. Who can tell?"

One of the "other equally interesting films" was Warners' *The Terror* (1928), directed by Roy del Ruth from a Harvey Gates screenplay based on an Edgar Wallace play. Barney McGill handled the photography, and May McAvoy headed the cast of Louise Fazenda, Edward Everett

OPPOSITE: May McAvoy helped usher in the era of sound films in her role as a ballet dancer in *The Jazz Singer* (1927).

BELOW: The cast of *The Terror*, with May McAvoy at center, holds a séance.

Horton, Alec B. Francis, Matthew Betz, Holmes Herbert, John Miljan, Otto Hoffman, Joseph Girard, and Frank Austin. To make sure that no one could accuse *The Terror* of not being completely "all talking," the film dispensed with all credits and subtitles. Conrad Nagel's voice not only read off the credits but also interrupted the action to inform the audience of any change of scene. May McAvoy fled down endless hidden halls and underground tunnels pursued by a hooded criminal called The Terror. The background score played on and on, and Louise Fazenda giggled at the sputter of every "spine-chilling Vitaphone effect." Carlos Clarens, in *An Illustrated History of the Horror Film*, commented, "The picture may have been full of sound, but it signified absolutely nothing. At one point, the leading lady lisped that she was 'thick and tired of thuch thilly antics,' and thus was lovely May McAvoy's doom sealed."

After *Caught in the Fog* (1928), her marriage to United Artists' vice-president G. Cleary led to her retirement from the screen. She returned in 1940, making uncredited bit appearances well into the fifties.

The hooded criminal known as "The Terror" threatens May McAvoy in his underground torture chamber in this scene from *The Terror* (1928). Note *Phantom of the Opera* touch—the organ in the background—and the overall similarity of this shot to Lon Chaney and Mary Philbin in the 1925 film.

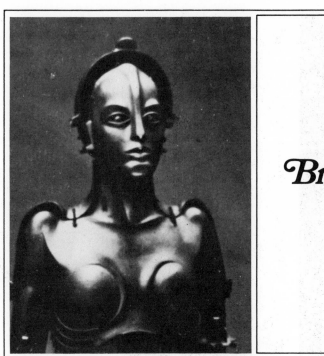

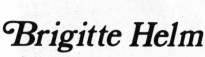

# Brigitte Helm

*B*y the time charming, golden-tressed, sixteen-year-old Brigitte Helm (real name: Gisele Eve Schittenheim) was cast as the female lead in Fritz Lang's *Metropolis* in 1926, horror-film Scream Queens were no longer unique. What is unique (among many other things concerning this film) is that her amazing dual role—as a human versus her evil android counterpart—is of itself historically important: it's one of the earliest filmic acknowledgments of a female being sociopolitically as viable as the male.

Regrettably, the only print of *Metropolis* always available—in the United States anyway—is a butchered ten-reel version, seven reels short of its original length. By some miracle, it still holds up as a classic, with most of its original logic and beauty intact (even though the American distributors idiotically believed that audiences would have found the original seventeen reel length "difficult to comprehend in toto").

Before too long into the story, Helm is established initially as an evangelical Sister Aimee type, out to help the helpless and soothe the unhappy underground workers of Metropolis who, as seen from the start, have much to be restless about. Right after opening credits, the workers are seen in all their unreal misery. Starting another ten-hour-day, they are seen descending from their bleak underground apartments, carried even farther below on huge elevators, heads bowed, spirits crushed. A few reels later, their working conditions are revealed in horrendous detail—a blight on mankind, resembling sheer hell on earth. Accidents are commonplace: a terrible explosion occurs, bodies fly about, and, matter-of-factly, the survivors carry away their comrades on stretchers.

Shortly after the opening credits (workers going below to work, *et al.*), the scene shifts far high above-ground to the near-celestial abodes of the upper class. who spend their lives in magnificent penthouses.

Seen are a number of the ruling class gamboling and partying; attention centers on the hero, Gustav Frolich (as Freder), son of Joh, Metropolis's ruler, played by Al-

fred Abel. Raised with a silver spoon in his mouth, Gustav has led a sheltered existence, shielding him from the grim reality of the workers' horrific conditions.

As the camera closes in, Frolich frolics around a fountain, playing tag with a pretty young lady, surrounded by an indoor garden, birds, and other flora and fauna. Who should butt in, breaking the mood, but Brigitte Helm (as the immortal Maria), entering through the main door and bringing with her a gang of pathetic little waifs holding on to her skirts. They are the children of neglect, victims of plutocratic apathy. Maria is guiding angel and conscience. In answer to Gustav's puzzled look, Brigitte says: "Look—these are your brothers!"

The jet-set crowd and Gustav are so stunned by the sight, no one protests at the intrusion. Gustav is subsequently informed by the head attendant that Brigitte Helm (Maria) is the daughter of a worker. But this short experience disturbs Gustav so much that he quickly breaks away from the party, deciding to find out what life is really like for the lower class by going far down below. It takes him only moments to realize that the workers live in a technological nightmare.

Herewith Fritz Lang presents sensitive insight into prevailing conditions—and an unnerving social and ecological preview of the near future: environmental pollution; hazardous working conditions; the destruction of individuality through intensive social alienation.

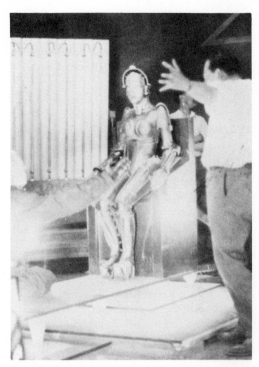

A production shot on the *Metropolis* set, with Fritz Lang directing.

Feder (Gustav Frölich) with Maria (Brigitte Helm) in *Metropolis*—their first intimate encounter.

OPPOSITE PAGE

TOP LEFT: The Golden Age of the German film industry: Max Schreck in *Nosferatu* (1922).

TOP RIGHT: Conrad Veidt and Lil Dagover in the German classic, *The Cabinet of Dr. Caligari* (1919).

BOTTOM LEFT: A view of the awe-inspiring décor of *Metropolis* (1926).

BOTTOM RIGHT: Paul Wegener in the title role of *The Golem* (1920).

Jarred by what he's just witnessed, Gustav runs to his father and wonders how anyone could *rule* with such flabbergasting stupidity. Again, the analogy here between fiction and reality is sharp and forceful. When his son is finished protesting over the plight of the poor, and accusingly states, "Where do they belong in your scheme?" his father answers characteristically:

"In their proper place—the depths!"

Gustav's immediate rejoinder is:

"What will you do if they turn against you some day?"

His father smiles smugly but offers no answer.

In ensuing scenes, Gustav goes back to the workers below and personally shares their suffering by working on one of the machines itself (a huge time-clock-type device whose immense hands Gustav tries to control). Joh (Alfred Abel), Gustav's father, meanwhile believes it's time to "control" the workers with shrewder tactics; he connives with Rudolf Klein-Rogge (playing Rotwang, a quasi-mad scientist)

to kidnap Brigitte because she's become a spiritual leader among the workers—à la Sister Aimee—who hold her in a kind of Virgin Holy Mother esteem. The main trick, though, is not just kidnapping but making an *android duplicate* of Brigitte—a duplicate in every physical respect except Brigitte's quality of mercy, which will be replaced by the android's diabolical nature.

The kidnapping of Brigitte is soon followed by a fantastic scene. She is next seen in scientist Rudolf's amazing, complex laboratory; her nude, comatose body is stretched out underneath a transparent capsule; her head is covered by a special helmet to which are attached wires. Rudolf broods, meditating a bit, then ponders over his next move, to pull the switches that will begin the transformation of an inert, metallic, inhuman-looking robot. He makes his decision. He pulls the switches. The transformation begins.

Standing there in the midst of his private, mind-bending lab, Rudolf Klein-Rogge watches while the robot form is gradually

Rotwang (Rudolf Klein-Rogge) unveils his creation to Frederson (Albert Abel).

encircled by a succession of magical-looking halos, shifting circles resembling hoops made of light. The robot begins to change; the face starts to alter, its inhuman quality slowly disappearing, resembling Brigitte more each second. The change is finally complete. The robot is now an android fully aware of its mission, and evil to the core.

The "evil" Brigitte goes out to foment unrest and trouble among the workers; and this is exactly the pretext needed by Metropolis's unscrupulous master, Joh, in order to destroy their rebellious incentives. There is evidence here of unusual insight into the nature of *agents provocateurs* (one of Lang's important stylisms) and about Nazism, due to appear soon around Germany's troubled corner. But even more uncanny is a nearly prophetic vision of more recent events: Chicago's monstrous political riots of 1968 and Watergate and "stonewalling." Even Alfred Abel as Joh is by temperament

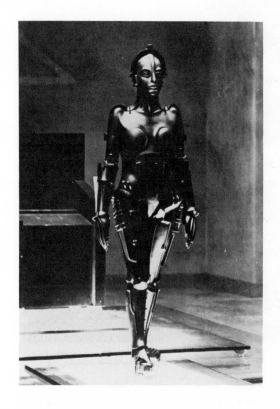

ABOVE: Rotwang's robot creation—the inspiration for the design of C3PO in *Star Wars* (1977).

BELOW: Rotwang casts his robot with the physical appearance of Maria (Brigitte Helm)—but minus her angelic qualities.

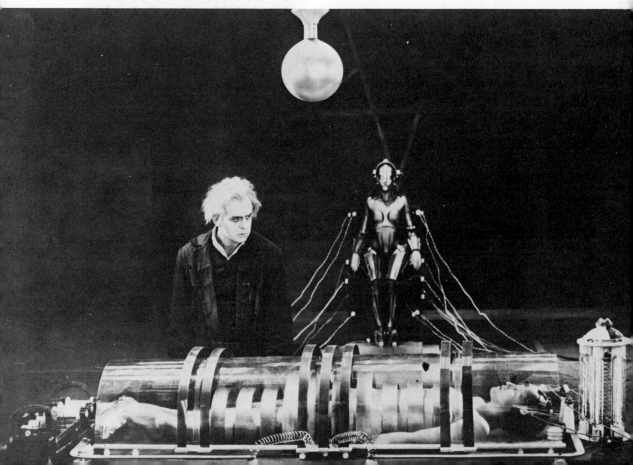

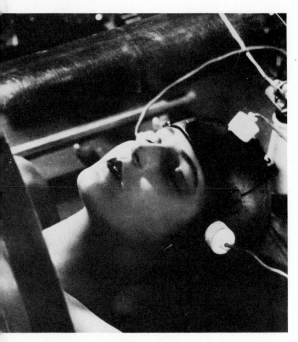

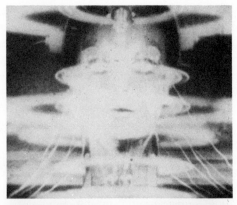

ABOVE: A close-up of Maria as the transformation begins.

RIGHT: Frame blow-ups detail the creation process of the robot Maria, also portrayed by Brigitte Helm.

and strategy and even in *appearance* almost a double for Richard M. Nixon.

After riots that threaten the very foundations of Metropolis, Gustav saves the "real" Brigitte from captivity. Both go out in an attempt to save the people, whose rage turns against the android Brigitte; they track her down and symbolically burn her at the stake. But even while the evil double wilts away under the fires of true justice, the mad scientist Rudolf runs after the innocent Brigitte. He realizes that all his dreams and plans are dead, and he pursues her in one of the finest chase sequences made; through an empty cathedral, up, above, and across parapets, and all over the tremendous Gothic structure; and as he is about to corner Brigitte, stepping between the two is the heroic, challenging figure of Gustav. Both pounce on each other, hero versus mad doctor, running across the cathedral's slanted eaves, while Abel looks up surrounded by the excited mob around him. Abel realizes he may have erred as he sees

Before and after—rehearsing and performing the nightclub act of *Metropolis*.

his son's life in the balance hundreds of feet aboveground. Rudolf and Gustav tumble over and over; the scientist now has the upper hand. Is all lost for her hero? Then, quickly, it's all finished. Rudolf starts to roll down the steep cathedral roof, totters just a second, then falls to his death.

In a strange kind of rapprochement, the big, burly Chief Foreman Grot (played with heavy beard by Heinrich George, resembling Laird Cregar)—who has made several other impressive appearances earlier in the story—leads a huge phalanx of the workers, walking toward Brigitte, Gustav, and Alfred, who stand at the top of the great cathedral's steps by its huge doors. Grot leaves the huge assemblage, goes up the steps, stands hesitatingly. Gustav overcomes his hesitation by gently taking his arm and placing the hand in his father's open palm. They both shake hands warmly, thus signifying that there is indeed a successful way of mediating between *the heart and the mind*. The film closes, almost abruptly, at this point.

In the whole genesis of great science-fantasy films, *Metropolis* is undoubtedly the definitive archetype, anticipating virtually all elements serving to guarantee the success of future classics such as *Things To Come, The Day the Earth Stood Still*, and *2001: A Space Odyssey*. When *Metropolis* opened in the United States (with altered character names), Mordaunt Hall, in *The New York Times*, offered this review:

Nothing like *Metropolis*, the ambitious Ufa production that has created wide international comment, has been seen on the screen. It, therefore, stands alone, in some respects, as a remarkable achievement. It is a technical marvel with feet of clay, a picture as soulless as the manufactured woman of its story. Its scenes bristle with cinematic imagination, with hordes of men and women and astounding stage settings. It is hardly a film to be judged by its narrative, for despite the fantastic nature of the story, it is, on the whole, unconvincing, lacking in suspense and at times extravagantly theatric. It suggests a combination of a preachment on capital and labor in a city of the future, an *R. U. R.* idea and something of Mrs. Shelley's *Frankenstein*. Its moral is that the brains and the hands fail when the heart (love) does not work with them. The brains represent capital, and the hands, labor. The production itself appears to have been a Frankenstein model to the story. Fritz Lang, the famous German director

53

who was responsible for the *Siegfried* film, handled the making of the photodrama. Occasionally it strikes one that he wanted to include too much and then that all one anticipates does not appear. But at the same time the various ideas have been spliced together quite adroitly. It is a subject on which an adverse comment has to be taken from the perspective of the enormity of the task, as most other pictures would fade into insignificance if compared to it. When one criticizes the halting steps of workmen, their stagy efforts to demonstrate fatigue and even the lacking details of life in this metropolis, one realizes that there is in this screen effort much that borders on symbolism.

The narrative is based on a novel by Mr. Lang's wife, Thea von Harbou, who also supplied the manuscripts for *The Indian Mausoleum and Siegfried.* . . . Metropolis is ruled by John Masterman, a man of great brain and whose only soft spot in his heart is for his son, Eric. This son falls in love with Mary, one of the workers, and he, in sympathy for those who work and dwell far under the ground, becomes one of the underlings, much against his father's wishes. . . .

Some idea of the prodigious work in this production can be imagined when it is said that about 37,000 extras were engaged in some of the episodes. Eleven thousand of the men have shaven heads. . . . The sequence in which Rotwang, the inventor, manufactures a double of Mary is put forth in a startling fashion. Rotwang first gives chase to the real Mary, and then puts her in a glass cylinder, around which appear circles of radium lights. To add to the impression, there are boiling liquids in glass globes, and finally the Mary without a soul is produced with the help of an iron Robotlike woman Rotwang had made previously. The artificial Mary, the "woman" who could walk and talk but possessed no soul, has queer drooping underlids to her eyes. She leers at those who approach her. . . . Brigitte Helm is extraordinarily fine in the rôles of the real and the artificial Mary. Alfred Abel gives a vivid portrayal of Masterman, and Gustav Froelich is excellent as Eric. Rudolf Klein-Rogge is splendid as the inventor. The cast is remarkably well chosen.

*Metropolis* was also described as follows in a program note during a special film-society presentation in 1960: "Remarkable in its horrific presentation of what well could be the great automated and dehumanized great city of the future, Fritz Lang's *Metropolis* is a significant example of expressionist film-making at its finest. A chilling portrait of a massive upper world of steel and concrete (Lang patterned the looming sets after seeing New York's skyline during a trip) ruled over by a cabal of evil, the film also pictures a lower city where masses of enslaved workers battle for survival in a jungle of machines. The social and ideological commentary of Orwell and Huxley; a vision of portent, and a warning. Though many critics contend the work to be proto-Nazi propaganda (this view is explored at length by the noted film historian Siegfried Kracauer in his epic study *The German Film: From Caligari to Hitler*), all concur with Dr. Kracauer that *Metropolis* is 'cinematically an incomparable achievement.' "

Although for reasons of his own, Lang's personal favorite was the Peter Lorre vehicle *M, Metropolis* is a monument to the late artist's directorial genius. Because of myopic critical opinion (at a time when critics were considered oracles) and poor overseas distribution—augmented by the butchery it suffered in the United States —*Metropolis* was a financial disaster. Its cost was estimated at approximately 3 million dollars (some say 4 million) during a period when Germany was bankrupt from a cataclysmic depression. This would be comparable today to somewhere in the vicinity of 25 or 30 million dollars.

Perhaps all this cost and opulence may not be very apparent during a screening, but it should be understood, of course, that at least seven of the original seventeen reels were chopped out for American distribution. Among major omissions, and apart from several integral subplots, there is a magnificent stadium scene (not unlike a portion of Riefenstahl's *Olympiad*); around sixty seconds of this were recently found and reinserted. In the original, Rotwang is far more sympathetic and far from being on the brink of derangement, especially during the film's last wild scene. Reediting has unfortunately given the story a slightly different interpretation. There has been serious discussion during the past few years of the possibilities of restoration to its original form, complete with a sound track and musical score.

Beyond exciting the imaginations of fantasy fans during the twenties, the picture brought acclaim to Brigitte Helm, establishing her overnight as one of Europe's leading stars. Within several years, Brigitte was the toast of Europe's theatrical culture and the darling of high society. But, above all, she was a laureated *artist*; and this is confirmed so well by the renowned film historian Paul Rotha in his excellent study, *The Film Till Now* (Spring Books, London, 1967), in describing the way director G. W. Pabst plied Miss Helm's talent in *Crisis* (1928):

. . . . (In) *The Joyless Street* . . . the centre of interest was the compelling fascination of Brigitte Helm's Myra. Pabst was the first director to reveal a rare side to this actress, a quality that was not apparent in *A Daughter of Destiny* [aka *Alraune*, 1928], *Metropolis*, *At the Edge of the World* [a 1927 futuristic tale] *L'Argent*, and her other pictures. In *Loves of Jeanne Ney*, Pabst was interested in the playing of Brigitte Helm as the blind girl. In *Crisis* (1928), he became absorbed in the personality of Miss Helm herself. He succeeded in making her every movement exciting. Her strange latent power and underlying neurosis were here given their freedom. Her vibrant beauty, her mesh of gold hair, her slender, supple figure were caught and photographed from every angle. The intensity of her changing moods, her repression and resentment, her bitterness and cynicism, her final passionate breakdown in the Argentine club; these were constructed into a filmic representation of overwhelming psychological power. Pabst analysed and dissected the remarkable character of Miss Helm and built up out of the pieces a unified, plastic personality. Her curious, fascinating power has never been exploited with such skill.

Even though she starred in many non-fantasy films, Brigitte Helm's reputation as a stellar heroine (or heavy) of the horrors would have been justified enough by being the female lead in *Metropolis*. Her genre status soared even higher in the leading role in *Alraune* (1928), later resuming the same part in the sound remake of 1930. In 1932, she starred in G. W. Pabst's *L'Atlantide*, and in 1934 had the female lead in *Gold*.

Under Henrik Galeen's direction, there's a quality of *déjà vu* in *Alraune* because Helm plays a role rather similar in character to her evil counterpart in *Metropolis*—even down to her creation by a well-meaning but, as usual, slightly off-the-wall scientist, depicted by the immortal Paul Wegener. Forecasting the possibility of creating test-tube babies (a popular topic of Sunday-supplement sensationalism of that day), Wegener succeeds in creating Alraune (Helm); but she carries evil genes and blood from a prostitute mother and a father executed for his crimes. Helm grows to beautiful womanhood, devoid of soul, by nature and talent a psychic vampire. She is emotionless, yet feigning warmth and masking soulless ruthlessness with her sensuous power, and one man after another falls desperately in love with her, ultimately ending in some terrible fate. Some scintilla of awareness, a lost ember of conscience grows inside her; eventually the ember turns into a consuming flame that she cannot put out; and, in the end, she destroys herself.

The subject awed audiences and critics alike; for, here was no Golem, robot, or unnatural monster—just a human-looking creature who, regardless of origin, reminded them of the self-destructive people and actual, social, psychic vampires met in everyday life. A box-office winner, *Alraune* was remade in 1930 and also in 1952. In her monumental work on early German films, *The Haunted Screen* (University of California Press, 1969), Lotte Eisner says: "If Galeen's silent *Alraune* of 1928 is so much superior to Richard Oswald's sound version of 1930, the reason is to be found not only in the greater talent of Galeen: the first *Alraune* has the benefit of silence to safeguard the tension inherent in an essentially fantastic subject. Even so, this film of

Creator and creation: Paul Wegener and Brigitte Helm in *Alraune* (1928).

Galeen's made during the period of decline lacks the quality of *The Student of Prague*, which the same director made in 1926 within the conventions of the Expressionist vision. By 1928 German filmmakers seldom dared to indulge in fantasy as completely as before, and elements of the 'new objectivity' mar the unity of a film like *Alraune*."

Helm's next important fantasy was *L'Atlantide* (1932). Lamentably, like numerous other films, this too (along with *Alraune* and *Gold*) is presumably lost. It had already been made in 1920 by director Jacques Feyder (his first film), based on Pierre Benoit's best-selling novel *L'Atlan-* *tide* (1919); production was at great expense, partly shot by Feyder in exotic Moroccan locales for authenticity. Since then, the Haggard-like theme has been re-adapted many times for the screen in various guises. The most notable one, seen frequently on TV, is *Siren of Atlantis* (1948), with the lovely Maria Montez in the title role heading a good cast consisting of Dennis O'Keefe, Jean-Pierre Aumont (once dubbed "the poor man's Jean Gabin"), Henry Daniell, and Morris Carnovsky—who are otherwise wasted. The film bore the touch and look of another Hollywood back-lot programmer. One of the last known versions was *Antinea, L'Amante*

Hildegarde Neff in *Alraune* (1952), directed by Arthur-Maria Rabenalt.

*della Citta Sepolta* (retitled for British release as *The Lost Kingdom* and as *Journey Beneath the Desert* for American distribution by Embassy). It was directed by Edgar G. Ulmer, a talent who raised the B film to high plateaus. (*The Black Cat, Bluebeard, Detour,* and *Ruthless*).

Covering *L'Atlantide* in his highly interesting survey, *Science Fiction in the Cinema*, John Baxter writes:

Feyder's *L'Atlantide* echoed its time and its filmic attitudes; fantasy was merely a matter of decoration, an excuse for weird *décor*. Pabst's *L'Atlantide* (1932), springing from a cinema no longer content with elaborate decoration for its own sake, has the erotic bite of the best German films, and a visual élan that makes it a modern classic. Predictably, Pabst's Antinea (Helm) is no simpering sex-pot but a cold and imperious queen who delights, like Brunhilda, in competing with her lovers and destroying those who cannot match her. Declining to become involved in the tedious details of the legionnaires' discovery of Atlantis, Pabst explores at length the story of Antinea's birth, the daughter of an Arab sheikh and a Parisian can-can dancer. As Antinea, Brigitte Helm is a worthy successor to the robot Maria of *Metropolis*, her axe-hard profile used by Pabst to good effect in a design that echoes it in a succession of huge images of her face filling the halls of lost Atlantis. Shot like Feyder's version partly in the Hoggar desert and other Moroccan locations, Pabst's film is in every way a superior work, one of the finest romances from the golden age of the German cinema.

*Gold* (1934) was one of Brigitte Helm's last starring roles, released in the second year of Nazism's rule over Germany. Heavy on hardware and elaborate pseudo-scientific but highly realistic apparatus, *Gold* is relatively simple and even a little old-fashioned in story structure: a scientist discovers a fantastically cheap method of making gold; he's opposed, then successfully thwarted in his endeavors lest he upset the world's economy. Brigitte Helm plays the scientist's daughter who falls in love with the hero. Part of *The New York Times'* review (November 22, 1934) had this to say:

This time the dream of many ancient, and some modern, would-be gold manufacturers is realized on the screen with a remarkable display of thrilling scenes involving excellent views of some fearful and wonderful machinery. . . . While there is no doubt from the very beginning that the stalwart and versatile Hans Albers will have his revenge upon the evil Scotch mining magnate (Michael Bohnen) for having caused the death of the former's fellow Berlin scientist in a gold-making experiment, the audience is kept interested in the steps leading up to the denouement, despite the inordinate length of the film.

The fine work of Albers and Bohnen is well supported by Brigitte Helm, as the Scots-

Elaborate production values highlight the German-made *Gold* (1934). Here is the underwater lab, complete with atomic reactor—a scene which intrigued Allied scientists.

man's daughter who apparently falls in love with the visiting German engineer at first sight, and by the appealing, little Ien Deyers, as his German sweetheart, whose blood saves his life when a transfusion becomes necessary following the destruction of the Berlin laboratory in the first part of the picture. But the outstanding merit of the production is to be found on its technical side.

Brigitte Helm stayed on in Europe throughout the war years; but just as entertainment media and, particularly, film culture were nearly irreparably disrupted by the war, so did Miss Helm's career go into limbo.

The irony of this, providing not only sad but heavy evidence of the monstrous effect of war, is how one of the world's finest dramatic artists—with most of her best years still ahead—could be celebrated one year but fade into obscurity in less than thirty months.

A great evaluation of Helm's personality and position in the arts was made by a contemporary eyewitness. Following is not merely a fine analysis of Brigitte Helm but a study of tremendous

sensitivity written by Robert Herring in early 1932, a remarkable film scholar of the day:

It is not generally known that Eleonora Duse, during the last years of her life, made a film. It was called *Ashes*. But it is not generally known because Duse had it destroyed; she was not satisfied with herself—at the end of her life she "recognised at once that a different training, a different technique was necessary for this new art. . . . I am too old for it—isn't it a pity?" she said two years before she died.

Duse, eight years ago, was found haunting the cinemas of Florence. If you know what those were like four years later, as I do, you will come a little nearer understanding her greatness in realizing cinema itself. For Duse had been born in the life of the theatre, she had lived in it all her life, and could not keep away from it; and yet, when she was sixty-two, with years of acclamation and success behind her, she said to someone, who reproached her for going to films, that "they are perhaps a genuine expression of the modern world. If I were twenty years younger I would begin all over again on the films and I am certain that I could do a great deal on them, and perhaps evolve something like a completely new form of art . . . one would have to forget the theatre entirely and learn how to express oneself in the language of the films, which is as yet undeveloped; but something quite different is needed from stage technique . . . a new and more effective kind of poetry, a new expression of the human soul. . . . I am too old for it, isn't it a pity?"

Duse, of course, never found the theatre she wanted. She was always searching for "new and more effective kind of poetry" in the theatre, and she lived long enough to glimpse it in cinema.

Brigitte Helm's is much the same trouble. She is born twenty years too soon, and faced with her, most directors can only turn that flaming spirituality into vamp roles, robing an icicle in satin, covering a flame with unneeded tinsel.

It always happens to me when I read of Duse; I think of Helm, and in writing of Helm, I want to write too of Duse. People will think that I am comparing them, which is absurd, the kind of thing that people would think. It simply is that if you are talking of the South Pole to someone, you presume some knowledge of the North Pole, though the two are quite different. There are, for instance, no bears in the Antarctic, far fewer flowers, and the Aurora Borealis is much poorer; on the other hand there are more and greater icebergs. They are "poles apart," but it is what lies between that makes simultaneous consideration possible, and I feel that there was Duse, whom I did just see, and here is Brigitte Helm, and everything else lies between. But that of course does not bring them together. An Arctic bird could not live in the South Pole.

But I am constantly surprised at how old-fashioned nearly everything that happens is—the way people live and their love-affairs, flying the Atlantic . . . the use of radio, the fact that women have not evolved either a useful or a beautiful costume, our treatment of such things as gases and "natives," the things we talk about and, can I believe my ears, the things we don't. And when I look back, there was Duse; accepting the cinema and realising it, and I look round again and find Helm, who does to me typify a lot that we call "modern." The things which, the more one grows accustomed to being alive, one finds one can use . . . zip-fasteners, the rock paintings at Makumbi, Heinrich Mann's *Berlin*, the outside of Selfridges, the colours and materials of the Central London railway, and the fact that a sunbeam could give a 120 mph aeroplane a start of five million

miles in a five million and one mile race and win. With all that Brigitte Helm fits in.

So when she arrived at Wembley, to do interiors on the four-tongued *City of Song*, I went down to see her. It happened that just before, some friends of mine were reading Ibsen, and as I had seen *The Lady from the Sea* acted by Duse, I was reading her life by Rheinhardt (Berlin, 1928; Secker, London, 1930) and perhaps because of association through Werner Krauss in *The Wild Duck*, though I think because I always, Duse apart, thought so, I was thinking of Helm in such plays as *Rosmersholm* and *The Doll's House*. Anyway, you see I was in a certain amount of muddle which Helm only increased by making it seem quite natural.

She has a gift for making things seem that. It seems quite natural to be sitting talking to her, although the prospect of meeting the trailing turbaned creature of German films with the sidelong glance is unnerving. It seems quite natural at the time to find that she is not this at all, though you only think that after. She is not in the least a star and not in the least indifferent. Her eyes are so blue and her skin so Germanic-gold that the steel-and-silver Brigitte Helm of the screen seems (what it is) a creation of her mind. Off the screen, even in make up and a long pale blue dress, she and her screen-self seem complementary but detached. What they call bi-polarity, I believe. But you see that the screen Helm is the clothing devised by the mind for her actual self, which is so friendly and radiant and lights up so gently when you mention Pabst, say you know Berlin or tell her she will soon see *Anna Christie*.

It is absurd to mitigate Helm's magnetism because they often put her in mediocre films. We are told she cannot be as good as we think she is; it is merely personality shining in a desert. But personality could not alone, at 22, have made Helm the most important actress in the European cinema, playing with equal insight young wives, girls and expensive prostitutes generally. Look at other people in mediocre films and see how mediocre they are. Think of Dita Parlo's failure to be anything but superficial in *Heimkehr*, think of how much more Helm did in *The Wonderful Life* than Parlo again in *Hungarian Rhapsody*, and, classic instance, think of Louise Brooks—*Lulu*. In a good film too, well a goodish one—think how much better even than Marlene Dietrich Helm would have been in all that is important. The trouble is that Helm in a bad film makes it seem much better. She gives it a vitality on a real, psychic plane. She brings motives and moods into play that never are brought into play except by her, though we know them in our daily lives, and she can give them with a sharpness which loses no delicacy and a fullness which is never broad. She makes a living woman in a film where no woman could live, and so, brought upon the slick interpretations, which give us no women at all, of Norma Shearer, Ruth Chatterton, Mary Brian, and the rest, who are so pleasant in their way, we rather tend to say that Helm is "exotic." Actually, she becomes only exotic when she has a bad director, and her cool ardour and sort of mystical matter-of-factness are diverted into vamp roles.

Duse, of course, acted in mediocre plays: Sardou, Dumas. She did Shakespeare, Ibsen, Goldoni, too, but *Heimat* and *La Dame Aux Camelia*, plays like that, were her repertory. Once again, those plays acted by ordinary players show Duse's greatness. I only once saw Duse, once only, in only one play, but the extraordinary thing is that having seen that, I have a good knowledge of what she would have been like in those other plays which I have seen actresses make nothing of. And why did she go on appearing in these plays? Rheinhardt's book says, "Because she felt that their conventional construction left the character parts undeveloped; they provided merely a framework in which she had room to create her own conception . . . acting was the creative expression of an inner discord which might have become pathological but for her gifts, a projection of split in the personality, a solution for her own problems." And Paul Schlenther wrote of her creations, "When one sees an actress like Duse taking all the crudeness out of those crude and mediocre plays one is compelled to admit that acting can be completely emancipated from poetry and to swear that it is a flow of changing plastics effects more akin to sculpture." Words which rather seem to fit what Helm does in the train sequence in *Alraune* and in *Abwege (The Crisis)* and in *The Wonderful Lie*.

Perhaps one of the reasons why I keep referring to Duse in what should be an interview with Brigitte Helm is that most of the things which were said of Duse's work seem as you see to apply to Helm. That uncanny quality which one can find no name for, one finds in a book on Duse that everyone felt in her "something of the elemental and indefinable," and

that is what you want for Helm's uncanny power.

That power is due to her spirit behind her parts. The ice-flaming presence we see on the screen flames, it seems to me, with mind. There is the glittering scythe and behind it the swing of the scythe. That is Helm, acting. Mind-acting. She makes herself a vehicle for it, as Duse felt herself a vehicle for a power greater than herself. They say that when, in the first act of *La Dame aux Camelias*, the dance is broken by a cough, "Duse merely stopped and looked nervous." That is a remarkable thing to do. I think only Brigitte Helm on the screen could do it. She is always at her best when she stops and looks nervous; that is to say, when her actual person stops and she is a vehicle for flowing mind. You are never taken in by the fact that Helm plays vamps so well, are you? So much the better than Garbo, for instance? She says, "I will play a vamp, of course, but she must have something here"— and she hits neither heart nor head, but her chest, meaning drive and the need to get something out. It seems she instinctively feels that crooks have their expression twisted, have the wrong outlet, and wants to know why that is so . . . because, like any creative worker, she wants to free herself.

To me, Brigitte Helm stands for an entirely peculiar type of acting which is not in the least exotic, but merely rare. It is simply that she goes further and takes things on to a higher plane. The things she is called on to do in her parts she does a little more sharply, she sees a little more clearly; and when she is to be exotic she carries exoticism a little further, because she is behind it and that is her mind's comment on it. But in simple parts or sophisticated parts, you can always find what she is doing, if you look, what she is searching for in the parts, the solution she is trying to achieve as she develops, and that "split in personality" that was so marked when I met her at Wembley that when I came on the phrase in the book, I got so muddled with Duse, and have written no interview at all.

But does that matter? I can tell you that she hated the *Yacht of the Seven Sins*; that she says everything is due to one's director, it is awful to work with a director who makes one do stupid things as some of them do; that she speaks two languages in *City of Song*, her first talkie, but plans to add French and English to these in her next film, to be made in Germany

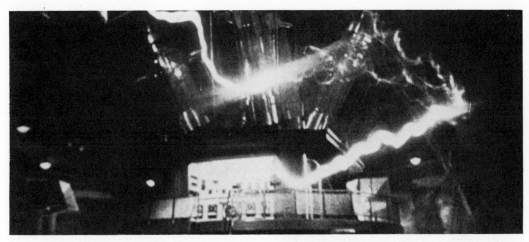

In the finale, the machine in *Gold* malfunctions, and the lab is flooded. This sequence was excerpted for use in United Artists' *The Magnetic Monster* (1953).

with Fritz Kortner. Then she plans to go on the stage, because she has been working since she was sixteen and has never had to speak and she feels the stage will give her voice-poise. She would like to go to Hollywood for no more than two films. She would learn a lot in Hollywood if she came back in time; and she thinks it a pity to work too long for one firm, because they get fixed in their ideas about you. And she wants a new type of part (in my opinion she needs a new kind of cinema, for the cinema which she represents, the psychological cinema, has not come into its own or even been properly born yet. Infant mortality in film psychology is high). But what is all that compared to the fact that meeting her one knows she can act Ibsen and that the real part for her is neither a Manolescu crook, nor a Grune miller's daughter, but a combination of both. Real simplicity, which is sophistication achieved. And compared to the fact that eight years ago an elderly actress was complaining that she was twenty years too old and that she would like to begin all over again on the movies, the only thing in acting that isn't old-fashioned between her and Brigitte Helm, now that the cinema talks, is going to the theatre to learn how to talk. I mean, do you see what I mean?

With Nazism bludgeoning its way to total control of Germany in 1933, Joseph Goebbels was installed as minister of propaganda, assuming full power over all media, especially filmmaking; most of the cream of German filmmaking had already left or were packing up for what freedom and sanity lay elsewhere. Many, like Fritz Lang, finally settled in Hollywood; others, staying behind, barely had time to run for cover or would perish under Nazi atrocities. Helm's heart and position were soon self-evident. If she had chosen to do so, she could have stayed on, feted and laureated, situated in the lap of Nazi luxury, as Thea von Harbou did by separating from Fritz Lang and embracing "the new order." But of her own accord (around the time of *Gold*'s completion) she and her "non-Aryan" husband took leave of their homeland one night without notice.

A report in the September 23rd, 1938, edition of *The New York Times* tells the rest:

Brigitte Helm, the siren princess of *Metropolis* [the writer was thinking of *L'Atlantide*] and the star of the *Lie of Nina Petrovna* has *disappeared* from the German screen. Guilty of "race defilement" because she married a Jew after the establishment of the Nazi regime, she has been working in Paris, where she made *Adieux les Beaux Jours* in 1934.

Not long after the war's end, Brigitte Helm returned to Germany, taking up residence in Munich and living in very affluent circumstances. She still maintains the same lifestyle, surrounded by many friends and undying memories.

# Mary Philbin

The still photograph of Mary Philbin reaching for Lon Chaney's mask in *Phantom of the Opera* (1925) might well be the most reprinted still from the silent days around today. One encounters it everywhere. Were it not for this one film, Mary Philbin would be almost totally forgotten, but, in this case, one is enough. There's no doubt Philbin qualifies as a Scream Queen—her reactions and screams in *Phantom of the Opera* are delivered with such intensity that one sometimes imagines her voice can actually be heard!

She was born in 1903. As a child in Chicago, she lived in a world of make-believe and fantasy. "I was always pretending I was a beautiful princess," she remembered, "begging mother to let me wear her long dresses and floating veils, and going through all kinds of romantic stories of my own imagining, always as the heroine, of course."

Mary's dolls did not sit idly with blank stares but were cast in roles in her fantasy plays. The dolls that weren't on stage became spectators in the audience. Whenever

there was an opportunity to see a motion picture, Mary went. "I suffered with the lovely ladies in distress and sometimes found myself acting with them. Then I'd go home and go through the play myself, standing before a mirror and seeing if I couldn't outact the screen player."

When the Elks Club and the Chicago *Herald Examiner* held a beauty contest with the winner to receive a Universal contract, young Mary Philbin, just out of high school, considered entering but then rejected the notion. "I was terribly anxious to enter," she recalled, "but when I looked over my photographs, I decided I hadn't a chance—each day the paper was printing pictures of girls so much prettier than I. So, rather tearfully, I gave up the idea of entering at all. Then a letter came saying my picture had been selected from some 5000 applicants and I was to come in person before the judges for a further elimination. I read the letter twice before I could believe my eyes, then ran to mother so excited I could hardly talk. She smiled and told me she had sent in an old photograph, one of those I had discarded as no good, for she knew how much I wanted to enter. That was a great day for me. Mother helped me dress, and I went to meet the judges."

One of the judges was Erich von Stroheim, and Mary made a strong impression on him. He thought she was the most attractive young woman in the room. "Mr. von Stroheim talked to a number of the girls, and then he saw me and came over and began asking me if I liked pictures. Finally, he asked if I had seen *Broken Blossoms* (1918), and when I said yes, and told him how wonderful I thought it was, he asked me to come into another room where we could have quiet."

Von Stroheim then suggested that she act out the scene from *Broken Blossoms* where Lillian Gish was threatened with a whipping. "At first I was afraid and self-conscious, but Mr. von Stroheim was so patient and so interested that I forgot myself and began to act as I had loved to act at home. He was wonderful—he told me he believed I had real talent. I was never so happy in my life."

Von Stroheim sent a cable to Carl Laemmle in Europe, and Laemmle signed Mary Philbin on as a Universal contract player. Time passed, but eventually she got the word and left for Hollywood. "Mr. von Stroheim wanted me for his *Foolish Wives* (1921), but there was some hitch there. The first part I played at Universal was in *The Blazing Trail* (1921). Other parts followed."

When von Stroheim scripted *Merry-Go-Round* (1923), he had Mary Philbin in mind when he wrote the character of Mitzi. Both Irving Thalberg and Carl Laemmle were doubtful, but the role became hers— and it was the turning point in her career. "I got my real break," she said. "I loved that part." The story took place at an expensive Hollywood reconstruction of the Vienna Prater fairgrounds. Philbin played the young innocent cranking the carousel organ, romanced by a young count (Norman Kerry), and secretly loved by a hunchback (George Hackathorne). Her father (Cesare Gravina) runs the puppet show, and her boss Huber (originally enacted by **Wallace Beery**) is a brutal sadist occasionally given to driving the caged gorilla into a frenzy and inflicting various torments on the employees of the amusement park. The

Mary Philbin in a gag studio shot about the time of her debut at Universal in *The Blazing Trail* (1921). The original publicity department caption read, "Mary Philbin, Universal star, sharpens her ax and fixes the turkey with a puissant glare as Thanksgiving Day draws near."

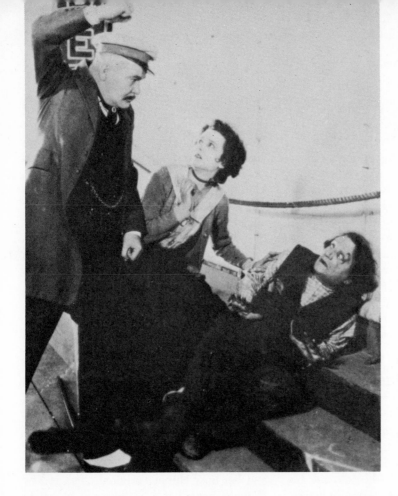

George Siegmann as carousel-owner, Mary Philbin as Mitzi, and Cesare Gravina as her puppeteer father in *Merry-Go-Round*. Siegmann replaced Wallace Beery in the role after Beery walked off the set when von Stroheim was fired by Irving Thalberg.

hunchback retaliates by opening the gorilla's cage. It roams about, finally strangling Huber while he sleeps. Mitzi promises to marry the hunchback, but, after World War I, the count returns to the fairground. After overhearing Mitzi accept the count's proposal, the hunchback commits suicide.

After five weeks of filming, von Stroheim was fired by Thalberg. Philbin collapsed into tears. "I can't act without Mr. Von," said Philbin. Wallace Beery walked off the set, refusing to continue without von Stroheim.

Work continued. Beery declined to return and was replaced by George Siegmann, an old enemy. Philbin and the others were retained. The directorial task was given to Rupert Julian, who would later direct *Phantom of the Opera*. Although scenes by von Stroheim were in the final release, the credit went to Julian. *The New York Times* reviewed the film:

*Merry Go Round*, the photoplay holding forth this week at the Rivoli, is a scintillating fascinating picture, skillfully directed by Rupert Julian. Some of the dramatic incidents call to mind thoughts of Vienna in merry and reckless prewar days, of Grimaldi, the famous clown of past years, and also Edgar Allan Poe's story, *The Murders in the Rue Morgue*. Running through the film is a charming love story, and, although the production is 10,000 feet long, the action is so swift and the interest so well sustained, that it hardly seems half that length. . . . There are a number of incidents in this production that will linger in one's mind for some time, especially where an old clown has been badly injured by a large plant pot pushed from a balcony by the villain, who owns a rival show. A second before the clown is making the children laugh at his antics, and while lying on the ground he courageously continues to amuse the little ones, until expression fades from his face and he is carried off unconscious in an ambulance. . . .

There is a great orang-outang—too big, but made to appear very real—whose cage-door is intentionally left open by the hunchback in charge. The beast climbs up a door post to the villain's sleeping quarters and—well, George Siegmann's part as Schani Huber comes to an abrupt end, but what happens is left to the imagination after the animal is seen in Huber's room. . . . Siegmann, as usual, makes a grim, convincing villain, always ready with a sneer and brutal rage. Miss Philbin is appealing as the simple girl in love with the gay young officer. Gravina gives a splendid portrayal of the clown. In fact, all the players deserve praise. They seem to have been carried away by the picture as much as those who will go to see it. *Merry Go Round* is so entertaining that the sets and scenes are almost taken for granted as the story runs along, and Mr. Julian has seen to it that there is movement even in a close-up, on the side of which one observes the stir in the street.

Mary Philbin was next seen in Henry Otto's *Temple of Venus* (1923), which had fantasy elements. *The New York Times* commented,

An extravagant production on which the director, or somebody else, has permitted a wild imagination to run riot was presented by William Fox as a successor to *Monna Vanna*. This film might be likened to a patchwork quilt, and in it a heroic effort has been made to link together as one story the most incongruous sequences, some of which are extraordinarily beautiful. One sees Greek gods and goddesses, life on a rock-ribbed island, a bevy of dancing nymphs, scenes of ultra-modern jazz existence, a love affair between an artist and an unsophisticated maiden, and truly marvelous pictures of seals. It would take a superbrain to weld together such a melange of matter, and even the ordinary spectator may find his head in a whirl trying to follow this two miles of celluloid as it is flashed upon the screen. This picture should be taken as a film folly without attempting to follow the narrative. Obviously it is meant to be a screen beauty show, but the shadow of the censor has restricted certain possibilities in this picture. The gowns in the jazz sequences are deeply decollette at the back, and a pretty woman is asked by her maid whether she wishes a lavender shower or a plunge in the perfumed pool. Apparently this lady fair chooses the latter as a vague outline of her figure is visible through the self-imposed censorial steam screen as she glides toward the sparkling water. . . . In an effort to sustain interest, but without an idea of suspense, the nether limbs of feminine players are shown in , a semi close-up as they descend the stairs on their way to a so-called "beach-warming" party.

The outset of this affair is on the order of the swimming pool scenes in most motion picture houses. One sees the hostess, satiated with dancing and long gowns, give the order to disrobe. So off come the frocks and finery, revealing dainty bathing costumes—"one-peach bathing suits" as a bit of pulchritude called them. The bored hostess takes all this as a matter of course. . . . There are a number of scintillating scenes with dancing girls in their filmy veils, and compelling shots of the rocks and the breaking seas, and the tinting and toning of these sequences is effective, especially in the double exposure parts where Moria (Mary Philbin) is shown talking on the picturesque rocks, the only person who can see the nymphs. . . . According to the story a young artist fed up with jollity and jazz flees to the rugged island and meets the fair Moria. In the opening to a cave on the brink of still, reflective waters, paying little heed to his canvas, he tells Moria about the prattling Echo, whom he is painting from memory of others' works. The film fades into his narrative and Juno, Jupiter, Thetis, Echo and others are introduced. . . . We cannot say much for the acting in this picture, the fault being largely with the direction, as most of the thought was devoted to the spectacle. Miss Philbin, who was loaned to the Fox organization by the Universal corporation, did splendidly in *Merry Go Round*; but in this film she appears with a mass of hair always floating around her shoulders, doing a great deal of posing.

*Temple of Venus* was followed by *Fifth Avenue Models* (1925), adapted by Olga Printzlau from the novel *The Best in Love* by Muriel Hine. *Phantom of the Opera* was made as a result of the success of *Hunchback of Notre Dame*. Since audiences had not forgotten George Hackathorn's hunchback characterization in *Merry-Go-Round*, obviously it was thought something unique would result from the teaming of Philbin, Cesare Gravina, director Rupert Julian of *Merry-Go-Round*, with Lon Chaney in a facial makeup even more bizarre than his *Hunchback* disguise. Also cast in *Phantom* was leading man Norman Kerry, who was in both *Merry-Go-Round* and *Hunchback*. Universal acquired the rights to the Gaston Leroux novel, written in 1908. The Universal set department

ABOVE: In this scene from *Phantom of the Opera* (1925), suitor Raoul (Norman Kerry) begs Christine (Mary Philbin) to reconsider, not knowing the sinister hold the Phantom has on her.

began work on an enormous reconstruction of the Paris opera house auditorium, stage, and lobby—complete with five tiers of cellars and catacombs.

When Julian started shooting, it was announced that Chaney's makeup was so horrible that no stills would be released until after the film had opened. Filming progressed for several months—with scenes involving three-color Technicolor, many extras, the special staging of the ballet sequences—and problems between the director and the star. This led to Chaney directing himself in some of the scenes and the eventual replacement of Julian by assistant director Edward Sedgwick (although Julian's name was retained in the final credits).

After the film was in the can, a new series of problems ensued—which writer Robert E. Sherwood in *Photoplay* referred to as The Phantom Jinx: "When *Phantom*

FIRST TIME AT OUR PRICES

CARL LAEMMLE
presents

# The Phantom of the Opera

with
## LON CHANEY
### MARY PHILBIN
and
### NORMAN KERRY

Directed by RUPERT JULIAN

From the internationally famous story by GASTON LEROUX.

## WILD
## WEIRD
## WONDERFUL

Feature Production Will Be Shown at 11.30 A. M.;
1.30, 3.35, 5.30, 7.35 and 9.45 P. M.

*MUSICAL FEATURES*

STANLEY SYMPHONY
ORCHESTRA
DAVID KAPLAN, Conductor

KARL BONAWITZ
Pre Eminent Organist
With an unusual offering

Christine's test: which lever to pull to save Raoul and the Prefect of Police?

*of the Opera* was first shown at previews in and about Los Angeles, the critics who were called in to appraise it voiced a vehement desire for more comedy relief. 'There's too much spook melodrama,' said they. 'Put in some gags to relieve the tension.' So Chester Conklin was hailed from the Sennett lot, and the picture went back into production with Conklin prominent in the cast. He contributed a great deal of monkey business, and answered the demand for a few laughs. Then it was found that new subtitles were needed, so one of the most reliable writers in Hollywood, Walter Anthony, was summoned. Again, *The Phantom* was completed, and sent to San Francisco for display. When it was shown there, it was received with some of the foggy chill for which that city is justly famed. 'There are some gorgeous scenes,' was the opinion in Frisco, 'but the story as a whole doesn't make sense.' Following this rather discouraging start, *The Phantom of the Opera* was crated and shipped to New York, where it was viewed by Mr. Laemmle,

R. H. Cochrane and P. D. Cochrane, the officials of the organization. As a result, the film was turned over to a new staff of editors and cutters who proceeded to hack it into a new form, and new title-writers came in to account for the numerous revisions made in the continuity. One of the elements that came out first was the comedy. Reversing completely the Los Angeles opinion, it was felt that the gags inserted at the eleventh hour merely clouded the issue. *The Phantom* was essentially a spook melodrama, in which there was no legitimate place for 'belly laugh.' So Chester Conklin, and all his scenes, were put under the knife —and his ludicrous face does not appear at all in the finished picture. Another casualty was Ward Crane, who played an important part in the earlier sequences of the picture. All the garden parties and duels were removed and with them went Ward Crane. Thus two large salaries, and a great many incidental expenditures, were wasted. At the last minute, *The Phantom* was again subjected to hasty revision, and whipped

67

into final shape, so that Universal's foreign representative, James Bryson, could take the finished print to England for presentation. Mr. Bryson had done wonders with *The Hunchback of Notre Dame* in Great Britain, and he had planned a tremendous promotion campaign for *The Phantom*. Unfortunately, he planned a little bit too well. He arranged for a military escort to accompany him and *The Phantom* from the dock in Southampton to London. His stunt worked beautifully, and occasioned a loud and painful squawk throughout the British press. An American movie person had insulted His Majesty's uniform! It was a frightful offense. British pride was heated to the boiling point, and scalded the unfortunate Mr. Bryson who, after all, had only done what any enterprising press agent would have done in his place. As a result of this outrage, *The Phantom of the Opera* was boycotted by many exhibitors in England, and the picture was withdrawn from the British market."

In the United States, however, the film outsold *Hunchback of Notre Dame* and wound up on *Film Daily*'s Ten Best list (which polled several hundred film critics). Others in the *Phantom* cast were Snitz Edwards, Gibson Gowland, John Sainpolis, Virginia Pearson, Arthur Edmund Carewe, and John Miljan. (For more details on *Phantom of the Opera*, including a detailed synopsis, see the Lon Chaney chapter of *Heroes of the Horrors*.) Reviewing the film in *The New York Times*, Mordaunt Hall observed:

Up to the present the motion picture producer cannot be accused of hiding his light under a bushel at the opening exhibition of one of his pet pictures. He prefers to spread the news by blinding arc lights, and when the surging, clamoring, curious crowd swarms into the theatre lobby a flashlight is taken of the event so that photographs of the occasion can be dispatched to the four corners of the earth. It was the usual, unrestrained scene last night at the Astor Theatre, where the Universal Pictures Corporation's latest screen effort, *The Phantom of the Opera*, was presented. *The Phantom of the Opera* is an ultra fantastic

melodrama, an ambitious production in which there is much to marvel at in the scenic effects. It has been produced with a sort of mechanical precision, and the story reminds one somewhat of a writer who always seeks for alliterative combinations. The narrative could have been fashioned in a more subtle manner and would then have been more interesting to the few. As it stands it will strike popular fancy, and the stage settings will appeal to everybody.

In this presentation one perceives an effect of the interior of the Paris Opera, with people peering from the boxes and flocks of faces in the orchestra seats. . . . There is the famous staircase, down which passes the Phantom,

BELOW: Christine is temporarily reunited with Raoul, as Eric the Phantom (Lon Chaney, Sr.) plans his next move.

OPPOSITE: The Phantom howls in triumph over his apparent victory.

who, in a cheery moment for the gala event, has decided to appear in flowing crimson and a mask of a death's head. There are the affrighted figurantes who whisper and blanche at the thought that this stalking figure may be the awful Phantom who dwells in the subterranean cellars under the Temple of Music. You see the bed once owned by Gaby de Lys, which resembles a boat swung from three pillars; then there is a coffin bed in which the Phantom is supposed to rest his weary limbs, and dozens of other interesting features which are flashed here and there on the screen.

Lon Chaney impersonates the Phantom. It is a rôle suited to his liking, and one which he handles with a certain skill, a little exaggerated at times, but none the less compelling. One has to remember that this is a fantastic tale and therefore strange things can happen; and they do. The idea is an excellent one, but the changes in the picture, and re-cutting it, have made some of the scenes abrupt. . . .

Mary Philbin fills the rôle of Christine Daae, with whom, for some mysterious reason, the Phantom has fallen in love. This strange person who is so much feared, is thought to be frightful of face, so forbidding that the few who have seen him have fled in terror. He wears a mask. Christine knew less about him than any of the other girls in the opera, and when a "voice like an angel" taught her from the other side of a wall how to sing, she never suspected that her benefactor and the Phantom were one. . . . The Phantom, or Erik, as he pleases to call himself at times, has an inclined plane to his underground domicile and when he beguiles the dazed Christine to come below with him he puts her on a horse and she is taken down, down and down, where we are told there is the seepage of the Seine, which river incidentally is more than a mile away from the Opéra. The Phantom is just as much at home on the roof of the Opéra as he is below and in this picture people are permitted to

wander at will through the building, and yet the police can't lay their hands on the hideous looking Phantom.

The most dramatic touch is where Christine in the cellar abode is listening to the masked Phantom—he wears a weird, childish-looking mask with plump cheeks—as he plays the organ. Then she steals up behind him, as he is apparently entranced with his own playing, and, after hesitating, suddenly snatches the mask from the Phantom's face and at once faints at the horrible ugliness of the man. In the theatre last night a woman behind us stifled a scream when this happened, as this is the first glimpse one has of the Phantom's physiognomy. He is hollow-eyed, with a turned-up nose which has long nostrils. His teeth are long and separated and his forehead is high. There is no doubt that he is a repellant sight.

Miss Philbin is only satisfactory in some of her scenes, and she ought to have been able to make many of them far more telling. Actually the outstanding performances in this production are delivered by Lon Chaney and Arthur Edmund Carewe, who is cast as the Persian, or the head of the secret police. This is a well-dressed thriller, with a capable acting by the villain, a stiff and stilted hero and an insipid heroine. So far as the story is concerned, it looks as if too many cooks had rather spoiled the broth . . .

Mary Philbin then turned up in *Surrender* (1927) based on the play *Lea Lyon* by Alexander Brady. "I enjoyed my work in *Port of Dreams* (1929), one of my late pictures," said Philbin. "Shortly before that I played in *Drums of Love* (1928) for the great Mr. David Wark Griffith! I had to pinch myself at times to be sure I was awake, it was just like a dream come true!" In 1928 she was also in *Love Me and the World Is Mine*, based on the Rudolph Hans Bartsch story *The Affairs of Hannerl*. This was directed by Ewald André Dupont, fresh from his triumph with the now-classic German silent *Variety* (1926). However, *Love Me and the World Is Mine* was so unsuccessful that it may have hastened his return to Europe.

In 1928 Mary Philbin co-starred with Conrad Veidt in Paul Leni's *The Man Who Laughs*, along with Olga Baclanova (see

Baclanova chapter, beginning on page 108). Also in the cast were her fellow players from *Merry-Go-Round*—Cesare Gravina and George Siegmann. Others in the cast were Brandon Hurst, Stuart Holmes, Josephine Crowell, Sam de Grasse, Edgard Norton, Torben Meyer, Nick de Ruiz, Julius Molner, and Zimbo the Dog. Director Leni began in Germany as a designer with Max Reinhardt and became a director in 1916 with expressionistic excursions that impressed Carl Laemmle. After *Waxworks* (1924), he came to Hollywood and made *The Cat and the Canary* (1927), which so pleased Laemmle that Leni was given more of the same—*The Chinese Parrot* (1927) followed by the grotesque *The Man Who Laughs*. In 1965 the film was remade in Italy with Jean Sorel and Ilaria Occhini.

With two horror films to her credit, Philbin was now identified with the genre. She was immediately cast in another horror, *Erik the Great*, which was soon retitled *The Last Performance* (1929). Written by James Creelman, who was to co-author the *King Kong* screenplay a few years later, the story had Philbin as a Trilby-like young woman in the thrall of a Svengali-styled mesmerist (Conrad Veidt). The director was the remarkable Paul Fejos. Fejos was born in 1897. He had studied medicine and worked in both film and theatre in Hungary before coming to the United States to join the Rockefeller Institution's bacteriological section. When Edward M. Spitz paid him five thousand dollars in 1927 to make an experimental film, Fejos responded with *The Last Moment*, depicting a suicide. It

OPPOSITE PAGE

TOP: The blind Dea (Mary Philbin) makes her way through the streets of London in *The Man Who Laughs*.

BOTTOM LEFT: Conrad Veidt, Mary Philbin, and Brandon Hurst in *The Man Who Laughs*.

BOTTOM RIGHT: Gwynplaine (Conrad Veidt) conceals his hideous grin from Dea (Mary Philbin) in this touching interlude from *The Man Who Laughs*.

The cast of *The Man Who Laughs* poses with their distinguished visitor: Carl Laemmle, president of Universal Pictures, with Mary.

was filmed in twenty-eight days with Georgia Hale of *The Gold Rush* (1924) and photography by Leon Shamroy, resulting in a Universal contract for Fejos. After the memorable *Lonesome* (1928), he made *Broadway* (1929), *The Last Performance*, and then soon returned to Hungary, where he ignored pleas by MGM that scripts were awaiting him in Hollywood. His work in documentaries for Svensk Filmindustri sent him throughout the world. In 1941 he became the Director of Research for the Wenner-Gren Foundation for Anthropological Research, and in 1955 advanced to become the president of this organization.

Photography for *The Last Performance* was by Hal Mohr, and joining Veidt and Philbin in the cast were Leslie Fenton, Fred Mackaye, Gustav Partos, William H. Turner, and Anders Randolf. It has also been seen under the title *Erik, The Great Illusionist*. Titles were by Walter Anthony and Tom Reed, but, coming at the transition of silents to talkies, it had added sound effects and dialogue. Little suspecting that

she would be remembered almost solely for *Phantom of the Opera*, Philbin enthusiastically raved, "The greatest thrill of my life came when I heard my voice from the screen in my first talking picture, *Erik the Great*. It all seems too good to be true."

She was in *The Shannons of Broadway* (1929), adapted by Agnes Christine Johnson from the play by James Gleason, and she was seen again in a 1930 reissue of *Phantom of the Opera* with added music and sound effects. New footage was shot for this version, written by Frank McCormack and directed by Ernst Laemmle. John Miljan was entirely cut out of the film, and Edward Martindel was added to the cast, replacing John Sainpolis. In years to come, it would not be this sound version but the original silent film that would be threaded constantly into projectors—making Mary Philbin the best-remembered Scream Queen of the silents and perhaps the most familiar dramatic actress of that period to young people today.

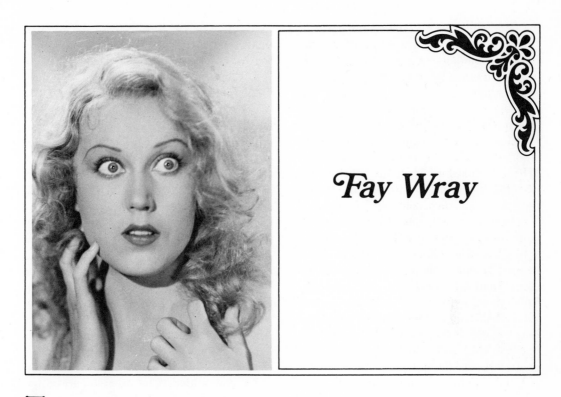

# Fay Wray

*T*he object of Kong's affections, Fay Wray, was born September 10, 1907, on her father's ranch, Wrayland, in Alberta, Canada. While she was very young, her parents moved to Los Angeles. Here she attended Hollywood High School, where she did her first acting—a role in the annual Hollywood Pilgrimage Play in 1923.

She began work in films almost immediately after graduating from Hollywood High. Her mother took her to the casting office of Century Studios, but they were given a quick brush-off. However, as they left the lot, she was eyed by a producer who offered the youthful actress a bit in a comedy. Her motion-picture debut was titled *Gasoline Love*. In the year that followed, Fay Wray worked as an extra and did bits in Westerns and comedies.

The turning point came in the spring of 1926 when she was brought into Erich von Stroheim's office by Mrs. Schley, a talent scout. Von Stroheim was searching for a female lead for his lavish Paramount production of *The Wedding March*, and, at this point, he had already rejected every young actress contracted to Paramount.

After only a brief interview von Stroheim cast Fay Wray as Mitzi. She remembered the experience this way:

The office was rather dark. Von Stroheim sat behind his desk, and in a corner sat his secretary. He didn't talk to me at all, but I knew he was watching me as he chatted with Mrs. Schley. Presently he said, looking at me at last, "Are you sure you can do the part?"

"I know I can," I replied, but I was all atremble.

Then he swung about in his swivel chair. "Whom does she look like to you, Mrs. Westland?" he asked. "Mitzi," answered his secretary. Not a word more. That was all. Then von Stroheim rose and approached me. He put his hand over mine: "Goodbye, Mitzi."

I broke into tears. I couldn't help it. That part was right for me. I knew I would get it when I read it. But when von Stroheim said, "Goodbye Mitzi," it was just too much. Mrs. Schley cried, and Mrs. Westland cried, and there were tears in von Stroheim's eyes. They left me there, and I sat weeping in the dark.

Filming began in June 1926, on thirty-six separate sets, a reconstruction of Vienna in 1914. Prince Nicki (von Stroheim) meets the poor Mitzi (Wray) when his horse injures her during the parade of Corpus Christi ceremonies. Attracted to Mitzi, he begins haunting her mother's wine garden, where Mitzi plays the harp in the orchestra. The relationship is discouraged by both sets of parents. Nicki's father, Prince Ottokar (George Fawcett), wants him to marry the crippled Cecilia (ZaSu Pitts), daughter of "The Cornplaster Magnate," Schweisser (George Nichols). At a brothel the two fathers sign a marriage contract.

Initially repelled by Cecilia, Nicki finally agrees to the wedding. The butcher Schani (Matthew Betz), learning of Nicki's interest in Mitzi, plans to wait outside the church and kill Nicki after the ceremony. Mitzi promises to marry Schani if he will leave Nicki alone. Nicki and Cecilia move into a castle. Schani and Mitzi marry. Seeing that Mitzi still yearns for Nicki, Schani goes to the castle and shoots at Nicki, accidentally killing Cecilia. Schani is killed while making his escape. Nicki and Mitzi

could now marry, but, instead, she enters a convent. World War I begins and Nicki leaves with his regiment.

Filming continued until February 1927, when it was discovered that *The Wedding March* costs had reached $1,125,000. Von Stroheim was ordered to stop shooting and begin editing. He succeeded in shortening the film from thirty-three hours to six hours, but, in October 1927, von Stroheim was taken off the editing by studio chief B. P. Schulberg.

In 1928, after editing by Josef von Sternberg and Julian Johnston, Paramount previewed a choppy version minus much of Nicki's establishing characterization. The film went back into the hands of von Stroheim. He restored footage, ending the story with the wedding. A Broadway opening for March 1928 was announced but then postponed. Instead, it was not seen until the fall of 1928. A synchronized music score on discs was added. The second part, originally intended to follow after an intermission, was not seen at all in the United States. Von Stroheim refused to permit its release because he had not controlled the editing. It was released in Europe in 1931 as *The Honeymoon* in its ten-reel mutilated

LEFT: Fay Wray early in her career.

RIGHT: As Mitzi, in the film that launched her career, *The Wedding March* (1928).

form. In 1954, after a transfer of the disc score to a sound track, von Stroheim assembled a definitive reconstruction of *The Wedding March* for the Cinémathèque Française, but *The Honeymoon* was later destroyed in a fire and is now lost forever.

Small-town exhibitors hated *The Wedding March*. The Cozy Theatre of Duchesne, Utah, reported, "The poorest Paramount picture I have played this year, not much of a story and has the poorest photography imaginable. There is about two hundred feet of Technicolor that is very foggy, makes you think your projectors are out of focus. I advertised this very highly and raised the price of admission. Only a few came and was glad of it. Any program picture that I have run this year is better entertainment."

"It's a fourteen-reel, messed-up picture," said the Dixie Theatre of Durant, Mississippi. "We had it booked for three nights, but we didn't have the nerve to offer to show it the second night. In London or in some foreign country, in a big city where are all classes of nationalities, it might be understood and called a big picture."

The Dixie's appraisal was accurate, for *The Wedding March* did fare better in larger cities. *Motion Picture News* offered a report from Cleveland: "The downtown first-run houses here continue to draw capacity attendance. Interest in the new sound pictures grows keener each week. . . . *The Wedding March* opened up very big at the Allen. Every local critic gave it a big boost, some saying it ranks among the best pictures ever made. Although no records were broken, it showed a good record at the end of the week." And in New Orleans: "Erich von Stroheim's masterpiece, *The Wedding March*, did the second best business of the week, being shown at Loew's State Theatre. The film, long awaited by movie lovers of New Orleans, was highly praised by critics and patrons alike."

The *Daily News* gave it four stars, and Bland Johaneson in the *Mirror* wrote, "Von Stroheim certainly knows how to direct women. He has done for the tepid and negative Fay Wray what he did for Mae Murray in *The Merry Widow*. She acts. If she never acts again, she'll have the delightful Mitzi to her everlasting distinction."

*The Wedding March* made Fay Wray a star, and she was also seen in three other 1928 Paramount releases—*Street of Sin*, *The First Kiss*, and *Legion of the Condemned*, teamed with Gary Cooper in the last two. *Legion of the Condemned*, produced and directed by William A. Wellman, had a screenplay by John Monk Saunders and Jean de Limur based on Saunders' original story. That same year Fay Wray married Saunders, a union that resulted in the birth of a daughter, Susan.

Her association with Merian C. Cooper and Ernest Schoedsack of *King Kong* began in 1929 when she appeared along with Richard Arlen, Clive Brook, William Powell, and Theodore von Eltz in the David O. Selznick production of *Four Feathers* for Paramount. Others in the cast were Noah Berry, Zack Williams, Noble Johnson, Harold Hightower, Philippe de Lacey, Edward J. Ratcliffe, George Fawcett, and Augustine Symonds. Originally filmed as a silent picture, with much African location footage, Selznick supervised the shooting of additional sound sequences back at the studio. After a reediting session Selznick sent a telegram to Schoedsack:

"PLEASE TAKE MY WORD ABOUT THE AUDIENCE REACTION. THE HIPPOPOTAMUS SCENES GOT GASPS AS NOW CUT INSTEAD OF LAUGHS AS PREVIOUSLY, AND WE ARE SURE THAT THIS IS TRACEABLE TO THE RECUTTING OF THE SEQUENCE AND ALSO TO ITS NEW PLACE IN THE STORY CONTINUITY. THIS IS FOR YOUR INFORMATION IN CASE YOU ARE TEMPTED TO DO ANY RECUTTING. ALL THOSE WHO WERE SKEPTICAL ABOUT THE PICTURE NOW BELIEVE IN IT WHOLEHEARTEDLY AND ARE CERTAIN OF ITS SUCCESS ONLY WITH THE SOLITARY FEAR THAT IT MAY NOT DO AS WELL AS IT WOULD HAVE A YEAR AGO BECAUSE OF THE TALKING-PICTURE SITUATION. HOWEVER, THERE IS NO QUESTION THAT THIS IS ONE STORY WHICH SHOULD BE BETTER WITH MUSIC AND SOUND EFFECTS THAN WITH MID-VICTORIAN DIALOGUE."

Josef von Sternberg also turned to talkies with Paramount's *Thunderbolt* (1929), the story of a Death Row convict, Thunderbolt (George Bancroft), who frames the suitor (Richard Arlen) of his girl (Wray) and plans to murder him on the eve of his own execution. Seen today, Wray's witness-stand histrionics seem overwrought and inappropriate to the film's *mise en scène*. *Pointed Heels* (1929), a Paramount musical comedy with color sequences, co-starred Fay Wray, Helen Kane of "Boop-Boop-a-Doop" fame, and William Powell. Fay rejoined Powell in *Behind the Makeup* (1930), a backstage romantic triangle drama for Paramount. The credited director of this film is Robert Milton, but it was actually directed by a woman—Dorothy Arzner.

Neither Fay Wray nor Gary Cooper thought they would fare too well in talkies when they were reunited in David O. Selznick's *The Texan* (1930), based on O. Henry's *A Double-Dyed Deceiver*. Others in the Paramount production were Emma Dunn, Oscar Apfel, James Marcus, Donald Reed, and Edward J. Brady. But both Wray and Cooper were seen together again in the all-star lineup of *Paramount on Parade* (1930), which featured a Dorothy Arzner-directed sequence.

Paramount's *The Sea God* (1930) was a South Seas adventure tale with Richard Arlen and Eugene Pallette. *The Border Legion* (1930), also at Paramount, was the third of the many film versions of this Zane Grey novel. In *The Finger Points* (1931), written and coproduced by Wray's husband, John Monk Saunders, she played the girl of a reporter turned crooked. Richard Barthelmess, Clark Gable, and Regis Toomey also starred. This Warner Brothers film was her first picture away from her home studio, Paramount. Years later, Fay Wray recalled the early thirties as a time when motion pictures were made "just like clockwork. I started a new film every four weeks."

In *The Conquering Horde* (1931), a Paramount Western, she was teamed once again with Richard Arlen. *Not Exactly*

*Gentlemen* (1931) was her first film for Fox, followed by *Three Rogues* (1931). *Dirigible* (1931) was initiated as a Paramount follow-up to the successful *Wings* (1927) with David O. Selznick telegraming B. P. Schulberg:

"EVEN IF WE STRUGGLE WITH THE NAVY'S DEMANDS AND SATISFY THEM ON EVERY STORY POINT, I DO NOT SEE WHAT THEY CAN GIVE US. THEY CERTAINLY WILL NOT ENDANGER A NAVY DIRIGIBLE, AND ANY SCENES OF VALUE WILL HAVE TO BE TRICKED IN ANY EVENT. . . . WE HEAR THAT HOWARD HUGHES HAS OBTAINED UNBELIEVABLY MAGNIFICENT DIRIGIBLE SCENES WITH THE USE OF A TWENTY-FIVE-FOOT MINIATURE DIRIGIBLE. HAVE HAD DISCUSSION WITH ROBERTS OF EFFECTS DEPARTMENT WHO IS CONFIDENT HE CAN GIVE US EVERYTHING WE NEED WITH DIRIGIBLES AFLIGHT, IN DANGER AT NIGHT, EXPLODING, ETC., WHICH WE SURELY CANNOT GET WITH REAL DIRIGIBLE."

The property was sold off by Paramount to Columbia, where Frank Capra directed both Fay Wray and a real dirigible. Filming took place in Lakehurst, New Jersey, at the same mooring mast where the Hindenburg burst into flames six years later. There *was* an accident during the filming of *Dirigible*—but of an entirely different nature. To get the effect of coldness at the South Pole, actors Hobart Bosworth, Ralph Graves, and Clarence Muse each had small cages containing dry ice in their mouths so their breath would show on film. Bosworth, annoyed that his cage was preventing him from speaking clearly, took the ice out of the cage and put it into his mouth. Screaming, he fell to the ground— with his jaws locked tight. The incident resulted in the loss of five teeth and part of his jawbone. *Dirigible* brought recognition to the struggling Columbia Pictures, with president Harry Cohn receiving a standing ovation at the April 18, 1931, Grauman's Chinese Theatre premiere. It was the first Columbia film to open at Grauman's.

Returning to Warners for *Captain Thunder* (1931), Wray starred as a bandit's girlfriend. Others in the cast were Victor

The climax from the Warner Brothers' early sound horror classic, *Doctor X* (1932).

Varconi and Don Alvarado. She was reunited with Clive Brook and Richard Arlen in Paramount's *The Lawyer's Secret* (1931). Addressing B. P. Schulberg, Selznick commented on the casting in another of his legendary memos: "As we have all long known, a good showman trick is the combination of one or more players of importance or even of moderate importance with one or more players on the downgrade, to give an effect of an all-star cast. Thus, putting Clive Brook and Richard Arlen with Buddy Rogers, Fay Wray, and Jean Arthur in *The Lawyer's Secret* probably gives the picture an appearance of importance, to exhibitors and public alike, way beyond its real strength if carefully analyzed. I feel that the picture is benefiting materially from this, and that it is helping get the public in to see a new Buddy Rogers. I wonder if we could not do the same for Bow by the use of such a trick, as we have done for Rogers. . . ." Selznick's brother, Myron, was Fay Wray's agent during the thirties. Myron Selznick was considered the most important agent of the time; his ability to

negotiate higher and higher salaries made him the enemy of producers throughout Hollywood.

In Ben Hecht and Charles MacArthur's *The Unholy Garden* (1931), about international criminals seeking sanctuary from the law in the Algerian city of Orage, Fay Wray played opposite Ronald Colman in her first film for United Artists. Also in 1931, she attempted Broadway in *The Brown Danube* without any noteworthy success. The 1931 play *Nikki* was written for her by her husband, Saunders, but when *Nikki* was sold to films, the role went to Helen Chandler.

After Universal's *Stowaway* (1932), she made her first horror film—Warner's *Doctor X* (1932), with Lionel Atwill donning synthetic flesh before he kills under the full moon. Others in the cast were Preston Foster and Lee Tracy. John Baxter in *Hollywood in the Thirties* calls it "one of the greatest of the classic horror films." In a reenactment of the crimes, Fay realizes that the person portraying the murderer is indeed the real murderer. Michael Curtiz directed in two-color Technicolor—although the Technicolor prints were seen only in certain first-run engagements.

The elements that would coalesce in *Kong* began to pull together even earlier in RKO's *Most Dangerous Game*, also directed by Ernest Schoedsack (with Irving Pichel) and also with Max Steiner music. Further, stars Wray and Joel McCrea were supported by Robert Armstrong and Noble Johnson, who were both in *Kong* the fol-

lowing year. The screenplay was by James Creelman, one of the *Kong* screenwriters. Based on a Richard Connell short story (later popularized on radio of the forties), the picture shows Wray and McCrea fleeing big-game hunter Count Zaroff (Leslie Banks), who has decided that the ultimate sport is hunting down human game. Wray's role was written into the story, originally an O. Henry Award winner from 1924. Footage from *The Most Dangerous Game* can

BELOW AND OPPOSITE: Zaroff (Leslie Banks) and his men: Wan (Noble Johnson), Scarface (Dutch Hendrian), and the Tartar (Steve Clemento) pursue Rainsford (Joel McCrea) and Eve (Fay Wray) in *The Most Dangerous Game* (1932).

also be seen in the 1945 remake, *A Game of Death*, and the screams of Audrey Long in *A Game of Death* were actually taken from old sound-track screams made by Fay Wray.

In *Vampire Bat* (1933), the tale of a doctor's insane experiments with blood chemistry that lead to murder, Wray was surrounded by the excellent cast of Lionel Atwill, Melvyn Douglas, and Dwight Frye. The film was a low-budget effort from the "poverty row" company, Majestic.

In Warner's *The Mystery of the Wax Museum* (1933), Wray was once again the female lead in a cast headed by Lionel Atwill and once again seen in two-color Technicolor under the direction of Michael Curtiz. William K. Everson commented, "The unrestrained yet slightly unreal color hues added to the nightmarish quality of the final laboratory scene, creating erotic as well as terrifying effects with its contrast of the pink flesh tones of a nude Fay Wray, strapped to an operating table, with the bubbling green fluid in Atwill's wax-embalming vats. A handsome production in every way (the laboratory set, with its cat-walks, machines, and vats of wax, was a

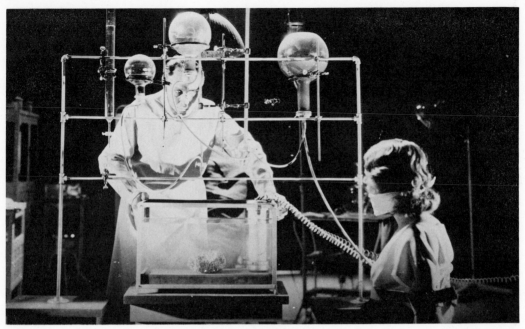

Fay in *Vampire Bat* (1933), with Lionel Atwill.

beauty) and directed with pace and style by the versatile Michael Curtiz, *The Mystery of the Wax Museum* was also well served by its cast. Fay Wray, obviously, was the ideal heroine for such a frolic. . . ."

For many years through the fifties and sixties, *The Mystery of the Wax Museum* was a "lost film," but it was finally rediscovered, eventually turning up on late-night TV in 1975. Everson, seeing the film again after a lapse of twenty-five years, was able to reassess its worth: "Fay Wray is brought into the film quite late (she has far less footage than Glenda Farrell, the wise-cracking reporter who cracks the case) and has really nothing to do other than providing a luscious victim for Atwill in the closing reels. Incidentally, Miss Wray—first seen doing her exercises in sweater and brief shorts—looks most fetching in Technicolor. She also doubles for the wax figure of Marie Antoinette in the opening reel—none too convincingly. Why Curtiz didn't shoot a few seconds and freeze-frame it, I don't know—the shot goes on endlessly, and Miss Wray can be seen all too clearly breathing, twitching, moving her eyes, and even allowing some muscle movement of

her right shoulder!" In 1953 *The Mystery of the Wax Museum* was remade as the 3-D *House of Wax* with Vincent Price in the Lionel Atwill role and Phillis Kirk in Wray's part. (See Vincent Price chapter of *Heroes of the Horrors*.) Yet another remake was the 1966 *Chamber of Horrors* with Patrick O'Neal and Suzy Parker.

With RKO's *King Kong* (1933), both Wray and the giant gorilla achieved immortality. Rudy Behlmer's liner notes for a condensation of Max Steiner's innovative score also neatly synopsize the story: ". . . You can immediately sense the apprehension as the ship approaches the ominous Skull Island; there is the distant chant—then the throbbing sacrificial music of the natives as they prepare to offer Fay Wray to the omnipotent Kong. As this frenzied ritual reaches its climax, three strokes on a gong summon the beast from the jungle. Percussive, thumping effects emphasize his approach, and finally Kong's three-note descending theme signals his initial entrance. Some of the agitated, dissonant strains composed to accompany the captured Kong in New York are next, and the finale—as a counterpoint to the horror—

ABOVE: A posed shot that was not in *King Kong*: Fay with Robert Armstrong (as Carl Denham).

BOTTOM RIGHT: A rare publicity photo shows producer and director Merian C. Cooper and his pipe dream.

underlines the Beauty and the Beast concept as Kong, barraged with gunfire from airplanes, gently puts Fay in a place of safety before toppling to his death from the pinnacle of the Empire State Building."

In the late sixties Fay Wray recalled the events that led to her accepting the part: "I knew two very fine producers—Merian C. Cooper and his partner Ernest B. Schoedsack—and I admired the work that they had done. Mr. Cooper said to me that he'd had an idea for a film in mind. The only thing he'd tell me was that it was going to have the 'tallest leading man in Hollywood' . . . Well, naturally, I thought of Clark Gable hopefully, and when the script came I was *absolutely appalled*! I thought it was a practical joke. I really didn't have much appetite for doing it, except that I did admire these two people, and I realized that it did at least have scope and a good imagination. It had dimension above anything else that has been tried in the film."

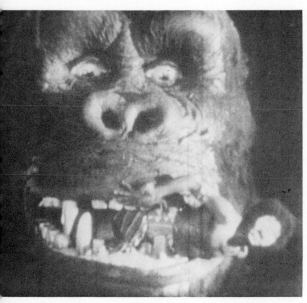

ABOVE: A cut scene from *Kong*, later replaced.

It took a full year to accomplish the *Kong* special effects—at a total budget of $650,000. Several new techniques of special effects were created during the course of filming. "The first shot RKO ever made in rear process is in *Kong*," said Cooper. "It's where Fay is on top of the tree and the dinosaur comes for her. That shot took us three days because none of us knew how to do it. We used the first miniature projection, which is the reverse of rear projection. We invented it for *King Kong*."

Six eighteen-inch-high Kong models were built for the model animation. Inside were moving metal armatures. The scene in which Kong removes Fay Wray's blouse was one of the scenes missing from the film until they were restored in the mid-sixties. Hidden wires pulled off her clothing. A film of this was projected, and a model Kong was animated in front of this.

However, when Fay Wray first spots Kong through the trees, this was a full-scale

BELOW: The fight in the forest with Tyrannosaurus Rex.

ABOVE: Kong, again victorious, returns to his prized possession—Fay. BELOW: Kong battles the pterodactyl.

construction of Kong's face. Including shoulders and the top part of Kong's chest, this mechanical monster was twenty feet high with a movable mouth. Bear skins were used for hair. Like Jessica Lange in the 1976 *Kong* remake, Wray was grasped by a full-scale hand. "The hand and arm in which my closeup scenes were made were about eight feet long," said Wray. "Inside the furry arm there was a steel bar and the whole contraption, with me in the hand, could be raised and lowered like a crane. The fingers would be pressed around my waist while I was in a standing position. I would then be raised about ten feet into the air in the ape's hand, but then his fingers would gradually loosen and begin to open. My fear was real as I grabbed onto his wrist, his thumb, wherever I could, to keep from slipping out of that paw! When I could sense that the moment of minimum safety had arrived, I would call imploringly to the director and ask to be lowered to the floor. I would have a few minutes rest, be resecured in the paw, and then the ordeal would begin all over again—a kind of pleasurable ordeal."

Fay Wray was destined to remain a Scream Queen for many years to come—even though she was never to have another role like the part of Ann Darrow in *King Kong*. Leslie Halliwell in *The Filmgoer's Companion* calls her "a great screamer," and *Kong* historian Steve Vertlieb comments that "few would doubt her right to the title of the world's most celebrated screamer." One of the picture's magnetic attractions is the fact that Ann Darrow, once she's seen Kong, never seems to stop screaming. Wray explained, "Well, I just imagined I was miles from help, and . . . well, you'd scream too if you just imagined that situation with that monster up there. And when the picture was finished, they took me into the sound room, and then I screamed some more for about five minutes—just steady screaming, and then they'd cut that and add it in."

What did it all mean? *New York* magazine quipped, "As if we didn't have enough to worry about during the Depres-

sion, this big ape had to show up and fall for Fay Wray. His death was a disaster for sanitation men." But what did it all mean *really*? Was there some hidden psycho drama of the collective unconscious in *Kong*? Andrew Dowdy, in *Movies Are Better Than Ever*, seems to think so: "Ever since King Kong got a whiff of Fay Wray and scaled the Empire State Building with her for a purpose just sufficently obscure to escape conscious recognition, Hollywood has proved adept at smuggling kinky stuff into otherwise straight films. Apes and dames. Monsters and maidens. Deserted islands of women abandoned by men, save one or two survivors of a nearby shipwreck. These were the tacky cheats of the fifties, the allowable mythology of the unspeakable, translated with weekly regularity out there in the pulsating darkness."

A love story, as suggested by Ivan Butler in *Horror in the Cinema*? "Kong himself radiates charm, and easily wins our sympathy from his captors, who deserve worse than they get. Fay Wray, the perfect heroine in such circumstances, would have softened tougher hearts than the old ape's, and their scenes together, as she lies cradled in his gentle palm, make us wish that he could have had a better chance of winning her over to a greater appreciation of his own warm regard for her."

Or, as Carlos Clarens has it in *An Illustrated History of the Horror Film*, a Freudian-dream diary? "The literal-minded among critics, probably misled by a realistic prologue laid in the contemporary Manhattan of breadlines and the starving unemployed, failed to perceive that *King Kong*'s logic is that of a dream, that the picture is a visualization of the most recurrent dream fantasies: Driscoll (Bruce Cabot) and Ann dangling from a rope over a precipice and being slowly hauled by Kong, their subsequent fall into a chasm, a race through the jungle with something large and terrifying in pursuit, one Cyclopean eye peering

OPPOSITE: Sketch of a deleted scene from *Kong*, later replaced.

84

through the window of a midtown hotel, dawn-of-the-world landscapes, dizzying heights, and so forth."

For Ray Bradbury, who saw *Kong* forty-three times (twenty times more than Rod Steiger), it had soul: "You can't invent soul, as we all know. It simply happens. Even Mr. Cooper and Mr. Schoedsack, after they birthed Kong from their hot-wired ganglions and the brighter bumps on their heads, could not conceive or deliver forth anything as grand, as beautiful, as touching or as perfect as this God of the Apes."

For Bruce Felton and Mark Fowler in Felton and Fowler's *Best Worst and Most Unusual*, *Kong* "has come to mean many things to many people—the Black Man enslaved, sexual frustration, the danger inherent in man's attempt to control nature. The phallic imagery of the finale, in which Kong scales the Empire State Building, is unmistakable, if unintended. David O. Selznick produced this classic, and Fay Wray screamed a lot."

Or was Kong symbolic of religious omnipotence, putting the "fear of Jesus into every heart" as in Dory Previn's song, *King Kong*?

Or was it the "perfect Depression movie," as indicated by writer Michael Valenti: "Except for a discordant prologue about breadlines and hunger, it was a nightmare fairy tale in which movie audiences took temporary respite from the gloom that prevailed beyond the marquee's circle of warmth."

*Kong* opened at both the Roxy and Radio City Music Hall shortly after the banks were closed by FDR, but it was an incredible hit nevertheless, grossing $90,000 during the first four days of its run in New York (comparable to about $500,000 in the 1970s). Three months later Fay Wray was menaced by a giant squid in Columbia's *Below the Sea* (1933), filmed in black and white with color sequences, and one week after that *Ann Carver's Profession* (1933), written by Robert Riskin, was released, followed by *The Woman I Stole* (1933) that same month. All three were for Columbia.

RKO's *The Big Brain* (1933) was followed by Paramount's *One Sunday Afternoon* (1933), based on the James Hagan stage play, and Fox's *Shanghai Madness* (1933) with Spencer Tracy. (Wray later said her favorite leading man was Tracy, not Kong.) In United Artists' *The Bowery* (1933), the story of Steve Brodie's legendary jump off the Brooklyn Bridge, Wray appeared with George Raft, Wallace Beery, and Jackie Cooper. Her final release of 1933, Columbia's *Master of Men*, brought the list of Fay Wray films that year to a startling total of eleven. Curiously, more than half of the titles on this 1933 list are totally ignored by TV and revival theatres today.

Universal's *Madame Spy* (1934) was directed by the Czech-born Karl Freund, best known for his horror direction of *The Mummy* (1933) and *Mad Love* (1935). This was followed by Columbia's *Once to Every Woman* (1934) and another Karl Freund film, *The Countess of Monte Cristo* (1934). In MGM's *Viva Villa!* (1934), the story of Pancho Villa, she appeared with

Scenes from lesser-known films featuring Fay Wray: BELOW: *Black Moon* (Columbia, 1934). OPPOSITE LEFT: *Melody for Three* (RKO, 1941). OPPOSITE RIGHT: *The Countess of Monte Cristo* (Universal, 1934), with Paul Lukas.

Wallace Beery and Leo Carillo; the film was nominated for a Best Picture Academy Award. United Artists' *Affairs of Cellini* (1934), based on Edwin Justus Mayer's play about Renaissance Man Benvenuto Cellini, featured Fay surrounded by the star-studded cast of Fredric March, Constance Bennett, Louis Calhern, and Frank Morgan (who was nominated for an Academy Award).

Clements Ripley's novel *Haiti Moon* provided the basis for the Wells Root screenplay used in Columbia's *Black Moon* (1934), the story of a woman who nearly sacrifices her daughter during a voodoo ritual. The theme was a subject of much popular interest after the publication in 1929 of William Seabrook's *The Magic Island*, illustrated by Alexander King. Directed by Roy William Neill, Jack Holt and Fay Wray headed the cast of Dorothy Burgess, Lumsden Hare, Cora Sue Collins, Arnold Korff, and Clarence Muse. Back at RKO, Fay was teamed with Joel McCrea again in *The Richest Girl in the World* (1934).

Only one year after *Kong*, Fay Wray acted in Columbia's mystery-adventure *The Captain Hates the Sea* (1934), with Victor McLaglen, Helen Vinson, and John Gilbert. Perhaps, as Michael Valenti put it, this was "the first ominous note that her career had gone from high gear to sudden eclipse. Hollywood's motto was that you were only as good as your last movie, and if you weren't even *in* your last movie. . . ." *The Captain Hates the Sea* was set aboard a liner headed for Europe. Universal's *Cheating Cheaters* (1934) was based on the play by Max Marcin. RKO's *Women in the Dark* (1934)—also known as *Woman in the Shadows*—featured Wray, Ralph Bellamy, and Melvyn Douglas in a film version of the Dashiell Hammett short story. After *White Lies* for Columbia in 1934, Fay headed for England to do two Gaumont-British films. In *The Clairvoyant* (1935), directed by Maurice Elvey, she played opposite Claude Rains in a story of a professional prognosticator who realizes that he has a genuine psychic gift; foreseeing his own death, he is powerless to prevent it. Based on a novel by Ernst Lothar, *The Clairvoyant* is remarkably similar to the Cornell Woolrich novel filmed as *The Night Has a Thousand Eyes* (1948). Others in the cast were Jane Baxter, Mary Clare, and Donald Calthorp. Walter Forde's *Alias Bulldog Drummond* (1935), for Gaumont-British was yet another in the long-run mystery series that had begun in 1929. *Come Out of the Pantry* (1935), for United Artists, was followed by *Mills of the Gods* (1935) and *Roaming Lady* (1936) for Columbia. A play by Charles Marlow provided the basis for the fantasy comedy *When Knights Were Bold* (1936), filmed by Capitol, a British-production company.

Dreaming of medieval times, a man fantasies that he is a rich nobleman. When he awakens, his dream literally comes true when he inherits property and marries a young woman of nobility. Fay played the female lead in the cast of Jack Buchanan, Garry Marsh, Kate Cutler, Martita Hunt, Robert Horton, Aubrey Mather, Aubrey Fitzgerald, Robert Nainby, and Moore Marriott. Jack Raymond directed.

In Columbia's *They Met in a Taxi* (1936), as a model accused of theft, she played opposite Chester Morris. *It Happened in Hollywood* (1937) was followed by *Once a Hero* (1937), both for Columbia. In Columbia's *Murder in Greenwich Village* (1937), she was teamed yet again with Richard Arlen, this time as a society girl suspected of killing a painter. *The Jury's Secret* (1938), for Universal, was a murder mystery in which she played opposite Kent Taylor. G-men and spies fought it out in *Smashing the Spy Ring* (1938); others in the cast were Chester Morris and Ann Doran.

In 1939 Fay Wray and John Monk Saunders were divorced. The low-budget *Navy Secrets* with Craig Reynolds and Grant Withers at Monogram was her only 1939 credit, due to her playwriting collaboration that year with Sinclair Lewis on *Angela Is 21*—a play that failed to reach Broadway. In 1940 Saunders died.

RKO's *Wildcat Bus* (1940) starred her in a story of a bankrupt playboy (Charles Lang) turned crooked. In 1941 her playwriting period ended with *Golden Wings*. Her work in radio included the lead role in "Welcome to Agnes," aired October 25, 1941, as part of the anthology series *Armstrong's Theater of Today* on CBS. She returned to film acting in Columbia's *Adam Had Four Sons*, a family drama based on Charles Bonner's novel *Legacy*. Of more notable quality than her many low-budgeters of the late thirties, *Adam Had Four Sons* received three stars from the *Daily News*. Ingrid Bergman, Warner Baxter, Susan Hayward, and Richard Denning headed the cast. She then joined Jean Hersholt in RKO's *Melody for Three* (1941), part of the

Dr. Christian series. In Columbia's *Not a Ladies' Man* (1942), she appeared with Paul Kelly and Douglas Croft in the weak melodrama of a district attorney who refuses to prosecute a gangster married to the attorney's ex-wife.

There were rumors of a romance with Howard Hughes at this time, but such talk dissipated when she married the distinguished screenwriter Robert Riskin, who had authored the Wray film *Ann Carver's Profession* nine years earlier. Academy Award winner Riskin was best known for his work as writer on the Frank Capra films at Columbia. Riskin and Wray had two children—Robert and Vicky—and the marriage also brought an end to her career. Eleven years passed before she was seen again on the screen. In 1944, however, the Wray-Sinclair Lewis play *Angela Is 21* was filmed by Universal as the musical comedy *This Is the Life*. Wanda Tuchock did the screen adaptation, and Felix Feist directed. Top-billed was Susanna Foster, fresh from her *Phantom of the Opera* (1943) success, and Donald O'Connor providing the hoofing. Also present was Patric Knowles, who had just been seen in *Frankenstein Meets the Wolfman* (1943).

During World War II Riskin was chief of the motion-picture overseas branch of the Office of War Information, forming Robert Riskin Productions at RKO after the war to film *Magic Town* (1947). In 1949 he created his own independent company, Equitable Pictures. After surgery in 1950, Riskin remained bedridden. Fay Wray decided to return to film acting.

In Fox's *Treasure of the Golden Condor* (1953), a period adventure about treasure hunters in Central America, she appeared with Cornell Wilde, Constance Smith, and Anne Bancroft. MGM's *Small Town Girl* (1953) was a musical comedy about the reaction in a small town when a playboy millionaire arrives on the scene. Jane Powell, Farley Granger, Ann Miller, and Bobby Van headed the cast with Fay as Jane Powell's mother. On October 2, 1953, she began a weekly TV series, *Pride of the Family*, playing mother to Natalie

Wood and Bobby Hyatt, with Paul Hartman as the bumbling Dagwoodlike husband and father; when the series moved from ABC to CBS in 1955 the title was changed to *The Paul Hartman Show*.

A widow in 1955, Fay Wray was also well established in the film industry after her successful comeback. She was exactly the right age for "mother" roles, and her return to films coincided with the release to television of *King Kong*. Suddenly, her name and face were known to an entire generation that had never seen her before.

MGM's *The Cobweb* (1955), based on the William Gibson novel, was a potent drama set in a mental institution, with Fay joining a heavyweight cast of Richard Widmark, Lauren Bacall, Charles Boyer, Gloria Grahame, Susan Strasberg, John Kerr, and Lillian Gish. At Columbia, she was in *Queen Bee* (1955), a melodrama about a destructive Southern belle with Joan Crawford recreating, in a fashion, Bette Davis' *Jezebel* role. Warners' *Hell on Frisco Bay* (1955), with Alan Ladd, Edward G. Robinson, Joanne Dru, and Fay Wray, was a throwback to the Warners crime dramas of the thirties. On August 20, 1955, she appeared in "There's No Forever" on CBS's *Damon Runyon Theatre*, followed by a role in "My Son Is Gone" on the syndicated *Studio 57*. On February 22, 1956, she was in "Times Like These" on *The 20th Century-Fox Hour* for CBS. After "Exit Laughing" for *Studio 57*, she was seen January 29, 1957, in "Killer's Bride" for NBC's *Jane Wyman Theatre*. CBS aired "The Iron Horse" with Fay on *GE Theatre* November 24, 1957, one week after her appearance on ABC's *Telephone Time* in "Alice's Wedding Gown."

After *Out of Time* (1957) she played John Saxon's mother in Universal's *Rock, Pretty Baby* (1957), the first of the "mild youth" genre that was heavily influenced by TV family-situation comedies of the time (*Ozzie and Harriet, Pride of the Family*, etc.). *Film Daily* commented, "It's sure to be a smash with the youngsters. At a special screening at RKO last week, the audience greeted the film with howls of delighted approval. Oddly enough, the picture, while aiming at the younger set, also has family appeal, for it presents an interesting and wholesome glimpse of family life in suburbia." In United Artists' *Crime of Passion* (1957), about an ambitious woman led to adultery and murder, Fay Wray was third-billed in the cast of Barbara Stanwyck, Sterling Hayden, and Raymond Burr. In the cornball *Tammy and the Bachelor* (1957) for Universal, she appeared with Debbie Reynolds, Leslie Nielson, Mala Powers, and Sidney Blackmer. Universal's *Summer Love* (1958) was a sequel to *Rock, Pretty Baby*. Her last motion-picture credit was American-International's *Dragstrip Riot* (1958) with Gary Clark, Yvonne Lime, and Connie Stevens. AIP described it as "the story of teenage youths who live as fast as their hot rods will carry them. Gary Clark as the newcomer to the gang is running away from his past, his flight being hampered by a gang of motorcyclists who throw a reign of terror over his very existence. Courage is measured as drag races are performed on railroad tracks, the climax building up to a free-for-all between the two gangs. All this is accomplished by rock-'n'-roll numbers and actual flat races at Santa Barbara, California."

She continued to work in television. After "Eddie" on January 22, 1958, for NBC's *Kraft Theatre*, she was third-billed in "A Dip in the Pool" for *Alfred Hitchcock Presents* on CBS on June 1, 1958. Coincidentally, this happens to be the only episode of Hitchcock's TV program in which he made a cameo appearance (his face on the cover of a magazine), as he had done for so many years in his motion pictures. In this show, Keenan Wynn stars as Rotibol, a loudmouth tourist on a cruise to Europe. After losing money at cards, he enters a betting pool on how many miles the ship will travel the next day, counting on a storm which will slow the ship. When he sees that the weather is good the next morning, he decides to jump overboard, hoping his rescue will cause a delay which will win him the bet. He picks a woman passenger as a witness, and jumps in. However, she is a mental patient, and her story of a man jumping overboard is not taken seriously. Others in the cast were Louise Platt, Philip Bourneuf, and Doreen Lang. Francis Cockrell did the adaptation from a Roald Dahl short story. "A Dip in the Pool" is one of the nineteen shows in the series which were directed by Hitchcock himself, and it can still be seen in syndication in many areas. In the same week that Wray was seen in the *Hitchcock* episode, she appeared in "The Case of the Prodigal Parent" on CBS's *Perry Mason*.

In 1959, her TV credits included "The Promise" on the May 5 *David Niven Show* for NBC, *Playhouse 90*'s "Second Happiest Day" for CBS, and a return to *Perry Mason* in "The Case of the Watery Witness" on October 10. "Bequest of Arthur Goodwin" was a March 9, 1960, episode of ABC's *Hawaiian Eye*, and the following month she appeared in "Flight from Terror" on ABC's *Islanders*. "Theatre in the Barn" was aired on ABC's *Real McCoys* May 18, 1961, followed by another *GE Theatre*—"Money and the Minister"—on November 26 of that year. For NBC's *Wagon Train*, she acted in "The Cole Crawford Story" on April 11, 1962. On January 22, 1964, she was seen in "You're So Smart" on NBC's *Eleventh Hour*. Another *Perry Mason* appearance was "The Case of the Fatal Fetish" on March 4, 1965.

Also in the mid-sixties she did an engaging *Today* interview reminiscing about her experiences with *King Kong*. Living alone in her Brentwood home overlooking Los Angeles (just down the road from where Jane and Peter Fonda grew up), she emerged to do extensive traveling during the sixties. One of her closest friends is Dorothy Jordan, widow of Merian C. Cooper.

Fay Wray made an appearance in 1976 at the third Telluride Film Festival in a *King Kong* tribute, along with Orville Goldner and George Turner, the authors of *The Making of King Kong*; special effects genius Linwood Dunn; Cooper's assistant Archie Marshek; Mrs. Merian Cooper, and Cooper's secretary Zoe Porter—the first person who was ever lifted in the life-size Kong hand. And, oh yes, the real Kong himself was also at Telluride, in the form of one of the original eighteen-inch-high minature armatures used in the film. During the panel discussion, Fay Wray picked up the naked armature and remarked, "We're good friends now." At that very moment, a hang-glider swooped down from one of the mountains nearby. Coming into a direct line above Fay Wray from the audience's point of view, the silhouette brought gasps, for it seemed to resemble a pterodactyl in flight. Legends never die, do they?

In *Castle of Frankenstein* #17, for October 1971, Phil Moshcovitz reported on the Madison Avenue return of Kong—a revival which included Fay Wray's daughter in one commercial: "Call it camp or just plain commercialism, but *King Kong* is making a comeback in advertising. A fair maiden is asked, 'Why does Almond Joy bar come in two pieces?' 'So I can share it,' she replies. 'There's a piece for me and a piece for my friend.' A giant ape gets his piece by reaching through her bedroom window after which his monstrous hand tickles her chin. *Kong* is also king in a few magazine ads. A spectacular two-page color ad in *Newsweek* is headlined, 'Don't monkey around.' He's high on the Empire State Building in pseudo-Peter Max pop style. Clutching a blond beauty while fighting an array of airplanes, his fanged mouth and blaring eyes add to the realism. Kong was also resurrected by Puerto Rican Rum for an ad showing a large ape fist grasping a frightened female as her boy friend tries to free her. 'Ron Rico? Didn't this girl have a strange animal magnetism?' reads the headline."

In 1971, Fay Wray's daughter, Victoria Riskin, appeared in a re-creation of her mother's escapade with Kong atop the Empire State Building. This thirty-second remake was a Volkswagen commercial by animator David Allen for the Doyle, Dane, and Bernbach agency, Kong and Vicky are circled by biplanes. Kong holds Vicky instead of putting her on the ledge. In the background is another change—the Pan Am building. "Forget this scene," says Kong. "Nothing stays the same in New York, I guess." He climbs to the street, muttering, "Hardly a red-carpet treatment. Last time I was here, half the whole city of New York was fleeing my wrath. Babe, we're splitting this town." He walks over to a thirty-foot high VW 311, puts Vicky in the passenger seat, and drives off. After several airings in 1971–72, the VW Kong commercial vanished from view.

Because of *Kong*, Fay Wray's fame is worldwide—with an endless parade of sequels, satires, remakes, and rip-offs. In *Queen Kong* there's a character called Ray Faye. Despite the heavy 1976 promotion of ex-fashion model Jessica Lange as Ann Dar-row, millions of viewers will always have an eidetic imprint of Fay Wray screaming as the airplanes launch their attack on Kong. As an illustration of Fay Wray's staying power in the original *King Kong*, it was she, and not Jessica Lange, mentioned in the song "The King Kong Dirge" as sung by Garrett Morris on *NBC Saturday Night Live* in November 1976, during the furious publicity surrounding the *Kong* remake. Morris stood behind a thirties-style microphone while giant slides of the original Kong holding Fay Wray were projected in the background. The song mentioned Fay Wray in the opening line.

Airplanes? It wasn't the airplanes. It was beauty that killed the beast.

The *Kong* legend, as developed in other films. BELOW: Michael Gough in *Konga* (1961); NEXT PAGE, TOP LEFT: It was not beauty in this case, but Richard—that is, Richard Einiger—who slew the beast; CENTER LEFT: Linda Miller in *King Kong Escapes* (1968); BOTTOM: *King Kong Versus Godzilla* (1963); TOP RIGHT: the 1966 animated *Kong*.

# Laura
# La Plante

*L*aura La Plante appeared in two of horror director Paul Leni's films—the first film version of *The Cat and the Canary* (1927) and *The Last Warning* (1929)—and a sequence from one La Plante picture turns up in the *Flash Gordon* serials.

She was born in 1904 in St. Louis, Missouri, and began appearing in the Christie Comedies at the age of fifteen. As she explained in the early thirties: "Mother, sister Violet, and I lived in San Diego, where, in spare time, I studied the violin. Each summer I went vacationing, a protracted visit with my aunt, who lived in Hollywood. As finances are something to worry about even when one lives with kind relatives, I always wanted to do my share to help with the bills. I just knew I could act, and the movies fascinated me. Finally, through a scenario writer who lived next door, I secured an introduction to the agent who was managing Priscilla Dean. This agent arranged for me to go over to the Christie Studio, where William Beaudine, the director, gave me my first screen test. After this I had more luck and did extra work right along. Then

came what I thought was a big chance. Christie's was making a series of two-reel comedies based on the cartoon *Bringing Up Father*, and I was cast as Jiggs's daughter. To use the movie term, the comedies were a flop, and when they were finished, I was out of a job. This was a great disappointment, but I was still determined to stick to it and make good in pictures."

She went back to doing extra work and bits. "Soon afterward I had the opportunity to play the sister part with Louise Glaum, who was starring in *Love* (1920). It was a slick part, and I thought sure I'd be a star overnight. But when I saw the picture, little Laura couldn't be found anywhere! However, I was not discouraged, and my agent secured me the feminine lead opposite Charles Ray in *The Old Swimmin' Hole* (1921). That was better. From there I went to Fox Studios, where I played the part of a blonde crook with Eileen Percy. After that I made several pictures with Tom Mix, Johnnie Walker, and Edna Murphy, and finally got a sympathetic part with Colleen Moore at the old Metro Studios. Then came

a series of two-reel Western pictures and two serials with Bill Desmond."

These were *Perils of the Yukon* (1922) and a 1923 Universal adaptation of Jules Verne's *Around the World in 80 Days*, updated by directors Reeves Eason and Robert F. Hill to *Around the World in 18 Days*. The grandson of Phineas Fogg (Desmond) traveled the globe on behalf of an international fuel corporation after the idea is suggested by his daughter (La Plante). She goes with him on the trek—which is accomplished with submarines, speed boats, crack express trains, airplanes, and other modes of transportation available in 1923. Others in the cast were Spottiswoode Aiken, William P. DeVaul, Wade Boteler, and William Welsh. The twelve chapters were titled: *The Wager, Wanted by the Police,*

LEFT: Laura La Plante in *The Cat and the Canary* (1927).

BELOW: The fake doctor (Lucien Littlefield) points a threatening finger at Annabelle West (Laura La Plante) in *The Cat and the Canary.*

*Apaches of Paris, The Man Who Broke the Bank at Monte Carlo, Sands of Doom, The Living Sacrifice, The Dragon's Claws, A Nation's Peril, Trapped in the Clouds, The Brink of Eternity, The Path of Peril,* and *The Last Race.*

"I was afraid I'd be classed as a serial actress after I had done two," recalled La Plante. "Hence, I raised my salary so high the serial producers just couldn't hire me. Hoot Gibson used me in a feature opposite him, but my big chance came when I finally got the lead with Reginald Denny in *Sporting Youth* (1924). It brought me a five-year contract, but how nearly I missed the opportunity! Mr. Denny wanted me for the picture, but Harry Pollard, the director, didn't. The director won and picked his own choice for the lead. A short trial convinced the director he had to have someone else. The studio called me at three o'clock one afternoon and told me to catch the six o'clock train for Del Monte, California, where the Denny company was shooting. I didn't have time to pack my best clothes, but I did catch the train! After a few days the director became reconciled to having me around, and things went swimmingly. It was my big chance, and I grabbed it. I was lucky. It's seldom those breaks come, you know." *The New York Times'* favorable review noted: "Laura La Plante is effective as Betty . . ."

She made *Smouldering Fires* in 1925. In 1926 she married William Seiter, her director in the films *The Fast Worker* (1924), *Dangerous Innocence* (1925), and *The Teaser* (1925). (Between 1922 and 1954 Seiter directed over eighty films of which the best-remembered is probably the Marx Brothers' 1938 *Room Service.*)

*The Midnight Sun* (1926), directed by Dimitri Buchowerzki, is the La Plante film that features the *outrè* Ballet Russe material seen over a decade later in *Flash Gordon.* After *Skinner's Dress Suit* (1926), she made *Poker Faces* (1926), *Her Big Night* (1926), *Butterflies in the Rain* (1926), *The Love Thrill* (1927), *Beware of Widows* (1927), and the extremely popular *The Cat and the Canary* (1927). It was

based on John Willard's 1922 play of the same title, and, as directed by Paul Leni (of *Waxworks* fame), it became the model for the many "old creepy house" comedy thrillers made during the thirties by Universal and others.

A synopsis of the story evokes the penultimate cinematic *déjà vu.* The credits are hidden behind cobwebs, and a hand brushes them away. The story begins: the

TOP: Fortunately, Laura can rest easy with a protector like Creighton Hale. Martha Mattox lingers sinisterly at the doorway.

BOTTOM: Lucien Littlefield continues with his doomsaying, this time throwing a scare into Annabelle's friend (Gertrude Astor).

eccentric millionaire Cyrus West had died fearing hereditary insanity and with much suspicion of his greedy relatives—whom he saw as cats hiding in the shadows of huge medicine bottles. On the twentieth anniversary of his death, at midnight, there is a reading of his will, conducted by lawyer Roger Crosby (Tully Marshall, at the West mansion overlooking the Hudson. Present are Annabelle West (La Plante), her childhood sweetheart Paul Jones (Creighton Hale), Aunt Susan (Flora Finch), Susan's niece Cecily (Gertrude Astor), and two cousins who are bitter rivals, Charlie Wilder (Forrest Stanley) and Harry Blythe (Arthur Edmund Carewe). It is announced that Annabelle is the sole heir; however, if the doctor (Lucien Littlefield) decides that she is insane, a second heir will be chosen, according to the will. Paul, Susan, and Cecily want to leave after being frightened by the strange housekeeper, Mammy Pleasant (Martha Mattox), but they are interrupted by the arrival of the warder (George Siegmann). The warder tells of the escape in the area of a criminally insane madman who suffers from delusions, believing himself to be a cat that enjoys mutilating canaries. When Crosby attempts to warn Annabelle that the envelope containing the name of the second heir has been opened, Crosby vanishes mysteriously and is later found murdered. Annabelle claims that she was menaced in her room by a hairy claw which stole part of her inheritance, a diamond necklace. This leads to the conclusion that Annabelle must be insane, and the doctor arrives. He says that she is insane. Accidentally, Paul stumbles on the truth—that all the mysterious events were arranged by cousin Charlie, hoping to drive Annabelle mad. After Charlie's arrest,

Creighton Hale temporarily loses control of the situation when the masked, unknown killer appears.

Annabelle and Paul remain happily at the West mansion with Mammy Pleasant.

The screenplay was by Robert F. Hill and Alfred A. Cohn, with titles written by Walter Anthony. Gilbert Warrenton handled the camera, and Charles Hall was the art director. Louise Bogan wrote in *The New Republic*: "Paul Leni, a German director imported by Universal Pictures, has done his best for *The Cat and the Canary*, a story full of complicated disappearances and such box-office horrors as long taloned hands appearing from wainscoting. He has invention—a turn for grim lighting and sinister composition not ineffective even when applied to this thin material—which should come through magnificently, given a picture of terrifying implications. *The Cat and the Canary* has several sets done in the best *Castle of Otranto* feeling. One, a long corridor lined with tall Gothic windows whose pale curtains blow out in the wind like shrouds, is shot from every angle—from above, as a woman moves along it carrying a lamp, from below, when figures seen against the narrow arches lean back in alarming distortion. Leni suggests action by shadows sliding against bleak, bright walls; he breaks up his scene into patterns by placing his actors behind barred chairs and lozenged windows. His talent, more discreet and less violent than Murnau's, is yet one that can save sets from their three-walled monotony, switch them into impressive design, give them tenseness and angularity. The possibilities of motion pictures as a medium for projecting horror have never been fully realized. *The Cabinet of Dr. Caligari* (1919) pointed the way, with its use of backgrounds pulled into the color of the action. Without screams or pistol shots, by arrangement and pattern alone, by a combination of pure realism and grotesque dream, the picture of pure horror is

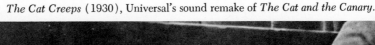

*The Cat Creeps* (1930), Universal's sound remake of *The Cat and the Canary*.

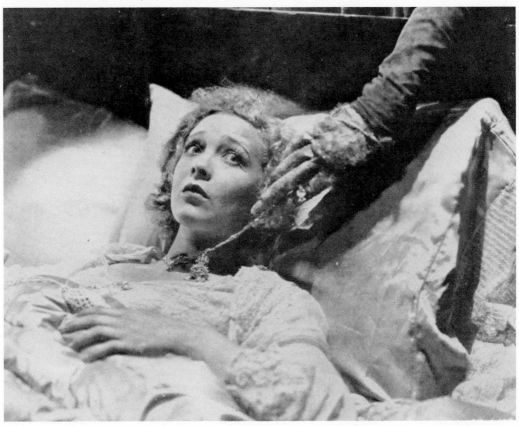

still waiting to be made. If any company wants to produce Poe, Paul Leni might very well be the man to take the work in hand. *The Narrative of A. Gordon Pym*, under his direction, should be a full adventure for the startled eye."

Leni, unfortunately, never had the opportunity to film Poe. In two years, after three more horror mysteries, he was dead of blood poisoning at the age of 44.

Beaumont Newhall, the director of Eastman House, was nineteen when he saw *The Cat and the Canary* at the Olympia Theatre in Boston. His study notes from December 1927, were not published until 1966: "The first scene showed some bottles, and a cat tearing a canary apart, or rather fighting with it. These bottles then changed in a startling manner to a castle high upon a hill. . . . There was a series of remarkable dissolves, the opening of a door, the entrance of a person to the assembled multitude. Mr. Leni was not at all wary about using that most valuable asset in the cameraman's bag of tricks, the trucking of the camera around the scenes. It seems that the will was to be read at twelve o'clock, so at twelve we see the mechanism of a clock striking out the hour. This slowly dissolves,

or is superimposed upon the scene showing the crabby lawyer reading the will. Mr. Leni places his camera near the floor and thus heightens the weird effects. A hand seizes a jewel around the sleeping woman's neck. She screams, and bolts upright in bed, a truck-in to her mouth, followed immediately by a title 'Help!' Very effective. The doctor examining the young heiress was inevitably a scene from the famous *Cabinet of Dr. Caligari*. There was the same type of cold impassionate mental doctor, spreading fear and mental disorder more than curing it. I have called this film 'à la *Caligari*' because there is so much insanity in it, and this feeling of insanity is heightened by the crazy sets. All honor to Mr. Leni for making a presentable photoplay from a maudlin stage thriller."

*The Cat and the Canary* was remade in 1939 with Bob Hope and Paulette Goddard. An earlier remake was *The Cat Creeps* (1930), directed by *Phantom of the Opera*'s Rupert Julian and featuring a cast of Helen Twelvetrees, Raymond Hackett, Neil Hamilton, and Jean Hersholt. Carlos Clarens calls the Leni original "the best of the three." Yet another version was *El Gato*, a 1930 Universal Spanish-language film shot simultaneously with *The Cat Creeps* and featuring Antonio Moreno, Lupita Tovar, and Manuel Granado.

La Plante was seen next in *Silk Stockings* (1927), adapted by Beatrice Van from

LEFT: Laura La Plante in blackface in the early thirties.

the stage play by Cyril Harcourt. In *Thanks for the Buggy Ride* (1928), with story and continuity by Beatrice Van, she was once again directed by her husband. After *Finders Keepers* (1928) and *Home James* (1928), she appeared in Paul Leni's last

The masked killer captured by Antonio Moreno in *El Gato* (1930), the Spanish-language version of the 1930 *The Cat Creeps*.

commercial film before his death. Ironically, it was titled *The Last Warning* (1929). *The Last Warning* depicted a series of macabre hauntings and visitations in a decrepit Broadway theatre, a story based on Wadsworth Camp's novel *House of Fear* and the play *The Last Warning* by Thomas F. Fallon. It was fully in the tradition established by *The Bat* and *The Cat and the Canary*, but the creepy catwalks and jack-in-the-box trapdoors evoked the atmosphere of *Phantom of the Opera*. Adapted to films by Alfred A. Cohn, Robert F. Hill, and J. G. Hawks, the screenplay of *The Last Warning* was credited to Cohn and Tom Reed. The eighty-eight-minute film had sound effects and recorded dialogue, and Joseph Cherviasky did the score. The art direction was once again by Charles D. Hall, and Hal Mohr was the director of photography. Comparing it with the earlier twenties adaptations of stage thrillers, Carlos Clarens notes, "It was the same formula and again, it worked, though in a more modest way. Leni had a visual wit as well

as a head for the macabre. . . . In *The Last Warning*, a shot of a theater front changing into a monstrous grimacing face is a humorous comment on *Metropolis*."

Reviewing in retrospect, David Robinson in *Hollywood in the Twenties*, observes that *The Last Warning*, seen today, "retains a good deal of its charm; the horror effects produced by the elaborate lighting and careful *mise en scène* are set off by pleasant comedy which compensates for the fading dramatic force of the film." La Plante was topbilled, and Montagu Love, Roy D'Arcy, Margaret Livingston, John Boles, Burr McIntosh, Mack Swain, and Slim Summerville completed the cast. Leni, before his death, worked on one more film for Universal, the all-synchronized experimental *Puzzles* (1929). In 1939 *The Last Warning* was remade as *House of Fear*, a programmer directed by Joe May, starring Irene Hervey and William Gargan.

When she appeared as Magnolia in *Show Boat* (1929), with her blonde hair dyed brunette, it became apparent that La

Plante and talkies fitted hand in glove. She commented, "Among my first all-talking pictures are *Scandal* (1929) and *Show Boat*. The latter play was taken from the book by Edna Ferber and furnished one of the greatest roles of my career."

After *Hold Your Man* (1929) and *Captain of the Guard* (1930), she took part in Universal's Paul Whiteman extravaganza *King of Jazz* (1930), which featured a spectacular fantasy stage setting of giant musical instruments, making the performers look like they have been transposed to the late fifties set of *The Incredible Shrinking Man*. In 1931 she appeared in *Lonely Wives, God's Gift to Women*, and *Men Are Like That*. Around this period she wrote, "Although a motion-picture career's worth it, anyone who feels that he or she can come out to Hollywood and go crashing over the top is laboring under a sad delusion! It's a hard life. The financial reward awaits the winner as it does in most any other profession, but the work is far harder and opportunity comes less and less each year to newcomers seeking to break into pictures." Reading between the lines, perhaps one can find a clue to explain why La Plante chose to abandon her high-ranking plateau in Hollywood, having already proved she was more than adequate for talkies. She traveled to Europe in 1932, divorcing Seiter in Riga, Latvia.

On June 19, 1934, in Paris, she married produced Irving Asher (who made, among others, the 1942 *Mr. and Mrs. North* mystery with Gracie Allen). Through the late thirties and early forties, the Ashers lived in London and then moved to Beverly Hills. She almost returned to films in 1943 as Nora Charles in *The Thin Man* series, as a replacement for Myrna Loy, who had grown restless with her MGM contract. Instead, her comeback waited until "She Also Ran" on a 1956 *Bell Telephone Hour*. It was the story of a suffragette running for President, and La Plante was cast along with silent star Aileen Pringle. On November 13, 1955, she appeared in "The Movie Star" on the NBC-TV series *It's a Great Life* with James Dunn, William Bishop, and Michael O'Shea. In 1957 she portrayed Betty Hutton's mother in Hutton's awkward attempt to establish herself as a dramatic actress in *Spring Reunion*. It was not only Hutton's last film but La Plante's as well.

In the sixties Laura La Plante began spending much time by her swimming pool at her desert home not far from Palm Springs. Her two children, Tony and Jill, both born in England, have worked in advertising. Tony Asher collaborated with Beach Boy Brian Wilson on several of the most popular Beach Boy tunes, including *Caroline No, Wouldn't It Be Nice?* and *Don't Talk—Put Your Head on My Shoulder* (available on Capitol Records' *The Beach Boys Pet Sounds*).

1933: The girls of the chorus stand in the back and are also seated at extreme left and right. *Seated, from left to right*: Holding the flowers is Olympic swimming champion Eleanor Holm, who appeared in such films as *Tarzan's Revenge* (1938) and married Billy Rose in 1939; Joe E. Brown, with his oft-caricatured mouth; Leo Carrillo, later famed as Pancho in *The Cisco Kid*; Bette Davis is seated next to Tom Mix, who made over 400 Western films before his auto accident death in 1940; next in line is Laura La Plante, who began to vanish from the screen about the time this photograph was taken. Standing behind Tom Mix is Doris McMahon.

# Mae Clarke

$M$ae Clarke, the female lead of *Frankenstein*, was born August 16, 1910, in Philadelphia as Mary Klotz. Because her father was a theatre organist, she grew up seeing films constantly. Having studied dance as a child, she began her career with a nightclub act at the age of thirteen. While performing as one of May Dawson's Dancing Girls in 1924, she was seen by producer Earl Lindsay, who cast her in a show at New York's Strand Theatre. This led to a small role in *The Noose* in 1926, followed by the musical *Manhattan Mary* (1927) and a tour in vaudeville. In 1928 she married Lew Brice, Fanny Brice's brother.

Her first film for Fox, *Big Time* (1929), was based on William Wallace Smith's story, *Little Ledna*. After *Nix on Dames* (1929), *Fall Guy* (1930) for Warners, and *Dancers* (1930), she and Brice were divorced. She later commented, "He hated being known as Mr. Mae Clarke, poor guy. But what man wouldn't?"

After *Men on Call* (1930), she created a strong impression as the prostitute Molly in the popular *The Front Page* (1931).

Then came *Public Enemy* (1931) and her famous grapefruit scene with Cagney, which seems to turn up in almost every television documentary about films of the thirties. Marjorie Rosen queries in *Popcorn Venus*, "If Hollywood's idea of portraying Depression hardship was for gangster Jimmy Cagney in *Public Enemy* to squash a grapefruit in Mae Clarke's face (vicarious vengeance, admitted director William Wellman recently, on the wife he was soon to divorce), or for ex-millionaire William Powell in *My Man Godfrey* to wander around as a butler, viewing the good life from the servant's shoes, how could we expect the industry to serve females any less exploitatively?" Also in 1931 were *Good Bad Girl*, *Reckless Living*, *Determination*, and British director James Whale's *Waterloo Bridge*.

In James Whale's *Frankenstein* (1931), Mae Clarke was third-billed in the cast of Boris Karloff, Colin Clive, Lionel Belmore, Edward van Sloan, Dwight Frye, John Boles, Frederic Kerr, and Marilyn Harris. The adaptation by Robert Florey (who

ABOVE: Mae Clarke, as she appeared in 1931 at the time of her appearances in *Fall Guy* and *The Front Page*.

BELOW: The famous grapefruit scene with Mae Clarke and James Cagney in *Public Enemy* (1931).

later directed Peter Lorre in the 1940 *Face Behind the Mask* and the 1946 *Beast with Five Fingers*) and John Balderston and the screenplay by Florey, Garrett Fort, and Francis Edward Faragoh, were based on Peggy Webling's play version of the Mary Shelley novel. Young Dr. Frankenstein, absorbed in the creation of life in an old tower on a hill, begins to ignore his bride-to-be, Elizabeth (Mae Clarke). Aided by his hunchbacked, stumbling servant (Dwight Frye), he has been digging up bodies. "I am not restoring life to the dead," he declares. "This creature never lived. I am creating new life!" In the midst of a thunderstorm, he succeeds in harnessing the electricity of the lightning. His creation twitches. It moves. It walks. But it is only a distorted parody of man—since the hunchback has substituted a criminal brain. The hunchback is killed by the creature. Dr. Waldman (Edward van Sloan), Frankenstein's old teacher, persuades him to allow the creature to be dissected for further study. Agreeing, Frankenstein and Elizabeth leave to be married. The Monster recovers from the drug it had been given and kills Waldman. Roaming around, it finds a little girl whom it plays with—and then

kills. At the Frankenstein home, plans for the wedding are in progress. When the Monster appears, the enraged villagers pursue it to an old windmill. Dr. Frankenstein and his creation struggle at the top of the windmill while the villagers, waving torches, mill around below. The Monster throws him to the ground, but his fall is broken. Then the windmill is set afire. The Monster, screaming inarticulately, is destroyed in the conflagration. Or so we think. Frankenstein and his bride live happily ever after—until the next picture.

As the female lead in *Frankenstein*, Mae Clark had a role that was somewhat disappointing compared to Helen Chandler's part as Nina in the Lugosi *Dracula*. This is loosely justified because their *filmic* characterizations are almost proportionately the same in the original book versions. In Mary Shelley's book, *Frankenstein*, Elizabeth is kept offstage part of the time, and she becomes known to the reader from young Frankenstein's affectionate descriptions and through extensive correspondence and, finally, through the consummation of a long-sought marriage that is quickly terminated by the Monster when he vengefully murders the young bride. Throughout all of Stoker's original book version of *Dracula*, though, Nina is not only *the* heroine-in-distress and, temporarily, main victim, but also the focal point of Dracula's own vampirical affection leading to his own destruction.

Director Tod Browning adheres rather faithfully to the original novel and play at least in spirit if not actual context—Nina is still centrally very important. And, of course, what other alternative does old Dracula have as one of fiction's greatest womanizers of all time?

By contrast, James Whale minimizes Elizabeth's position, reducing her almost to the level of an overexposed bit player during most of *Frankenstein*. This is obviously deliberate, even if crude; Whale saves his ammo, focusing all energy and attention on van Sloan, Clive, Frye, and Karloff. Though some of the other cast members are dimensionally cardboard-like, Mae Clarke does show some color and spirit in several important sequences. Shortly after the tale unfolds, she expresses grave concern over Clive's (Henry Frankenstein) progressive isolation; her solicitude is shared by van Sloan and John Boles, and all proceed to become unwelcome visitors at Clive's desolate, country retreat.

Mae's best scene comes much later. The wedding plans, now disrupted by the awful news that the Monster is nearby and on the loose, Clive and friends hear Karloff bellowing wildly somewhere in the chateau, probably in the basement to which they head. Meanwhile, Mae's in her bedroom sulking, unaware that the Monster is at that very moment coming in behind her through the window. One of the all-time fright scenes, the moments that follow, as Monster and Mae face each other, hits the peak of horrific perfection.

In 1932, Clarke was in *Final Edition*, *Three Wise Girls*, *Impatient Maiden*, Hobart Henley's *Night World*, *Breach of Promise*, and RKO's *The Penguin Pool Murder*, a mystery about a man found murdered in an aquarium's penguin tank. In 1933 there were *Fast Workers*, *Parole Girl*, *Made on Broadway*, *Turn Back the Clock*, *As the Devil Commands*, *Penthouse*, and *Lady Killer* (co-starring with Cagney once again.)

In 1934, her films were *Flaming Gold*, *This Side of Heaven*, *Nana*, *Let's Talk It Over*, *Operator 13*, and *Man with Two Faces*. The latter was an especially significant mystery (with horror undertones) about an evil hypnotist (Louis Calhern) who uses his high-society contacts to lure female victims until the intellectually superior Edward G. Robinson turns the tables against him.

*The Daring Young Man*, *Silk Hat Kid*, and *Hitch Hike Lady* followed in 1935. In Republic's *House of a Thousand Candles* in 1936, Clarke starred with Phillips Holmes in a tale of a young man who takes up residence in an incomplete mansion to fulfill the terms of his grandfather's will. The year 1936 brought *Hearts in Bondage*, *Wild Brian Kent*, *Great Guy*, and *Hats Off*. In

1937 she made *Trouble in Morocco* and *Outlaws of the Orient*. Also in 1937, Clarke married Stephen Bancroft. They were later divorced. Her third marriage, to Herbert Langdon, also ended in divorce. She next made *Women in War* in 1940; *Sailors on Leave* in 1941; *Flying Tigers* and *Lady from Chungking* in 1942; *Here Come the Waves* and *And Now Tomorrow* in 1944; *Kitty* in 1945; and *Daredevils of the Clouds* in 1948.

In 1949, Mae Clarke was the heroine in Republic's science-fiction serial, *King of the Rocket Men*, directed by Fred Brannon and written by Royal Cole, William Lively, and Sol Shor. Special effects were by the Lydecker brothers, Howard and Theodore, who had earlier accomplished some of the most convincing flying effects ever done for the Republic serial *The Adventures of Captain Marvel* (1942). No one has ever surpassed the Lydeckers in creating intricate special effects on a limited budget. Franklin Adreon was the associate producer. Stanley Wilson scored, and the chapters were edited by Cliff Bell and Sam Starr. The twelve chapters were titled *Dr. Vulcan-Traitor, Plunging Death, Dangerous Evidence, High Peril, Fatal Dive, Mystery of the Rocket Man, Molten Menace, Suicide Flight, Ten Seconds to Live, The Deadly Fog, Secret of Dr. Vulcan, and Wave of Disaster.*

Chapter One begins with the death of Professor Drake and the near death of Professor Millard (James Craven). The man behind this is the sinister Dr. Vulcan. Glenda Thomas (Clarke), photographer of *Miracle Science* magazine, heads for the desert to see the independent research project of Millard's Science Associates. Here she meets Jeff King (Tristram Coffin), also working on the project, and the publicity director Burt Winslow (House Peters, Jr.). Two of Vulcan's men

OPPOSITE: Two views of the Frankenstein Monster's encounter with Elizabeth (Mae Clarke). She falls unconscious. The Monster (Boris Karloff) then heads off as his pursuers go in the opposite direction.

attack Jeff, and after he gets rid of them, he goes to the isolated cave where Millard is hiding out from Vulcan. Together, Jeff and Millard have perfected a flying suit propelled by rockets. When Jeff dons the suit, he becomes Rocket Man! Vulcan attempts to take over Science Associates but is always foiled by Rocket Man. The connection becomes clear to Vulcan—he deduces that Jeff and Rocket Man are the same. (Since Jeff is always missing whenever Rocket Man is zipping around in the air, not too much brainpower was expended in figuring this out.) Tony Dirken (Don Haggerty), another of Vulcan's men, captures Jeff during a moment when he is totally engrossed in the new Science Associates gadget, the Sonutron. But Dirken splits

Top Secret!

The brains and brawn of America combine to hold off the madmen who would rock the world in disaster!

KING OF THE ROCKET MEN

featuring
TRISTRAM COFFIN · MAE CLARKE
DON HAGGERTY · HOUSE PETERS, JR.
I. STANFORD JOLLEY

Mae Clarke twists Tristram Coffin's dials.

when, to his amazement, Rocket Man unexpectedly appears to rescue Jeff. Inside the suit is Millard, and they return to the cave.

Another Millard machine is the Decimator, which disintegrates rocks. Vulcan appropriates the Decimator and demands a billion dollars from the mayor. When his ransom is ignored, Vulcan creates a tidal wave and an earthquake in the New York harbor. Another Science Associates device is brought into play. It locates the island where Vulcan has the Decimator. Rocket Man heads for the island—but so do a number of bombers, something nobody bothered to tell Jeff about. Rocket Man knocks out both the Decimator and Vulcan and manages to get away just as the bombs fall. Vulcan and his men die in the barrage of bombs.

Also in the cast of *King of the Rocket Men* were I. Stanford Jolley, Douglas Evans, Ted Adams, Stanley Price, Dale Van Sickel, Tom Steele, David Sharpe, Eddie Parker, Michael Ferro, Frank O'Connor, and Buddy Roosevelt. The serial was released as a feature film titled *Lost Planet Airmen* in 1951. It also spawned a number of sequels: the 1952 *Radar Men from the Moon* (same suit but Rocket Man was now known as Commando Cody), the 1952 serial *Zombies of the Stratosphere* (same suit but the hero is now Larry Martin of the Inter-Planetary Patrol; one of the Zombies, believe it or not, is none other than Leonard Nimoy), and the 1953 TV series *Commando Cody, Sky Marshal of the Universe*. Mae Clarke, fortunately, was associated with none of the sequels.

Also in 1949 she appeared in *Streets of San Francisco* and *Gun Runner*; in 1950, *Annie Get Your Gun* and *The Yellow Cab Man*; in 1951, *The Great Caruso, Mr. Imperium, The People Against O'Hara, Callaway Went Thataway*, and *The Unknown Man*; in 1952, *Because of You, Horizons West, Singin' in the Rain, Thunderbirds*, and *Pat and Mike*.

On May 2, 1954, she was in "The Judgment" on *The Loretta Young Show* on NBC, in addition to being in the film *Magnificent Obsession* for Universal. More television work followed—"Man in the Cellar" on *Four Star Playhouse* (September 30, 1954), "Gunpoint" on *Public Defender* (January 20, 1955), and "When I Was Young" on *Medic* (October 24, 1955). She had four 1955 motion-picture releases—*Women's Prison, Not as a Stranger, Wichita*, and *I Died a Thousand Times* (a remake of *High Sierra*).

In 1956 her films were *Come Next Spring, Mohawk, The Desperadoes Are in Town*, and *Ride the High Iron*. On December 5, 1956, she appeared in "Front Page

Everybody gets a good push as Don Haggerty threatens Mae Clarke and Tristram Coffin in this scene from *King of the Rocketmen*.

Father" on ABC's *Ford Theatre*, followed by "Killer's Pride" on the February 9, 1957, *Jane Wyman Theatre* and "A Greater Strength" on the February 23, 1958, *Loretta Young Show*.

After the 1958 alcoholic drama *Voice in the Mirror*, she was seen in *Ask Any Girl* (1959), *Big Hand for the Little Lady* (1966), *Thoroughly Modern Millie* (1967), and *Watermelon Man* (1970). Today, she lives alone in a North Hollywood apartment, where she works on her colorful Klee-like paintings between film roles.

# Olga Baclanova

When Olga Baclanova moved before the cameras, she walked in beauty and could add a new meaning, if not dimension, to the words "I am woman—female through-out." Undoubtedly, Baclanova's very attractive presence and superb sense of motion were unique on the screen because of her creative background. The Russian ballerina-actress was born in 1899. After her education at the Cherniavsky Institute in Moscow, she began acting at the Moscow Art Theatre at the age of sixteen. She appeared in featured roles in many stage productions —*The Daughter of Madame Angot, Carmencita and the Soldier, The Miracle* (as The Nun), *Grand Hotel, Idiot's Delight, 20th Century, The Cat and the Fiddle.* She traveled to the United States with the Moscow Art Theatre in 1926, electrifying New York with *Carmen.*

In 1927 she was seen in the Mauritz Stiller film, *Street of Sin,* written by Josef von Sternberg, and she followed this with a strong appearance in von Sternberg's *The Docks of New York* (1928), appearing with George Bancroft and Betty Compson. Her presence added to the murky waterfront atmosphere. Marjorie Rosen comments in *Popcorn Venus,* "An important distinction existed between saucy con girls and vicious predators like Olga Baclanova. . . . These females, modern neorealistic heirs to the vamp, antedated the full-blown and bitterly realized Evil Woman who would become a staple of late thirties' melodrama."

In *The Man Who Laughs* (1928), based on the Victor Hugo novel, Baclanova portrayed a duchess both repelled by and attracted to the circus performer Gwynplaine (Conrad Veidt), whose face has been frozen since childhood into a hideous, grinning clown visage. The role had originally been planned for Lon Chaney. The story is set in seventeenth-century England; Gwynplaine is discovered to be an English earl, kidnapped as a child. In one horrific scene, Gwynplaine is tortured in an Iron Maiden. Carl Laemmle produced for Universal, and the silent-horror director Paul Leni fashioned the film from a J. Grubb Alexander screenplay based on an adaptation by Charles E. Whittaker, Marion Ward, and May McLean. The titles were by Walter Anthony, but synchronized music and sound effects were added to thrust *The Man Who Laughs* into competition with the talkies. Others in the cast were Mary Philbin, Josephine Crowell, George Siegmann, Brandon Hurst, Sam De Grasse, Stuart Holmes, Edgar Norton, Julius Molnar, Jr., and Frank Puglia.

In 1928 she was in Victor Schertzinger's *Forgotten Faces* for Paramount, followed by *Avalanche*, based on the Zane Grey story. After *Wolf of Wall Street* (1929), she starred as a *femme fatale* creating conflicts with Clive Brook and Neil Hamilton in the African setting of *Dangerous Woman* (1929). Baclanova was in William Wellman's *The Man I Love* in 1929, written by Herman J. Mankiewicz of *Citizen Kane* fame. Richard Arlen, Mary Brian, and Jack Oakie were other headliners in this Paramount production about a prizefighter infatuated with a high-society lady. She also appeared in *The Great Lover*, a 1931 MGM drama. By the time of *Freaks* she was well established in "other woman" roles.

In *Freaks* (1932), for which she is best remembered for her role as the trapeze artist, she starred with Wallace Ford and a collection of genuine circus performers— the Siamese twins Violet and Daisy Hilton, Martha the Armless Wonder, Randian the Living Torso, Johnny Eck, who had only half a body, and the well-known German midget Harry Earles. It was, in fact, Earles who suggested the Tod Robbins short story *Spurs* to horror director Tod Browning. Willis Goldbeck, Leon Gordon, Edgar Allan Woolf, and Al Boasberg then did the screenplay for the MGM production. Cedric Gibbons handled the circus atmosphere art direction, and Merritt B. Gerstad photographed.

The story tells of a circus midget (Earles), hopelessly in love with the attractive Cleopatra (Baclanova), who spurns him until she learns he is heir to a fortune. She then agrees to marry him and lures him away from his midget fianceé (Daisy

TOP: A 1928 photograph of Baclanova, taken not long after she defected from the Moscow Art Theatre to join the Hollywood colony.

BELOW: Baclanova added her glamor and Russian soul to the underworld of Josef von Sternberg's Paramount film, *The Docks of New York* (1928).

OPPOSITE PAGE

TOP LEFT: A posed publicity shot of the circus performers in *Freaks* (1932). Seen in the doorway of the circus wagon is Johnny Eck, billed professionally as "The Half-Man." At one time he led his own orchestra. In the background, standing behind Slitzy, are the famed, fifty-eight-pound thin man, Pete Robinson, and the half-woman, half-man known as "Josephine-Joseph."

CENTER LEFT: Prince Randian, the Armless Wonder, talks with Matt McHugh in *Freaks*. A Coney Island attraction for many years, Randian was married, had two children and four grandchildren. Born armless and legless in 1871 in British Guiana, Randian was brought to this country by P. T. Barnum. He was often billed as either "The Caterpillar Man" or "The Snake Man."

TOP RIGHT: Harry Earles and Olga Baclanova.

BOTTOM: Ed Brophy, Josephine-Joseph, and Matt McHugh.

BELOW: Henry Victor (the circus strong man) and Olga (the trapeze artist).

Earles). Together with her lover, the circus Strong Man (Henry Victor), she plots a slow poisoning, planning to inherit the midget's money after his death. The others in the circus manage to overcome their dislike of Cleopatra and decide to admit her to their clique, celebrating with a banquet for the newlyweds. But the drunken bride rebuffs them, screaming venomous insults, and storms out. The others do not forgive her.

Keeping a close watch, they learn of her evil plans. On the night of an intense storm, Cleo and the Strong Man prepare to murder the midget, but other circus people arrive in time to prevent the mayhem. Ocarina accompaniment is heard behind the movie's most terrifying scene (which also might be considered one of the most brilliantly executed scenes in the history of the horror film), as they chase the trapeze artist through the dark, rainswept woods.

111

Flashes of lightning glint on their knives. Wriggling and crawling along the ground, hiding under the wagons, they slither in an inexorable pursuit, finally ensnaring her. Exactly how they wreak their revenge is not seen, but the unforgettable finale and epilogue show that Cleopatra has been transformed into a freak like the others—placed on exhibit as a disfigured, squawking chicken woman. As originally filmed, the Strong Man was emasculated.

The film was previewed in San Diego, and, during this showing, a woman found Browning's vision so disturbing that she fled up the aisle, screaming wildly. This was a portent of things to come—for many exhibitors found *Freaks* so revolting that they refused to show it. Or, if they did, it might be cut heavily. In England it was banned for thirty years.

Critical opinion was sharply divided. The *New York World-Telegram* took note of this in their comment, "A field day for lovers of the macabre. . . . To some it will be fascinating; others will find it revolting," as did *Variety*: "As a horror story, it is either too horrible or not horrible enough, according to the viewpoint." The *New York Herald Tribune* opined, "Mr. Browning has always been an expert in pathological morbidity, but after seeing *Freaks*, his other films seem but whimsical nursery tales."

"The difficulty," said *The New York Times*," is in telling whether it should be shown at the Rialto Theatre—where it opened yesterday—or in, say, the Medical Center. *Freaks* is no normal film, but whether it deserves the title of abnormal is a matter of personal opinion." The critic of *Harrison's Reports* found it "so loathsome that I am nauseated thinking about it. The producers give the excuse that these creatures are all in the circus. . . . But this does not give them the right to do with them as this picture does." The idea was revived in the 1963 *House of the Damned*, but the concept of a full cast of freaks was not attempted again until *The Mutations* in 1974, followed by *The Sentinel* (1977).

Writing in the fourth issue of *Castle of Frankenstein*, Ken Beale reviewed in retro-

The wedding celebration: Angelo Rossitto pours champagne, and the Siamese twins Violet and Daisy Hilton offer a musical duet while Johnny Eck and Roscoe Ates look on. The Hilton sisters were well known as a vaudeville team. Rossitto later appeared in the 1956 *Carousel* and *Frankenstein Versus Dracula* (1971).

spect: "Out of all the many horror films, one stands out. Not so much for its mood of terror (although there is plenty of that in the eerie climax) but because of its unique quality. There was never a picture like *Freaks* before; there will probably never be again. The screen has seen monstrosities aplenty: crawling, creeping, slimy horrors without number; deformed and hideous specimens of alleged humanity in as wild an array of shapes as the imagination can conceive. But audiences, watching these horrible creations, somehow were not too strongly affected. They knew that beneath the crippled exteriors lurked entirely normal actors, rendered hideous by the makeup man's art. Or else, that the grotesque creatures were animated models, brought to life by the magic of the camera. But *Freaks* was different. Its chills had an extra quality, for its monstrosities were living, breathing human beings, deformed into their strange shape by a vagary of nature. Despite Browning's practiced hand, *Freaks* was not a success. It was a little *too* horrible. Audiences did not enjoy this particular brand of fright. Throughout the years, this picture has built up an almost legendary reputation, as the 'ultimate' horror film. It has been revived occasionally, and the audience reactions have proven it has not lost its chilling power. But a large-scale revival was never undertaken, and, as far as the staff of *Castle of Frankenstein* can determine, it has never been seen on television." Throughout the years it has also been seen retitled as either *Nature's Mistakes*, *The Monster Show*, *Barnum*, or *Forbidden Love*.

One of the most acclaimed creators of macabre films, Tod Browning was born in Louisville, Kentucky, in 1882 and joined a traveling carnival at the age of sixteen. He became a skilled comedian, touring many countries with a show called *The World of Mirth*. With sixteen years of experience in vaudeville, circuses, and carnivals, it was only natural that these later surfaced as major themes in his movies. In 1914 he arrived in Hollywood and began work in silent comedies. The following year he worked as an assistant to D. W. Griffith on *Intolerance*. In 1918 he began directing the Priscilla Dean adventure melodramas, such as *The Virgin of Stamboul* (1920) and *The White Tiger* (1923). Doing character bits in these films was Lon Chaney, and, beginning with *The Unholy Three* (1925), Browning directed Chaney in a number of thrillers and horror films. After *Dracula* (1930) and *Freaks*, Browning continued to make horror films through the thirties until his last, *Miracles for Sale* (1939), about a magician exposing a fake medium. Browning then announced, "When I quit a thing, I quit. I wouldn't walk across the street now to see a movie." He kept his word— almost. After the death of his wife in 1944, he lived alone at Malibu, refusing to see even films made by his close friends. But later he acquired a TV set, and, in the years prior to his death in 1962, he stayed awake

The wedding celebration takes an abrupt and unexpected twist: A loving cup is sipped in turn by each celebrant. "We accept you! We accept you!" they chant. But Cleo (Baclanova) is repelled.

all night long recapturing the years through Late Late Shows.

In 1933 Olga Baclanova appeared with Robert Armstrong (who was reading his *King Kong* reviews that same year), Constance Cummings, and James Gleason in *Billion Dollar Scandal*, based on the Teapot Dome scandal. During the late thirties she conducted a radio program, and in 1943 she was in the film version of Rose Franken's novel and play *Claudia*. She surfaced again in the late sixties to do a half-hour interview with Richard Lamparski for his WBAI-FM radio series, *Whatever Became Of . . .?*

Olga Baclanova had a son, Nicholas (Soussanin Jr.) Saunders, by her second marriage to actor Nicholas Soussanin. Her third husband was Richard Davis, a foreign-film distributor and the former owner of New York City's Fine Arts Theatre. On September 6, 1974, Baclanova died in Vevey, Switzerland, and was buried there.

# Elsa Lanchester

$E$lsa Lanchester was born in London on October 28, 1902, the illegitimate daughter of Edith Lanchester and James Sullivan (who did not believe in marriage). The pacifist, vegetarian, and socialist leanings of her parents led to her enrollment at a Summerhill-like boys' school run by a socialist, Mr. Kettle. For seven years Elsa Lanchester was the only female on the campus of this progressive school, and she also went to classes in Chelsea conducted by Isadora Duncan's brother, Raymond—a situation that led to young Elsa's receiving a scholarship to study with Isadora Duncan in France. When World War I began, the Duncan school dissolved, and Lanchester returned to the Kettle school in London. At the age of eleven, she formed her own dance classes, The Classical Dancing Club, going on to become a student teacher at the Margaret Morris Dancing School in Chelsea.

At fifteen she was living on Baker Street when she launched a dance group known as The Happy Evenings Association, which evolved into a children's theatre in Soho between 1918 and 1921 until it closed after a run-in with child-labor laws. Lanchester and her partner, character actor Harold Scott, then turned The Children's Theatre into an after-theatre nightclub called The Cave of Harmony, which was successful due to the participation and assistance of H. G. Wells, Aldous Huxley, Evelyn Waugh, and various West End actors who put in appearances.

Lanchester's West End debut was in April 1922, in *Thirty Minutes in a Street*, and she made a striking impression in *The Insect Play* the following year. Her reputation continued to grow over the next few years in productions of Congreve's *Way of the World*, Sheridan's *The Duenna*, *The Cobra*, the *Riverside Nights* revue, *The Midnight Follies* at the Cafe Metropole, *Cautious Campbell*, and *The Pool*. In 1926, she appeared opposite Charles Laughton in Arnold Bennett's *Mr. Prohack*.

During this same period Lanchester began in films with a 1924 short involving

ABOVE AND OPPOSITE PAGE: Elsa Lanchester in *Bride of Frankenstein* (1935).

the talents of Evelyn and Alec Waugh and director Terence Greenidge. Her first professional film was *One of the Best* (1927), a period-crime drama, followed by a bit in *The Constant Nymph* (1928), and a group of silent shorts, *Bluebottles*, *The Tonic*, and *Daydreams*, written for her by H. G. Wells, and another short, *Mr. Smith Wakes Up* (1929). Laughton appeared in bits in two of these comedies. Laughton and Lanchester also appeared together singing duets at The Cave of Harmony, but the club shuttered in 1928. On February 9, 1929, Laughton and Lanchester married. "If I had not been full of a sort of respectful awe, we should not have had any relationship at all," she wrote later.

Portraying a prostitute, she was a success in the 1929 play, *The Outskirts*, followed by *Ten Nights in a Barroom*. Lanchester and Laughton appeared as themselves in the revue film, *Comets* (1930). Her 1931 films were *The Love Habit, The Stronger Sex, Potiphar's Wife*, and the female lead in *The Officer's Mess*. That same year she appeared on stage as Little Lord Fauntleroy in *Little Lord Fauntleroy*, followed by a role as the twelve-year-old daughter of a murderer (Laughton) in *Payment Deferred*, a production that traveled on to New York. This was filmed in 1932 with Laughton but minus Lanchester.

After the success of *The Private Life of Henry VIII* (1933), and a season of Shakespeare with the Old Vic, Lanchester was signed to an MGM contract. Her first MGM film was *David Copperfield* (1934), followed by *Naughty Marietta* (1935). MGM agreed to end the contract at three films by loaning Elsa to Universal for *The Bride of Frankenstein* (1935). Today it is her best-known role, and she says, "Television runs the old picture every Halloween, I think. It's nice to be remembered for one part. I don't mind the trademark."

James Whale, whom she knew from the Cave of Harmony days, directed and also came up with the idea that she play the dual role of Mary Shelley and the bride of Frankenstein's monster. "The most mem-

orable thing I did in that film, I believe, was my screaming. In almost all my movies since, I've been called upon to scream. I don't know if it's by chance, but I would like to think that I'm not hired for that talent alone."

John Baxter, writing in *Hollywood in the Thirties*, commented, "The momentary invitation to laugh is stifled by her magnificent performance as the awakening creature, quick, twitchy, birdlike movements of the head, and the low-angle shooting by John Mescall to show the scars on her throat emphasizing her alien quality, the white streaks in her bush of hair providing a sort of visual exclamation point to our surprise." Three hours were spent each day in the application of the monster makeup along with an additional hour for the wrapping of the bandages.

In 1975 she recalled, "Children recognize me in the market and say, 'There she goes!' I don't mind that so much. But it annoys me when mothers drag the poor dears to me and demand the children say something to Frankenstein's bride. . . . I could appear on more talk shows, but I don't like stressing the Frankenstein picture. Can you imagine an actress being overexposed by a picture she made forty years ago?"

She and Laughton returned to England after *Bride of Frankenstein* and his final scenes for *Les Misérables* (1935). Lanchester signed a contract with Alexander Korda, first appearing in the short film *Miss Bracegirdle Does Her Duty* (1936), followed by a cameo as a dinner guest in René Clair's fantasy-comedy, *The Ghost Goes West* (1936). The Laughtons then appeared together in *Rembrandt* (1936) for Korda. Lanchester had the title role of the annual London stage production of *Peter Pan* with Laughton as Captain Hook. When it closed, Laughton left to work on the never-completed Josef von Sternberg *I, Claudius*, and Lanchester took *Peter Pan* on tour.

Laughton became partners with *Caligari*–producer Erich Pommer, forming the Mayflower Pictures Corporation. The first

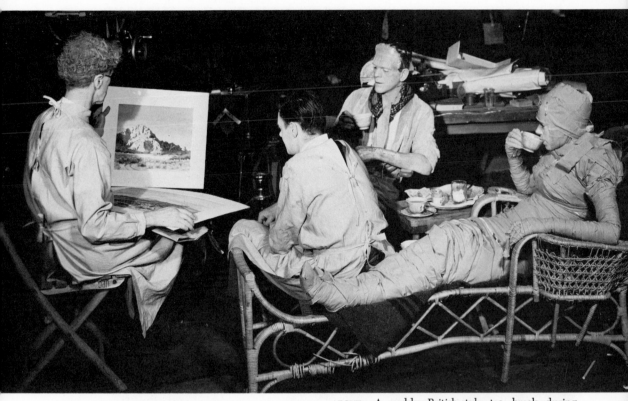

ABOVE: A veddy British-style tea break during *Bride of Frankenstein. Left to right*: Ernest Thesiger, Colin Clive, Boris Karloff, Elsa Lanchester.

production was Somerset Maugham's *Vessel of Wrath* (1938), retitled *The Beachcomber* for the United States release. Lanchester's interpretation of strait-laced missionary Martha Jones pleased the critics and brought Hollywood offers. But she later commented, "Ever since I played Miss Jones in *The Beachcomber* with Charles, picture companies have been offering me spinster parts. You can't imagine what awful parts they are. Miss Jones, being a Somerset Maugham character, was drawn with truth. But those other parts! They were named 'Miss Steel' or 'Miss Iron' or something of the sort." In 1939 Elsa Lanchester wrote the biography-autobiography, *Charles Laughton and I*, published by Harcourt Brace and Faber and Faber. "I write like a comedienne, too," she said years later. "I wrote a book about Charles in 1939. It was humorous of course. I didn't try to write like I was Lady Macbeth!"

With the approach of World War II, the Mayflower company was dissolved and the Laughtons went back to Hollywood. In

BELOW: Syd Roye's ad art for a double bill.

117

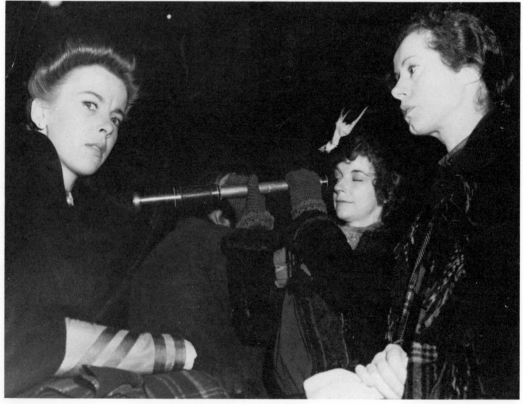

May 1941, Lanchester portrayed the lead in a Broadway mystery drama, *They Walk Alone*. It was not successful, and she returned to Hollywood for the role of Emily Creed in Columbia's *Ladies in Retirement* (1941), directed by Charles Vidor. That same year she began her 15-year association with the Los Angeles Turnabout Theatre. "Before coming to The Turnabout," she said, "I was very dissatisfied with Hollywood. When you work in a studio, you are the servant of a company. You're not in control of what you're doing." Instead, at the 160-seat theatre, she felt she "had the great satisfaction of being kept continuously busy at work I enjoy."

Her first film for Fox was *Son of Fury* (1942) as a prostitute, followed by the all-star anthology film, *Tales of Manhattan* (1941), also for Fox. She was a waitress in RKO's *Forever and a Day* (1943), a singer in Republic's *Thumbs Up* (1943), Roddy McDowall's mother in *Lassie, Come Home* (1943), a charwoman planning to assassinate Hitler in the 1944 *Passport to Destiny* (a.k.a. *Passport to Adventure*), a cook in RKO's *The Spiral Staircase* (1946), a secretary in Fox's *Razor's Edge* (1946), a chaperone in Republic's *Northwest Outpost* (1947), and a maid in RKO's *The Bishop's Wife* (1947), a fantasy about an angel returning to earth to offer an assist to a bishop. In *The Big Clock* (1948), an engaging thriller directed by John Farrow, Laughton played a publishing tycoon who commits murder and attempts to frame an innocent man; Lanchester was an oddball artist. In MGM's *The Secret Garden* (1949), adapted from Frances Burnett's children's mystery classic, Lanchester was a maid once again, and she was again seen as an artist in Fox's *Come to the Stable* (1949), a film that brought her an Academy

Award nomination. After the Danny Kaye comedy *The Inspector General* (1949), she was in *Buccaneer's Girl* (1950), *Mystery Street* (1950), *The Petty Girl* (1950), and *Frenchie* (1950). That same year Lanchester introduced her nightclub act, eventually appearing in every major American city with her specialty songs and comedy.

She was a spinster college president in Fox's *Dreamboat* (1952); Madame Magloire in Lewis Milestone's *Les Misérables* (1952) for Fox; Megaera in RKO's Shaw adaptation, *Androcles and the Lion* (1952); a singing housekeeper in Paramount's *Girls of Pleasure Island* (1953); Lida O'Reilly in Republic's *Hell's Half Acre* (1954); a bearded lady in the Martin and Lewis comedy, *Three Ring Circus* (1954). In 1954 she began working in television, eventually appearing on *Alfred Hitchcock Presents*, *Studio One*, *Hallmark Hall of Fame*, *Burke's Law*, *The Ed Sullivan Show*, and many others. Her guest star role in "The Brain Killer Affair" on *The Man From*

At the *Tomb of Ligeia* Hollywood premiere, Elsa looks as if she just dropped by for the fun of it. However, Carol Borland (standing next to Vincent Price at far left), reliving her famed vampire role for *Mark of the Vampire* (1935), appears to have taken up permanent residence in the dungeons beneath the theater.

OPPOSITE PAGE

TOP: Elsa eyes Eugene Pallette in this scene from René Clair's *The Ghost Goes West* (1936).

BOTTOM: Ida Lupino, Edith Barrett, and Elsa Lanchester in *Ladies in Retirement* (1941). In an off-screen moment, Elsa waits patiently while Edith plays with a telescope and Ida Lupino looks at the photographer with seeming irritation.

*U.N.C.L.E.* prompted one critic to pen, "If they ever give Emmys for Villain of the Year, Elsa Lanchester deserves one for her portrayal of Dr. Dabree."

She was the evil stepmother in MGM's Cinderella remake, *The Glass Slipper* (1955). Both she and Laughton were nominated for Academy Awards for their roles in Billy Wilder's *Witness for the Prosecution* (1957). In 1958, she and Laughton returned to the London stage in *The Party*, directed by Laughton, and that same year she was a witch in Columbia's *Bell, Book, and Candle*. After her specialty music material was recorded, she toured her one-woman show, *Elsa Lanchester—Herself*, directed by Laughton, from 1959 to 1961. It was their last work together; Laughton died of cancer on September 15, 1962.

In 1964 she portrayed yet another maid in MGM's *Honeymoon Hotel* and became a series regular on *The John Forsythe Show*. "I accepted the role because I needed a regular life. I needed the routine of seeing people every day." *Mary Poppins*

(1964) began her decade-long association with Disney. After *Pajama Party* (1964) for AIP, she was a busybody neighbor in *That Darn Cat* (1965), a teacher of yoga in *Easy Come, Easy Go* (1967), a descendant of Blackbeard the Pirate in *Blackbeard's Ghost* (1968), a housekeeper in *Rascal* (1969), and a landlady in *Me, Natalie* (1969). She was in the 1969 made-for-TV movie *In Name Only*, and she also participated in a PBS documentary special on Korda and the ill-fated *I, Claudius* film of the thirties.

In the seventies Lancester embarked on a number of Cinerama horror roles, none of which can stand alongside her now-classic *Bride of Frankenstein*. In *Willard* (1971), the Daniel Mann-directed tale of a boy who uses rats to gain revenge, Lanchester was a nagging mother. In *Terror in the Wax Museum* (1973), John Carradine is murdered in his own wax museum and Lanchester, portraying Julia Hawthorn, takes over. The film involved a set in which wax statues were intermingled with actors

Elsa Lanchester as Julia in *Terror in the Wax Museum*.

Elsa as Hester, the eccentric spinster who talks to anything alive—or dead—in the Cinerama mystery comedy, *Arnold* (1974).

using shallow breathing techniques. Supposedly, Lanchester walked onto the set at Paramount, sat near a figure that appeared to be waxen, and nearly fainted when the "wax criminal" stepped down from the pedestal and walked past her. In Cinerama's *Arnold* (1974), directed by George Fenady, Lanchester played Hester, Arnold's eccentric sister, in this tale that harkens back to the "reading of the will in the old house" dramas of the twenties.

In 1976 she portrayed Dame Jessie Marbles, "England's most famous distaff sleuth," in Neill Simon's *Murder by Death*, directed by Robert Moore. During filming, she said, "In this picture I let out a few little screams, but not any really important ones. The secret of a good scream is its un-expectedness. I always keep a little reserve of air in my lungs. I can be in the middle of a sentence and produce a hair-raising scream without pause."

Living alone in Santa Monica, Lanchester had, for many years, planned a second Laughton biography. In 1975, she said, "Women shouldn't write about their husbands because they can't be totally honest. The quality of loyalty doesn't change, if you know what I mean." Rather than a new book, it turned out that Lanchester had been working on research and an introduction for Charles Higham's *Charles Laughton: An Intimate Biography*, published in 1976 by Doubleday. "I'm still very active," she told feature-writer Vernon Scott. "This book occupies a great deal of my time.

Elsa as Dame Jessie Marbles in Neil Simon's *Murder by Death* (1976).

While it isn't quite honest, it is more so than most people would expect. Charles died in 1962, you know. We were married in 1929. My problem is that I never collected any of his memorabilia, and Charles threw everything away. So I must depend on my memory. I have total recall, which helps a great deal. I'm working with a professional author who is doing the research of Charles's life before I came into it. And we've gone to libraries for research. Fortunately, I've kept a good many news cuttings. There will be no gilding of the lily. Charles was fat. He was not a matinee idol. His career twisted in unusual directions. . . . The new biography is both humorous and serious. Readers will be surprised at some of its contents, but then Charles Laughton was a most surprising man."

Equally surprising is Elsa Lanchester, whose career has spanned six decades and diverse media—stage, film, TV, print, night-clubs, and recordings. "I'm a comedienne, really. And I do what people expect of me. When I leave the house I'm on stage. It's a bit of a strain, so I stay home a lot."

"I have never had a complex about growing old," she said in 1971. "I will accept any role if it's interesting, and the age of the character has nothing to do with it. Of course, you make much more of birthdays in the United States than we did in England, but I tell my friends not to think about age. Charles and I believed we shouldn't make a fuss about growing old so we never exchanged birthday gifts. I believe one should prolong youth as long as possible, but not fret when it's gone. Many actresses my age are living with memories of the past rather than enjoying the present."

Bruce Davidson and Elsa in *Willard* (1971).

# Joan Crawford

With a career that spanned decades, Joan Crawford was the only major silent-film female star still a persistent image in the sixties and seventies. This was partially due to horror films, beginning in 1962 with *What Ever Happened to Baby Jane?*.

She began life as Lucille LeSoeur on March 23, 1904. When she was just a few weeks old, her parents were divorced, and she did not meet her father until twenty years later. "I was born in San Antonio, Texas," she wrote in the early thirties, "and like most any other kiddie spent my early teens mastering the mysteries of the three 'R's.' But after school hours and during vacation periods, my thoughts always strayed to a secretly cherished dream of someday becoming a great actress."

She was raised by her mother and stepfather, Henry Sassin, who owned a Lawton, Oklahoma, theatre. Adopting her father's surname, she was known as Billie Sassin. After a move to Kansas City, her mother and stepfather also separated. Nine-year-old Lucille waited on tables while going to school, and her mother opened a laundry. As a Kansas City salesgirl, Lucille won a Charleston contest. Then, the way she told it, "I ran away from home. As I look back I can see that it was indeed a foolhardy venture for a young girl, untrained in the ways of the world, to alone seek her livelihood in a strange city: Good luck was with me from the outset, and I landed my first job with a revue in Chicago. That was in 1922. During this engagement I acquired much experience that was to prove invaluable in later years. My next jump was to New York, where I appeared in the Shubert production, *Innocent Eyes*. The theatre program listed me as Lucile Le Sueur. It seemed too good to be true. At last I was really in the theatre. Next came a part in *The Passing Show* at the Winter Garden. Little did I suspect that I was to dance my way right out of this show into the movies. But that's just exactly what happened when Harry Rapf of the Metro-Goldwyn-Mayer studios saw the show one evening and offered me the chance to enter motion pictures. Was I thrilled? Why, I was so excited I could hardly talk. I wondered what Hollywood was really like. Would I be a star with my name in electric lights or just another girl among a legion of failures? These thoughts ran through my mind as I packed for the westward jaunt. I hoped for the best. Upon my arrival in the movie city I was given six months of intensive training in the art of screen acting."

In *Lady of the Night* (1925), Lucille doubled for Norma Shearer, who had a dual role, and then she was seen in *Pretty Ladies* (1925). "I was extremely happy even though my part was only that of an extra player. I learned that extra work was the foundation upon which some of our greatest artists have built their careers. Perhaps I too would be so fortunate. My optimism knew no bounds when I was picked for an important part with Jackie Coogan in *Old Clothes* (1925). My work in this production seemed to settle my future as a featured player, and I was tendered a long-term contract to which I happily and hurriedly affixed my signature."

Another walk-on was *The Only Thing* (1925). A fan mag contest gave her a new name—Joan Crawford. "Next I was cast for one of the leading roles in *Sally, Irene and Mary* (1925). In 1925 I was chosen as a Wampas Baby Star—'WAMPAS' meaning the Western Association of Motion Picture Advertisers. There are two pictures to which I owe much in the matter of making my name known to the film fans. They are *The Boob* [1926] and *Paris* [1926]." She was also loaned out that year for *Tramp, Tramp, Tramp* with Harry Langdon.

In 1927 she was in *The Taxi Dancer, The Understanding Heart, Twelve Miles Out, Spring Fever,* and her first horror film —playing opposite Lon Chaney in *The Unknown.* One of the most bizarre stories ever filmed, it was directed by Tod Browning, who was happiest when juxtaposing circus, carnival, and stage-magic environs with *outré* plots. *The Unknown* and *Freaks* (1932) were his two most successful forays in this direction. Waldemar Young did the silent scenario from Browning's story. *Photoplay* commented:

Some of the New York critics said that Lon Chaney has overreached himself in playing the armless Alonzo of *The Unknown.* (No punning intended, of course.) We think you will like it as an unadulterated shocker. Alonzo is the armless star of a small circus. He isn't really armless, for he keeps his real ones strapped to his sides. Still, he has developed great skill in using his toes in place of his fingers. In fact, he is the star knife thrower of the show. Estrellita, a beauty of the circus, is loved by Alonzo. The girl has a complex against arms, grown out of her hatred of men. So she is drawn to the 'armless' Alonzo. To gain her heart, the knife thrower hies himself to a hospital and forces a surgeon to amputate his arms. Thus his distorted mind fancies to win the girl. When he returns to the circus, he finds that Malabar, the circus strong man, has overcome Estrellita's complex. In fact, she's in love with Malabar. So Alonzo starts out to eliminate the strong man. See *The Unknown* and follow the story from there. Like the other Chaney pictures directed by Tod Browning, this has a macabre atmosphere. If you wince at a touch or two of horror, don't go to *The Unknown.* If you like strong celluloid food, try it. It has the merit of possessing a finely sinister plot, some moments with a real shock, and Lon Chaney. Besides, Joan Crawford is an optical tonic as Estrellita.

Lon Chaney and Joan Crawford in *The Unknown* (1927).

The photography was by Merritt B. Gerstad, and the film was edited by Harry Reynolds and Errol Taggart. The titles were by Joe Farnham, and Merritt Gerstad handled the camera. Others in the cast were Norman Kerry, Nick de Ruiz, John George, and Frank Lanning. (For a more detailed synopsis of *The Unknown's* story, see the Lon Chaney chapter in *Heroes of the Horrors*.)

In 1928, after *Rose Marie, Across to Singapore, The Law of the Range*, and *Four Walls*, she became a star in *Our Dancing Daughters*. There were two more silents —*The Duke Steps Out* (1929) and *Our Modern Maidens* (1929)—before she was heard singing in *Hollywood Revue of 1929*. (That same year she married Douglas Fairbanks, Jr.) *Untamed* was followed by *Montana Moon* and *Our Blushing Brides*, all in 1930. In 1931 she appeared in *Paid, Dance Fools Dance, Laughing Sinners, This Modern Age*, and *Possessed*; in 1932 *Grand Hotel, Letty Lynton* (adapted by Wanda Tuchock from Marie Belloc Lowndes' novel about the Madeleine Smith case), and *Rain* (still seen today at revival theatres). Crawford was now number three on the box-office attraction list. Crawford and Fairbanks were divorced. In 1933, she was in *Today We Live* and *Dancing Lady*, in 1934, *Sadie McKee, Chained*, and *Forsaking All Others*. She married her *Sadie McKee* co-star, Franchot Tone. In 1935, there were *No More Ladies* and *I Live My Life*; in 1936, *The Gorgeous Hussy* and *Love on the Run*, in 1937, *The Last of Mrs. Cheyney* and *The Bride Wore Red*.

She renegotiated a new, five-year MGM contract, but her box-office pull had diminished sharply. In 1938, she appeared in *Mannequin*; in 1939, *The Shining Hour* and *Ice Follies of 1939*. She and Tone were divorced. She made a strong comeback in *The Women*, followed by *Strange Cargo* (about an escape from a penal island) and *Susan and God* in 1940.

In *A Woman's Face* (1941), directed by George Cukor, the Crawford image of dark psychological undercurrents began to surface. She played the nursemaid Anna Holm, who travels down a shadowy prison hallway into the bright lights of a courtroom to tell her strange story in flashback. Because she had been scarred as a child, her bitterness led her into a criminal situation in Stockholm, where Torsten Barring (Conrad Veidt) persuades her to murder the boy she supervises so Barring will inherit a fortune. But plastic surgery brings a personality change. Revelry and sleigh-ride merriment counterpoint the climax—she murders Barring instead. Donald Ogden Stewart and Elliot Paul did the screen adaptation from the play *Il Etait Une Fois* by Francis de Croisset, a property that had previously been a successful vehicle for Ingrid Bergman in Sweden. Bronislau Kaper provided the music score.

After *When Ladies Meet* (1941), she married Philip Terry. In 1942 she was in

Joan's Charleston dance in *Our Dancing Daughters* (1928).

*They All Kissed the Bride*; in 1943, *Reunion in France* and *Above Suspicion*; in 1944, *Hollywood Canteen.* She won an Academy Award for her performance in *Mildred Pierce* (1945), a role Bette Davis had turned down (and one that almost went to Barbara Stanwyck). With Ranald Mac-Dougall and Catherine Turney adapting, director Michael Curtiz adeptly realized James M. Cain's story of an ambitious woman (Crawford) and her vicious daughter (Ann Blyth), who both fall for the same man (Zachary Scott). Max Steiner did the music, and others in the cast were Eve Arden, Jack Carson, Bruce Bennett, George Tobias, Lee Patrick, and Butterfly Mc-Queen. Crawford also won the National Board of Review Best Actress Award. The film was nominated for a Best Picture Oscar but lost out to *Lost Weekend.* *Mildred Pierce* was so successful that a Mildred Pierce Restaurant opened in Hollywood with various items on the menu named after the characters. The tone of many Crawford films to come was fully established.

She divorced Terry; they had had one child—Christopher. Crawford's other, adopted, children were Christina, Cathy, and Cindy. With *Humoresque* (1946) she signed a new $200,000-per-picture contract with Warners—where Davis had reigned for so many years. *Possessed* (1947) was not a remake of her 1931 *Possessed* but a Silvia Richards/Ranald MacDougall adaptation of the play *One Man's Secret* by Rita Weiman, a story about a schizophrenic woman hallucinating the murder of her stepdaughter. Curtis Bernhardt directed, and the music was by Franz Waxman. Others in the cast were Van Heflin, Raymond Massey, Geraldine Brooks, Stanley

Ridges, Moroni Olsen, and Douglas Kennedy.

In 1947 she starred in *Daisy Kenyon*; in 1949, *Flamingo Road*; in 1950, *The Damned Don't Cry* and *Harriet Craig*; in 1951, *Goodbye, My Fancy*; in 1952, *This Woman Is Dangerous.* Crawford was nominated for an Academy Award for her performance in RKO's suspense thriller *Sudden Fear* (1952) and was chosen for the Best Feminine Performance in *Film Daily*'s annual poll of film critics. She played Myra Hudson, a playwright who learns that her husband (Jack Palance) and his girl friend (Gloria Grahame) are plotting her murder. Others in the cast were Bruce Bennett, Virginia Huston, and Touch Connors. Elmer Bernstein provided the stinger chords. David Miller directed, and the Lenore Coffee-Robert Smith screenplay was based on a story by Edna Sherry. The success of *Sudden Fear*, which the *Daily News* gave four stars, thrust Crawford back into the limelight.

She then made her first color film, MGM's *Torch Song* (1953), followed by the offbeat Western *Johnny Guitar* (1954). She continued as a potential murder victim in *Female on the Beach* (1955) and *Queen Bee* (1955). In 1956 she made *Autumn Leaves*; in 1957, *The Story of Esther Costello*; in 1959, *The Best of Everything.* In 1955 she married Pepsi Cola president Alfred Steele. After his death in 1959, she was elected to the Pepsi Cola Board of Directors. New York papers on June 1, 1959, carried the headline: "JOAN CRAWFORD BROKE." "I haven't a sou to my name. Uncle Sam has every penny. Alfred thought he was leaving me plenty, but it wasn't to be that. It all went for income taxes and debt." she told Louella Parsons.

*What Ever Happened to Baby Jane?* (1962) was a peak in the "Horror of Personality" genre (as defined by Charles Derry in his 1977 book, *Dark Dreams*, published by A. S. Barnes). *Cinema* magazine commented, prior to the film's release, "What happened is Robert Aldrich's cinematic incision into a young beauty who has grown old, into a grease-paint that has

Paranoia in *Female on the Beach* as Crawford misconstrues Jeff Chandler's motives.

faded, into a child's doll-like mind that had been plucked, powdered, eyelined, rouged, curled and twisted by the face of glamour into a mask of horror. In telling the story of how the past glory of Hollywood crippled the lives of two sisters, Aldrich has selected two performers, Joan Crawford and Bette Davis, who demonstrate how the past has also served the present. The audiences that worshipped the images of *Now, Voyager*, of *The Letter* and *Of Human Bondage* will, upon seeing *Baby Jane*, realize that they were even then looking past the glamour of the surface to the beauty within. Bette in all her tragic horror again creates a villain with the proportion of a monster, a character perfectly tragic and evil, a perfomance perfectly beautiful. Joan Crawford is perfect. *What Ever Happened to Baby Jane?* is Aldrich's first encounter with the pure horror film, and with it he brings new dimensions to his credits and to the genre."

Bette Davis and Crawford, as two feuding ex-movie-queen sisters, explored the very *mythos* of the Crawford-Davis publicity, transforming it into a horror film that scored at the box office. The Lukas Heller screenplay, based on a novel by Henry Slesar, was directed with a campy intensity by Robert Aldrich. Crawford was the bedridden Blanche Hudson, tormented by Davis as Baby Jane, planning her hoped-for triumphant return to motion pictures, rehearsing her outdated song-and-dance with pianist Edwin Flagg (Victor Buono). Clips from older films showed Davis in Warner's 1933 *Parachute Jumper* and Crawford in *Sadie McKee*. Norma Koch's black-and-white costume design won an Oscar.

Like Davis, Crawford was suddenly turning up in a succession of horror-oriented films. In *The Caretakers* (1963) she was the head nurse teaching judo at a mental institution. In *Strait-Jacket* (1964), scripted by Robert Bloch for William Castle, things got more mental. The psycho, revealed at the climax, turned out to be not Crawford but her daughter (Diane Baker). John Benson, reviewing in *Castle of Frank-*

*enstein* #5, commented, "Decapitation by axe seems to be a currently popular theme; this form of gory thrill is featured in both *Dementia 13* (1963) and *Strait-Jacket*. *Strait-Jacket* is, of course, the major production with the big buildup, familiar producer-director William Castle and famous star Joan Crawford, but the other film ultimately stands up as a better production. The press sheets at the preview of *Strait-Jacket* said that after seeing the ending, viewers will want to see the film again to see if any scenes 'cheated.' I doubt if many viewers would want to go through such

TOP: Pepsi-Cola director Joan Crawford buys the first ten shares of the newly formed PepsiCo, Inc., with the help of Merrill Lynch, Pierce, Fenner & Smith manager Douglas Milne. PepsiCo, Inc. was formed by the merger of Pepsi-Cola and Frito-Lay. The stock replaced both Pepsi-Cola and Frito-Lay on the New York Stock Exchange, and Joan Crawford continued as a member of the board of directors of Pepsi-Cola.

BELOW: In *Strait-Jacket*, Lucy Harbin (Joan Crawford), released on probation from a mental institution, returns home. The next morning she examines a bust of herself as she looked twenty years earlier, sculpted by her daughter Carol (Diane Baker).

Lucy awakens the next night, hearing the chant "Lizzie Borden took an ax, and gave her mother forty whacks." Two heads lie on the pillow next to her, but when she leaves the room, they vanish.

needless torture, especially since the denouement is fairly obvious throughout most of the film, and one can see that, in a sense, there *was* some 'cheating.' (The good surprise-ending film depends on a number of scenes which seem to lead to a false ending but which would also seem perfectly natural in a new way to a person who knew the final outcome. *Strait-Jacket* has some scenes that, while not actually contradicting the conclusion, did not play well to a person who knew who the murderer was.) The point is that the press sheets were suggesting that the main attraction of the film was a 'trick ending.' Even more significantly, the ads suggested that *Strait-Jacket*'s main attraction is crude, direct gore and sadism, with the ad line, '*Warning! Strait-Jacket vividly depicts axe murders!*' In between the murders, the production is as halfhearted as a tired burlesque comedian killing time between the stripper's numbers. Only during the 'shock' sequences do things come to life; camera and lighting values become competent, the editing becomes tight and craftsmanlike, and the sound reaches its creative peaks. Joan Crawford struggles with the script and the hack dialogue but does not come near her great performance in *What Ever Happened to Baby Jane?* Except for George Kennedy, who gives an interesting performance as a sinister hired hand, the rest of the cast is pretty weak." The rest of the cast was Leif Erickson, Howard St. John, John Anthony Hayes, Rochelle Hudson, and Edith Atwater. The music was by Van Alexander.

*Hush . . . Hush, Sweet Charlotte* (1965) was planned as a film that would bring the

OPPOSITE: The killing of the hired hand, Krause (George Kennedy), in *Strait-Jacket*.

130

*Baby Jane* team of novelist Henry Farrell, director Robert Aldrich, screenwriter Lukas Heller, Bette Davis, and Crawford back together again. However, Crawford became ill. The insurance company then had an option to allow for either a period of recasting or a cancellation of the production. Aldrich stated, "Our position was that the whole reason for making the picture was to rejoin Crawford and Davis, so we couldn't just substitute anybody." The only two actresses that the production company felt ranked along with Crawford were Katharine Hepburn and Olivia de Havilland, so Aldrich went to Switzerland and talked de Havilland into replacing Crawford.

Crawford, instead, turned up next in another William Castle programmer, *I Saw What You Did* (1965). *Castle of Frankenstein* commented, "William Castle pays homage to Hitchcock (notably a shower-murder à la *Psycho*) with well-acted but somewhat routine suspenser from the novel *Out of the Dark*. First-rate premise has

teenage telephone prankster calling random numbers and whispering film's title, finally hitting psycho John Ireland, who has just knocked off his wife. Joan Crawford, Leif Erickson, Andi Garrett, Sarah Lane." William McGivern did the screenplay from the Ursula Curtiss novel.

In 1967, she did a guest appearance in "The Karate Killers" on *The Man from U.N.C.L.E.*, followed by *Lucy Show* and *Secret Storm* episodes in 1968. *Berserk!* (1967) was a British film produced by Herman Cohen and directed by Jim O'Connolly from a story and screenplay by Cohen and Aben Kandel about a series of grisly murders. Appearing with Crawford were Ty Hardin, Diana Dors, Michael Gough, and Judy Geeson. Frances Herridge, reviewing it in the January 11, 1968, issue of the *New York Post*, gave this opinion:

A flock of poodles provides the most engaging moments of *Berserk*. . . . Certainly they are the liveliest performers in the circus that

Michael Gough and Joan Crawford look on as an accident brings the circus spectacle to a halt in *Berserk* (1967).

provides the setting for this suspense melodrama. And best of all they don't talk. The trite
dialogue is the principal flaw in the film. It's
not spoken, but declaimed, without much facial
expression—like bad dubbing. Another flaw, of
course, is the plot itself, which offers a series of
bizarre murders among the traveling troupe,
explained in a twist ending that twists any surviving credibility into a corkscrew. Joan Crawford is sleekly groomed and brightly brittle as
the tough circus owner and one of the prime
suspects behind the deaths that always work to
her advantage. Other suspects are clumsily
worked in too—also a few circus acts to fill out
the waiting time between murders.

On November 8, 1969, Crawford
starred in the debut of *Night Gallery* as a
wealthy blind woman who buys a poor
man's eyes so she can have several hours of
vision, during a period that coincides with
the New York City blackout. The Rod Serling script was directed by nineteen-year-
old Steven Spielberg, six years before his
*Jaws* triumph. Writer Tom Allen saw this
debut as Spielberg unveiling "the adven-
turous, eclectic visual style that will flourish
later in *Jaws*, including disorienting jump
cuts, a montage scene of Joan Crawford
unbandaging her eyes in a manner that is
reminiscent of Eisentein's cream separator
in *The General Line*, and a finale of abstract but symbolic crashing glass that's
assembled along the lines of one of Slavko
Vorkapich's ripest passages in the early

In *Trog* (1970), when three university students are attacked by an apelike creature in a desolate
cave, Dr. Brockton (Joan Crawford), an eminent anthropologist, enters the cave and photographs
the creature (Joe Cornelius). She believes the strange being is a troglodyte, a primitive cave-
dweller.

thirties. The flashy visuals are neither arty nor typical of Spielberg's general TV career. They are, rather, off-the-cuff, apt responses to the generally lurid turns of Serling's script; but, in any year, on any show, they are extraordinary passages in made-for-TV work, which is normally no more daring than cookie-cutting patterns."

Spielberg, who had signed a Universal contract that same month, was making his debut as a director. In an interview with filmmaker David Helpern, Spielberg remembered, "My first professional film was *Night Gallery* with Joan Crawford. It was the pilot, the trilogy. She played a blind dowager in Manhattan during the New York blackout. It was a clever Rod Serling piece which was hard for Joan to memorize. She couldn't remember words like transcendental and esophagus . . . I signed the contract and within four weeks I was on the stage with Joan Crawford, so it was massive culture shock, hemorrhaging, you know, my first day. . . ."

*Night Gallery* was followed by a January 21, 1970, role in "Nightmare" on NBC's *The Virginian*. In *Trog* (1970), she was the anthropologist-author of *Social Structures in the Primates*, Dr. Brockton, who studies the pre-Ice Age troglodyte (Joe Cornelius) at England's Seaton Marshes. Sam Murdock (Michael Gough) has plans for a housing development in the area and doesn't like the kind of publicity monsters always bring. He stirs up the critter, which then kills several locals and kidnaps a child. Robert L. Jerome, in *Cinefantastique*, re-

viewed, "Miss Crawford, bristling authority, rescues the child from the still obedient Trog, but the military insists on destroying both the cave and the creature. When a reporter asks her for a comment on this calamity, she simply pushes him aside, as deftly and defiantly as the Crawford of yore faced those gangster's bullets in *The Damned Don't Cry* decades ago. . . . In a role that would surely defeat a lesser actress, Miss Crawford manages to look dignified, and she puts her indelible stamp of authority on all the foolishness. One can imagine that Shelley Winters or Bette Davis might have given the role a saving sense of 'camp,' but La Crawford gives it class." Freddie Francis directed the Herman Cohen production for Warner Brothers release, and Aben Kandel did the screenplay from a Peter Bryan-John Gilling story. Others in the cast: Bernard Kay, David Griffin, and Kim Braden.

On September 30, 1972, Crawford appeared in a *Sixth Sense* episode on ABC. Other TV credits include "Because I Love Him" on CBS's *Mirror Theatre* September 19, 1953; three *GE Theatre* roles in 1954, 1958, and 1959; *Della* in 1959; two *Zane Grey Theatre* guest-star roles in 1959 and 1961; and "Same Picture, Different Frame" on *Route 66* in 1963.

On May 10, 1977, Joan Crawford died alone in her New York apartment. She is survived by her four children—Mrs. Cathy Lolonde, Mrs. Cynthia Crawford Jordan, Christina Crawford, and Christopher Crawford—and four grandchildren.

# Bette Davis

$A$cclaimed as a legend in one's own time, especially at an early age, is a rare privilege, but becoming a reestablished legend several times in one's life, as Bette Davis has, is phenomenal.

Davis was born in Lowell, Massachusetts, in 1908, and from girlhood had her heart and mind set on a stage career. After attending a series of productions touring in the New England area, she became entranced by a Boston performance of Ibsen's *The Wild Duck* with Peggy Entwistle as Hedvig. "Mother!" Bette exclaimed emotionally after the play, "Some day I'll play Hedvig." Not many years later Bette's dream was fulfilled.

Bitten by the acting bug, the young Massachusetts girl slowly inched her way closer to her goal, participating in school plays, absorbing all she could by reading famous playwrights' works, and studying dance. Her first serious romance happened while attending Newton High School when she met Harmon Nelson; they eventually

ABOVE: Bette Davis in *Hush . . . Hush, Sweet Charlotte.*

married in 1932, at the time when he organized and led his own orchestra. Meanwhile, she went to a famous finishing school in Ashburnham, the Cushing Academy.

John Murray Anderson's school is thought to have helped Bette in that he emphasized studies into every possible area of dramatic art, including film acting. "There were classes in everything," Bette said, "including the bar sinister movies. We made one two-reeler that season and we acted in a play a week."

Imbued with renewed spirit after finishing Anderson's school, Bette got further encouragement from noted actor Frank Conroy. He gave her a letter of introduction to young stage entrepreneur George Cukor, who later became one of Hollywood's greatest directors. Cukor had a successful repertory company. During the fall of 1928 in Rochester, New York, Bette joined his group, co-starring with Louis Calhern and Miriam Hopkins in several productions, each lasting one day. Bette's engagement with Cukor's group lasted about a week, but she considers this to be one of her most invaluable experiences. She rejoined Cukor the following season. In between, Bette worked during the summer at the Cape Playhouse in Dennis, Massachusetts. Her reviews in Rochester were generally excellent. Louis Calhern, though, twice her age, looming hugely over her petite figure, decided capriciously that Bette was physically unfit to play opposite him in married roles. Without any warning, Cukor acceded to Calhern's quirk, firing Bette on the spot.

James Light, a producer at the New York Provincetown Playhouse, cast her in some of his company's productions, including Ibsen's *The Wild Duck*. While this prestigious Village group wasn't exactly Broadway, it attracted Hollywood scouts who were always searching for new faces. Bette was soon approached by one, representing Samuel Goldwyn, to appear in a Paramount film test in New York. She was badly depressed by her first close contact with film bureaucracy: "It was ghastly," she exclaimed. "I wondered how Hollywood ever discovers anyone. Actors with no knowledge of the screen are shoved in front of a lens and told to act. No thought is given to makeup. I suppose they reason that if the result is remotely favorable, you will be a sensation after they have worked on you."

She starred in *Broken Dishes*, and then co-starred with Richard Bennett in *The Solid South* to excellent notices. Another talent scout, this time from Universal, approached. Now, in 1930, at the age of twenty-two, Bette was offered a three-month contract with a renewal clause. Bette was aware that most film actresses were highly limited, inexpressive, and inarticulate during the "talkies" early period; filmmakers needed talent badly. Besides, with the Depression going full blast and theatres dropping dead, Hollywood money never looked better.

Finishing *Bad Sister* (1931) as her first for Universal, she was seen the summer of 1931 in two other films for Universal—*Seed* and *Waterloo Bridge*. After RKO's *Way Back Home* (1931) and Columbia's *The Menace* (1932), she appeared in Capitol's *Hell's House* (1932). She came within a hair of beginning her film career as a horror-

OPPOSITE: Bette, as rendered by artist Grant Mac-Donald for *Movies* magazine. Note that names of both Fredric March and Weissmuller are misspelled.

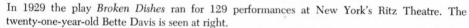

In 1929 the play *Broken Dishes* ran for 129 performances at New York's Ritz Theatre. The twenty-one-year-old Bette Davis is seen at right.

15¢ **BROADWAY** and **HOLLYWOOD**

# MOVIES

*August*

Bette Davis

GRANT MACDONALD

In This Issue:
**FREDERIC MARCH**
and
**How to Swim**
by
**Johnny Weismuller**

137

film star. Liking what he saw of Miss Davis on the screen, director Robert Florey was considering her for the heroine role in his *Murders in the Rue Morgue* (1932), but, Carl Laemmle, head of the company, insisted on Sidney Fox instead.

In his generally very fine, informative volume, *Mother Goddam*, written with Bette Davis's aid, Whitney Stine mentions Bette's loss of the *Rue Morgue* part: "As it turned out, this was one of the wisest decisions ever made. Otherwise Davis might have gone on at Universal as the Egyptian girl friend of *The Mummy* and ended up as the assembled *Bride of Frankenstein*."

Bette was on the brink of returning to the New York stage when George Arliss offered her a starring part in *The Man Who Played God* (1932). A popular play, remade several times for the screen (and for TV, starring Karloff), the story has famed musician Arliss losing his hearing, though others are unaware of his disability since he has mastered lip-reading. Arlisss puts his ability and eagle eye to *outré* use by focusing on peoples' private lives and problems through the use of binoculars. Eventually, with his personal influence and money, he is able to affect others' affairs. Bette plays Arliss' loyal and dedicated student. All Arliss movies were prestige films and big at the box office, but this one won especially good reviews, thanks to Bette's role, and Warner's signed her to a long-term contract. Arliss later wrote about Bette: "I think that only two or three times in my experience have I ever got from an actor at rehearsal something beyond what I realized was in the part. Bette proved to be one of those exceptions."

Bette commented: "It is probable that *The Man Who Played God* was my most important picture. I did others that I liked better and which were more significant, but there was something about appearing as Mr. Arliss's leading lady that gave me standing."

That same year, 1932, was Bette's first big contract year, and a very busy one involving her in eight productions, though few were of lasting significance. But several

starred some of the best actors available: George Brent, Barabara Stanwyck, in *So Big*; Ruth Chatterton, George Brent in *The Rich Are Always with Us*; Spencer Tracy in *20,000 Years in Sing Sing*, one of 1933's best grossers and a top favorite in rereleases over the next ten years. There were also *The Dark Horse*; *Cabin in the Cotton* with Richard Barthelmess; *Three on a Match*, directed by Mervyn LeRoy; *Parachute Jumper* (1933) with Douglas Fairbanks; and *The Working Man* (1933) with Arliss. After *Ex-Lady* (1933), though, Bette enforced a clause in her contracts that stipulated, "No pinup pictures!" Her last 1933 release was *Bureau of Missing Persons*. In 1934 she appeared in *Fashion Follies of 1934*, *The Big Shakedown*, *Jimmy the Gent* with Cagney, William Dieterle's *Fog Over Frisco*, and *Housewife*.

*Of Human Bondage* (1934) hit all-time-best lists throughout the world, but most of the Warners stuff was el junko programmer material—except for *Dangerous*, for which she won her first Academy Award. It was the right milieu for her talents: Bette plays Joyce Heath, an alcoholic actress on the skids. The critically acclaimed *Bordertown* (partly remade in 1940 as *They Drive by Night*) was made the same year.

Released in December 1935, *Dangerous* was followed in a month by *The Petrified Forest*, adapted from Robert E. Sherwood's prize-winning play. It co-starred Leslie Howard, with Humphrey Bogart establishing his hard-boiled gangster image by repeating his role from the Broadway version. Bette's notices were again raves, but little came of it—Warners, typical of hard-headed big business, continued to feature her in the usual thirties mindless programmers.

After *The Golden Arrow* (1936), she appeared in *Satan Met a Lady*, an adapatation of Dashiell Hammett's *The Maltese Falcon*. Bette temporarily severed her Warners agreement and sailed off to England in the summer of 1936 to connect with a film planned by a close associate of Alexander Korda, Ludovico Toeplitz. War-

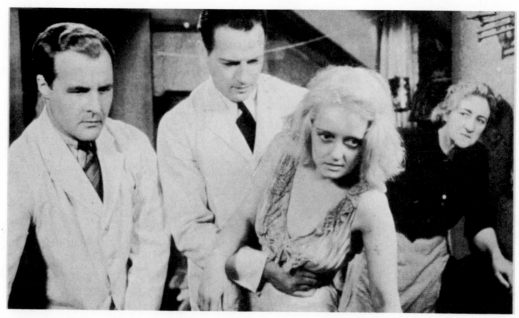

Reginald Sheffield, Reginald Denny, Bette Davis, and Tempe Piggott in *Of Human Bondage* (1934).

ners promptly brought an order of restraint against her. She lost the case, and the litigation costs were rumored to be in excess of $85,000. Her 1937 films were *Marked Woman* with Bogart, *Kid Galahad* with Bogart, *It's Love I'm After* with Leslie Howard, and *That Certain Woman* with Henry Fonda. Bette was now guaranteed better roles in better films, evidenced by *Jezebel* (1938), which got her a second Oscar. Most if not all her films were now streaked with dark, moody, often Gothic tones. *The Sisters* (1938) had Bette, as one of three sisters, leaving her old small town to marry dashing, devil-may-care but quite irresponsible reporter Errol Flynn, who deserts her just before the Frisco earthquake. It had an early, minor disaster-film quality and Victorian settings.

*Dark Victory* (1939) is one of the best and most memorable Bette Davis films. While MGM was expertly creating a whole string of very neatly made two-handkerchief medical *sob-operas* with their Dr. Gillespie/Kildare series, *Victory* hit the jackpot with a highly literate story worthy of at least five monogrammed hankies and a whole box of Kleenex. Around reel two we learn that Bette (as rich, frivolous playgirl Judith Traherne) is incurably ill of a brain tumor. *Juarez* (1939) is a little jewel mounted on a vast tableaux loaded with cornball subplots. Someone damaged the film's potential in the editing, reducing portions to absurdity and boredom. Bette bitterly complained that some of her own scenes were ruined in the cutting room. Several months later, theatres everywhere revealed Bette as an unmarried woman aging on into middle age in *The Old Maid* (1939). Good Edmund Goulding direction, tenderly scored by Max Steiner, carried off this epic of unrequited love and lost youth to good reviews and rewards.

After Errol Flynn had so heroically and messianically fought for all underdogs and thwarted evil in England in *The Adventures of Robin Hood* (1938), he came close to gaining the throne of England and sharing it with Queen Bette in *The Private Lives of Elizabeth and Essex* (1939). His adoring public, tantalized beyond control by Warners' huge advance promotion, were looking forward to a Flynn-Davis liaison with great anticipation. Believing the ending too gruesome and not what Errol's public might like to see, Warners deleted the final sequence showing his full execu-

Bette Davis and Geraldine Fitzgerald in Edmund Golding's *Dark Victory* (1939).

tion. Bette's first Technicolor film had all the majesty and opulence that Warners could command, under Michael Curtiz's expert direction, with an excellent Erich Wolfgang Korngold score. Missing are the sweeping adventure-spectacle and swashbuckling expected in a period film starring Errol Flynn.

Gothic overtones affected much of the ambience of *All This and Heaven Too* (1940), but Anatole Litvak's ho-hum direction, uninspired enough as it was, was hurt by Charles Boyer's presence. In her most

OPPOSITE PAGE

TOP LEFT: Bette with Dick Foran in *The Petrified Forest* (1936).

TOP RIGHT: Bette Davis and Henry Fonda in William Wyler's *Jezebel* (1938).

BOTTOM: Anita Louise, Bette Davis, and Jane Bryan in *The Sisters* (1938).

unsympathetic role since *Of Human Bondage*, Bette was a blackmailing, faithless wife in *The Letter* (1940). Highly stylized and sensitively paced under director William Wyler's complete control, *Letter* went up (with *All This and Heaven Too*) for Oscar nominations. Bette and her co-stars were wasted in her next two films, *The Great Lie* (1941) and *The Bride Came C.O.D.* (1941). Meanwhile, Bette went into her second marriage—with Arthur Farnsworth on December 30, 1940.

*The Little Foxes* (1941) had the inimitable teamwork of director William Wyler, Gregg Toland—who had just completed his lensing of an even greater classic, Welles' *Citizen Kane*—and Lillian Hellman, scripting her own adaptation of her stage hit. Writers Dorothy Parker, her husband Alan Campbell, and Arthur Kober added embellishments by creating a new character and scenes for Richard Carlson, who plays the boyfriend of Bette's daughter. The film was further buoyed dramatically by having five members of the original stage

*The Little Foxes* (1941).

cast—Charles Dingle and Carl Benton, as Bette's brothers and partners in evil; Dan Duryea, in his film debut, as the dishonest, weakling nephew; Patricia Collinge, the broken-hearted, alcoholic aunt; and John Marriott as the loyal black family servant. The play's title (from the *Song of Solomon*) was suggested by Lillian Hellman's close friend Dorothy Parker: "Take us the foxes, the little foxes that spoil the vines, for our vines have tender grapes."

*Foxes* is set in the post-bellum South. The Civil War's ravages have drifted away into the past. The parasites, the carpet-baggers—*the little foxes*—live off the fat of a land injured far worse by them than by any war. It is this heritage of uselessness, of self-destructive exploitation, in which Regina Hubbard Giddens (Bette Davis) and her family have roots. The whole family reeks of smug, mongooselike covetousness endemic among uncreative, power-hungry despots in any profit-motivated society; but in the South it has its own kind of mint-juleps-and-magnolias decadence, embodied in the works of Hellman, Faulkner, and Williams. Balancing out regionalism, the Hubbards of *Little Foxes* have their Northern counterpart in the Minafer-Ambersons of Orson Welles' *The Magnificent Ambersons* (released by RKO less than a year after *Foxes*). The Ambersons wallow in

self-destructive decadence, in an opposite direction, heading toward ruination thanks to George Minafer Amberson's blind, head-strong arrogance. *Foxes* and *Ambersons* are alike, though, in exemplifying the qualities that dominate powerful people who, un-trained for anything but parasitism, have only one of two directions to follow. The Hubbards of *Foxes* avoid decline by first trying to ravenously tear down each other in a power struggle, in the end losing to Medea-like Regina (Bette Davis). The Ambersons are spoiled in the lap of luxury, untrained for anything but sumptuous par-tying and self-admiration, watching their once-affluent resources diminishing with the years, one family member after another taken by age or failing health, with the Amberson family's great white hope, George, matured into a successful psychic vampire. After breaking both legs in an auto accident, he is shocked into awareness while contemplating his poverty in a hospital.

Evil is more prevalent in *Foxes*. Bette is worse than a black-widow spider, trying to cannibalize all those around her. After a series of vicious power plays, she attempts to secure a firm position that will put her in dominant financial control over her entire family. In the film's most memorable moment, her gentle, knowledgeable but ailing husband, Herbert Marshall, comes by de-grees to the realization that she whom he's called his wife is no woman but a monster. But it is too late in the day to undo her evil; he is crippled by a heart condition. Should he die, Bette will achieve everything she wants. Ruthlessly, she raves about her de-sires. Quietly, he refuses to relinquish his control. This only brings more venom out of her. A seizure suddenly takes hold of Marshall. He begs her to bring him his medicine—the only thing that might save his life. Only a little earlier she had cursed him with a passion: "Ah hope you die. Ah hope you die very soon. I'll be waitin' for you to die." Now, she stands by coldly, the epitome of inhumanity, watching her hus-band painfully die. She now has every-thing, all the power and wealth she ever

Paul Henreid, Bette Davis, and John Loder in *Now, Voyager* (1942).

wanted. In the final scene, though, no one wants her.

Wanting a change of pace, she influenced Jack Warner to buy film rights to *The Man Who Came to Dinner* (1941), and then followed with *In This Our Life* (1942). *In This Our Life* is perfectly dark, grim, and nasty enough to create a feeling of manic depression even in a confirmed optimist. As a good study of an extremely dark but plausible side of the human condition, it falls into the same groove as the *Guest in the House* (1944), with evil excellently portrayed by Anne Baxter, or lies parallel to Gene Tierney's escalating depravity perhaps in *Leave Her to Heaven* (1945). Bette seemed to hate the film, however: ". . . [it] was mediocre . . . a box-office failure." Crowther of *The New York Times* wasn't too enthusiastic but agreed that few could do so well on screen as Bette in her milieu: ". . . she plays as poisonously as only she can . . . ," adding ". . . her evil is so theatrical and so completely inexplicable that her eventual demise in an auto accident is the happiest moment in the film. That, indeed, is what probably provoked the audience to cheer."

*Now, Voyager* (1942) was another big theatrical success, with Bette playing the part of a young woman whose life is all but ruined because of possessive mother-smother love.

Just months before *Voyager*'s release, Arthur Farnsworth—her husband of only a few short years—suddenly collapsed screaming on Hollywood Boulevard and lapsed into unconsciousness. Bette was at his side in the hospital, but Farnsworth never regained consciousness. An autopsy showed evidence of an early head injury—specifically, an unknown blood clot., As Bette described it in her autobiography: "Farney had fallen down the stairs at Butternut [Bette's country house] the previous summer. We thought nothing of it at the time as he was not injured. It was unbelievable that he was gone—just like that. And so young. It didn't seem fair. It was my first actual experience with death. I was in a state of real shock."

Still mostly undated and one of the great literate films of the forties, *Watch on the Rhine* (1943) had behind it the combined talents of director Herman Shumlin (who had directed the original stage ver-

143

sion), script adaptation by Dashiell Hammett from Lillian Hellman's Broadway hit, and one of Max Steiner's best scores. Villains, intrigue, and Nazis abound in prewar Washington, D.C., but they are only part of the action. More important, the film is a grand testimonial to a man's moral character and uncompromising integrity. Included were four members of the stage production: Paul Lukas, Donald Buka, Eric Roberts, and George Coulouris. Moving, powerful, courageous, and timeless in its message, *Rhine* offers a sweeping array of unforgettable actors giving their very best. For his excellent presence, Paul Lukas won the Oscar as Best Actor of the year.

Bette proved she could jitterbug and sing ("They're Either Too Young or Too Old") in *Thank Your Lucky Stars* (1943), Warners' star-loaded, vaudeville style "war effort" extravanganza. She was next reunited with Miriam Hopkins in *Old Acquaintance* (1943). The two were novelists who are lifelong rivals, trying to remain friends while involved with the same man (John Loder). *Mr. Skeffington* (1944) is veritably a soft-pedaled version of Wilde's *The Picture of Dorian Gray*, coincidentally being produced at the time by MGM. It was followed by *Hollywood Canteen* (1944) and *The Corn Is Green* (1945).

In the fall of 1945, Bette met William Grant Sherry, a professional artist who was to become her third husband. In the meantime, her mother Ruthie would also remarry. Only a month after they met, Bill and Bette married on November 29, 1945.

Once more, in *A Stolen Life* (1946), Bette is in her natural element—well, almost. What could have been a powerful macabre adventure was tamed down in the usual Warners manner. Never identified as a studio interested in catering to fantasy-horror (especially after *Dr. X* and *The Mystery of the Wax Museum*), Warners exercised particular restraints on any film

Bette inspires poor Welsh mining-town student John Dall in *The Corn Is Green* (1945). Dall is also well remembered for his roles in *Gun Crazy* and Hitchcock's *Rope*.

properties that might have had the slightest true-grue genre connotations. *A Stolen Life*, adapted from a novel by Karel J. Benes, is an excellent example. Bette Davis plays two sisters in a dual role (almost anticipating *Dead Ringer*); one is all sunshine and light, the other predisposed to evil. Even after bad Bette succeeds stealing away good Bette's fiancé, her marriage is a bickering, mean-mouth failure. As tradition also has it even in real life, good Bette plays the happy martyr suffering her vicious sister's excesses; they even go out one bright, sunny day on a sailboat cruise. As luck would have it, bad weather arises out at sea, and mean, nasty Bette falls overboard to disappear forever. Back on shore, all think that it's bad Bette who survived. Bette goes along with the confusion, takes her sister's place, and tries making up for all the unhappiness her brother-in-law suffered in the past. He, of course, can tell the difference and stays happy with it. Of important significance is the fact that this was also Bette Davis's first film as a producer.

*Deception* (1946) is almost, though not quite, as formidable as the title may sound. Thanks mostly to a wonderful Korngold score, the film is worth *listening* to. Otherwise, it's one more story involving passionate musical virtuosos loving the same woman, Bette. During filming, Bette learned that she was pregnant.

Bette's luck with films continued to diminish from 1945 to 1949—especially in 1947, when she was absent from the screen. Her main consolation was her daughter, Barbara, born in May 1947. *Winter Meeting* (1948) was a harrowing excursion into triviality—Bette is a young woman who falls in love with a young, bright-eyed Navy man. *June Bride* (1948) was the only bright film moment in the four-year drought. Bette plays a magazine editor, with writer Robert Montgomery assigned by her to cover an important wedding taking place in June. Because of printing schedules, it must be rehearsed six months in advance—the heart of winter. Good, sophisticated writing made this a winner. Bette's sole 1949 appearance was in the tumid and miscast *Beyond the Forest*. She said in a 1972 interview: "My contract still had ten years to run. Ten years! . . . I was tired of fighting, and I thought, why should I if they keep putting obstacles in my path! If, after all these years, I'm still being given scripts like *Beyond the Forest*, then to hell with it."

Jack Warner granted her wish, and Bette was released from her contract. In order to get it, Bette was forced to apply pressure. She threatened that she would walk out on *Forest* in the midst of production, something she would never have dreamed of doing in the past. Warners was rapidly becoming a corporate mess. Her private life was also disturbed in 1949, and in a matter of months she would divorce William Grant Sherry.

Imagine their shame and chagrin when the Brothers Warner found that Bette, barely months out of contract with them, was already in hot demand by not one but two of their strongest rivals, RKO, and

Bette in King Vidor's *Beyond the Forest* (1949).

Zanuck of 20th Century-Fox. RKO's *Payment On Demand* (1950) stars Bette in a familiar role and atmosphere—as an aggressive, ruthless woman who uses her husband (Barry Sullivan) to scale the ladder of high society.

Within five days of terminating her work on this RKO production, Bette got a call from Darryl F. Zanuck over at 20th. He wanted to know if she were available and willing to appear in an especially prestigious film. The role was, of course, the part of Margo Channing in what has become one of the most-loved film classics, *All About Eve*. Eve was scripted with supreme skill and genius by Joseph L. Mankiewicz—his background and reputation had been the envy of the whole film world. He had been multifacetedly involved in fantasy and nongenre hits such as writer for *The Mysterious Dr. Fu Manchu* (1929), producer of *Strange Cargo* (1940), writer-director of *Dragonwyck* (1946, starring Vincent Price), *The Ghost and Mrs. Muir* (1947), and many other successes. *Eve* was a big Academy Award winner with an Oscar for Best Production, Mankiewicz awarded two (for screenplay and direction), one for Best

Costumes, and one to George Sanders for Best Male Supporting Role. But 1950 was an unusually good year, with competition from such future classics as *Sunset Boulevard* and *The Third Man*, not to overlook winners such as *Harvey, Cyrano de Bergerac, Destination Moon, Samson and Delilah*, and *King Solomon's Mines*, which won Oscars in different categories.

Until her next film—*Another Man's Poison*, 1952—Bette settled down to enjoy a sweet respite with her new husband, Gary Merrill, spending time in their rented cottage in Green Farms by the Connecticut seacoast. Meanwhile, Gary was under contract with Fox, appearing in *Decision Before Dawn*, a war film being shot in the Virgin Islands, about frogmen in World War II. Bette suddenly felt cut off and alone when she learned that Gary would be filming in Germany. By now, the Merrills numbered four, with a new member in their family, Margot, a newborn girl whom they had adopted.

California appeared more suitable now, so Bette decided to look for a home in Malibu, the ideal place to welcome back daddy Gary from Europe. Time seemed to

Hugh Marlowe, Anne Baxter, Gary Merrill, and Bette in *All About Eve* (1950).

whiz by, and before long, she and Gary received an offer from United Artists to star in *Another Man's Poison*. The film had wonderful potential. Bette is a mystery-story writer who has no qualms about carrying on with another man because her husband is serving a prison sentence; however, he returns unexpectedly and starts causing trouble, and Bette is forced to poison him. An old friend (Gary Merrill) of her husband's drops by unexpectedly while she's trying to find a way to get rid of the body. He learns what she's done, but mutual dislike seems to change to mutual admiration, and Gary helps Bette dispose of the corpus delicti. She cannot hide her unease with Gary around, especially when he decides to pose (with her consent) as her husband. Her unease verges on panic when kindly local veterinarian Emlyn Williams suspects something. Bette fixes the car's brakes so that Gary has an accident, but he survives. Bette decides then to poison him, too. When Williams drops by again, he tells Bette he knows *everything*. She faints, but is revived as Williams gives her some brandy—the drink containing the poison. Sensing the irony of her condition and realizing she's dying, Bette laughs ravingly. The final shot shows her face caught in a macabre grimace. With all its fine elements and perfect semi-Gothic setting (English countryside, lonely old house), it should have been a marvelous terror-shocker. It wasn't. It was stagey and uninterestingly chatty, and even the murders seemed like throwaway bits. "We had nothing but script trouble. Gary and I often wondered why we agreed to make this film after we got started working on it," said Bette in *Mother Goddam.*

*Phone Call from a Stranger* (1952) is an episodic melodrama in which Gary Merrill plays the sole survivor of a plane crash. Having been friendly with several passengers, he wishes to meet their families and learn more about them. Bette appears in different segments that trace her personal life from running off with a lover to the time she has a bad injury, up to the mo-

ment Merrill interviews her while she lies paralyzed in an iron lung.

Several months after that film's release, Bette made her first TV appearance on April 21, 1952, on *The Jimmy Durante Show*. *Daily Variety* noted that she seemed nervous in front of live TV cameras at times, including one long, nonstop routine lasting some fifteen minutes. One "classic" bit on this show had her reading a commercial: "I'll take two cans of Pet Milk. . . ."

That summer the Merrill household enlarged by one more with the adoption of Michael, who had been born on January 5, 1952. "He was a blond bomber at birth and has stayed so ever since," said Bette in her 1961 autobiography.

Hoping to match *All About Eve*'s success by creating another film in almost the same image, 20th Century-Fox offered *The Star* (1953). The story concerned the passing glory of a screen great (Bette Davis as Margaret Elliott) who watches the cruel progression of time catching up with her.

Bette marked time in the inspiring quietude of New England life, settling with Gary and her brood in Yarmouth, Maine. But even in the midst of bliss, unhappiness unexpectedly hit home again—it was discovered that beautiful little Margot, now three years old, was retarded and would have to be sent away to a special institution, the Lochland School in Geneva, New York.

Fox beckoned with the lead in *The Virgin Queen* (1955), practically a sequel to Warner's *Elizabeth and Essex*. This time, good Queen Bess has involvements with Sir Walter Raleigh (Richard Todd) who, youthful hot-blood that he is, goes a bit too far and is ordered to go to America.

Bette was now heading toward the most agonizing slump in her career. There was *Storm Center* (1956), a film too engrossed in imparting a message to be entertaining at the same time. By 1956 Bette was into her sixty-eighth film, cast as the famous Bronx mom in Gore Vidal's screenplay adaptation of Paddy Chayefsky's original teleplay classic, *The Catered*

Queen Elizabeth I (Bette Davis) exercises her authority in *The Virgin Queen.*

*Affair.* "Without doubt one of the most against-type characters I ever attempted."

She did not appear in another film for three years—she was now deep in the heart of a professional depression. But her name and fame burned brightly, and she made a number of prominent TV appearances: guesting in her own home in Maine on Edward R. Murrow's *Person to Person* (September 1956); *GE Theater* (March 20, 1957) in "With Malice Toward None"; "For Better, For Worse" on the *Schlitz Playhouse* (March 22, 1957); "Footnote on a Doll" (as Dolly Madison) on the *Ford Theatre* (April 24, 1957); "Stranded" (the real-life experiences of Beatrice Enter, who was trapped in a 1940 snowstorm with her pupils at an isolated schoolhouse) on *Telephone Time* (May 9, 1957).

Contracted to appear on Broadway in *Look Homeward, Angel,* Bette broke her back on June 23, 1957, and was replaced by Jo Van Fleet. Early in 1958, Bette was back in action as the host-narrator of *Whispering Streets,* a daily radio soap opera. She returned to TV with "The Cold Touch" (foreign intrigue in Hong Kong) on *GE Theatre* (April 13, 1958); "Fraction of a Second" on *Suspicion* (April 21, 1958);

"The Starmaker" on *Studio 57* (August 10, 1958); "Out There—Darkness" (working with two of her old friends, director Paul Henreid and photographer Ernie Haller) on *Alfred Hitchcock Presents* (January 1, 1959); "The Ella Lindstrom Story" on *Wagon Train* (February 4, 1959); "Dark Morning" (as a teacher protecting a young girl accused of homicide) on *The June Allyson Show* (September 28, 1959); and "The Elizabeth McQueeney Story" on *Wagon Train* (October 28, 1959).

She left for England to receive $50,000 for four days' work in *John Paul Jones* (1959), followed by co-billing with Alec Guinness in *The Scapegoat* (1959). "A more unhappy set I have never worked on, and a duller film, when it was finished, would be hard to find. If you sneezed while watching it, I had disappeared!"

She appeared again on TV in "The Bettina May Story" on *Wagon Train* (December 20, 1961), and she toured with Gary Merrill in *The World of Carl Sandburg.* She leased a New York townhouse for a year, but *Sandburg* ran only four weeks in New York. Her marriage to Merrill was at an end. She wrote her autobiography, *The Lonely Life,* published by Putnam in

148

The Street People of *Pocketful of Miracles*. Angelo Rossitto is seen with accordion. Ellen Corby stands at center with Edgar Stehli at her right.

1961. "The offer to write a book, with the cash advance, was a lifesaver at that point, financially."

As filming on Frank Capra's *Pocketful of Miracles* (1961) was nearing completion, Bette received the worst news of her life— the one person she loved the most and to whom she owed her entire career, her mother Ruthie, had just died. Broken from within, agonizing silently over her loss, Bette stayed on to finish the film despite her personal pain; then, after her final take, she flew back East to join her family.

Rehearsals meanwhile were underway for the Chicago opening of Tennessee Williams' *The Night of the Iguana* (November 21, 1961). Bette starred in the role of Maxine Faulk. Following its highly successful twenty-eight-day run, the play opened on Broadway at the Royale Theatre on December 28, 1961. The critical response was positive, particularly from Walter Kerr. But, dissatisfied with certain conditions and the leading man, Patrick O'Neal, Bette surprised the theatrical world by announcing that she was giving up her role and leaving in April 1962. "I don't want to go on for another six months," she said. "I'm going to

rest and walk in the country for about a hundred miles a day."

Even as she was leaving *Iguana*, Bette received a script from director Robert Aldrich for her approval. Did she like it, and would she like appearing with Joan Crawford as her co-star in *What Ever Happened to Baby Jane?*. Not long after, when she signed contracts, the world knew her answer.

Without Robert Aldrich's interest and energy from the very beginning, there would never have been any *Baby Jane*—at least not on film. Hardly past the halfway mark in directing a gigantic biblical epic in Europe titled *Sodom and Gomorrah* (1963), he received a copy of Henry Farrell's horror-shocker novel, *What Ever Happened to Baby Jane?*, for consideration as a screen property. The next problem was convincing the money men. Story rights were available for only $10,000. The price rose to $61,000—apparently insiders along the filmmaking grapevine heard about the story property and started questioning. Renowned for his gambling predilection, Joe Levine bought up the rights with Aldrich; scripting chores went to Lukas Heller.

Bette in her transformation from Apple Annie to lady in *Pocketful of Miracles*.

So far so good. Then a rift arose between them, and Aldrich bought out Levine's interest in the story, but now the price soared to $85,000 because it included Heller's script. With limited cash reserves, Aldrich's next dilemma was contracting Joan and Bette at a price he could live with, and far below their usual scale. As an inducement, to clinch the deal, they agreed to accept a small salary plus a neat percentage of the film. Raising capital was the next and hardest move. Of seven large film companies contacted, all reacted with the usual narrowness or coldness—Bette hadn't had a hit in ages, and Joan wasn't much better off either; one of these firms said they might reconsider if Aldrich would "agree to cast younger players." Just when it seemed that the deal would fall apart,

hope appeared. Seven Arts, having a controlling interest in Warners, responded with interest but confided that they considered it a "high-risk venture."

Bette was now back at Warners for the first time in fourteen years. Smiles beamed, laughter rang in the air, and Jack Warner, looking more like Smilin' Jack than ever, was delighted to hear that no one hated his guts. It was like the good old days again . . . well, maybe also like the bad ones, too, depending on what one chose to reminisce about. Part of the production team consisted of Ernie Haller, the great cinematographer who worked on some of Joan's films and fourteen of Bette's.

Whether a publicity gimmick or not, a "feud" was rumored to be developing between the women. Even if the rumor

Bette as Baby Jane.

Baby Jane (Davis) is "writing a letter to Daddy."

lacked credence, Bette cast oil upon the waters: "We wouldn't have one. A man and a woman, yes, and I can give you a list, but never two women—they'd be too clever for that." And now—lights, camera, action: finding her mark and ready before the camera, Bette stood wearing long, blond curls around her cadaverously made-up face. Eyes bright, head alert, and in complete control of herself, she looked like a combination of a scrofulous, overripe Shirley Temple and Marcel Marceau gone sour. And she loved every minute of playing the bitchy, vile-tempered, loud-mouthed, mad-as-a-hatter Baby Jane Hudson.

The time is 1923. Making appearances around the country in variety shows and in vaudeville as a solo act, spoiled, ill-mannered Baby Jane, age seven, is adored by her public; in one scene she brings the house down when, in cutsey-poo style, she sings her theme song, "I've written a letter to dadd-dee. . . ." She also supports her father and dutiful, wise-looking older sister Blanche, very plain in appearance but temperamentally the opposite. As Baby Jane grows older, she loses all her appeal.

By contrast, Joan Crawford as Blanche, has blossomed into beautiful womanhood and becomes a top film star. She sees to it

that her sister also has a film career as well, but Bette's films are potboilers of lasting insignificance. At the height of her career—returning with a drunken Bette one night from a party—their car pulls up to their driveway; one of them goes out to unlock the gates. Suddenly, the car speeds into the gates and smashes up, permanently crippling Joan. As the years pass, guilt-ridden Bette dedicates herself to caring for Joan, convinced the accident was caused by her in drunken jealousy. Her incessant guilt has affected her physically and mentally; her clothing is as out of style as the car she drives. Time has been unkind to her looks, also aided by an affinity for liquor. Because Joan controls most of the purse strings, Bette's financial dependence makes her more irritable and dishonest; she makes out checks forging Joan's signature, when she's not ordering things over the phone and charging them to Joan by imitating her voice.

Living alone in a Hollywood house, they are visited occasionally only by cleaning woman Maidie Norman. When Bette's eccentric behavior becomes worse, as does her drinking, Maidie becomes concerned, especially since she knows that Joan plans to sell the house and perhaps place Bette in a home. When Bette learns of this, she turns Joan into a prisoner, cutting off her extension phone. Joan, denied food almost completely, turns into a wreck. Giving way to empty delusions of grandeur, Bette believes she should revive her Baby Jane act after more than thirty-five years. She hires unemployed pianist Victor Buono. Dressed up in her Baby Jane getup, Bette welcomes him, then shocks him by doing her old routine, singing in a strident dissonant voice, "I've written a letter to dadd-dee. . . ." He goes along with the madness, hoping it will prove profitable.

Maidie criticizes her one day, and Bette fires the cleaning woman. Sensing that something is terribly wrong, Maidie sneaks back into the house. Unlocking Joan's door, she gasps in horror. Crosscutting reveals that Bette is meanwhile downtown cashing another forged check. Unfortunately, Maidie doesn't leave soon enough for help and is surprised by Bette's return. While Maidie turns for a moment to phone, Bette bears down with a vicious hammer blow to the head, killing her instantly. She later disposes of the body elsewhere. A drunken Buono arrives for a visit, thinking he can pick up a little cash. Bette welcomes him cheerfully. While they talk, Buono hears Joan upstairs and swaggeringly pushes his huge shape past Bette, heading to Joan's room. Thinned down by starvation, eyes sunken, skin gray and deathly pallid, Joan, bound and gagged,

moans weakly for help. The sight restores Buono to sobriety. He rushes down the steps and out of the house, yelling, "My God—oh my God!"

Reduced to childish confusion, Bette is a pathetic figure, calling out pleadingly to the fleeing Buono to come back. One thing she is aware of—she must leave the area quickly or face some punishment. Packing Joan's inert body into the car, Bette drives off to the beach, and spends the whole night there with Joan by her side. The morning sun reveals a gay, carefree Bette; lying next to her is a living but corpselike Joan. It is a warm, pleasant day—people begin to arrive. Basking in the sun's warm rays, Bette stares absent-mindedly as if without a worry in the world. Without turning her head, she hears Joan moan: "I'm dying, I'm dying." Wanting to think only of pleasant, little-girl thoughts, she feigns nonchalance, but her face screws up in annoyance. Her gaze still averted, she hears Joan confess a terrible, long-hidden fact. Joan, who blames herself for Bette's mental condition, reveals that on the night of the accident, Bette was too drunk to drive and was never behind the car's wheel. Joan then had deliberately plotted it all, sending Bette in her groggy, drunken state to open the driveway gate, then aiming the car to run her down, intending later to tell authorities that Bette's death was accidental. What altered this insidious scheme was that Bette was only slightly brushed by the car, which smashed into the gates with terrific impact, crippling Joan. Due to her foggy, besotted confusion, neither Bette nor the authorities ever suspected the truth, attributing Joan's accident to Bette's drunken driving. Joan thus shows herself to be the true monster who tried to avenge herself for all the years she felt humiliated living in her sister's shadow when they were youngsters. As a cripple, Joan found a way of destroying Bette psychologically by inculcating in her false impressions of guilt, never realizing that in the long run her victim would become her tormenter.

As this terrible revelation sinks slowly into her mind, Bette tries shutting out the

Blanche is subjected to Baby Jane's torture.

sounds, covering up her ears with her hands the way a child would, and then removes them reluctantly. Like a kind unguent, truth now becalms her tortured spirit. Eyes that bulged from the shock of awareness soften; tension subsides—Bette now relaxes, turning her averted face to Joan with a stunningly benign smile creasing her features, saying, "You mean, all this time we could have been friends?"

Bette rises to her feet and runs off down the sand dune heading to an ice-cream stand. She orders two ice-cream cones as she might have done long ago when she and Joan were little girls. Wending her way back happily through the sand, a gentle surf rippling nearby, sun beaming all over, Bette attracts a small, growing crowd. They are curious at the sight of this eccentric, middle-aged woman, dressed and acting like a child. With cones in hand, she feels they are watching because she's the famous, cute, darling little Baby Jane. They're her audience. To please them, she

goes into a little dance. The police, who have been nearby, arrive. Elsewhere, another crowd is seen gathering around Joan's body.

A sweeping, overhead shot scans the whole beach scene. Sounding rhythmically like a musical heartbeat, a full orchestra underlines this closing scene, then swells with a poignantly dramatic variation of "I've Written a Letter to Daddy."

The film became an unusual financial success, eliciting this reaction from *Hollywood Reporter* in a page-one headline article:

"*Jane* Recoups Cost In 11 Days: First Film Shown Under TOA's 'Hollywood Premier' Plan Makes Hollywood History. . . . *What Ever Happened to Baby Jane?* made film history by amassing through the weekend $1,600,000 in film rental, putting the Warner-Seven Arts Association and Robert Aldrich picture into the profit column in less than two weeks. Negative cost was $825,000; the rest went for prints, advertising, and other expenses."

Off screen, Bette stumped around doing personal tours to promote *Baby Jane*. In the New York City area alone, in three days, she appeared in seventeen theatres showcasing the film, starting on November 6, 1962. Joe Morgenstern eulogized the event in his *Herald Tribune* column (November 11, 1962): "She ranged as far as White Plains and as wide as Astoria. She subjected herself, not merely willingly but gleefully, to a sight-seeing tour of New York by day and night, on which she saw the same sights seventeen times; movie palaces in various states of splendrous decay suddenly came alive again with throngs of fans who had paid to see a fabled chatelaine in the flesh. 'It is awesome,' Miss Davis said at mid-tour, 'the interest in Hollywood. . . . The tour is good for the picture, and important to me because people get a terrific surprise to find that I'm not ninety, despite the fact that I've been around for a thousand years.' . . . She gave the audience advice on how to imitate her: 'Puff the cigarette like mad, roll the left elbow like mad, and say Peetah.'" In a clever promotional gimmick that Warner created for her New York tour, Bette would announce from the stage that anyone finding a lucky envelope under the seat won a Baby Jane doll. The gentle tumult that followed throughout the theatre tickled Betty's fancy: "It's as if I had just shouted *bottoms up*."

Lukewarm though Crowther's *Times* review may have been, the *Times* did an about-face eight years later in its *New York Times Guide to Movies on TV*—with an introduction by Bosley Crowther: "Fine, horrific fun, with one eye closed. Take it straight, as could hardly have been intended—but as it frequently appears—and you'll recoil from a murderous duel of snarls, shrieks, moans, and rattlesnake repartee. . . . Yet, as shrewdly directed by Robert Aldrich, and played by the two ladies as though it were the last film for each, it is a genuinely gripping horror exercise, with a sufficient story surprise toward the end. . . ."

". . . . *Baby Jane* is a grand horror movie for adults," said Judith Crist, "made remarkable by the no-holds-barred performances of old-pros Bette Davis and Joan Crawford in their Guignol perfection. Miss Davis triumphs on two levels, capping her insane villainies with a lyrical pathos that is unforgettable. . . ."

Pauline Kael asked, "Was it possible that audiences no longer cared if a film was so untidily put together that information crucial to the plot or characterizations was obscure or omitted altogether? *What Ever Happened to Baby Jane?* was such a mess that *Time*, after calling it 'the year's scariest, funniest, and most sophisticated thriller,' got the plot garbled." Kael also felt baffled and upset over an article in *The New York Times* that endorsed *Baby Jane* and rebuked the companies that refused to invest in the film: ". . . but how could businessmen, brought up to respect logic and a good commercial script, possibly guess this . . . would delight the public?"

Highly favorable reviews were in the majority. Paul Beckley in the *Herald Tribune* said: "If Miss Davis' portrait of an outrageous slattern with the mind of an infant has something of the force of a hurricane, Miss Crawford's performance as the crippled sister could be described as the eye of that hurricane. . . . Both women are seen in the isolated decay of two spirits left to dry on the desert by the receding flow of fame. 'I didn't forget to bring your breakfast because you didn't eat your din-din,' Miss Davis tells Miss Crawford. She then howls a witch's laugh that would frizzle the mane of a wild beast. It is the mingling of baby talk and baby-mindedness with the behavior of an ingenious Gauleiter that raises the hackles."

Why a minority of critics and viewers had difficulty assimilating and enjoying *Baby Jane* is understandable. The film works extremely well as entertainment, but its elusive message can be easily misjudged and overlooked by anyone failing to see the true horrors for the shrieks. On the surface, entertainment level, it succeeds on all counts. In another, almost insidious way, it's even more horrific, playing subliminal head games with its audience, creating uneasy awareness of transitory or enduring love-hate experiences that can arouse homicidal tendencies.

Of immeasurable value is *Baby Jane's* B-film look and ambience. Aldrich, like Roger Corman, is primarily a director who feels at home and works like a genius on small-budget films but may get rattled with larger structures (e.g. 1977's disappointing *Twilight's Last Gleaming*). The warm, direct personal touch achieved in B-films is the substance and essence of ideal filmmaking—its sensibility and mystique can best be illustrated by the undying appeal of such classics as *Carnival of Souls* (1962), *Night of the Living Dead* (1968), *The Texas Chainsaw Massacre* (1974), *The Little Shop of Horrors* (1960), to name a few. Lots of money can spoil something potentially great. Clive T. Miller's excellent piece, "*Nightmare Alley*: Beyond The Bs," in *Kings of the Bs*, states it well: "*Nightmare Alley* (1947) is the quintessential B movie spoiled by an A production. If the studio . . . had left well enough alone, *Nightmare Alley* would have been hard and nasty. Or if they had turned it into a full-fledged A project, it would have become a classic. Instead, they went halfway and ruined it, the deprived bastard child of a millionaire. The amazing thing is that they didn't turn it into a mess."

Bette Davis was now back on her feet in 1962, surrounded by success. Her autobiography, *The Lonely Life*, was a top-ranking best-seller. *What Ever Happened to Baby Jane?* was a box-office smash hit, winning an Oscar nomination and reputedly bringing her close to a million dollars. Bette was openly disappointed at not winning the Oscar. In a 1970 interview she said: "I was positive I would get it. So was everybody in town. I almost dropped dead when I didn't win. I wanted to be the first actress to win three times, but now it's been done (by Hepburn), so I may as well give up."

She was also back on the tube: "The Accomplice" on *The Virginian* (December 19, 1962) and "The Case of the Constant Doyle" on *Perry Mason* (January 31, 1963).

With TV, *Baby Jane*, and her book, Bette felt financially secure enough again to move back to Hollywood and buy a cute New England-type home a stone's throw from the heart of fashionable Bel Air. More important, she was now on the Hollywood Top Stars list and, after sixteen years' absence, receiving the red-carpet treatment again from Warner's, who were readying

A dual role in Paul Henreid's *Dead Ringer* (1964). The seated Bette Davis doesn't seem consoled by the backing up she's receiving from that other Bette Davis, as her scheming twin sister.

her for her next assignment, the lead—actually, the double lead—in *Dead Ringer* (originally titled *Dead Pigeon* and a.k.a. *La Otra* when it was made as a Mexican film with Dolores Del Rio sixteen years earlier).

For *Ringer*, Bette succeeded in looking nearly twenty years younger thanks to makeup wizard Gene Hibbs, whose famous specialty was in "youthifying" aging screen queens. *Dead Ringer* started production in July 1963, and was released in February 1964. In her strange dual role, Bette visits her twin for the first time in eighteen years. The occasion is her brother-in-law's funeral —cause of death, an unexpected "heart attack." Originally he had loved Bette-1, but was forced by Bette-2 (who coveted his wealth) into a marriage when she faked a pregnancy.

Meanwhile, unmarried Bette has owned a cocktail lounge all these years. When she learns the truth about how her twin cheated her out of true love, she decides to murder widow Bette, then take her place as a wealthy widow and respected matron—after all, they're so identical, who'll ever find out? Though a police lieutenant, Karl Malden, is interested romantically in the unmarried Bette, her mind is elsewhere. Later, she lures her widowed sister to her apartment, writes a suicide note claiming business troubles as the cause for taking her life, then kills Bette-2. After she has changed her clothes and appearance enough to leave no doubt about her new identity, she eases into her sister's lifestyle. Her staff is puzzled by small inconsistencies, but they're of small consequence. The one she can't convince is Peter Lawford, her sister's unprincipled lover. He tells Bette he "knows everything" and threatens to take away the whole fortune. To keep him quiet, she gives him a few jewels, which he later pawns. This alerts the police, who search his room and find arsenic. A quarrel between Bette and Lawford results in Bette's huge hound attacking and killing Lawford. By now the police have become interested in the cause of the husband's death—an autopsy shows traces of arsenic. Bette is then arrested on suspicion of murder. She first confides to Malden who she really is, but he scoffs at her revelation. Bette keeps her true identity secret and marches off to the gas chamber.

*Dead Ringer* was directed by Bette's old friend, Paul Henreid. The supporting cast included Estelle Winwood, Jean Hagen, Philip Carey, George Macready, George Chandler, and Bert Remsen. Next to *Baby Jane*, *Dead Ringer* was disappointing, held up primarily by Bette's bravura tricks and polished artistry, but neither her presence nor a highly competent cast could pull this above its average mundane contrivances and predictable plot. "The original script . . . was appallingly bad," Bette revealed. "Paul and I worked very hard to make it plausible at all. We did not completely succeed. . . ."

The reviews were obviously mixed, but none were unkind and some surprisingly good. *Variety* commented, "Aggressive salesmanship and the Bette Davis name will probably have to carry the box-office burden for this old-fashioned suspense melodrama. . . . The story doesn't hold up very well under scrutiny. . . . [It] will have to rely on the support of the less-discerning, less-selective picture-goer, and the incurable Bette Davis buff. . . . She achieves good contrast in her dual portrayal and carries on gamely and with considerable histrionic relish in the combination assignment. . . . The most impressive thing is the rich and macabre musical score composed for the occasion by Andre Previn. It is the most virile aspect of the picture."

*The New York Times* said, "Her mammoth creation of a pair of murderous twin sisters not only galvanizes this uncommonly silly little film, but it is great fun to watch. . . . [It is] creaky on . . . plot . . . but it has all the extra accoutrements the studio used to supply in her dramatic heyday. . . ." *Motion Picture Herald* remarked, "Exhibitors scarcely need to be told that Miss Davis zoomed in public interest through her sensational return to the screen in *Baby Jane*. Following on that, David Wolper made her screen career the subject of his effective documentary on network television, *The Indestructible Bette Davis.*" The *N. Y. News'* Wanda Hale loved it and gave *Ringer* three and a half stars: "Bravo, Bette Davis! It's so gratifying to those of us who admire perfection to see the old pro at work . . . giving an unerring performance."

Bette was soon off to Rome to star as Horst Buchholz's mom in *The Empty Canvas* (1964), produced by Joseph E. Levine and Carlo Ponti, directed by Damiano Damiani. Adapted from Alberto Moravia's acclaimed novel, the story underwent considerable change in an unsuccessful New Wave styled transition to the screen. The story mostly concerns young artist Horst Buchholz unhappy in art and love— unhappy in art because his heart was never in it. He's not too happy either about returning to the big villa of his wealthy, widowed mother, Bette Davis. . . . *Canvas* was Bette's emptiest film since her *Baby Jane* comeback. She seemed to dislike it intensely: "No doubt about it, mincemeat was made of Mr. Moravia's classic book about an Italian family. . . . I actually never understood why I was asked to be in *The Empty Canvas* at all. . . ."

*Motion Picture Exhibitor* commented: "Bette Davis is seen in a minor role that does nothing for her. . . ." *Time* magazine had a good time panning and describing *Canvas*: "It is chiefly notable for the fun of watching Davis breast the New-Wave plot with bitchy authority. In a blonde Dutchboy bob, Bette looks like a degenerate Hans Brinker. . . . In his mother's bedroom, crowning a marriage proposal to the girl whose favors can be had for the price of an espresso, (Horst) generously covers her nude body with some of mama's 10,000 lire banknotes. The door opens. In sails Bette, rococo-eyed, jewels a-jangle, a one-woman spectacular. She sees her darling at play, drops into her deep-fried Southern drawl, and issues what must be the last word in ultrapermissive momism: 'Please put the money you don't want back in the safe—I don't want the maid to find the room in this curious state.' "

Bette's "baby" daughter, B.D., meanwhile turned sweet sixteen and in January

1964, married Jeremy Hyman (nephew of Elliot Hyman, president of 7-Arts) at the Beverly Hills Episcopal Church. The union brought Bette a grandson, Ashley.

Bette next came under the capable direction of Edward Dmytryck in Joe Levine's production of *Where Love Has Gone* (1964). Based on Harold Robbins' bestseller, *Where Love Has Gone* reaped an ample share of good and bad reviews; but, at least, most conceded it was earthier, better entertainment than pseudo-arty *Empty Canvas*.

*Hush . . . Hush, Sweet Charlotte* (1964) was an inspired encore to *What Ever Happened to Baby Jane?*, based on an original story by the same writer, Henry Farrell, and adapted for the screen by him and Lukas Heller. Hoping to repeat *Baby Jane's* success, plans for teaming up Joan Crawford and Bette Davis together again fell through when Joan fell suddenly ill. Stepping in to fill Crawford's spot was Olivia de Havilland, who at first objected to the role but finally gave in to Aldrich's sweet persuasion. *Charlotte's* story begins in

Bette Davis, Horst Buchholz, and Catherine Spaak in *The Empty Canvas* (1964).

1927: The young daughter of a wealthy Southerner (Victor Buono) plans to run away with Bruce Dern, though he's still married to Mary Astor. Buono puts a stop to the plan, and later in the darkened greenhouse, Dern is found decapitated. The daughter's mind is seriously affected, and no one is certain whether or not she did it. Father Buono prevents further scandal by sending his daughter out of the country until the fuss has simmered down. In 1964 the girl, now an aging Bette Davis, is facing eviction from the big mansion to make way for a road. She sends for her only living relative, cousin Olivia de Havilland. Family doctor Joseph Cotten has also been of much help during her periods of stress. While de Havilland ostensibly contrives to help Bette and get her out of the house, she and Cotten team to drive her mad so that she will be committed and they can take over her fortune. Agnes Moorehead, the slovenly but faithful housekeeper, suspects de Havilland and is killed when she threatens to reveal what she knows. Meanwhile, retired insurance investigator Cecil Kellaway arrives from England to delve into the case that has never been closed, and Bette, Mary Astor, and others confide in him, with Astor giving him an envelope to open in the event of her death. Bette continues to be driven closer to the edge of madness—or so it seems—while secretly overhearing Cotten and de Havilland discussing their conspiracy. While they talk below on the patio, Bette pushes stone decorations off the balcony, killing the evil, scheming twosome. At about the same time, Mary Astor dies from her illness, and Kellaway learns that it was she who had killed Dern many years ago. De Havilland (who knew the truth) had been blackmailing her through the years. Kellaway hands the note revealing the true state of affairs to a composed Bette as she is being taken away.

When Bette appeared in England to begin work on *The Nanny* (1965), she spoke about *Sweet Charlotte* in a BBC radio interview: ". . . I made a tour of theatres in New York City with *Charlotte*, and I suggested to the audience, when they asked me about horror films, to start reading Shakespeare again. You know, everybody acts in the press today as if anything that involves any kind of murder, legitimate or not, or any kind of tragedy, is a 'horror' movie. *Charlotte* was not a horror film. It was the study of a very sad woman who had a terrible thing happen in her life. And I'm not saying this was written like Shakespeare. *The Letter* was never criticized as a horror film—was it? Well, at the start of *The Letter* I'm plugging a man with six bullets. *The Little Foxes* was never called a horror film, and I let a man die of a heart attack."

The general critical response to *Sweet Charlotte* was quite good, despite some obvious dissatisfaction among those who believed that angelic-faced Olivia was too gentle looking, compared to Crawford, who could turn beauty and meanness on or off like a faucet. *Motion Picture Exhibitor* commented: "It's well done in all areas of execution even though the darkness is a bit much, and the length is a bit excessive. A sneak-preview audience seemed properly impressed with the good acting and the quality production and direction, with interest evident throughout. . . ."

Kenneth Tynan wrote, "An accomplished piece of Grand Guignol is yanked to the level of art by Miss Davis's performance as the raging, aging Southern belle; this wasted Bernhardt, with her screen-filling eyes and electrifying vocal attack, squeezes genuine pathos from a role conceived in cardboard. She has done nothing better since *The Little Foxes*. Arthur Knight in *Saturday Review*: "Once again he (Aldrich) is aided immeasurably by the gutsy, free-wheeling performance of Bette Davis, with her incredible ability to abandon all consciousness of self in the full realization of a role that ranges from youthful, wide-eyed innocence to the stark terror of a middle-aged woman helplessly in the grip of a nightmare, both real and imagined."

With cofinancing coming in from 7-Arts in the United States, Hammer of England was now beginning to branch out from its familiar Gothic horror image. *The Nanny* had the creative support of veteran Hammer names such as Jimmy Sangster (who produced and scripted), with direction by Seth Holt. Bette was costumed and made up as a very homely, aging governess —she had rarely looked more unglamorous. While Bette was working on the set one day, a lady who had long admired her came right up to her and said: "Oh, it's a pleasure to meet you, Miss Davis. You look great." Bette found this incident very funny and later said to some colleagues: "I almost killed her!"

The story starts in a contemporary English setting. Bette is a nursemaid and general all-around servant in the home of wealthy James Villiers and his delicate wife Wendy Craig. All three are awaiting the arrival of their ten-year-old boy, William Dix, following a two-year stay at a school for disturbed children. Craig is apprehensive about his return, recalling that he was involved in the drowning death of his younger sister in the bathtub—the reason why they sent him away. Back home now, Dix refuses to let governess Bette touch, help, or feed him. Meanwhile, Villiers must go abroad on business. Craig is visited by her sister, Jill Bennett, who has a weak heart and needs medication to stay alive. Little Dix makes friends with Pamela Franklin, an older girl in the upstairs apartment, and relates how his sister fell into the bathtub, hit her head, and was drowned when Bette carelessly turned on the water without noticing the small unconscious child. Bette was the one who convinced the authorities that little Dix was responsible. Suddenly Craig is taken ill by food poisoning—the finger of suspicion points to Dix again. While Craig is hospitalized, Jill Bennett moves in to watch Dix—she sees Bette acting suspiciously outside Dix's door. Jill has a heart attack, and Bette refuses to give her the pills. As Jill Bennett dies, Bette confesses that she was responsible in a way for the little girl's death. She feared that someday Dix would be believed, which would mean that she would lose her comfortable job. She next goes after little Dix, and

struggles with the boy until he bangs his head. Bette drags his body to the bathtub, filling it with water and holding his head under. Realizing suddenly the horror of her deed, she saves the boy and revives him. Returning to full consciousness, Dix runs away. Bette then packs her belongings and prepares to leave. Dix goes to the hospital to visit his mother, his conscience clear of any wrongdoing.

Said *Variety*, "It's not necessary to be an astute student to guess that Bette Davis as a middle-aged Mary Poppins in a fairly fraught household will eventually be up to no good. . . . *The Nanny* is a superior psycho-thriller . . . Miss Davis handles her assignment with marked professionalism

Bette with Wendy Craig in *The Nanny*.

and copes with plenty of knowhow competition, up against two of Britain's outstanding young femme thesps, but it is Miss Davis's restrained yet compelling performance that makes the whole thing jell. . . ." *Time* magazine commented, "Having mopped up in three earlier blood-letters, moviedom's Ace Bogeywoman, Bette Davis, now goes about her grisliness with quiet, unruffled efficiency." *Boxoffice* said, "Bette Davis is chillingly polished and gives the controlled performance always expected of her. . . ." Based on an original novel, *The Nanny* was authored by Evelyn Piper, who also wrote Otto Preminger's *Bunny Lake Is Missing*. *Nanny* was a mild but not a big box-office success.

Bette remained active the following year in television, cohosting *The Mike Douglas Show* for a week in April and celebrating her birthday on it. She was next on *Gunsmoke* (October 10, 1966). On *The Milton Berle Variety Show* (October 7) she brought the house down with a hilarious parody, *The Maltese Chicken*.

Various projects were discussed, including the role of Helen Lawson in *Valley of the Dolls* (1967) eventually assumed by Susan Hayward. Robert Aldrich's *The Killing of Sister George* (1968) was also another production being considered. The role finally went to Beryl Reid.

Next year Bette was offered the option of starring in the Hammer screen version of the London stage hit, *The Anniversary*, but she rejected the offer. After Jimmy Sangster made a number of major changes, Bette liked what she saw and accepted the role. The role of the monstrous Mrs. Taggart seemed tailor-made for her. There could be no dispute that this was perhaps the quintessentially evil possessive mom to end all similar filmic personifications. In its very own way, *Anniversary* is so *uniquely* different that is almost without any known precedent, with the exception perhaps of *Moss Rose* (1947) and the aptly titled *Female Trap* (1968).

Bette (as wealthy Mrs. Taggart) continues to celebrate her wedding anniversary though her husband has been dead for ten years. Each year she expects and virtually dictates the presence of her three sons: Jack Heldey, the middle one married to Sheila Hancock; the youngest, Christian Roberts, engaged to pregnant Elaine Taylor; and James Cossins, the eldest, who doesn't care for women but has a thing for dressing like one. Hedley, Hancock, and their five children plan to emigrate to Canada; when they tell this to Bette, she's livid with rage. She pulls a sick joke on them by telling them that the children were in an accident with Cossins, who was bringing them home in his car. When the shock effect of the news wears off, she sadistically admits it was a fraud in order to punish them for their arrogance. Roberts tries breaking the news of his engagement softly so that it will be acceptable to Bette, but she treats fiancée Taylor with contempt, discovering the girl has deformed ears (which she tries to hide in her hairdo) and loudly playing it up, then relays some news about Roberts' former girlfriends to frustrate and torment her further. Regarding Cossins, Bette has been condoning and encouraging his transvestite practices to keep him with her. It comes out at the gathering that Bette has been paying Hedley a thousand pounds each time he makes Hancock pregnant, hoping that she will suffer a heart attack during one of her pregnancies.

Cossins, meanwhile, returns breathless from a lingerie raid on neighboring clotheslines, just eluding the police. However, he had to abandon Hedley's car at the scene. Bette insists that the car owner will be blamed and jailed, and Hedley agrees to give up going to Canada if she will get him out of the predicament. Bette also demands an IOU from them for the money she's given them for the children. Bette's attempt to cause Taylor to miscarry backfires, and Roberts and Taylor stalk off, determined to get married. When Hedley hears her admit that she has always hated him, he and Hancock leave, determined to really go to Canada. Bette doesn't give up that easily and phones her attorney to lodge a complaint with the emigration authorities about the IOU. She also arranges to see that Tay-

lor gets a large amount of money as a wedding gift, which will create a wretched existence for Roberts. She is sure that all her sons will be with her next year for her anniversary.

Great as it is, *Anniversary* received an unjust share of downgrading reviews. That the film is flawed cannot be denied, but its minute drawbacks cannot alter the fact that the film states its thesis with clear, groin-level clarity that some have consciously or

LEFT: Bette in Roy Ward Baker's *The Anniversary* (1968).

BELOW: A shot of Bette with Ernest Borgnine in *Bunny O'Hare.*

unconsciously resented. The grim fact is that *Anniversary* is *too* clinical, too direct in saying that a home is not always a home, and that the most abhorrent murderer of mind and spirit can be mom, country, and apple pie—especially when good old mom is the mediator for all of the contrived social demands that destroy individuality and wilt creativity.

Frances Herridge said in *The New York Post* (March 21, 1968): "Bette Davis fans are being shortchanged. Not that she doesn't give her all. But the direction and filmscript smother what might have been a dandy black satire on Momism. If the direction had been more subtle, the dialogue less heavy, Miss Davis' impersonation could well be an entertaining archetype of the possessive mom. . . ."

One of the few with a positive statement, Judith Crist exulted: "Bette Davis emerges as pure Mama Sin in *The Anniversary*. . . . It is a triumph of star over vehicle, with Miss Davis sporting several changes of eyepatches to match her stylish wardrobe."

"It may not be the greatest movie ever made," Bette said in a March 10, 1968 *Times* interview, "but it's a good old-fashioned Bette Davis movie. I waited two years for a part like this. . . . This is the age of horror films. The world is pretty horrible. . . ." She assailed some of her sixties films: "I did four or five stinking pieces of trash in a row. . . . *Baby Jane* was a challenge and fun. *The Anniversary* was fun. *Sweet Charlotte* I liked up to a point. . . ."

In 1969 she went over to London to star with Sir Michael Redgrave in *Connecting Rooms*. In the story she plays a fifty-year-old musician living next door to Redgrave in a dumpy little London boarding house. She attempts to pursue her profession as a concert cellist, while Redgrave has his own problems as a professor who gets ousted from his position when it's discovered he's homosexual. The film suffered distribution problems and never received a general release in the United States. On January 26, 1970, she was seen in "A Touch of Magic" on *To Catch a Thief* as an elderly safecracker. She then teamed with

Ernest Borgnine for *Bunny O'Hare* (1971).

*Madame Sin* (1972) with a budget of $1.7 million was at that time one of the most expensive made-for-TV movies on record. Madame Sin, a Eurasian mastermind à la Fu Manchu (Davis), headquartered in a remote spot in Scotland, is busily conspiring to bring the world to heel, thanks to her own intrepid but evil scientific genius—not to mention a touch of sadism mixed with sardonic cynicism so that she can stay in character. While walking around London's Piccadilly Circus, ex-CIA man Robert Wagner is kidnapped by some very unholy, phony nuns. Bound and gagged, he is trundled off to the Scottish highlands to "Serpentine," sinister Bette's spacious fortress of fear. It turns out that another former agent, Denholm Elliott, had to abduct Wagner "for his own good" after Wagner refused to enlist in the great-mysterious-cause. Before Wagner learns much, his mind almost boggles from all the gadgetry and experimentation he witnesses, such as Sin's main project, a machine guaranteed to create total contentment by erasing nasty old memories and replacing them with new ones. Bette reveals her master plan to Wagner: utilizing his ex-CIA, pre-Watergate, post-Kennedy know-how, he must help her capture a Polaris submarine, which fits into Bette's *grand scheme*.

All should go well, since the Polaris's commander, an old friend of Wagner's, won't suspect a thing, especially once the old reliable memory machine mangles his mind. Wagner is suddenly horrified to learn he's been a bigger dupe than seemed possible—his beautiful girlfriend, Catherine Schell, never got killed, as everyone in the weird castle said she had. What a dope—it was the old atomic shell game all the time. Schell had been secretly incarcerated in the castle's most remote area. Meanwhile, Madame Bette shows him the sights, such as an insidious sonic device, explaining, "Music is food for the hungry soul. Don't you agree, Mr. Lawrence? The world of sound vibrations is relatively unexplored. I find it endlessly rewarding. In art it has the power to soothe, but in science it has the power to *hurt*." About ready to save the girl and bring Bette's evil to an end, Wagner is thwarted horribly; during her imprisonment, Catherine underwent a *mind change*, turning into Mme. Bette's pawn. Catherine poisons Wagner, then sadly waves good-by as she, Bette, and Elliott make their getaway.

The pity of *Sin* is that it appeared late in the day (1972) after James Bond, *The Man from U.N.C.L.E*, and so many others in the mastermind-versus-spy field milked the genre dry. Some of the critical opinions were colder than a hit man's heart, if not hypercritical to a fault. *Films and Filming* uncharitably remarked: "*Madame Sin* is the Women's Lib answer to Ernst Blofeld, Dr. No, and all those other descendants of Jules

Inside her castle headquarters in Scotland, Bette, as the leading woman of evil, operates the controls of her electronic devices in *Madame Sin*, her first motion picture made for television, aired January 15, 1972 on ABC.

Verne's Captain Nemo. . . . Bette Davis has her moments, chief among them the classic delivery of leaden lines which on (her) lips take on a Wildean ring. Otherwise, she is reduced by the limitations of the script to a meticulously orating gargoyle." Richard Combs of BFI's *Monthly Film Bulletin* was more didactic: "The evil mastermind ('a genius, a philosopher, an abstract thinker') has lost most of his mystery and allure since he also turned technocrat and bureaucrat and declined into the bloated comic-strip villains of the Bond films. *Madame Sin* half-heartedly tries to pump some life into the new formula, but the film is defeated by the trite mechanics of the plotting and by the fact that surprisingly little personality is evident behind the mask-like immobility of the Bette Davis role or the occasional 'beast of prey' symbolism that (coauthor and director) David Greene supplies." Greene also made other notable fantasies: *The Shuttered Room* (1966), *Sebastian* (1968), and *Godspell* (1973). *Madame Sin* was first shown in the United States on January 15, 1972, on TV as an *ABC Movie of the Week*, and released theatrically in Europe the following May.

Bette next received word from Universal to appear as a retired lady judge in *The Judge and Jake Wyler*. Projected plans called for this to be another pilot for a possible series, but like so many similar plans, this too was aborted after the initial airing. In the story, she portrayed a very eccentric hypochondriac constantly afraid of germs. This was a two-hour *NBC Movie of the Week*, aired December 2, 1972.

Breezing through a guest spot in March, in a TV special, *Johnny Carson Presents the Sun City Scandals '72*, (singing "Just Like a Man"), she then hopped off to a health spa near San Diego for a much-needed several weeks' rest. During her vacation, Dino De Laurentiis' office called on her with a script titled *Lo Scopone Scientifico* (*The Scientific Cardplayer*, a.k.a. *The Game*). She liked it, and in less than three days set foot in Rome in preparation for production. Though not supernaturally inclined like Pushkin's *The Queen of Spades*,

163

*Scopone* bears some resemblance to it with a black-comedy tone mingled into a socio-humane message. Bette is an elderly, wealthy American, wheelchair-ground and fanatically engrossed with card playing. Joseph Cotten is her constant, timorous companion and partner. Allegorical morality counterpoints much of the action against a background of social problems in an Italian slum setting. In this atmosphere, Bette plays cards and wins. Her main targets are Alberto Sordi and his wife, Silvana Mangano, who provide most of the film's black comedy. Ambition and greed around the card table create suspense—tension heightens in anticipation of huge winnings. Before Bette decides to leave the scene by jet plane, Sordi's strange daughter presents Bette with a parting gift: a cake baked with her own hands and loaded with poison. *Scopone* won highly critical praise in key European situations, and was one of Italy's biggest box-office hits, though the film has not yet received American distribution as of this writing.

Possessive momism was the substance of a TV pilot next on Bette's roster. Titled *Hello Mother, Goodbye*, it co-starred Jimmy Stewart, and was produced by MGM-TV for NBC. Bette was overwhelmed by the friendly vibes created by the MGM people—overhead, spread clear across the studio lot driveway, was a great banner saying "Welcome Bette and Jimmy." The *Hello Mother* pilot was coscripted by Buddy Freeman and Jack Sher, and directed by Peter Hunt, who had also directed the Broadway and film version of *1776*.

On Sunday, February 4, 1973, Bette appeared before a packed audience at New York's Town Hall for a historical occasion: an evening of Bette Davis. The entire program was loaded with warm nostalgic moments plucked out of numerous film clips from her movies. The first one unreeled (from *All About Eve*) brought rapturous cheers from the crowd. The final clip was also from *Eve*, followed by more than an hour of questioning by John Springer, who hosted and produced the event. The audi-ence kept on reacting with such obvious love and admiration that Bette seemed profoundly moved. When it had subsided, she responded with deep affection: "What can I say?" Remembering the event the following year in *Mother Goddam*, she said, "All the blood, sweat, and tears of forty-three years were suddenly worth it for a reception like this."

After being the subject of a delightful roast on *The Dean Martin Show* (September 27, 1973), Bette went into another *ABC Movie of the Week*, titled *Scream, Pretty Peggy*. Direction was by Gordon Hessler, known for other genre productions such as *The Oblong Box, Scream and Scream Again, Cry of the Banshee, Murders in the Rue Morgue*, and *Sinbad's Golden Voyage*. Others in the cast were Sian Barbara Allen and Charles Drake, with Ted Bessell playing Bette's psychopathic son. Never one for investing much depth and substance in any of his films, Hessler was at least competent enough to combine some average feeling for action-suspense with a degree of interesting visual sense.

*Peggy*, though, was hardly even fair Hessler, but considering the scripts' quality, it would have proved trying even for a Franju or De Palma, who have turned even the most routine situations into artistic horror. *Peggy* is little more than an unabashed, turned-around swipe of *Psycho*, coauthored by Jimmy Sangster, whose long association with hardcore genre films would ordinarily belie such execrable rehashing. In this tale, Bette has problems with her son, Ted, who is infatuated with Sian. In the guest house is Ted's mad sister, whom no one has seen in years. Meanwhile, Ted putters away sculpting while Bette seems to be shielding him from some "unmentionable" confrontation with reality. Outcries from the guest house grow in frequency. Tension increases, and Bette grows more concerned. In ninety minutes, though, little else occurs, outside of several audible off-screen quarrels between Ted and his unseen sister. Only toward the end are matters more animated: Ted goes to calm down his sister. A disquieting silence follows—Ted is either

Mrs. Elliott (Bette Davis), the mother of a famous sculptor absorbed in depicting evil—both in his work and in real life—in the *ABC Suspense Movie* titled *Scream, Pretty Peggy*, originally telecast November 24, 1973.

disabled or killed. Sian rushes over to investigate, but Ted is nowhere to be found. Only a vague female form can be seen at the end of the room. It's Ted in drag, as violently mad as they come. On the verge of being murdered, Sian is saved when Bette shoots poor Ted to death. The film is a sheer shameful waste of talent, and other *Psycho* rip-offs have been infinitely better. The film was aired on ABC-TV November 22, 1973.

Finishing one long run of her one-woman lecture-film road tour, Bette began work on *Burnt Offerings*. The film was produced and directed by Dan Curtis, who achieved fame on TV in the late sixties with the daily Gothic soap opera, *Dark Shadows*,

two theatrical spin-offs of the show (one fair, the other poor), unexciting TV adaptations of *The Picture of Dorian Gray* and *Frankenstein*, and an unusually good *Dracula* starring Jack Palance.

*Burnt Offerings* had been more than five weeks in production around San Francisco by early October 1975, and Bette was fidgeting noticeably, upset by what she considered chaotic working conditions. Karen Black turned up pregnant, and the cameraman bungled and ruined the rushes, setting back production two weeks. And the ultimate tragedy: Curtis's daughter committed suicide. Production had to be halted a full week. No one connected with the production could ever remember so many things going wrong on a film. There was also Oliver Reed's carousing—"Oliver Reed comes piling into the hotel at five A.M., and he's on the set at six with the hangover of the world. He fell down a mountainside the other night playing bagpipes," Bette revealed. "I said I'd never do another horror film after *Baby Jane*, and here I am in the biggest horror of them all."

*Burnt Offerings* begins as Black persuades her husband (Reed) to rent an old mansion for the summer from Eileen Heckart and her crippled brother, Burgess Meredith. Karen and Oliver then move in with their son, Lee, twelve, and aunt Bette Davis. The only provision is that Karen prepare meals for the unseen elderly invalid mother of the owners. Karen becomes obsessed with beautifying the place, and Oliver, in the pool with Lee, nearly drowns the child. Bette ages very rapidly and dies after Oliver witnesses an apparition of a ghastly looking chauffeur he had encountered as a youth at his mother's funeral. Oliver tries to leave with Lee, who also survived a gas-filled room. When the pool threatens to engulf Lee, Karen dives in to save him and then goes upstairs to visit the recluse. When Oliver goes searching for his wife, he is horrified to see that Karen has taken on the appearance of the weird old recluse. He then leaps to his death. Lee is also killed as the house crumbles. Owners Heckart and Meredith, who had been dead, rejoice as the house restores itself.

Since Bette gets a hefty flat fee for her services, it really didn't matter that *Burnt* was char-broiled by a few reviewers, with cool box-office results. Most horror buffs believed the film dragged a little, lacking punch here, zap there and a feeling for conflict. One factor, of course, may have been that director Curtis, having sustained a personal tragedy, was working under a terrible strain. *Boxoffice* commented: "Horror is implied and rarely shown in a lengthy (116 minutes) thriller. The title (from Robert Marasco's novel) has no meaning, except in a poetic sense. The film has many effective moments and compact performances from an equally compact cast. While few can ac-

cept Oliver Reed and Karen Black as a typical American married couple, the bizarre situations will engross audiences. Bette Davis makes a welcome return in a too limited part. . . . [It] can be called a thinking person's chiller. . . ." Archer Winsten of *The New York Post* said, "Either you believe a house can have that kind of effect—I mean lethal—or you don't. If you do, the picture can pump up your blood pressure to new highs. If you don't, you'll be thinking you've wasted your money. . . . The best [I] can say is that Bette Davis died horribly in paroxysms worthy of that great actress, that Oliver Reed achieved an athletic and bloody death photographically most spectacular, and that Karen Black can look awfully mean when she wants to. . . ."

Next came NBC-TV's Hallmark production of *The Disappearance of Aimee* (aired in December 1976). Allen Macaulay, who interviewed her for *The Record*, said: "Aimee Semple McPherson is a part that Miss Davis has wanted to play for a long time. But the evangelist was at the peak of her popularity in the thirties, and no studio would touch the story—'The censors would just not have allowed it,' Miss Davis said. So time, in a manner of speaking, has passed her by—but she does get to play the preacher's mother, Minnie 'Ma' Kennedy, who was a lot of offstage help to her daughter's career."

Macauley had first met Bette during the premiere of *Baby Jane* in New York: "[Her] face, incidentally, has changed little in the fourteen years since her near-Oscar performance in *Baby Jane*. . . . It's when the questions touch on her private life that the bars go up. She parried a question on whether she'd marry again with, 'That's the most flattering thing you could say!'

"She lives alone. Period. It's not her life's ambition, but she is reconciled to it: 'I knew for a long time that I'd end up as a lonely old lady,' she said. . . . She has her house to occupy her time. 'I'm a schizo hausfrau,' she said. 'I spend all day cleaning and dusting and washing. But I can't clean a stove,' she said, making vigorous scrubbing motions in the air. 'Once a week a bunch of people come in and clean the house top to bottom.'"

On following weeks, Bette made the rounds plugging *Sister Aimee* with great faith and sincerity, showing up on *Tomorrow* (December 17, 1976) with Tom Snyder, and interviewed the next morning by jocose Gene Shalit, who could make even a funeral oration seem like an opening scene from a Mel Brooks movie:

GENE: Do you ever get weary of living up to what has become a kind of a Bette Davis legend?

BETTE: I don't think you can become a legend until you're in your coffin. But there's a whole new thing today about *living* legends and *dead* legends—so, I'm supposedly one. I think it's terribly important in any way of life to just be yourself. Some people will like you, some people won't.

GENE: A whole generation of impersonators has made a living just doing Bette Davis.

BETTE: The first impersonation was Arthur Blake in *The Letter*. . . .

GENE: Can you impersonate yourself doing that? . . . Show me, okay?

BETTE: Well, it's very simple. All you do first is this with your arm [turns it around pretentiously in a circular motion]—and then you do this [puffing on her cigarette several times]. And then you say, "Pee-tahh!" All you have to do—so simple.

GENE: Now that line, "Peter, come here, I

Oliver Reed, Lee Montgomery, Bette Davis, and Karen Black stand in the main floor of the house with a life all its own in Dan Curtis's *Burnt Offerings*.

want you"—isn't that about what the line is?

BETTE: I always just say, "Peter"—I never said it that way in my life in the first place.

GENE: Well, who is he?

BETTE: I swore I never worked with a character named Peter. Finally, a fan letter came from a woman who said, "You did in a film called *In This Our Life*. The hero, Dennis Morgan, was called Peter." But, no—each impersonator makes it a little more and a little more, so now that's all you have to do.

*Aimee* was aired that evening. It was a crashing two-hour bore. Except for Bette's presence, and a good supporting performance by Barry Brown as a persistent news reporter, the moments seemed to pass like hours. Perhaps an interesting film of the famous evangelist's life could be made, but this wasn't it.

In January 1978, Bette appeared in a two-part NBC-TV movie, *The Dark Secret of Harvest Home*, adapted from the excellent, atmospheric Tom Tryon novel, *Harvest Home*. Bette starred as the Widow Fortune in this tale about a 1978 urban family who move into a house in a secluded New England village and encounter weird local customs. The production, off-beat and anachronistic, attempted to combine a sense of past and present, and is reminiscent of *The Scarlet Letter* and other Nathaniel Hawthorne tales in mood. Garbed in Puritan style, Bette plays a sedate and seemingly benign witch-like leader of a cult that consists of nearly all the town's inhabitants. It was regrettable that NBC's Programming Practices Department radiated its uncreative control, ruining any potential for quality terror and suspense by reducing nearly everything to Nancy Drew proportions. But the dilution is offset to some degree by Tryon's unique premise: a rural farm location complements a supernatural atmosphere and rites; the cult's *outré* ceremonies take place in a bizarre corn-and-wheatfield setting. There is a feeling of some impending evil that will transform the Thanksgiving ambiance into a nightmare, a surreal pagan harvest-home rite rather than the usual Satanism format—a refreshing departure from the cycle of films dealing with unoriginal devil-worshiping and exorcism themes.

The American Film Institute selected Bette Davis as the 1977 recipient of their AFI Life Achievement Award. The four previous recipients of the Award were John Ford, James Cagney, Orson Welles, and William Wyler. In announcing the unanimous decision of the institute's trustees, AFI director George Stevens, Jr., said: "Bette Davis was chosen for her surpassing talent, which has enlivened motion-picture screens for four decades, and for her professional courage and independence, which have marked her career." This is, of course, the least that those representing the world of entertainment can do for one of their greatest.

# Veronica Lake

*H*er real name was Constance Ockleman. Under the name Constance Keane, she appeared in three films in 1939 and 1940. In 1940 producer Arthur Hornblow, Jr., renamed her Veronica Lake, and a star was born.

Constance Ockleman was born November 14, 1919, in Brooklyn, New York. Film books today continue to publish misinformation about her life based on studio-concocted press releases of thirty years ago. The truth is that her mother, Constance Charlotta Trimble, had an Irish immigrant background, and her German-Danish father, Harry Ockleman, was a seaman on the Sun Oil Company's tankers. After her father's death in February 1932, her mother remarried a year later. Her stepfather, *New York Herald Tribune* staff artist Anthony Keane, had lung problems, which resulted in moves to Montreal and Florida, where high school student Connie Keane became a beauty-contest winner.

In 1938 she arrived in Hollywood, where she enrolled in the Bliss Hayden School of Acting on Wilshire Boulevard. Her debut was as an extra in *Sorority House* (1939), followed by a bit in a Leon Erroll RKO three-reeler titled *The Wrong Room* (1939) and *All Women Have Secrets* (1939). During the filming of *Forty Little Mothers* (1940), director Busby Berkeley created her famous trademark, the "peekaboo" hairstyle covering her right eye. As Veronica Lake, on a salary of $75 a week, she was billed seventh in the cast of *I Wanted Wings* (1941). But newspapers and magazines generated such publicity that she was considered a rising star, and her salary was upped to $300 a week. At the insistence of Preston Sturges (despite flak from Paramount), she was cast as The Girl in his *Sullivan's Travels* (1941), now a classic seen continually in revival houses. Marjorie Rosen, in *Popcorn Venus*, writes: "Veronica Lake, petite and frail as the actress who minces about like a waif in hobo clothes in *Sullivan's Travels*, played out peekaboo fantasies with her silky blond pageboy gliding like a curtain over one eye." In the film version of Graham Greene's *This Gun for Hire* (1942), she played nightclub singer and magician Ellen Graham. Her salary was raised again to

169

Veronica Lake and William Holden in *I Wanted Wings* (1941).

Veronica Lake in René Clair's *I Married a Witch* (1942).

$350 a week, and she studied magic from professional magician Jan Grippo. With Alan Ladd making his mark as a psycho killer and horror-actor Laird Cregar in his black, silk pajamas, some critics compared *This Gun for Hire* to Hitchcock. Paramount immediately teamed Ladd and Lake again in a remake of Dashiell Hammett's *The Glass Key* (1942).

Her major fantasy role is Jennifer, the witch in René Clair's *I Married a Witch* (1942). She went to Clair and asked for the part. He refused. She then went to Preston Sturges and asked him to speak to Clair. Sturges did, but Clair still was adamant, claiming she couldn't play comedy. With much reluctance Clair finally cast her. After two weeks of shooting, he apologized, stating, "You are a hell of a good comedienne. I'm sorry."

*I Married a Witch*, based on Thorne Smith's *The Passionate Witch*, follows the adventures of an attractive witch (Lake) who was burned in Puritan times but has returned to Earth. After an initial invisibility, she materializes to torment the descendant (Fredric March) of those who persecuted her. She takes to the air on broomsticks and in automobiles, flying around a clock tower to check out the time.

Eventually, she winds up married to her intended victim after accidentally drinking a love potion.

During filming, March was subjected to Lake's practical jokes. In the scene in which he carries her off, a cameraman helped her rig a forty-pound weight under her dress. The scene was shot three times, with the unsuspecting March breathing heavily and gradually losing his strength. After the last take, the diminutive Lake looked at him, said "Big bones," and walked away. When March learned the truth a few days later, it irritated him to such an extent that he never spoke to her thereafter. According to Lake, the reason for the jokes was that "he treated me like dirt under his talented feet."

Another *I Married a Witch* incident with March is described in her autobiography, *Veronica*: "The shot was medium, showing only the two of us from waist-high. We were into the scene, and he came close to me. He was standing directly in front of the chair. I carefully brought my foot up between his legs. And I moved my foot up and down, each upward movement pushing it ever so slightly into his groin. Pro that he is, he never showed his predicament during the scene. But it wasn't easy for him, and I

delighted in knowing what was going through his mind. Naturally, when the scene was over, he laced into me. I just smiled."

Catherine de la Roche's British Film Institute *René Clair* index contains this summary: "In *I Married a Witch* Veronica Lake's witchery often seems essentially natural and the machinery of modern society absurdly artificial—hence the logic, credibility, and humor of a screenplay in which fantasy and reality are neatly balanced."

The original story of the novel was summed up in the back-cover blurb of the August 1946 Pocket Book reprint of *The Passionate Witch*:

*One Nude Brunette + One Vegetarian = ?* It all began when T. Wallace Wooly, Jr., the soul of propriety and vegetarianism, rescued the nude, strangely unharmed, and smolderingly attractive Jennifer from the burning hotel. It was no time to quibble about how he would look in front-page photos coming down the stairs with a nude girl slung over his shoulders. But when he discovered a week later that he had married the lady, he seriously wished he had shown more discretion and less valor. For there was something extremely unconventional about Jennifer's antics. In fact, Mr. Wooly soon realized that the yellow-eyed Jennifer was a witch —the kind who would leave you in peace only when she lay buried at a crossroads with a stake

TOP: Cecil Kellaway, Veronica Lake, Fredric March, and Robert Benchley in *I Married a Witch*.

BELOW: Fredric March and Veronica in *I Married a Witch*.

through her heart. And the kind who made it necessary for Mr. Wooly to forsake carrot juice and seek peace in some most monumental binges.

After Thorne Smith's death in 1934, the book had been completed by Norman Matson and published by Doubleday in 1941. Following the success of the *Topper* series, also adapted from Smith, *The Passionate Witch* was to provide René Clair the opportunity to recoup after the unsuccessful *Flame of New Orleans* (1940) with Marlene Dietrich, his Hollywood directorial debut. (That film would have a later success in France.) Clair explained, "I was looking for a film to make, any film after the flop I had had. Some people say I gave a chance to Veronica Lake, but the contrary is true: *she* gave me *my* chance, because at that time Veronica Lake was a promising young actress under contract to Paramount. Once I met Preston Sturges, who was a great friend of mine and a top director at Paramount at that time, and I told him the story . . . I just took the first three pages of the whole book. And then Preston said, 'That might be a good part for Veronica Lake because Paramount would like to make a star out of her.' Then we talked together with the head of Paramount. Which is why I say I was put under contract, more or less, by Veronica Lake."

In another interview Clair again emphasized this point (which seems to run contrary to Lake's own account): "Paramount had been trying to find something right for Veronica Lake, who had been receiving lots of publicity, partly because of her beautiful hair. They didn't want an ordinary role for her, and Preston convinced them that *I Married a Witch* was just what they needed. That's what did it. Veronica Lake got me that job. She was a lot more important to Paramount than I was, believe me."

Charles Higham and Joel Greenberg, in *Hollywood in the Forties*, note, "The film is one of Clair's happiest productions, gently satirical, playfully bizarre, and full of a mocking though never malicious wit. Its special magic is (Cecil) Kellaway's pixyish sorceror, revelling in his white magic and bringing the picture to a chuckling close with his tipsy ditty coming from a rocking liquor bottle in a cleverly constructed cage."

In 1943 her career peaked—she won the Army Poll as the most popular actress, and *Life* voted her the top female box-office attraction. She appeared again with Ladd in *Star Spangled Rhythm* (1943). Then came *So Proudly We Hail* (1943), *The Hour Before Dawn* (1944), *Bring on the*

Franchot Tone with Lake in *The Hour Before the Dawn* (1944).

*Girls* (1945), *Out of This World* (1945), *Hold That Blonde* (1945), and *Miss Susie Slagle's* (1945). *Duffy's Tavern* (1945) had both Ladd and Lake in cameos. In *The Blue Dahlia* (1946) she continued her association with both Ladd and the *film noir* genre. The screenplay, written in an alcoholic haze by Raymond Chandler after the film had actually begun shooting, concerns an ex-serviceman (Ladd) who is suspected of murdering his unfaithful wife. In *Ramrod* (1947), she was directed by her second husband, Andre De Toth, who is best remembered as the director of the first major studio 3-D horror film, *House of Wax* (1953). Another film with Ladd, *Saigon* (1947), was followed by *Variety Girl* (1947), *The Sainted Sisters* (1948), *Isn't It Romantic?* (1949), *Slattery's Hurricane* (1949), and *Stronghold* (1951).

In 1951 she and De Toth filed for bankruptcy after their home was seized.

The great screen team of Ladd and Lake, seen here with Luther Adler in *Saigon* (1947). The actress was teamed with Alan Ladd for a total of eight films.

They owed $60,000 in back taxes. The couple separated, and, although scripts were being offered to her at this time (contrary to some written accounts), Veronica Lake walked out on Hollywood. "I realized I really didn't want to go back through the grind of playing sexy sirens in grade-B thrillers all for the silk purses of the studio management."

In the three months that followed she lived in total isolation (except for a mule) in a cabin on St. George Mountain in the Sierras. At the end of this period she moved to New York. Just before boarding the plane, she turned and delivered her good-by to the cinema capital: "The hell with you, Hollywood, and fuck you too."

Living in Greenwich Village with her children, she began a new career in theatre and live television. Her TV credits between 1950 to 1954 include "Beware This Woman" on NBC's horror-thriller anthology, *Lights Out* (December 4, 1950); "Flight Overdue" on ABC's science-fiction show *Tales of Tomorrow* (3/28/52); and "Gramercy Ghost" on *Broadway Television Theatre* (1/4/54.) Her work in theatre in the fifties included touring in *Peter Pan* in the title role.

A broken ankle in 1959 kept her out of work through 1960 and 1961—while medical bills piled up. Even producers of summer stock began to forget about her. She took a job pasting felt flowers on lingerie hangers in a south Broadway factory. (Others who have held this job refer to the place as "The Flower Factory.") At this point she "felt I'd outlived my stay with friends," and she moved into the Martha Washington Hotel on East 29th Street, where she took a job as barmaid in the hotel bar to pay the rent. Although she worked there only for four months, *The New York Post* discovered her there, and ran the item as an important story. It was

173

A throat-clutching moment from *Isn't It Romantic?* (1948), in which Veronica Lake appeared with Mona Freeman, Billy De Wolfe (at center), and Mary Hatcher.

headlined in papers all over the world, but she had no use for anyone's pity, simply stating, "I really enjoyed that job. Sure, I needed the money. But I liked the people there. . . ." In 1963 she worked as a waitress in a Greenwich Village cafe. Also in the early sixties she hosted the *Festival of Stars* Saturday night movie series on WJZ-TV in Baltimore. One film in this series was *I Married a Witch*, which Lake introduced with much enthusiasm and nostalgia.

The role of Charlie the ghost in a 1965 Miami production of *Goodbye, Charlie* eventually led to a permanent move to Florida. In 1967 she repeated the role in Plymouth, Massachusetts. In the late sixties, after a sixteen-year absence, she returned to films—with two pictures in the horror-thriller genre. As she puts it, "Some day soon, perhaps on your local television station during their daily horror-film show, you'll be able to see my two latest films. Fortunately, I did not have to return to Hollywood to make these films. They were

produced in Canada and Florida, and, in vogue with today's trend of putting older stars in horror movies, both these efforts are designed to turn your knuckles white, set your heart pounding, and cause your girlfriend to cuddle up close in sheer terror." The first is the low-budget *Footsteps in the Snow* (1967), made in Montreal, for which she received $10,000 plus expenses.

This was followed by the 72-minute *Flesh Feast* (also titled *Time Is Terror*), filmed in Florida and released by Cine World (Viking International) in 1970. Lake, in addition to starring and co-producing (with Brad F. Grinter), apparently also took part in the scripting (which is credited to Grinter and Thomas Casey). In her autobiography she referred to herself as the "titular producer and director." At a cost of $20,000, 130,000 feet of 35mm in color was shot but, according to Lake, there were editing problems because the film's first director refused to shoot master shots. The story began at the Miami airport with the

174

murder of a reporter who had been following Carl Schuman back from South America. Schuman gets in touch with Dr. Elaine Frederick (Lake), who has checked out of a mental institution in order to perfect her new youth restoration process involving the use of flesh-eating maggots. Kristine, a detective posing as a student nurse, supplies the doctor with corpses for the experiments. Schuman arrives with an important patient who is strapped to the table. In the final scene this patient is revealed to be none other than Adolf Hitler. He wants to return to Germany but is worried about being recognized. Dr. Frederick states that Hitler was the cause of the torture and murder of her mother during World War II. She then pours the maggots all over him, while laughing maniacally at his pain as the film ends. *Boxoffice* reviewed, "Veronica Lake returns to the screen after an absence of 19 years . . . Miss Lake has shed her long hair and is an attractive, mature woman . . . Her new vehicle has a minimum of gore and drags throughout, although there is a unique plot twist and revelation at the end. While this cannot qualify as a class horror film . . . it is fine for horror shows and Friday the 13th bookings. Its catchy title and the return of Miss Lake could generate interest." Others in the cast were Phil Philbin, Heather Hughes, Martha Mischon, Yanka Mann, Dian Wilhite, and Chris Martell.

Makeup and maggots were provided by the Florida monster-maker Douglas Blake Hobart. In an unpublished manuscript, Fred Olen Ray, who has worked on several Florida productions, offered this account of Hobart's procedures: "The maggots were raised in Doug's backyard by leaving open for one day a garbage can with five pounds of hamburger in it. This was covered with a screen. Soon the stars of the film were born. The most difficult obstacle Doug encountered on *Flesh Feast* was the placing of live maggots on the faces of the various actors. The fact that they were a bit squeamish is an understatement. Doug soon qualmed fears by taking an inventory check on which maggots went here or there—and he made sure to get the right number back! Additional maggots were provided by Uncle Ben's Converted Rice, although I always thought that went against the grain."

In the early seventies Lake made a nostalgic and striking appearance on *The Dick Cavett Show*, evoking extended applause for her casual "take-it-or-leave-it" attitude. It was the first time some viewers had seen or heard of her in decades. Her autobiography (with Donald Bain) was published by Citadel in 1971, followed by a Bantam paperback edition in January 1972. She died in 1973.

Richard Widmark and Veronica Lake in *Slattery's Hurricane* (1949).

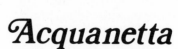

$E$ven if she could never attain superstar status, there is no question that Burnu "Acquanetta" Davenport possessed all the physical endowments that brought fame and fortune to other screen beauties. Hindsight now makes it obvious that her sensuous charm and earthy looks were not quite in vogue in an era that spawned actresses in the mold of Hedy Lamarr, Myrna Loy, Loretta Young, and other "high society" types. For over a generation Hollywood had invested much time and money creating an illusion of unmolestable virginity. Audiences flocked to theatres in overwhelming numbers, and few filmmakers cared to be *too daring* about production themes or most star personalities; nylon-hosed Betty Grable and satin-gowned Rita Hayworth were about as *far* as they went. And, of course, Mae West's libidinous style of acting and delivery was almost always a taboo subject. Not until television became a serious, viable entity did the major studios force themselves into changing to avoid perishing.

Whether Acquanetta was a misfit by being a "type" who was born too soon or a victim of poor management, her career was notably brief, ending as quickly as it started, puzzling her many new fans in the bargain.

Coming into Hollywood almost out of nowhere, she gained some recognition after producer Walter Wanger cast a friendly eye on her in a bit part in his production of *Arabian Nights* (1942)—she appeared as one of the harem girls. Even before the film's release, Universal liked what they saw in private screenings and signed her to a contract. However, her stunning looks were still far above her limited acting ability; her background had been primarily in modeling. Early reports stated that she commanded some of the highest modeling fees in New York before leaving for Hollywood.

As various reports indicated, stories of Acquanetta's origin often conflicted, and one journalist observed, "Burnu's origins are veiled in mystery." This was a valid observation—varying stories and publicity releases stated she was (a) a torrid Latin temptress from Venezuela; (b) originally born near a reservation of Arapaho Indian

Acquanetta and ape in a posed publicity shot of a sequence not to be found in *Captive Wild Woman*.

parents in Ozone near Cheyenne, Wyoming, in 1920; (c) from a Pennsylvania mining town. Sooner or later she would good-naturedly admit in certain interviews—especially to some astute, prying interviewers—that some of the so-called publicity and stories about her, such as her exotic Venezuelan background and the thick Spanish accent that she soon dropped, were sheer fabrication, largely from her own vivid imagination. Beyond a certain point, however, she was quite reluctant to speak of her past and would change the subject.

Soon after Wanger discovered her, her first major role was in Universal's *Captive Wild Woman* (1943), co-starring with John Carradine, Evelyn Ankers, and Milburn Stone; the director was Edward Dmytryk. When Ankers realizes her sister is ailing from some glandular disorder, she takes her to Dr. Carradine, whose experience is profound in other areas as well. Ankers invites Carradine to attend the circus, where her fiancé, Stone, runs a sensational wild-animal act. In one of the cages lives Cheela, a large female ape, who, needless to say,

The ape about to be transformed into Acquanetta by mad doctor John Carradine in *Captive Wild Woman.*

has special affection for Stone—a crush on him, so to speak. Carradine connives to kidnap the big ape. His great plan is to turn the ape into human form by some means or another—via gland transplants and injections, as long as the script's credibility could last. His nurse, though, threatens to expose him, and Carradine kills her. Later, he transplants the nurse's brain into Cheela the ape, who soon starts to look like Acquanetta. Pleased nearly to the point of sanity, Carradine takes Cheela (now in fetching femme form) back to the circus to see how well she mingles with humans. At home in familiar surroundings, Acquanetta amazes everyone by mystically placating some excitable beasts. Such phenomenal

ability being quite rare, she is hired by the management as an animal trainer of sorts. Eyeing Evelyn Ankers accompanying her fiancé Stone, however, arouses the green-eyed monster of jealousy in her—in this case, it's the ape of wrath. And, as all fantasy film buffs know all too well, certain creatures of ambivalent character should never lose their tempers, since it signals the last reel before "The End." That night she tries to kill Ankers, but is interrupted and kills another woman before fleeing. Reverting to apehood, Acquanetta is taken in tow by Carradine for rehabilitation and resumes human form. By now Ankers realizes Cheela and Acquanetta are one and the same; but Ankers is in more danger

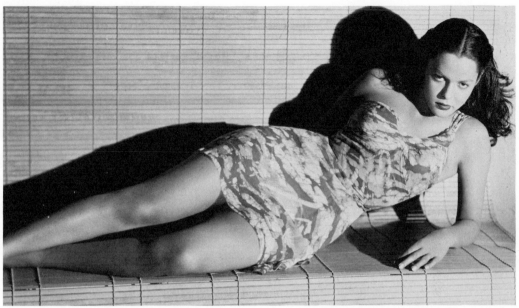

An alluring Acquanetta in a studio pinup shot from *Jungle Woman* (1944).

from Dr. Carradine, who now wishes to experiment on her in his lab. Cheela turns heroic in a crushing death struggle with Carradine, saving Ankers' life and then rushing to the circus just in time to stop a lion from killing her true love, Milburn Stone. She's shot, however, by a cop who misconstrues the ferocious-looking ape's honest intentions.

Around the same time, during the spring of 1943, Acquanetta was also seen in a silly little papier-mâché island-jungle tale, *Rhythm of the Islands*. In this was a fine cast starring Allan Jones (in sad decline since *The Great Victor Herbert* and *The Boys from Syracuse*) singing with lovely Jane Frazee, attended by Andy Devine and Ernest Truex as colorful characters and comedy relief. Acquanetta's true love this time is lovable, fumbling, porcine Devine— but he doesn't know his love may bring trouble. Her father is king of the cannibals, and Andy looks like very attractive soup stock. Just in time, Acqua intervenes, saving Andy from the kettle in this small-budget potboiler.

Meanwhile, *Captive Wild Woman*'s good reviews encouraged Universal to create a sequel. With *Jungle Woman* (1944),

Acqua resumed her ape woman role once more, becoming truly the first and, apparently, only film-horror female in history to become identified with an *established* monster character, as Karloff and Lugosi were identified with the Frankenstein Monster and Dracula, respectively.

Acquanetta in her famous metamorphosis in *Captive Wild Woman*.

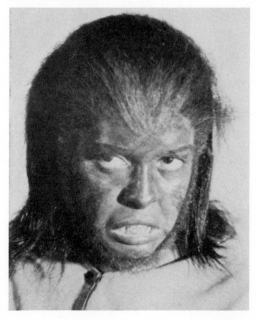

Carrying on where *Jungle Captive* left off, J. Carrol Naish (as a doctor) admits during a coroner's inquest to having killed Acqua, whose body has been found on the grounds of his sanatorium. Despite prodding by district attorney Douglas Dumbrille, Naish at first refuses to testify in his own defense, but the coroner eventually persuades him. A strange account unfolds through flashbacks and is corroborated by animal-trainer Milburn Stone and Evelyn Ankers, who is now his wife. Naish relates that Acqua was a homicidal human of super strength, changed from gorilla to human form through glandular transplants and delicate surgery. Acqua tries to kill Dr. Naish's daughter out of jealousy (basically the same story as in *Jungle Captive*, but reprised slightly differently); Naish tries to recontrol Acqua, but kills the ape woman with an overdose of adrenalin. When they reexamine Acqua's body in the morgue, it proves the doctor's story; the body has half reverted into a gorilla.

Even though *Jungle Woman* is hardly more than a thinly disguised rewrite job, it's a pleasant and compact time-waster. As with the majority of such low-budgeters, it ran only an hour, as had its predecessor; Acqua plays her part without any lines, just as she did in her previous ape role. The studio was fully aware of her physical attributes as well as her dramatic limitations that they had hoped she would eventually overcome.

She next had a supporting role as an artist's model in *Dead Man's Eyes* (Universal, 1944), starring Lon Chaney as the artist in love with Jean Parker. Lon loses his sight because Acqua blinded him with acid in a jealous fit. His doctor reveals that vision can be restored by transplanting corneas from a dead man's eyes. Jean Parker's father forthwith makes out a will bequeathing his eyes to Lon. Out of guilt and remorse, Acqua becomes Lon's nurse; she's also loved by Paul Kelly, a family friend. All are suddenly shocked to discover that someone has murdered Jean's father; Lon is an obvious suspect because he was the only one near when it happened. Detective Thomas Gomez steps in about the time Lon undergoes the corneal transplant. Lon pretends he's still blind, though the operation was successful. When Acqua is about to reveal that Kelly is the murderer, Kelly kills her. Carrying out his blind man's game, Lon traps Kelly, who is arrested just before he has a chance to kill Lon.

A disquieting hiatus developed in Acquanetta's career. Universal didn't seem interested in extending any further offers. Then, RKO put her under contract for a starring role in one of their most important films for 1946: *Tarzan and the Leopard Woman*.

The Tarzan films (starring Johnny Weissmuller) had been creaking badly for several years; originally starting on a very high, almost classical level, with *Tarzan the Ape Man* (1932), the series went on a gradual decline in the early forties. Though *some* segments shone brightly as topnotch adventure fare, they did little to avoid a "kiddy matinee" look; when it began to appear that Johnny Sheffield as Boy and Cheetah the Chimp were interminably involved in jungle picnics, jungle high jinks, and jungle bungling, the series seemed in danger of dying from terminal idiocy. Even while they declined in quality, and Cheetah threatened to upstage Weissmuller as a star, the above-average Tarzans showed there was yet some hope of life left.

*Tarzan and the Leopard Woman* (1946) was the elixir the series badly needed during its lowest period. Its director was Kurt Neumann (1908–1958), thirty-eight years old at the time, with an erratic and undistinguished record of mostly forgettable el cheapos behind him. He was now developing his talents and proving much of the potential he would demonstrate years later with such genre gems as *Rocketship X-M* (1950, brilliantly scored by Ferde Grofé), and *The Fly* (1958), which he also scripted and produced.

Acquanetta's first and only starring role in a big-budget production received favorable reactions from audiences and critics. Gabe Essoe, in his book *Tarzan of the Movies* (Citadel, 1968), says: ". . . Neumann's

Johnny Weissmuller, Johnny Sheffield, and Acquanetta are seen in this ad for the 1946 *Tarzan and the Leopard Woman.*

direction worked the situations in Carroll Young's original script to full advantage. The introduction of a female menace, Lea (Acquanetta), high priestess of the leopard cult, was all to the good. Reminiscent of Queen La of Opar, she seemed an extension of actual Burroughsiana."

Rich with adventure and characterizations, *Leopard Woman* does well in creating a semilost civilization atmosphere. There are also several fine villains played by veteran heavies Edgar Barrier and Anthony Caruso. The story tells of terrorism spread by a resurgent cult of leopard men, led by priestess Acquanetta, and goaded by the evil Barrier and Caruso, who fear civilization's inroads will wrest from them their control over the people. Dressed in leopard skins, armed with deadly steel claws and knives, the Leopard Men spread fear all around. Involved in all this is Tommy Cook (as Acqua's younger brother and about Boy's age), a forties juvenile who is best remembered for unsympathetic, often vicious, portrayals. Cook leaves the Leopard Men's city and seeks out Tarzan's home. He tries to ingratiate himself with Tarzan's family in order to slay them in some unguarded moment. Doing her best to inspire her special killer minions to carry out orders, assisted by her evil mentors, Acqua pontificates ceremoniously during unholy services. Cook's attempt to hurt Boy and kill Jane is aborted by Tarzan, and he flees back home. Tarzan tries to strike back in revenge but falls into a well-laid trap and becomes a prisoner to be offered later to the leopard god. Who should step in to undo Tarzan's bonds and indirectly aid in bringing an end to evil, but good old Cheetah. Despite this slight recidivistic quality (mainly because producer Sol Lesser wanted Cheetah to *star* in all his Tarzans), the film got fine notices in trade publications, e.g., *Variety*: "There isn't a dull moment in it," and the *Hollywood Reporter*: "One of the best adventures of the jungle man."

*Tarzan and the Leopard Woman* may be regarded as Acqua's last bid for fame before drifting practically overnight into obscurity. Occasionally she appeared in small supporting roles that were hardly more than walk-on cameos. In *Callaway Went Thataway* (1951), her role was so small that most reviews do not count her in the cast credits; the film is memorable, however, as one of the best comedies (along with the 1950 *Champagne for Caesar*) about TV in the early fifties. In *Lost Continent*, Cesar Romero and a rocket scientist team up and lead a crew to trace an experimental rocket loaded with valuable data; the rocket has disappeared on a "Lost World"-type plateau in a remote South Seas island. The action and story are good for an otherwise familiar story of this type—Acqua is a native girl who leads Romero and his group. Amid spliced-in footage of prehistoric monster scenes from *One Million B.C.* (1940), they all battle their way bravely; the island erupts into a volcanic holocaust, while Romero and those left alive, along with Acqua, paddle off in a canoe into the sunset.

There can never be any doubt that Acqua's acting experience and ability were virtually nil at the start of her film career— and the reason why they gave her no lines but told her to play her role mute in her two films as Cheela the ape woman. But neither can it be denied that throughout film history there were hordes of raw, untrained ingenues who in the long run learned their craft and matured into box-office superstars, or who could at least derive long-term livelihoods as secondary luminaries. Whatever the reason, Acquanetta's sudden fade-out at age twenty-six is as strange as it is saddening.

If it is of any consolation, she didn't suffer from any lack of personal attention. In 1945 she formed a romantic liaison with wealthy Mexico City manufacturer Ludwig Bashuck. Five years later, Burnu Davenport (or Mildred Davenport as per a *New York Times* report) filed suit for divorce, asking for the custody of their five-year-old son, Sergio. The suit fell through when Bashuck countercharged that their marriage was not legal. On March 24, 1951, the press announced her marriage to the well-known painter-designer, sixty-eight-year-old Henry Clive. Having had a penchant for show-biz beauties, Clive had been previously married to Ziegfeld Follies star Helen Cunningham and to actress Jean Williams. In the same year, Acqua divorced Clive on grounds of incompatibility.

Personal tragedy visited Acqua in 1952, when Sergio died. When the insurance company refused to pay off on his life insurance policy, she won out after a stiff court battle.

Through the years she made several comebacks around the film capital, and then hosted a TV and radio show on a local Arizona channel representing her current husband's Lincoln-Mercury dealership. "She has four sons by her present marriage," states Richard Lamparski in the *2nd Annual Whatever Became of . . . ?* (Bantam, 1977), and she "does not smoke or drink alcohol, tea or coffee. On weekends she and her husband fly their own plane to San Diego, where they keep a yacht that will sleep twenty-seven."

BELOW: Jungle heroines have continued to vine-swing through film history from the earliest days. *Left to right*: Enid Markey played the first Jane opposite Elmo Lincoln in *Romance of Tarzan* (1918). Frances Gifford was the jungle girl in the 1940 *Jungle Girl* serial. Mia Farrow's mother, Maureen O'Sullivan, was the most famous Jane of the Tarzan series. In *Perils of Nyoka* (1942) Lorna Gray befriended an ape played by Emile Van-Horne. (In later years VanHorne had a beauty-and-the-beast nightclub act until his ape costume was stolen, leading to unemployment and an eviction from his apartment in Pensacola, Florida. He then took to living in the streets in New Orleans' French Quarter while doing bit roles in films shot on location in New Orleans, such as *Hotel*. He died in the late sixties in New Orleans Charity Hospital.) Natives manhandle Lois Hall in *Daughter of the Jungle* (1949). Last picture in this strip shows Eurasian actress Mei Chen in *Luana* (1968).

ABOVE: Explorers found Acquanetta on a dinosaur-ridden plateau in Robert Lippert's *Lost Continent* (1951).

# Anne Gwynne

Anne Gwynne, one of the leading Scream Queens of the forties, was born December 10, 1918, in Waco, Texas. Her real name is Marguerite Gwynne Trice. After graduating from San Antonio High School, she went to Columbia, Missouri, where she enrolled in Stephens College, a school with a noted drama department. After her freshman year she accompanied her father to a Los Angeles convention, where his position with Catalina Swimwear led to work for her as a swimsuit model. Standing 5′ 5″, weighing 117 pounds, and topped off by her flaming red hair, she found no difficulty getting roles in West Coast theatrical productions. Her stage credits include *The Colonel's Lady, Stage Door,* and *Inside Story.*

In June, 1939, after a thirty-minute interview, she was signed to a Universal contract with a beginning salary of seventy-five dollars a week. She debuted in *Charlie McCarthy, Detective* (1939), followed by *Unexpected Father* (1939), *Sandy Takes a Bow* (1939), and the mystery *Honeymoon Deferred* (1940). Her career in horror began in 1940 when she was fifth-billed in

Arthur Lubin's *Black Friday* with Boris Karloff, Bela Lugosi, Stanley Ridges, Anne Nagel, James Craig, Jack Mulhall, and Paul Fix. Written by Curt Siodmak and Eric Taylor, this seventy-minute gangster-science thriller concerned a criminal's brain transplanted by Karloff into the head of auto-accident-victim Ridges; all efforts to save Ridges's life go awry when the brain's evil tendencies start to surface. Gwynne then got a respite from horror with roles in *Sandy Is a Lady* (1940), *Spring Parade* (1940), and *Give Us Wings* (1940).

She played opposite Buster Crabbe in Universal's twelve-chapter serial, *Flash Gordon Conquers the Universe* (1940), directed by Ford Beebe and Ray Taylor. When Ming the Merciless (Charles Middleton) starts spreading the Plague of the Purple Death, Flash (Crabbe), Dale (Carol Hughes), and Dr. Zarkov (Frank Shannon) head for the planet Mongo. Joined by Prince Barin (Roland Drew) and Aura (Shirley Deane), they launch an attack on Ming's palace and then take off for Frigia in hopes of mining Polante, an antidote for the Purple Death Plague. Dale and

Dr. Zarkov are captured by Torch (Don Rowan), Thong (Victor Zimmerman), and Sonja (Anne Gwynne). Confronted with an electrical death ray, Flash nevertheless manages to rescue Dale and Zarkov before squelching Ming's power-mad dreams by destroying the emperor's stronghold with a solarite explosion. Based on the Alex Raymond comic strip, this was the last of the three *Flash Gordon* serials.

In 1941 Anne Gwynne made *Nice Girl*, *Washington Melodrama*, *Tight Shoes*, and *Mob Town*. Her contribution to horror in that year was *The Black Cat*, a film that has no connection with the classic Edgar G. Ulmer-directed *Black Cat* of 1934, even though Bela Lugosi is in both. The 1941 title, directed by Albert S. Rogell, is yet another in the overworked reading-of-the-will-in-the-creepy-mansion genre. Gwynne was sixth-billed in the cast of Basil Rathbone, Hugh Herbert, Broderick Crawford, Lugosi, Gale Sondergaard, Alan Ladd, Gladys Cooper, and Claire Dodd.

The fan magazine, *Hollywood Who's Who for 1942*, wrote about her: "Nimbly fingers a violin and piano and wields a bowling ball and tennis racket right out of this world. Reads everything she can lay her hands on. Cherishes a 125-year-old Bible and Italian earbobs above all else— save her career." Her films that year were *Jail House Blues*, *Ride 'Em Cowboy*, *Broadway*, *Men of Texas*, and *Sin Town*. *The Strange Case of Dr. Rx* (1942) was another brain transplant affair—this time the idea is

Anne Gwynne (*center*) in *Flash Gordon Conquers the Universe* (1940).

to put the brain into the head of a gorilla. William Nigh directed the Clarence Upson Young screenplay. Gwynne had the female lead in the cast of Patric Knowles, Lionel Atwill, Paul Cavanagh, Leyland Hodgson, Mantan Moreland, Samuel S. Hinds, and Shemp Howard.

In 1943 she made *Frontier Badmen* (a Western with Lon Chaney, Jr.), *We've Never Been Licked,* and *Top Man.* After *Ladies Courageous* (1944), she played opposite Lon Chaney, Jr., in *Weird Woman,* adapted by W. Scott Darling with a Brenda Weisburg screenplay, based on Fritz Leiber's novel *Conjure Wife.* College professor Chaney suspects his new bride (Gwynne) of witchcraft, something she picked up from the natives during her childhood on a South Sea island. This was the second in Universal's *Inner Sanctum* series, a tie-in with the *Inner Sanctum* mystery novels and the *Inner Sanctum* horror-mystery-thriller

ZOOMING OFF THE EARTH!

New Thrills...
New Marvels
New Wonders

FLASH GORDON
CONQUERS THE UNIVERSE

with LARRY "Buster" CRABBE
as FLASH GORDON
CAROL HUGHES as Dale Arden
ANNE GWYNNE as Sonja
CHARLES MIDDLETON as Emperor Ming
FRANK SHANNON as Dr. Zarkov

12 NEW DYNAMIC EPISODES

radio program that had debuted on January 7, 1941. Also in the cast of *Weird Woman* were Evelyn Ankers and Lois Collier—who have both maintained friendships with Gwynne until the present day. Others in the cast were Ralph Morgan, Elizabeth Russell, Elisabeth Risdon, Kay Harding, and Harry Hayden. Special effects were by John P. Fulton, and Paul Sawtell was the music director. Sixteen years later Leiber's novel was adapted for television under its original title as part of NBC's *Moment of Fear* series, airing July 8, 1960. The following year saw yet another interpretation in the British-made *Burn Witch, Burn,* starring Janet Blair and Peter Wyngarde. With the Charles Beaumont/Richard Matheson/George Baxt screenplay retaining much of the flavor of Leiber's original story, this is easily the best of the three versions. Leiber did not publish another supernatural-horror novel until 1977, but his genuinely frightening *Our Lady of Darkness,* set in contemporary San Francisco, is larded with so much occult terror that it seems obviously destined for future filmic treatment.

In *Murder in the Blue Room* (1944), about a mysterious room with various ghosts and hidden passageways, Gwynne headed a cast of Donald Cook, John Litel, Grace McDonald, Betty Kean, June Preissler, Regis Toomey, and Emmett Vogan. Leslie Goodwin directed the I.A.L. Diamond-Stanley Davis screenplay. The sixty-minute programmer was based on Erich Philippi's novel, *Secret of the Blue Room,* which had been filmed twice previously by Universal—first as *Secrets of the Blue Room* (1933) with Paul Lukas, Lionel Atwill, Edward Arnold, and Gloria Stuart. A remake in 1938, *The Missing Guest,* starred Paul Kelly, Constance Moore, and William Lundigan. Of the three versions, the earliest stands out today, mainly due to a quaint early thirties naïveté that permeates the production and some hyperactive performances that attempt to transcend the static set-ups and staginess.

In Universal's *House of Frankenstein* (1944), Gwynne found herself smack dab in the middle of *all* the monsters—Dracula

(John Carradine), the Wolfman (Lon Chaney, Jr.), the Frankenstein monster (Glenn Strange), a "mad doctor" (Boris Karloff), Professor Bruno Lampini (George Zucco) and his Chamber of Horrors, and a psycho hunchback (J. Carrol Naish). The title is misleading, for there are no members of the Frankenstein family in this sixth semisequel, directed by Erle C. Kenton from an Edward T. Lowe screenplay based on a Curt Siodmak story. Others in the cast are Peter Coe, Lionel Atwill, Frank Reicher, Elena Verdugo, Sig Rumann, Philip van Zandt, Julius Tannen, Olaf Hytten, Brandon Hurst, Dick Dickinson, Charles Miller, George Lynn, Michael Mark, Belle Mitchell, and Eddie Cobb.

That same year Anne appeared in ads, clad in shorts and holding a gigantic bottle of Royal Crown Cola, giving the soft drink her enthusiastic endorsement: "Royal Crown Cola is tops! I know because I took the famous cola taste-test. I sampled leading colas in paper cups and found Royal Crown Cola best-tasting. When it comes to flavor, Royal Crown Cola is certainly in a class by itself!"

In 1945 Gwynne married a theatrical attorney, and her friend Evelyn Ankers was the bridesmaid. In *The Glass Alibi* (1946), with a reporter attempting to pull off the perfect crime, she starred with Paul Kelly and Douglas Fowley. Monogram's *Fear* (1946), with Peter Cookson, Warren William, and Gwynne, was an updating of Dostoyevsky's *Crime and Punishment* with an impoverished medical student beating a professor to death. In Republic's *The Ghost Goes Wild* (1947) Gwynne and James Ellison headed a cast of Edward Everett Horton, Grant Withers, Lloyd Corrigan, and Jonathan Hale in a Randall Faye and Taylor Caven screenplay based on a story by Faye. Directed by George Blair, the horror-comedy tells of a real ghost that intervenes when an artist-turned-spiritualist sets up a fake seance. Joseph Dubin and Morton Scott did the music score.

In RKO's *Dick Tracy Meets Gruesome* (1947), based on the Chester Gould comic strip, Gwynne held down the female lead while Boris Karloff dignified the burlesque by giving the famous one-and-a-half-dimensional cop (Ralph Byrd) a hard time with instant paralysis bombs. Robertson White and Eric Taylor wrote the screenplay from a story by William H. Giaffis and Robert E. Kent. John Rawlins directed, and the special effects were by Russell A. Cully. Others in the cast were Howard Ashley,

Anne Gwynne in *Weird Woman* (1944).

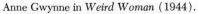

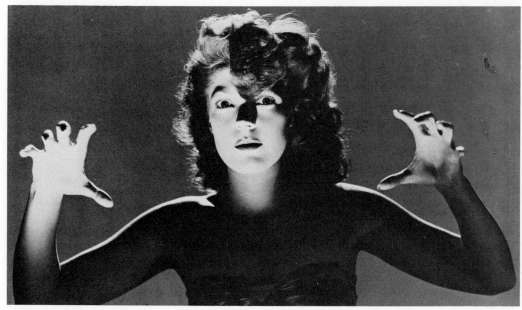

ABOVE: *House of Frankenstein* (1944). John Carradine, as Count Dracula, has Anne Gwynne hypnotized by his ring. His intentions are to make her Mme. Dracula.

June Clayworth, and Milton Parsons. There had been several earlier *Dick Tracy* Republic serials—*Dick Tracy* (1936), *Dick Tracy vs. Crime, Inc.* (1941), and *Dick Tracy's G-Men* (1939). All three starred Ralph Byrd, and the lead actress of the last-named was Phyllis Isley—none other than Jennifer Jones before she became Jennifer Jones.

Gwynne then appeared in *Enchanted Valley* (1948), *Panhandle* (1948), *Arson, Inc.* (1949), *Blazing Sun* (1950), *Call of the Klondike* (1951), and *Breakdown* (1952). *Meteor Monster* (1957), also titled *Teenage Monster*, stars Gwynne in a Ray Buffum screenplay about a boy who gets a full dosage of rays from a meteor. When puberty arrives, he not only grows more

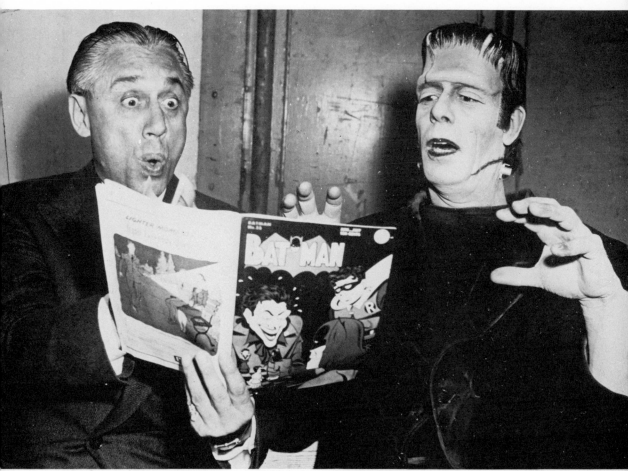

On the set of *House of Frankenstein*: Ole Olsen (of *Hellzapoppin* fame) discusses real horrors as he attempts to explain the business of comic-book distribution to The Monster (Glenn Strange).

hair than is the adolescent norm, but he turns into a monstrous psychotic killer. What's a mother to do? Jacques Marquette produced and directed with music by Walter Green. Gilbert Perkins played the monster, and others in the cast were Gloria Castillo, Stuart Wade, Steven Parker, Charles Courtney, Gaybe Mooradian and Frank Davis.

Widowed in 1965, Anne Gwynne drifted away from film acting and into secretarial work but emerged for a bit in *Adam at 6 AM* (1970). Today, she lives alone in the San Fernando Valley.

RIGHT: Anne's co-stars in *Dick Tracy Meets Gruesome* (1947): Skelton Knaggs, Boris Karloff, and Lex Barker.

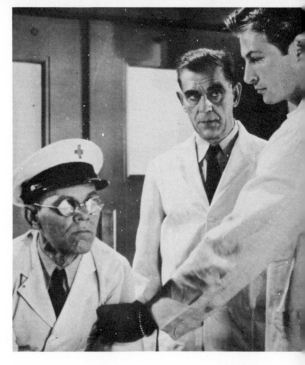

# Shelley Winters

Shirley Schrift was born August 18, 1922, in St. Louis, Missouri, where her father, Jonas, was a tailor's cutter. Her mother, Rose Winter Schrift, had performed with the St. Louis Municipal Opera Company before her marriage. At the age of four, young Shirley made her debut—walking on stage unannounced to sing "Short'nin' Bread" at a St. Louis theatre amateur night. The family moved to Jamaica, Long Island, and, when Shirley was ten, they moved to Brooklyn. In high school she appeared as Katisha in a production of *The Mikado*.

In the garment district she spotted a notice for a production of *Pins and Needles* being staged by the International Ladies' Garment Workers' Union. Lacking an Actors' Equity card, she was turned away, but shortly afterward she began acting lessons in the evening at the Drama Workshop of the New School for Social Research. Later she studied with Elia Kazan at the Actor's Studio, and, in Hollywood, with Michael Chekhov and Charles Laughton.

Reflecting on her high school days as a salesgirl, Winters recalled, "I worked in a Woolworth's store on Chestnut Street in Brooklyn, when I was going to Thomas Jefferson High School, from one to ten every night—in the Christmas bulb department. And also the hardware department— because I wasn't pretty enough to be in candy. The pretty girls they put up front in the candy. . . . When I worked in the five-and-ten, I was about fourteen or fifteen. They were paying us very little, and they were selling German bulbs. And it was the beginning of World War Two. So I organized the kids, and every time they sold one, they broke one. And before they could fire me, I called a strike. I really did. And then once we had the strike, I didn't know what you did, so I looked up in the Yellow Pages the CIO-AFL. I was trying to find out what you did once you were out on strike. They came, and they argued the thing. They settled the strike, and gave them more money and unionized it, but they had one condition to settle the strike—I had to go. The union wasn't going to do it, but by that time I was a model. And I was going to dramatic school, so I said, 'Okay.' "

Six months before her high school graduation in 1939 she began modeling, changing her name to Shelley Winter (without the "s") by combining the name of her favorite poet with her mother's maiden name. She later claimed that she made the name "Shelley" fashionable as a female first name, a claim confirmed by a recent study on the popularity and trends in given names.

In the summer of 1939 she worked in summer stock, earning ten dollars a week. That fall she became a chorus girl at the nightclub La Conga, later recalling, "I was probably the world's worst chorus girl." Spending much of her time waiting in offices around Broadway, she eventually landed a role in *Conquest* in April, which closed during its Delaware tryouts. Her Broadway debut came in 1940–41 with a role in *The Night Before Christmas*, and an understudy assignment in *The Time of Your Life*, followed by a bit in a *Rio Rita* revival and the touring production of *Meet the People*. A supporting role in the operetta *Rosalinda* led to a $150-a-week Columbia Pictures contract and her uncredited film debut in *What a Woman* (1943), a comedy about a female author's agent (Rosalind Russell), from a screenplay by Therese Lewis and Barry Trivers.

In 1943 she married salesman Mack Paul Mayer. Years later, she said, "We were married during the war. I can't remember. I didn't know what marriage was all about. He was sent overseas. We hardly lived together. There was nothing. I forget when we were divorced. Last time I saw him was in court after the war. Jerry Giesler got the divorce for me. I haven't seen Mack since. I understand he married an Italian girl and has three kids, and they live in Chicago."

After *Stepping Out* (1943) and *She's a Soldier, Too* (1944), there was *Sailor's Holiday* (1944) about wartime stateside. She had a strong role in the Maxwell Anderson-Kurt Weill musical, *Knickerbocker Holiday* (1944). *Tonight and Every Night* (1945) was a Technicolor story about the musical that played every night in wartime London during the bombings, with Shelley singing and dancing.

In 1945 she appeared as a harem girl

Winters and Ronald Colman in a scene from *A Double Life* (1948), Winters' first big movie.

with Cornel Wilde in the fantasy *A Thousand and One Nights,* about Aladdin and his magic lamp. Long before the TV debut of *I Dream of Jeannie*, this Samuel Bischoff color production cast the genie as a female —in this case, Evelyn Keyes. Shelley Winters was ninth-billed in the cast that also included Phil Silvers, Adele Jergens, Dusty Anderson, Philip Van Zandt, Nestor Paiva, and Rex Ingram. Directed by Alfred E. Green, the screenplay was by Richard English, Jack Henley, and Wilfrid H. Pettit from a story by Pettit.

With a career that had never really taken off, Shelley Winters' option was dropped by Columbia. Undaunted, she began dancing lessons, had her teeth straightened, and studied speech and acting with Charles Laughton while testing for various roles at Fox, Warners, and MGM; she was also making nightclub appearances under another name. As Shelley Winters (for the first time), she was well down in the cast listing of Allied Artists' *The Gangster* (1947), a psychological portrait of a New York City mob leader, and attracted

Shelley Winters wooed by Gary Merrill and
Michael Rennie in *Phone Call from a Stranger*
(1952).

scant notice in the postwar Gene Kelly
MGM musical comedy *Living in a Big Way*
(1947). So she left for New York to play
Ado Annie in the Theatre Guild production
of *Oklahoma*, then in its fifth year.

When Garson Kanin and George
Cukor were casting Universal's *A Double
Life* (1947), Winters returned to Hollywood, and her career finally got under way
with full intensity. The Kanin-Ruth Gordon
screenplay concerned an obsessed actor
(Ronald Colman) who gets the fantasy of
his stage life—as Othello—confused with
his real life. He finally loses touch with reality and commits murder. Winters was
fourth-billed as the waitress murdered by
Colman, and her performance brought her
critical attention. One critic wrote, "She
gave a strong blend of sex, humor, loneli-

ness, and desperation." Colman won an
Academy Award, and so did Miklos Rozsa,
who composed the score. Winters did another version of *A Double Life* ten years
later—January 6, 1957—on NBC's *Alcoa
Hour*, recreating her original role opposite
Eric Portman.

She hung out with tough guys in both
*Larceny* (1948) and *Cry of the City*
(1948). But even while playing leads she
appeared uncredited in the cast of the
Western classic *Red River* (1948). She was
back with the gangsters in *Johnny Stool-
Pigeon* (1949). Also in 1949, she had a
minor part in *The Great Gatsby* and then
played a murder victim in *Take One False
Step*, an Irwin and David Shaw story of a
college professor involved with murder.
After *South Sea Sinner* (1950) and appearing as a saloon singer in *Winchester '73*
(1950), she was scheduled for *Little Egypt*

(1951). But she was fed up with B pictures, and she tried to get out of them. Universal Studios casting executive Monique James remembered, "Shelley was cast in *Little Egypt*, for example, but, by the time we got around to testing her doing a belly dance, she had acquired enough rolls of fat on her belly to get turned down for the part. She then asked if she could be loaned out to another studio to do a good picture, *He Ran All the Way* [1951], with John Garfield. That's one of the ways she kept licking the system."

At Universal, where Winters was known as "The Blonde Bombshell," she had a seven-year contract, but two years of that contract were on suspension because of her occasional conflicts with the front office. "I don't know why I have the reputation of being difficult," she said many years later. "In Hollywood I was on suspension for two years. I only got paid for five. But I made thirty-six pictures—starring roles. How difficult could I be?"

She next made her memorable appearance as the pregnant factory worker Alice Tripp in George Stevens's *A Place in the Sun* (1951). Once again she was a murder victim—in a moody, atmospheric scene shot on location at Lake Tahoe. As Montgomery Clift silently rows through the dark, still water, she slowly begins to comprehend that she may be headed to her death. Oscars went to Stevens, cinematographer William Mellor, costumer Edith Head, editor William Hornbeck, composer Franz Waxman, and screenwriters Michael Wilson and Harry Brown. Both Clift and Winters were nominated for Academy Awards, losing out to Marlon Brando and Vivien Leigh in *A Streetcar Named Desire*.

Winters had overcome casting doubts by putting on weight. Stevens recalled, "I had turned her down to play the part of a plain-looking, chubby factory girl opposite Elizabeth Taylor because she was almost as glamorous-looking as Taylor. But Shelley asked to meet me at the Hollywood Athletic Club one day. I sat next to her in the lobby for a half hour without recognizing her. She had made herself so plain and

Shelley was the object of the affections of Frank Sinatra, Raymond Burr, and Alex Nicol in *Meet Danny Wilson* (1952).

chubby that I honestly didn't know who she was until she told me."

Afterward there was the title role in *Frenchie* (1951), followed by *Behave Yourself* (1951), *The Raging Tide* (1951), *Phone Call from a Stranger* (1952), *Meet Danny Wilson* (1952), *Untamed Frontier* (1952), and *My Man and I* (1952).

She married Vittorio Gassman in 1952, a union that brought Winters a daughter, Vittoria. In 1972 Winters said, "When did I marry him? Who knows? I've been married so much I can't keep track. Anyway, Vittorio was my second husband. I married him in 1952, around there. . . . My daughter Tory is a wonder. She speaks five languages. The relationship she has with her father is great. She's going with Massimo Arcoli—who knows how to spell it? He's the son of Vittorio De Sica's cutter. What can a mother do? Children grow up. They go off."

One of Winters' earliest TV roles was "Mantrap" on the January 28, 1954, *Ford Theatre*, followed by the TV version of "Sorry, Wrong Number" on the November 4, 1954, *Climax*. Recreating the character made famous on radio by Agnes Moorehead and later essayed in the 1948 film by Barbara Stanwyck, Winters played an invalid who overhears a telephone conversation in which her own murder is being plotted. Winters' films in 1954 were *Saskatchewan, Tennessee Champ, Executive Suite,* and *Playgirl,* and that same year she and Gassman were divorced.

In 1955 she returned to Broadway in *A Hatful of Rain,* prompting one critic to write, "She comes magically and honorably close to breaking your heart." On February 7, 1955, she helped introduce color television as one of "The Women" on NBC's *Producers Showcase.* After *Mambo* (1955), she was in *I Am a Camera* (1955), based on the Christopher Isherwood stories that later became *Cabaret* (1972).

In *Night of the Hunter* (1955), the only film directed by Charles Laughton, Winters was the widow murdered by psycho preacher Robert Mitchum. Written by James Agee, *Night of the Hunter* was something of a curiosity in the mid-fifties, doing so-so business and ignored by the Academy Awards. It was, however, one of the last great Expressionistic black-and-white horror films made in Hollywood.

*I Died a Thousand Times* (1955) was a remake of *High Sierra* (1941) with Winters in the Ida Lupino role and Jack Palance in Bogart's part, and, also in 1955, Winters appeared with both Lupino and Palance in *The Big Knife,* Clifford Odets' story of the struggles between a Hollywood star and producer. After *The Treasure of Pancho Villa* (1955) and *Cash on Delivery* (1956) for RKO, Winters returned to the stage in *Girls of Summer.* On August 30, 1956, she was seen in "Dark Wall" on *Climax.*

In 1957 she married her *Hatful of Rain* co-star, Anthony Franciosa, and the event was surrounded by much newspaper publicity. She talked about the marriage in 1972 with Lloyd Shearer: "Who was my third husband? What's the matter with you? Have you been frozen? You been in jail, or something? Tony Franciosa. A marvelous man. Very sexy. But a very stormy temperament. The trouble with our marriage was that he wouldn't give up his acting career. Selfish." By 1960 they were divorced.

She did much work on television in 1957: "A Double Life" in January; "Inspired Alibi" on February 13 for CBS's *U.S. Steel Hour;* "Don't Touch Me" on April 4 for *Climax;* "The Ruth Owens Story" on October 9 for NBC's *Wagon Train;* "Smarty" on October 11 for CBS's *Schlitz Playhouse of Stars;* "Beyond This Place" on November 25 for the CBS *Dupont Show of the Month;* and "Polka" on December 18 for *Kraft Theatre.*

In 1959 she toured with *A Piece of Blue Sky* prior to Broadway. The film version of *The Diary of Anne Frank* (1959), directed by George Stevens, brought her a Best Supporting Actress Academy Award for her third-billed role as Mrs. Van Daan. Stevens said, "For *The Diary of Anne Frank* she again proved to me she could be a fat *hausfrau.* This time the thirty extra pounds helped her win her first Oscar."

Winters' struggles had finally brought her to the very top, and she told a friend, "I wanted to be a star so that everybody would love me. Now they only love me because I'm a star."

Commenting on Mrs. Van Daan, she said, "The woman I played was quite a woman to begin with. Spoiled, a little self-centered maybe, through some of her life. But in her experiences during the occupation, I think she gained strength and insight. The woman—actually the real one—had quite a poignant history. She lived through the war and the concentration camp and the terrible experiences, and then was freed and died in the ambulance on the way to the hospital. Someone who knew her came and told me after the picture opened—a distant relative of some kind.

Shelley Winters and Jack Palance in a scene from *The Big Knife* (1955).

Shelley, as James Darren's mother, in a scene from *Let No Man Write My Epitaph* (1960).

She had that kind of strength. It wasn't evident when she was younger and she'd been a rich girl, and her father and her husband catered to her. And she liked frivolous things. But somehow her basic strength came out in those terrible experiences, and she was quite marvelous in the concentration camp and almost survived. But didn't."

She was fourth-billed in *Odds Against Tomorrow* (1959) from the William P. McGivern novel about a bank robbery. In *Let No Man Write My Epitaph* (1960), a sequel to *Knock On Any Door* (1949), she played James Darren's mother, who becomes a junkie. *The Young Savages* (1961) was based on Evan Hunter's *A Matter of Conviction* about juvenile delinquency. In Stanley Kubrick's *Lolita* (1962), Winters was Lolita's mother. Darryl F. Zanuck's *The Chapman Report* (1962) was based on

the Irving Wallace novel. She did two 1962 *Alcoa Premiere* dramas, "The Cake Baker" on January 2 and "The Way from Darkness" on December 13, and, that same year, she replaced Bette Davis in the Broadway run of Tennessee Williams's *Night of the Iguana*.

*The Balcony* (1963), based on the Jean Genèt play, was produced by Joseph Strick and Ben Maddow with direction by Strick and music by Stravinsky. Winters headed the cast of Peter Falk, Lee Grant, Ruby Dee, Kent Smith, Jeff Corey, and Joyce Jameson. Winters had seen *The Savage Eye* (1959), a film that had taken Strick and Maddow five years to make. She had also seen stage productions of *The Balcony* in both New York and Hollywood and "thought it was very exciting." A friend of hers spoke to Strick, who called her in New

195

York and asked, "Would you like to do it?" She negotiated arrangements for a percentage of their company and the film.

The film was made in the KTTV television studios in Hollywood—studios that were transformed into a brothel. Winters told an interviewer from *Cinema* magazine, "Most playwrights today write about the twist in the sexual life that's going on. Genêt traces it to an environment, and it's a brothel with a revolution going on outside. And that sort of describes the state of the world right now. We try to be healthy, but it's pretty difficult to be healthy in a sick world."

Her interpretation of *The Balcony* was that it concerned "the gray areas. There is no right or wrong. There is no good or bad. The good side is bad, and the bad side is bad. And, in a sense, I think Genêt is saying truly what has sort of happened. He picks the brothel as his setting because there the disturbances that are magnified in every other area of life are revealed most meaningfully. To me, he says the maps to make this a better world aren't written yet. In *The Balcony* the revolution which would abolish the dictatorial and cynical practices of the aristocracy and the dictators is just as bad or almost as bad as the dictators. In the last speech I have in the movie, I turn and talk to the audience. I say, 'Examine it and make it better. Change it.' . . . I think that he's holding a mirror up to nature and, as in most of his works, he's using a form which kind of reveals a self-degradation. In this story about a brothel—if that's what it's about—the men are as much or more degraded than the women."

She expressed admiration for her director: "Strick is very interesting. He's very smart about camera and the technical things and kind of—the styles—the visual style of the film. With *The Balcony* there's a great, harsh thing he gets. A toughness, cruelness—it works. I've seen the rushes.

OPPOSITE PAGE

TOP: James Mason and Winters in *Lolita* (1962).

BELOW: Winters as the madam in the brothel of *The Balcony* (1963).

The terrible, frustrating thing about a movie, if you're an actor, if you're not a director, you don't really know how it will turn out, what the whole impact will be, until you see it. I get to the point where I don't read the rest of the script. I just read my scenes. I mean, I read it once, but—you know, until you see it. . . . I don't know if it's a great movie, but it's an exciting one. You just can't tell. It's certainly a tough thing to put on film, Genêt. It's not realistic dialogue, it's poetic, and it's a sort of bizarre situation."

Before release of *The Balcony*, she seemed to have some doubts: "I'm thinking what I did in *The Balcony*. I'm wondering whether I really had a line to follow— whether I managed to do it. I always try to. Though I'm very occupied with the Method, and I've studied acting a great deal, in the last few years I've realized that no matter what you do, it has to be related to the total framework of the material. If you're lucky, you get a fine director who guides you. And, if not, you have to figure out for yourself what the playwright is saying to the audience, why he doesn't just save your salary. And the choice you make for each scene has to further that. And now that *The Balcony* is finished, I'm wondering if I did that. I hope so. If there's meant to be any positive person in the thing, it's the role I play. And I hope that comes through, and I haven't just played the cynicism. Now I wonder—I won't know now until I see the rough cut of the movie."

After *The Balcony* she left for New York to "go study at the Actors Studio and go to the gym and get myself ready for *Wives and Lovers* (1963) with Edith Head's costumes and—heaven help me, in Technicolor!"

In 1964 she won an Emmy for her January 31 performance in "Two Is the Number" on the *Bob Hope Chrysler Theatre* and went from another brothel (the 1964 *A House Is Not a Home*) to the Bible (the 1965 *The Greatest Story Ever Told*). She commented, "I've got two markets cornered —prostitutes and mothers. There must be some connection in men's minds between

Sam Norkin's caricature of *A House Is Not a Home*: Cesar Romero, Broderick Crawford, Shelley Winters, and Robert Taylor.

the two. The only mother I haven't played is the Virgin Mary, and I was all set to play her in *The Greatest Story Ever Told,* but then the director, George Stevens, got chicken." Instead she portrayed the "woman-of-no-name." After "A Disease of the Heart Called Love" on the November 23, 1964, *Ben Casey* series and "Back to Back" on the October 27, 1965, *Chrysler Theatre,* she won the Best Supporting Actress Academy Award for the second time with *A Patch of Blue* (1965). In 1966, there was *Harper, Alfie,* and the Italian-made *Time of Indifference,* along with "The Greatest Mother of Them All" for *Batman* on October 5 and 6. In 1967 she made *Enter Laughing;* in 1968, *The Scalphunters* for United Artists and *Buona Sera, Mrs. Campbell* for Universal, plus "The Ninth Month," a November 26 episode of *That's Life* on ABC. Also that year Winters crash-dieted from 156 to 126 pounds.

American-International's *Wild in the Streets* (1968) was sociological science fiction in which teens take over the world by putting everyone over thirty into concentra-tion camps. Robert Thom based his screen-play on a short story he had written in 1955. Paul Frees narrated, and Shelley Winters headed the cast of Christopher Jones, Diane Varsi, Ed Begley, Hal Holbrook, Millie Perkins (who was married to Thom at the time), Pamela Mason, Walter Winchell, Richard Pryor, Bert Freed, Kevin Coughlin, Larry Bishop, Dick Clark, Army Archerd, Melvin Belli, and Louis Lomax.

Renata Adler, reviewing in *The New York Times,* wrote, "Blunt, a little preachy, a product of American International Pictures (of beach party and teenage were-wolf fame), the movie is philosophy with dual exhausts and a very clear logic about where things lead. . . . The script is rather heavily weighted against the old. When the pop singer's mother, played with wonderful exaggeration by Shelley Winters, recognizes him on a television program—a recognition she manages only by consulting an old family photograph—she crows, 'I'm a celebrity.' When she drives to see him, she manages to run over a child and cripple her husband. The only dated thing in the picture is the treatment of the very young. The kid insurgents feel a certain amount of pressure from the three-year-olds ('That's right. They're better than we are,' Diane Varsi, as Mr. Jones' freaked-out girlfriend, says) but they are very kind to them. One realizes that last year's flower children have also been overtaken by events; they seem as dated as the sweet vegetarian brontosauruses. The writing is often marvelous. There are some monotonous ringing banalities spoken by the young, but there are other lines: when the liberal senator (played with power-corrupt cool by Hal Holbrook) visits Miss Winters to complain that her son is paralyzing the country, she answers with the dignity of any up-against-the-wall mama. 'Senator,' she says, in what might be a slogan for our times, 'I'm sure my son has a very good reason for paralyzing the country.' "

Pauline Kael, in her famous "Trash, Art and the Movies" essay, used *Wild in the Streets* as an example of a movie that is enjoyable without needing to be called "art": "It's a blatantly crummy-looking picture," she wrote, "but somehow that works for it instead of against it because it's smart in a lot of ways that better-made pictures aren't. . . . It's a paste-up job of cheap movie-making, but it has genuinely funny performers who seize their opportunities and throw their good lines like boomerangs —Diane Varsi (like an even more zonked-out Geraldine Page) doing a perfectly quietly convincing freakout as if it were truly a put-on of the whole straight world; Hal Holbrook with his inexpressive actorish face that is opaque and uninteresting in long shot but in closeup reveals tiny shifts of expression, slight tightenings of the features that are like the movement of thought; and Shelley Winters, of course, and Christopher Jones. . . . It's not so terrible—it may even be a relief—for a movie to be without the look of art; there are much worse things aesthetically than the crude good-natured crumminess, the undisguised reach for a fastbuck, of movies without art. . . . *Wild in the Streets* is a fluke—a borderline, special case of a movie that is entertaining because some talented people got a chance to do something at American International that the more respectable companies were too nervous to try."

Although *Wild in the Streets* garnered mixed reviews, Winters was the object of special mentions from several film critics. Vincent Canby in *The New York Times* remarked that, "Robert Thom has written a role for her that is not very big, but it is one that dominates the film and gives the movie its marvelously (and seriously) lunatic direction. I have a feeling that Mr. Thom didn't write Shelley's dialogue, but somehow 'received' it—whole—like a poetic image. In the film she's the kind of frumpy, middle-class mother who puts plastic covers over the furniture and remains serenely unaware that her sweet-faced, antisocial son is in the basement cooking up a mess of LSD and dynamite. . . . When, finally, she is being carted off to a concentration camp (at her son's direction) for the over-30s, she utters what is probably the theme of her performance. 'I'm the biggest mother of

them all!' she cries, and it's the comic measure of the film, and of her performance, that the line sounds both appealing and obscene."

Winters took her role in *Wild in the Streets* over the objections of her agent: "They sent me the script, and I liked it, but my agent didn't want me to do it. I was told that AIP shoots pictures in five days and all that sort of thing, but I wanted to do it, so I said I would. And then I cast it. I called up Hal Holbrook and Ed Begley and Chris Jones and Diane Varsi and told them I was going to do it and got them to also. They all had clauses in their contracts saying that they didn't have to do it if Shelley Winters wasn't in it. . . . It's amazing how many people take the picture seriously,

"The biggest mother of them all." Shelley is rounded up for the Paradise Camp in *Wild in the Streets*.

when really it's a great put-on. Even so, it's a lot more valid than that Generation Gap thing in *Life* magazine. . . . And, although the movie is a satire, it is in the realm of possibility. George Murphy is a tap dancer, and he's a senator. Ronald Reagan is on the Late Show, and he's Governor."

Columbia's *The Mad Room* (1969) was an updating of the Reginald Denham-Edward Percy play, *Ladies in Retirement,* filmed in 1941 by Columbia. Stella Stevens and Shelley Winters headed the cast of Skip Ward, Carole Cole, Severn Darden, Beverly Garland, and Michael Burns. The screenplay by Bernard Girard and A. Z. Martin concerned children, thought to be psychotic, who are accused of murdering their parents. Just prior to filming, Winters said in New York, "Before I came East I visited the set, and there was a little dog running around with a plastic reproduction of my hand in its mouth. It's that kind of picture."

A few days later Bobby Kennedy, a friend of Winters', was assassinated. Winters had been campaigning for him. As one of the leaders in a Hollywood group vowing not to make any more violent films and also a participant in the Committee for a Federal Gun Control Law, Winters attempted to withdraw from the cast of *The Mad Room.* Referring to RFK's assassination, she explained at the time, "When it happened, I tried to quit *The Mad Room,* but I couldn't. I mean, who needs it? But now I'm trying to talk them into making it into a satire. It's funny anyway. We go to the rushes every night and laugh—I mean two kids who think they've murdered their mother! You can't take it seriously, except Stella Stevens does. She's actually the murderer, and she wanders around the set in this mauve thing, playing it all very, very sympathetically, as if everybody should understand. . . ." (But in testimony prior to the November 1976, acquittal of high school student Peter Reilly, falsely accused of matricide and intimidated into signing a confession, such a situation *was* taken seriously—until writers Joan Barthel, William Styron, and Arthur Miller took an in-

terest in the case and it was discovered that prosecutor John Bianchi had withheld evidence exonerating Reilly. See Barthel's 1976 book, *A Death in Canaan,* published by Thomas Congdon Books/Dutton and, more recently, the 1978 CBS made-for-TV movie of the same name).

During this same period in 1968, Robert Thom had completed a screenplay for *Bloody Mama,* the story of Ma Barker, which American International planned to film with Winters in the lead. In a July 7, 1968, interview with Vincent Canby, she said, "That title, *Bloody Mama,* has got to go, and I think I'm going to have some trouble with American International Pictures about the whole thing. Their idea is another *Bonnie and Clyde* thing, but Robert Thom, who also wrote the script for *Wild in the Streets,* has done something entirely different. It's on three levels, like *Trans-Europe Express* [written and directed by Alain Robbe-Grillet in 1966]. Did you see that? We open with the director and the actors talking about the Barker gang, and why such people became folk heroes, and what the violence means. Then it goes into the story of the Barkers. In the first shot of me as Ma Barker I'm delivering my fourth son myself—and it goes downhill in violence from there. But then it also becomes a sort of collage, attempting to interrelate the other events of the times—like Sarah Bernhardt traveling around with her coffin, you know what I mean? It's really a very serious exploration of the meaning of violence. Not just another gangster story, which I'm afraid is what AIP wants. . . ."

After the violent events of 1968, American International, which usually made a practice of taking its cues from the headlines, suddenly became reluctant to enter production on *Bloody Mama.* Winters,

however, felt the multi-level messages in Thom's screenplay provided reasons for embarking on Barker. "I've just this minute come from a big razzmatazz with AIP! We were all yelling at each other, but I think everything will work out all right. Now they're saying that this isn't the time for such a film. For God's sake, now *is* the time. They can't get it through their heads that the script that Robert Thom wrote is *about* the *reasons* for violence. It doesn't glorify it! But then they're afraid it's too arty and nobody will understand it. It really was a razzmatazz, but I like them anyway. I think they'll change their minds."

Instead, AIP sent out the following press release: "American-International Pictures has canceled August production plans for filming of *Bloody Mama*, dealing with the life of the notorious Ma Barker, due to excessive violence inherent in the story, it was announced by AIP heads Samuel Z. Arkoff and James H. Nicholson."

But this was only a postponement. The film was finally made and released in 1970 (with Winters, Don Stroud, and Bruce Dern). *Sight and Sound* offered the following abbreviated review: "Sensually photographed by John Alonzo, Roger Corman's compelling and uneasily comic tale of Ma Barker and her boys eschews the glamour of Penn's *Bonnie and Clyde* and dwells instead on the outlaws' twilight passions—incest, sodomy, addiction, masochism: a destruction from within that leads inexorably to their brutal elimination at the vengeful hands of the society without."

She was third-billed as flighty bohemian artist Lena Marvin in the Jackie Gleason comedy, *How Do I Love Thee?* (1970) and fourth-billed as callhouse madam Dorothy Bluebell in Carol Reed's *Flap* (1970). *Variety* noted that Winters, in *Flap*, "manages to steal scenes as she devours the scenery."

After the British-made *Arthur! Arthur!* (1971), Winters co-starred with Debbie Reynolds in Curtis Harrington's period Hollywood horror, *What's the Matter with Helen?* (1971). The screenplay was by Henry Farrell, the creator of *What Ever Happened to Baby Jane?* "The whole conflict was between a life force and a death force," said Harrington. "Debbie Reynolds played a character with a will to live, and Shelley Winters played a character with the will to die. Everything else grew from that. I worked very closely with Henry Farrell on the screenplay. George Edwards and I had developed the project when we were under contract at Universal, and we had to buy it back from them. Of the films I've made, this is the one I'm most happy with. But Martin Ransohoff interfered with it. My cut would have been an R rating, and for some reason he wanted a GP. So the murder sequence was only a shadow of what I had intended it to be. It was much bloodier the way I shot it, very much like the shower scene in *Psycho*. Ransohoff also cut out all of my dissolves. He doesn't like dissolves. I wanted to get the feeling of Los Angeles in the thirties. Gene Lourie and I looked at a lot of buildings that had been built in the 1820s in the Spanish style. It was important for the plaster to be just right. I like the look of the film." So did critic Robert Mundy, who wrote, "*What's the Matter with Helen?* is Harrington's most achieved film: the strongest dramatically, psychologically the most complex, with a depth of character that *Games*, for instance, doesn't possess."

The story opens with black-and-white newsreels of the thirties, a sequence that wraps up showing the midwest trial of teenage Leopold-and-Loeb-like murderers. The film changes to color as the teens' mothers, Adele (Debbie Reynolds) and Helen (Winters), after receiving threatening phone calls, head for Hollywood, where they open a dancing school for tots. Hamilton Starr (Michael MacLiammoir) joins up to teach drama. When the phone calls continue, Helen turns to Sister Alma (Agnes Moorehead), an Aimee Semple MacPherson-type evangelist. Adele falls for Texas millionaire Lincoln Palmer (Dennis Weaver), the father of one of her pupils, Winona Palmer (Sammee Lee Jones). At the climax Helen goes totally mad.

*Variety* critic Murf stated, "Miss Winters' role is one she can do in her sleep, though she is mostly awake herein." Robert L. Jerome, reviewing in *Cinefantastique*, commented, "Director Curtis Harrington, a stylist on other occasions (*Night Tide, Games*), attempts to give the film the feel of a seedy *Sunset Boulevard*, but his stars, looking uncomfortable in the midst of horror, resemble bugs trapped in Lucite—cold and uninvolving to the onlooker. The suspense is minimal, and no shock in the film quite matches the report that Miss Reynolds commissioned this unattractive portrait of herself by financing the project to the tune of $800,000."

"To me," said Harrington, "the film was a very affectionate re-creation of a period in Los Angeles history, which I have my own tremendous feelings of nostalgia for. I was trying to show lives on the fringe of Hollywood in the thirties, not within the industry. I had tremendous feelings of sympathy for both characters in the story." David Raksin composed the nostalgic score.

Near the end of the year, Shelley Winters did the TV-movie *A Death of Innocence*, aired on CBS on November 26, 1971. This was followed by the ABC TV-movie, *The Adventures of Nick Carter*, a February 20, 1972, reprise for the famed pulp detective. Winters stated, "Television still is a mystery to me, and I don't like those quick, backbreaking production schedules. But I've learned that to survive as an actress today, you've *got* to do it. So I try to get at least one movie-of-the-week a year. Last year I did two, *Death of Innocence* on CBS and *Revenge* on ABC. Do you know how important TV is? I use the Ralph's Market test. I can come out in a big picture like *Alfie*, and no one pays any attention to me when I shop in the market. But whenever

Judge, jury, inquisitor: Shelley as Mrs. Hilton, out to punish the man (Bradford Dillman) responsible for her daughter's death in the TV-movie, *Revenge* (1971).

I do a TV show, the people all recognize me and swarm around. I even get mobbed after ten minutes on *Mike Douglas*."

Not long after the completion of *What's the Matter with Helen?*, Winters asked Harrington to direct her again in *The Gingerbread House*, an early twenties-period horror reworking of *Hansel and Gretel*. "I did it because Shelley Winters asked me to," said Harrington. "I had little influence on the script." The screenplay was by Robert Blees and Jimmy Sangster from a David Osborn story, and Gavin Lambert supplied additional dialogue. When the film was released in late 1971, it had been retitled *Who Slew Auntie Roo?* Harrington explained, "The film, while in production, was called *The Gingerbread House*. This was an appropriate title, and it was the title I gave the script. *Who Slew Auntie Roo?* was the producers' idea of a commercial title. It is my opinion that it harmed the commercial chances of the film."

Auntie Roo (Winters), an American widow living in England during the twenties, was once a music-hall dancer married to a well-known English magician. In a tragic 1913 accident she lost her daughter Kathryn. Unable to face the reality of this situation, she not only tries to reach the Other Side through seances—conducted by an alcoholic fake medium, Mr. Benton (Ralph Richardson), but she also keeps Kathryn's rotting corpse around. Every Christmas Auntie Roo invites eight children from the local orphanage over to her house. Becoming fond of young Katy (Chloe), she decides to kidnap the girl as a replacement for her daughter. Whit, reviewing in *Variety*, commented, "She sees, in the little girl she kidnaps, her own daughter. Actress has the talent to establish this sort of character and, at first, make it believable; later, it's anybody's guess what's in the character's mind."

Auntie Roo's plans are foiled by the arrival of Katy's brother, Christopher (Mark Lester), who believes that Auntie Roo is the witch of *Hansel and Gretel*. Finally, they escape by locking her in the pantry and setting the house on fire.

Interviewed by Dale Winogura in 1974, Harrington said, "I was approached by American-International to do the film. Also, Shelley Winters, who had worked with me on *What's the Matter with Helen?*, asked me to direct her in it. It was not a project that I personally wanted particularly to do. . . . There is one cut in the film that was imposed by the producer—the abrupt end of the confrontation scene between Auntie Roo and her servant. I also did not approve of the casting of the actor who played the servant. That was also imposed by the producers. . . . I did no actual writing on the film, though I did suggest some of the plot elements—especially the idea of Auntie Roo keeping the mummified body of her dead child, having been unable psychologically to bury her. Gavin Lambert contributed quite a bit of the dialogue. The first draft of the script was laid in the present day, and it was my idea to place it in the early twenties. I have a great fondness for all the imagery and quality of the traditional Victorian Christmas celebration. I tried to put as much as I could of that in the film. I added a great deal to it. It was just a thin little fable. I found Shelley Winter's mad behavior vastly amusing."

The main exterior set was Auntie Roo's house—in actuality, the administration building at Shepperton Studios after a face-lifting by art director George Provis. At a cost of around $800,000, the film had a 40-day shooting schedule. When it was released, a point arose over the wording used in the title. As a result, the film has *two* titles—*Who Slew Auntie Roo?* and *Whoever Slew Auntie Roo?*—one used in the advertising and one that appears on the print of the film!

Harrington had even more compliments for Winters: "We seem to understand each other. She is sometimes a difficult, headstrong actress, but she is also extremely talented. She makes wonderful 'choices' as an actress, and has an unerring sense of dramatic truth. The little displays of temperament are easy to cope with when you know you are getting something worthwhile on the screen. . . ." David Bartholomew, however, writing in *Cinefantastique*, disagreed: ". . . several of Shelley Winters' scenes are simply embarrassing to endure." But *Who Slew Auntie Roo?* owes a lot to Winters' performance—alternately obsessed, hysterical, pathetic, and riveting. Try watching the film during one of its late-night TV showings; you may drift toward sleep during the commercials, but when Shelley is on you're sitting bolt upright, and it's impossible to turn off the set until the film ends.

In the early seventies Winters set forth on a new career—writing. She said, "I'm working on my autobiography. I've become

RIGHT: Shelley Winters as Rosie Forrest, who cannot accept the death of her only daughter in *Who Slew Auntie Roo?* (1971). Rosie is seen here with a poster of her deceased husband.

BELOW: Introduction of Chris (Mark Lester) and Katy (Chloe Franks) to Rosie at the Christmas party.

a writer, or don't you know? I've already become a playwright. I had three short plays put on at the Actors Playhouse, off Broadway, in New York. They were called *One Night Stands of a Noisy Passenger*. I wanted to make a statement. About what? About me, about a liberal and the shift in political position from World War II through the Korean War, down to this war." Critics weren't kind to Winters' semi-autobiographical plays. One wrote, "Miss Winters makes sex so ugly and dull that even the most ardent voyeur will be turned off by this trio of tawdry peep shows."

She signed with Lippincott, receiving a five-thousand-dollar advance for her autobiography. In 1973, Winters said, "I've already written sixty pages, and I'm still not out of St. Louis, where I was born." By the end of 1976, Lippincott was still waiting for delivery of the manuscript (a book that, logically, could only be titled *Winters' Tale*).

In the Irwin Allen production of *The Poseidon Adventure* (1972), Winters, at the age of fifty and weighing in at 193 pounds, played ex-Olympic swimming champion Belle Rosen. "You want to know why I got this fat?" she asked Lloyd Shearer in Hollywood in the summer of 1972. "I'm naturally fat to begin with. Then my agent called; 'Shelley,' he said, 'the world's greatest part. You must play it. It's great. Absolutely great. But you've got to gain twenty-five pounds.' I guess I gained a little more than twenty-five pounds. You see, I play this fat woman, fat, an ex-Olympic champion. I have to hold my breath for three minutes. I've got to swim with this rope to the other side or somewhere. I lead these people out of the ship. I die in the end. It's a great part. The picture will cost five and a half million. Unheard of in Hollywood these days. They'll need about fifteen million before they come out, before they show a profit. Who could afford to turn this part down? That's why I came back here. Also I'm tired of New York. Listen, do you know anyone who'd like to rent my apartment? It's beautiful, nine rooms, Central Park West. I spent a fortune refur-

nishing it. You want to rent it? You know somebody? It's a great buy. I don't need it anymore. But I couldn't afford to turn down this part."

In 1973, she joked, "I was so heavy when I made *The Poseidon Adventure* that Gene Hackman looked at me and said, 'Somewhere in there is Shelley Winters.'" Based on a novel by Paul Gallico, *The Poseidon Adventure* told of an underwater earthquake stirring up a monstrous tidal wave that capsizes an ocean liner. Partially filmed aboard the Queen Mary, the Fox release was directed by Ronald Neame, and in the cast were Hackman, Ernest Borgnine, Red Buttons, Carol Lynley, Roddy McDowall, Stella Stevens, Jack Albertson, Pamela Sue Martin, Arthur O'Connell, Eric Shea, Fred Sadoff, Sheila Mathews, Jan Arvan, Byron Webster, John Crawford, Bob Hastings, and Leslie Nielson. The film was a tremendous popular success, launching the mid-seventies wave of "disaster" pictures. *Variety* critic Whit commented, "Borgnine and Miss Stevens are well teamed as a loving but constantly battling couple, and Shelley Winters and Jack Albertson [are] a married couple on their way to see their grandchild in Israel. Both are particularly strongly cast. Miss Winters, who, in the finale leading to her death rescues Hackman trapped underwater, is seen in a role of possible Academy proportions." Winters was nominated for an Oscar, but the award went to Eileen Heckart. Winters said, "I walked into the show with my agent and saw Hecky sitting behind us, and I said to my agent, 'Hecky's going to win.' I told her, 'Hecky, if I don't get it, you can have it.' My agent thinks I have ESP." David Bartholomew in *Cinefantastique* compared *The Poseidon Adventure* to earlier sea disasters: "the more brilliant examples of the disaster-at-sea film like Roy Ward Baker's remarkable and observant *A Night to Remember* (1958) or even *The Last Voyage* (1960), in which director Andrew Stone utilized, damaged, and eventually sank a real honest-to-God ship, the *Ile de France*." Bartholomew concluded that *The Poseidon Adventure*'s "special effects are, of course, the only valid reason for seeing it."

Early in 1973, Shelley Winters toured as Beatrice in *The Effect of Gamma Rays on Man-in-the Moon Marigolds* in Miami, Milwaukee, and at the Paper Mill Playhouse in Milburn, New Jersey, and the Playhouse on the Mall in Paramus, New Jersey. (Joanne Woodward played the role in the 1972 film version.) Other Winters stage works during the years have included productions of *Born Yesterday, A Streetcar Named Desire, Two for the Seesaw,* and *A View from the Bridge.*

Her major motion-picture role of 1973 was the part of Mrs. Cramer in Paul Mazursky's *Blume in Love.* Sylvia Millar,

reviewing in the *Monthly Film Bulletin,* called it "a witty cameo by Shelley Winters, keeping a fine balance between scabrous satire and honest emotion." She weighed 140 in this film.

In one project of this period, Winters hoped to have a woman director—Lee Grant. "A bunch of old broadies like me got together, and we found a wonderful script and we decided to make a picture in which none of us would have to wear face lifts. Lee Grant was going to direct. But could we swing it? No. Lee Grant is better than any director around, but we couldn't get financing. Why? Just because she's a woman. And the industry is controlled by a bunch of male chauvinist pigs. All they're

Shelley Winters, Carol Lynley, Roddy McDowall, and Stella Stevens ponder their next move to safety in *The Poseidon Adventure* (1972).

As Lenny Baker's overprotective mother in *Next Stop, Greenwich Village* (1976).

interested in is our bosoms and our behinds. Do you know there's only one woman cameraman and one woman director in the whole industry?"

In *The Devil's Daughter*, a 1973 made-for-TV horror movie, Winters, weighing 160, co-starred with Belinda Montgomery. Filmed in the wake of *The Exorcist*, the story concerned the Devil taking possession of Montgomery. Jeannot Szwarc directed. "This kid," said Winters, referring to Szwarc, "just tried to tell me that the women's lib movement is even causing *Italian* men to lose their virility. Impossible! Why, I had to chase *mine* with scissors to keep them away from me."

Filming took place in the giant Paramount Sound Stage 30. After one scene that Winters felt she could improve, she asked for another take. "Sure," said Szwarc, "and we'll rebuild the set for you, too."

"Kid," she smiled, "If this were a movie for theatres, you would now hear screaming and yelling like you never heard before. But since it's a movie for TV, I acknowl-

edge that you don't have much time to reshoot scenes—so let's proceed to the next one."

Winters called TV horror movies "the networks' way of getting around the anti-violence pressure. If you get garroted by a ghost, it's okay."

With *Next Stop, Greenwich Village* (1976), Shelley Winters made her second film for director Paul Mazursky. Murf, reviewing in *Variety*, had the following praise: "An outstanding cast of New York players, plus Shelley Winters in one of the most superb characterizations of her career, gives the 20th-Fox release a wonderful humanity and credibility. . . . In dark hair, Winters has managed to escape her near-formula mother role into new creative territory."

Her next role, in the French-made *The Tenant* (1976), directed by Roman Polanski, was even more offbeat. Timid filing clerk Trelkovsky (a brilliantly conceived empatic interpretation by Polanski) bribes a concierge (Winters) to see Mr. Zy (Mel-

Shelley Winters with John Huston in *Tentacles* (1977).

vyn Douglas) and inquire about an apartment. He learns that the previous tenant, Simone Choule (Dominique Poulange), is in the hospital after having thrown herself out the window. Trelkovsky goes to the hospital to see her and meets her friend Stella (Isabelle Adjani). When Simone dies, he moves into the apartment—where he suffers a Kafkalike persecution from the neighbors. Obsessed with Simone and the various objects she left there, he begins dressing up like her and experiencing paranoid delusions that the others in the building are driving him to suicide. After a car accident, Trelkovsky hurls himself—twice in succession—from the window. The film, based on an eldritch and psychologically taut novel by *Fantastic Planet* animation designer Roland Topor, plays like a male version of Polanski's own *Repulsion* (1965). Winters is suitably dominant as the Concierge, with her authoritative manner and bulk providing a nice contrast with the frail, nervous Polanski character. In one of the film's best moments, she shows Trel-

kovsky the window as her rising hand near his shoulder subtly suggests how easily he could be pushed out. But the film, unfortunately, makes it quite clear that Trelkovsky is a paranoid, while Topor's provocative novel has a constant edge of ambiguity, hinting that the neighbors are a genuine threat.

In the summer of 1976, Winters joined Henry Fonda, Bo Hopkins, Brian Keith, and Sherry Buchanan for the filming of American International's *Tentacles*, directed by Oliver Hellman. At the end of 1976, she went to Rome for a role opposite Alberto Sordi in Mario Monicelli's *Have a Nice Day*, and then joined the cast of the Disney film *Pete's Dragon*.

Free-associating on a March 1977 *Tonight* show, Shelley noted, shortly before Oscar night, that she had not been nominated: "But I did a very good picture, *Next Stop, Greenwich Village*. I gotta tell you how it happened. They changed the rules. They always change the rules. And I think this is how it happened. I gotta tell you

209

something—everybody votes for their friends. No, you don't. No, you don't. You vote for who you think is the best. But you've got to put down Best Actress or Supporting Actress, and my agent, who's a very good agent, who keeps me working a lot. . . . Hey! I love to do this show! Whenever I do this show, when I'm in my dressing room, I get an offer for a picture. April first I'm going to Italy or the Disney Studio, I don't know which. I have to read both—it happens to me all the time. It's really very lucky for me to do this show. I always get an offer for a movie. But I'm a villain in both of them. I don't know, I have to make up my mind. I'll read the scripts tonight. I don't know. What was I saying? Oh, yes, I wasn't nominated. Yes. The studios and your agent take out ads with the quotes from different—from your mother and your aunt and your boy friend—no, no, from famous critics about what they thought of your performance, but you have to say, 'Nominated for Best Actress, Supporting Actress.' Jack said to me, 'Well, I think you should go for Supporting Actress.' And I said, 'Well, I don't want to go for Supporting Actress. I have two Oscars for Supporting Actress, and I've got four nominations in that category, and only one nomination in Best Actress. After all, the lady who won for *Cuckoo*, Louise Fletcher, had really a small part in that picture, and she won the Oscar. He said, 'Well, I don't know. I would if I were you.' And then I couldn't quite make up my mind. So by the time the ad came up all I could write down was 'for your consideration.' So I got half the votes for Best Actress and half for Supporting Actress. This is the nominating—it's just like primaries for the President, you know. It works the same way except you get a different prize. . . . It's terrible not to be nominated. This is the first year in ten years I haven't been nominated. . . . Charlie Chaplin never won an Oscar and neither did Greta Garbo. I think the biggest Oscar is when they pay that money to see you. But that statue looks so pretty on your mantelpiece. I don't care. I'm not going to cry. Oscar night when I'm watching it on television, I'll just say, 'Who needs it?' "

In 1977 she appeared in *Journey into Fear* with Sam Waterston, Zero Mostel, Yvette Mimieux, Scott Marlowe, and Vincent Price. In *Pot Luck* (1977), co-starring with Max Von Sydow, she was directed by Mauro Bolognini. And on February 6, 1978, she played the part of Mrs. Hunter, an evil sorority housemother, in the ABC movie *The Initiation of Sarah*, with Tony Bill, Kathryn Crosby, and Kay Lenz.

Today Shelley Winters, as an actress, continues to surprise with her versatility in a wide range of roles. The days when she was typecast in roles of gun molls, whores, and mothers seem to be past. Now, no one can predict in just what guise she will turn up next.

As a real-life human being, she remains an active supporter of many causes—the Heart Fund, Israel Bonds, Fight for Sight, and others. Scheduled to speak at a hotel for the Heart Fund not long ago, she reported that she "got off the elevator, walked into a ballroom, and made my speech. They were happy to see me and applauded and were very nice. . . . And I was at the wrong lunch."

# Agnes Moorehead

*P*ossessing a rich multimedia background that few of her contemporaries ever had, Agnes Robertson Moorehead belongs in that pantheon that includes only the most select, great ladies of the screen.

She was born December 6, 1906, in Clinton, Massachusetts, but grew up in Reedsburg, Wisconsin, where her father, the Reverend John Henderson Moorehead, was a Presbyterian minister. When she was very young, she took part in church pageants. "My father never discouraged me from the theatre," she recalled, "but he never encouraged me. He said one thing and that was 'I want you to have an education first and then you can do what you want, try your wings.' . . . My father was a brilliant man, and so understanding but very disciplined. He was English."

Agnes Moorehead was graduated from Muskingum College in Ohio, and she then went to the University of Wisconsin, where she received a master's degree in English and public speaking, and, eventually, a Ph.D. "Do you know that I never had a date by myself until I was in college? I was always chaperoned. There were parties,

dances, and great sleigh parties, but always there were older people with us but not hampering us. Oh, we had great times. You know, I said to someone recently, 'Let's have a taffy pull,' and they looked at me as if I were crazy. Well, it's high time we had one. No one does these things anymore. Kids don't know what they're missing. You know, I feel so sad for these youngsters today. You should see them along Sunset Boulevard, they look like they were out of the pit."

For a period she taught speech, drama, and English, and, in Paris, she studied pantomime with Marcel Marceau. In 1919 she made her professional debut as a dancer-singer in the chorus of the St. Louis Municipal Opera, where she performed for four seasons. In 1923 she made her radio debut as a singer on a St. Louis radio station. After saving some money, she headed for New York and the American Academy of Dramatic Arts, from which she was graduated with honors. Throughout the twenties, she was seen on Broadway in such hits as *Marco's Millions, All the King's Horses, Candlelight* (with Gertrude Lawrence),

211

and *Soldiers and Women.* She joined the American Academy of Dramatic Art Stock Company in 1929. She married the actor John Griffith Lee in 1930, and they adopted a child, Sean.

The Depression brought hard times. Her Broadway parts slackened. "I remember once going four days without food until someone gave me a big box of rolled oats, which I lived on for two weeks. I know what a penny means." To survive she turned to radio.

During the thirties she was heard on a wide variety of radio dramas, mysteries, and serials. She made appearances on the *Ben Bernie* show of the early thirties and the NBC Blue Network's *The Orange Lantern*, a 1932 Fu Manchu-type mystery series. On *The March of Time*, which began in 1931, she portrayed Eleanor Roosevelt, and she also had roles on the historical *Cavalcade of America* and the documentary *America's Hour*. On *The Phil Baker Show*, which began in 1933, she played Mrs. Sarah Heartburn, and she was also Ma Hutchinson on *The Mighty Show*, about circus life. She brought to life the comic-strip characters of Min Gump on the 1934 *The Gumps* and the Dragon Lady on *Terry and the Pirates*, beginning in 1937, and also Margot Lane on *The Shadow* of the pulps. On the serial *This Day Is Ours*, which began in 1938, she was Catherine Allison, and the played opposite Van Heflin on the *Way Down East* serial. She was Rosie on *Dot and Will* and was also in the cast of CBS's 1938 *Joyce Jordan, Girl Interne.*

Years later, comparing television with radio, Agnes Moorehead observed, "Fantasy is being taken away from children. The cards must be on the table. Fantasy is out. But children *like* to dream. Every child wants to live in a world that's not this world. That's part of their childhood. That was one of the great things about radio. You had to use your imagination, and sometimes those radio fantasies seemed very real. With TV, everything is there for you, and you can just sit there like a lump. A lot of parents today don't let their kids read Grimm's *Fairy Tales* because they're

Agnes Moorehead as she appeared during a CBS radio broadcast in the thirties. Her best-known radio drama was "Sorry, Wrong Number" on *Suspense.*

too 'horrible', but of course they want to tell them the facts of life at ten. *Listen*, I was brought up on Grimm, and I never had a trauma. I used to get all excited about things coming around the corner, but I wasn't scared. My mother says I was constantly pretending to be someone else. Once my mother found me crying in the corner because I had read *The Poor Little Match Girl* and was pretending to be cold and hungry too. She didn't stop me. I used to come home after school with great tales about people I saw in the street. I'd tell my father, and he'd say, 'Yes, and then what did they do?' He never stopped me. Parents have to take time with children. My father never turned me down when I asked him to read to me, and he read me all the classics."

It was radio that brought her into contact with Orson Welles who, during the mid-thirties, appeared as an actor on many of the same programs that Moorehead was cast in, such as *The Shadow* and *March of Time.* "We met on a soap opera, and I was immediately intrigued with him. He was very conservative, sat in a corner constantly reading classics. He had a marvelous voice. We became extremely good friends, and later, while I was on *March of Time*, he

212

Agnes Moorehead's association with Orson Welles began during the thirties on radio programs such as *March of Time* and *The Shadow*. Here Welles performs some legerdemain for film mogul Cecil B. De Mille and Loretta Young during a break in the rehearsals of the *Lux Radio Theatre* (April 1945).

asked me to join him and Joe Cotten to do classics on WOR. That was the start of the *Mercury Theatre.*"

When Welles began *The Mercury Theatre on the Air* in 1938, she was one of the leading female members of the group. The Halloween broadcast of H. G. Wells' *War of the Worlds* brought front-page attention to the *Mercury* radio shows in 1938. By December of that year the program had both a sponsor, Campbell's Soups, and a new name—*The Campbell Playhouse*. Within a few months Welles had a $100,000 per-picture contract with RKO, and he arrived in Hollywood July 20, 1939. *The Campbell Playhouse* moved to the West Coast that winter, and Welles arranged for his *Mercury* radio company of Joseph Cotten, Agnes Moorehead, Ray Collins, Paul

Stewart, Everett Sloane, and George Coulouris to also be put under contract at RKO. After much delay, Welles finally, in 1940, began work on the first Mercury-film production. It was the "prismatic" *Citizen Kane*, and Agnes Moorehead, along with many other cast members, made their astonishing debut in films, creating a cinema classic that gains in reputation each year. Moorehead was 34 when she played the 28-year-old mother of the young Kane. "That's why he's going to be brought up where you can't get at him," she says slowly, over and over again as projector reels turn a million times. "That's why he's going to be brought up where you can't get at him." At the film's end the scorch rises on the sled and Moorehead's brief scene is suddenly recalled as one of the more memorable ones

213

in the film, anticipated at the next viewing.

In *The Magnificent Ambersons* (1942), however, she made an even stronger impression. Many would call *Ambersons* her best film. David Thomson, in his *Biographical Dictionary of Film*, asks, "What are the two most indelibly humane moments in the work of Orson Welles? There is a case for saying that Agnes Moorehead figures in both: in *Kane*, the scene with Kane's mother opening the window to call in her son from the snow so that he may advance on his destiny; and in *Ambersons*, where Aunt Fanny watches Georgie devouring her strawberry shortcake, pleased to be useful, thrilled by his appetite but knowing that he does not need her, deeply aware that her vibrant romantic hopes are being made shrill by neglect. It is hardly coincidence that these are moments of loss and frustration that stay with us long afterwards. . . ." The kitchen scene in *Ambersons* lasts over three minutes without a cut, a feat that must have seemed remarkable at the time, but was merely part of the film's style, capturing the slower pace of an earlier time. Moorehead's truly unforgettable moment comes later on the staircase. Joseph McBride calls it "one of Agnes Moorehead's greatest scenes. She simultaneously conveys profound anger at George, envy of Isabel, transparent self-pity, and sympathy for George." *Ambersons* brought Moorehead an Oscar nomination, the 1942 New York Film Critics Award for Best Feminine Per-

TOP LEFT: Agnes Moorehead in the first Mercury film production, *Citizen Kane* (1941), as the mother of Charles Foster Kane.

TOP RIGHT: Agnes Moorehead with Harry Shannon in *Citizen Kane*.

BOTTOM: A rare production still showing the filming of the famous *Citizen Kane* "Rosebud" sled scene in front of "Mrs. Kane's Boardinghouse—High Class Meals and Lodging." The eight-year-old Charles Foster Kane (Buddy Swan) cringes as his mother (Agnes Moorehead) and father (Harry Shannon) turn him over to Thatcher (George Coulouris), who takes him away for his future education. "Come on, Charles," says Thatcher. "Let's shake hands. . . . Sleds aren't to hit people with. Sleds are to sleigh on."

formance, and a National Board of Review Best-Acting Award.

She was seen next in RKO's *The Big Street*, adopted from Damon Runyon and starring Henry Fonda and Lucille Ball. She joined other Mercury actors for *Journey into Fear* (1943), written by Joseph Cotten and Welles with direction by Norman Foster. Welles explained, "For the first five sequences I was on the set and decided angles. From then on, I often said where to put the camera, described the framings, made light tests. . . . I designed the film but can't properly be called the director."

Commenting on Welles's later career, Agnes Moorehead said, "When one has genius, one always has it. If a picture is not of great consequence, there are always one or two great moments. Sometimes you have to take people you don't want or you don't have enough money and you can't do anything about it. Look at Olivier and Gielgud. They're not always at their best."

After MGM's *The Youngest Profession* (1943), a comedy about movie fan clubs, featuring a roster of guest stars, Moorehead returned to RKO for *Government Girl* (1943) about Washington in wartime. In 20th's *Jane Eyre* (1944) she was once again in a cast with Orson Welles, a brooding and atmospheric production directed by Robert Stevenson.

During this time she continued to appear on radio. On December 9, 1938, she appeared with Margaret Sullavan, Ray Collins, and George Coulouris in the *Mercury* production of Daphne du Maurier's *Rebecca*. David Thomson later wrote, "Mrs. Danvers in *Rebecca* on radio showed her flair for melodrama and, in truth, she may be best confined to brief passages where her intensity is limited." On May 5, 1939, she headed *The Campbell Playhouse* airing of *Wickford Point*, co-starring with John Cravens in *Our Town* the following week. She portrayed Homer's mother in *The Aldrich Family*, which began in 1939 on radio. She was the mother-in-law in the 1939 serial *Brenda Curtis*, Mrs. Riley in the serial *Life Begins* (later titled *Martha Webster*), which began in 1940, and the

Meeks' first maid in the 1940 *Adventures of Mister Meek* radio-situation comedy. She was heard in the *Bulldog Drummond* mysteries that began in 1941. Her comedic character of Marilly (playing opposite Lionel Barrymore) on *Mayor of the Town* on CBS, beginning in 1942, was, perhaps, her best-remembered radio series characterization. She was also Mrs. Townsend in the serial *The Story of Bess Johnson*, a 1941 NBC serial set in a boarding school (continuing the narrative begun in 1937 under the title *Hilltop House*).

On May 25, 1943, Moorehead starred in a segment of radio's *Suspense* that is considered today one of the great classics of radio drama. Her bravura portrayal of a woman who overhears a phone conversation of her own impending murder was titled "Sorry, Wrong Number," although apparently this was a last-minute title change from "She Overheard Death Speaking." The taut drama by Lucille Fletcher had a high pitch of hysteria that seemed to crystalize the fears of women left alone by the war. Throughout the half-hour, Moorehead attempts to make a telephone connection with someone who would help her. As the killer enters the house, she hears him pick up the extension downstairs. Finally, she is connected with the police department at the exact moment of her death. Frightening screams by Moorehead blended into the sound of a passing train. Then a male voice tells the police, "Police department? I'm sorry. Must have got the wrong number. Don't worry. Everything's okay." "Sorry, Wrong Number" had several repeats during the decade. It was filmed in 1948 by Anatole Litvak for Hal Wallis Productions with music by Franz Waxman. Lucille Fletcher was retained to embellish her story further, but the Moorehead role went to Barbara Stanwyck. Moorehead's superb radio interpretation is readily available, fortunately, for $6.70 from Radiola, Box H, Croton-on-Hudson, New York 10520, on an LP of the original *Suspense* backed with another radio classic aired on *Escape*.

After United Artists' wartime stateside drama *Since You Went Away* (1944),

Moorehead was in MGM's *Dragon Seed* (1944), adapted from Pearl Buck. MGM's *Seventh Cross* (1944) told of an escape from a Nazi concentration camp. MGM's *Mrs. Parkington* (1944) was adapted from Louis Bromfield and directed by Tay Garnett, and it brought Moorehead another Academy Award nomination. United Artists' *Tomorrow the World*, from a Broadway hit, concerned Nazism on the homefront when an American family adopts a German lad (Skippy Homeier) indoctrinated with Master Race-power dreams. MGM's *Keep Your Powder Dry* (1945) had Moorehead in a cast line-up of Lana Turner, Laraine Day, and Susan Peters. Then came MGM's *Our Vines Have Tender Grapes* (1945) and the MGM comedy *Her Highness and the Bellboy* (1945). RKO's *The Stranger* (1946), directed by Welles, had a role of a war-crimes commissioner tracking down a Nazi in Connecticut; the part was originally written with Moorehead in mind but was eventually played by Edward G. Robinson. She was filmed as part of the cast of MGM's *The Beginning or the End* (1947), the story of the development of the atom bomb, but her scenes were deleted from the final release print.

In Warner's *Dark Passage* (1947), directed by Delmer Daves, she was third-billed with Bogart and Bacall. Bogart played an escaped prisoner hiding under plastic surgery while attempting to prove his innocence. As the vicious Madge Rapf, Moorehead falls to her death. Charles Higham and Joel Greenberg, in *Hollywood in the Forties*, call Moorehead's performance in *Dark Passage* "a definitive portrait of bitchery."

In Universal's *The Lost Moment* (1947), adapted from Henry James and directed by Martin Gabel, Moorehead was a convincing 105 years old, and in Rouben Mamoulian's *Summer Holiday* (1948), an MGM musical of Eugene O'Neill's *Ah, Wilderness!*, she was the unmarried aunt. In Warner's *Woman in White* (1946), a revival of the Willkie Collins mystery classic, she played Countess Fusco as the menacing Count (Sydney Greenstreet) conspires with Sir Percival Glyde (John Emery) to acquire a family fortune by murdering one of twin sisters. Higham and Greenberg comment that Moorehead "brought a rich presence to a tiny part, especially in the climactic scene in which she silences her husband's insufferable dwelling on some jewels' attraction with a dagger planted deep in his back."

After RKO's Western-mystery *Stations West* (1948), she was fourth-billed as Aggie McDonald in the Oscar-nominated *Johnny Belinda* (1948), starring Jane Wyman as a deaf mute. She was also fourth-billed as Ma Stratton in MGM's *The Stratton Story* (1949), a biography of baseball pitcher Monty Stratton. She played a pawnbroker in MGM's *The Great Sinner* (1949), a Robert Siodmak-directed biography of Feodor Dostoevsky. Christopher Isherwood, who was never too happy about the way films he had worked on turned out, contributed to the writing of *The Great Sinner*. He said, "I only came in on *The Great Sinner* to lend a hand. It should have been much better than it was. I still think it was an amusing idea to show what happened to Dostoevsky while he was writing *The Gambler*; but apart from a few good scenes, it was neither Dostoevsky's story nor the story of Dostoevsky."

After United Artists' *Without Honor* (1949), came the bleak womens' prison drama *Caged* (1950), which was nominated for three Oscars. She was fifth-billed as Mrs. Cosick in 20th's *Fourteen Hours*, a man-on-the-ledge suspense drama. After MGM's *Show Boat* (1951) and RKO's *Blue Veil* (1951) she appeared in the French-made *Adventures of Captain Fabian* (1951), an Errol Flynn-starrer involving witchcraft in New Orleans. *Captain Blackjack* (1952), produced in Spain, concerned dope smuggling. Paramount's *The Blazing Forest* (1952) had Moorehead amid lumberjacks and flaming timber.

In 1952 she and John Lee were divorced. The following year she married actor and TV director Robert Gist (who later directed the 1966 *An American Dream*). Touring the United States in 1951 and 1952 was the Drama Quartette—Agnes Moorehead, Charles Laughton, Cedric Hardwicke, Charles Boyer—with its acclaimed "reading" production of George Bernard Shaw's *Don Juan in Hell*. Moorehead appeared on stage in a pastel pink satin gown with a prism crown atop her piled hair. Critics were bowled over by the Drama Quartette, and one wrote that Moorehead had "the crisp, clean elegance of a lily. She [fell] into exquisite poses and [moved] like a self-appointed queen, to give the play its chief visual attraction."

In 1953 she appeared in "Lullaby", an October 3 production on CBS' *Mirror Theatre*. MGM's *Story of Three Loves* (1953) was followed by *Scandal at Scourie* (1953) and *Main Street to Broadway* (1953), also both for MGM. Then came *Those Red-*

Charles Laughton, Charles Boyer, Agnes Moorehead, and Sir Cedric Hardwicke in *Don Juan in Hell.*

On April 17, 1958, Agnes Moorehead and Paul Douglas appeared together in "The Dungeon" on CBS-TV's *Playhouse 90* dramatic series.

*heads from Seattle* (1953), *Magnificent Obsession* (1954), *Untamed* (1955), *The Left Hand of God* (1955), and an April 10, 1955, appearance in "Roberta" on NBC's *Colgate Comedy Hour*. In 1956: *All That Heaven Allows* (which brought her an Oscar nomination), *Meet Me in Las Vegas, The Conqueror*, "Greybeards and Witches" on NBC's *Matinee Theatre* (May 1), "Teacher" on *Studio 57* (October 28), *The Revolt of Mamie Stover, The Swan, Pardners*, and *The Opposite Sex*. In 1957: *Raintree County, The True Story of Jesse James, Jeanne Eagels*, "The Life You Save" on *Schlitz Playhouse of Stars*, "False Witness" on CBS's *Climax* (July 4), and "The Mary Halstead Story" on NBC's *Wagon Train*.

In Warner's *Story of Mankind* (1957), a fantasy inspired by the Henrik Van Loon book, Moorehead appeared along with other guest stars Vincent Price, Virginia Mayo, Peter Lorre, John Carradine, Dennis Hopper, Ziva Rodann, Henry Daniell, and many others. Produced and di-

rected by Irwin Allen, the story had a representative man (Ronald Colman) defending the human race against the Devil (Price) in a Heavenly Court as the entire history of the world is reviewed.

In 1958 Moorehead and Robert Gist were divorced. On television that year she was seen in "A Tale of Two Cities" on CBS's March 27 *Dupont Show of the Month*, "The Dungeon" on CBS's *Playhouse 90* (April 17), "Protege" on NBC's *Suspicion* (May 12), and she jointed Carol Lynley for "Rapunzel" on *Shirley Temple's Story Book* (October 17).

In 1959 she appeared in *Night of the Quarter Moon* (also titled *Flesh and Flame*); *The Tempest*; "Deed of Mercy" on CBS's *GE Theatre* (March 1); "Man of His House" on NBC's *Alcoa Theatre*; and a December 6 episode of NBC's *The Rebel*.

She co-starred with Vincent Price in Allied Artists' *The Bat* (1959), written and directed by Crane Wilbur from the famed mystery novel by Mary Roberts Rinehart and play by Rinehart and Avery Hopwood. The title of the original novel was *The Circular Staircase*. A killer with claws on his gloves stalks a mansion. The supporting cast consisted of John Sutton, Gavin Gordon, Lenita Lane, Elaine Edwards, Darla Hood (of *Our Gang* fame), and Robert B. Williams. First filmed in 1915 by the Selig Company as *The Circular Staircase* with Eugenie Besserer, the Rinehart play was remade as a silent film a second time in 1926 under its original title with Louise Fazenda starring. Chester Morris and Una Merkel had a crack at it in 1930 with *The Bat Whispers*. By 1959 it wasn't just the staircase that creaked—so did the dialogue and plot—but Moorehead gave her all. Author Cornelia Van Gorder (Moorehead), with her companion Lizzie Allen (Lenita Lane) and her staff, moves into a summer home, The Oaks, rented by Mark Fleming (John Bryant). Mark's uncle, bank president John Fleming (Harvey Stephens), who owns The Oaks, was not in favor of the place being rented. The servants aren't too happy about the idea either after they learn about a maniacal killer called The

Bat, who is rumored to be in the area. While the banker vacations with Dr. Wells (Price), Victor Bailey (Mike Steele), a cashier at the bank, uncovers a million-dollar shortage. At their cabin, Fleming tells Dr. Wells he embezzled the million. He proposes a split of it with the doctor if Wells will murder their guide and return the body to Zenith as the banker's corpse. Then, he will secretly return to Zenith, pay Wells $500,000, and disappear forever. Wells agrees.

A forest fire breaks out. The doctor sees an opportunity to get all the money, and he kills Fleming. Young Bailey is arrested for the theft at the same time Dr. Wells returns with the charred body. Wells's story is that Fleming perished in the fire. At Cornelia's house, the mysterious figure known as The Bat puts in an appearance, frightening all in the house. To add to the middle-aged ladies' fears, Lizzie is bitten by a flying bat. Alarmed, Cornelia phones Dr. Wells and detective chief Andy Anderson (Gavin Gordon).

Anderson, just previous to his arrival at The Oaks, had entered Dr. Wells' laboratory and found caged live bats as well as a plastic replica of the human Bat. Meanwhile, two young women, Mrs. Dale Bailey (Elaine Edwards), wife of the imprisoned bank official, and Judy Hollender (Darla Hood), have gone to The Oaks. Now the ancient house has four women, the somewhat mysterious chauffeur (John Sutton), and the hardfaced housekeeper (Riza Royce) living in it. Dr. Wells is convinced that the stolen money is hidden in The Oaks. Mark Fleming thinks his uncle stole the money, and he too believes it is in the mansion. Just as Mark discovers the large secret panel behind which the money is hidden, he is murdered by The Bat. Lieutenant Anderson is summoned and assures the terrified women that he will maintain a close watch outside the house. Another detective (Robert B. Williams) is assigned to spend the night there. A sound awakens Judy and Dale, who investigate. As Dale opens a door, she is seized by The Bat, who throws her to the floor. He runs quickly

Former Mouseketeer Darla Hood, Agnes Moorehead, and Lenita Lane listen to mysterious sounds emanating from the top floor in this scene from Allied Artists' *The Bat* (1958).

into the hallway, where he murders Judy.

Later, The Bat is trapped by Dr. Wells in his own lab. Wells reveals he is going to find the hidden fortune and kill The Bat, but, in a swift move, The Bat kills Dr. Wells. Cornelia now decides to take matters into her own hands. She discovers the secret panel and enters it, becoming trapped in the airtight compartment. The others finally free her. Meanwhile, The Bat enters stealthily, and they see him in front of the safe. Sensing their presence, he turns quickly and shoots the guard. He then announces that since Cornelia, Lizzie, and Dale have seen him, he is going to kill them all. At that moment, three shots ring out, and The Bat

JOSEPH COTTEN  THOMAS MITCHELL  AGNES MOOREHEAD  PATRICIA MEDINA

IN

*Prescription: Murder*

The cover of the souvenir program book from the early sixties' Broadway production of *Prescription: Murder*. Mercury Players Joseph Cotten and Agnes Moorehead were reunited in this play by producer Paul Gregory.

falls over dead. The Bat was . . . Lieutenant Anderson!

*The Bat* opened for the first time as a play at New York's Morosco Theatre on August 23, 1920. Oddly enough, during one of its many revivals, it was also the first Broadway play that Vincent Price ever attended. Few literary or stage properties had ever been so well milked; even after it had begun dating terribly, it was still bringing in performing-rights royalties. All total, *Bat*'s rights brought in more than $1 million to Rinehart.

During the fifties, Moorehead conducted private acting classes out of her Beverly Hills home. Around 1959 she had

hoped to direct a film, and stated: "I feel I could give certain pictures that 'woman's appeal' which producers say is so important. I would like to codirect, with a man, first. I have, of course, directed a number of stage productions and also on radio. But I don't know whether I'll ever get a chance to direct pictures. It seems definitely to be a man's world. I know that in silent pictures there were several successful women directors, but with talking pictures they seem to have faded away."

In Walt Disney's *Pollyanna* (1960) Moorehead played the self-pitying invalid Mrs. Snow. The film was directed by David Swift, who had begun with Disney as an

Perhaps the best-remembered single episode of Rod Serling's 1959–61 *Twilight Zone* fantasy series was Agnes Moorehead's all-pantomine role of a woman whose home is attacked by two creatures from another planet ("The Invaders") and who does everything possible to get rid of the intruders. The punch ending reveals that Moorehead is an alien giant of another planet, and the UFOnauts are from Earth. This half-hour film gave Moorehead a one-shot TV credit as memorable as her "Sorry, Wrong Number" performance had been a decade-and-a-half earlier on radio.

office boy in the late thirties when Moorehead was already well established as a radio performer. Her television credits of 1960 were "Closed Set" on NBC's *Ford Star Time* (February 16), "Millionaire Katherine Boland" on CBS's *The Millionaire* (April 20), "Trial by Fury" on NBC's *Mystery Show* (August 7), "The Land of Oz" on NBC's *Shirley Temple Theatre* (September 18), "The Irishman" on ABC's *Adventures in Paradise* (October 31), "There's No Fool Like an Old Fool" on ABC's *Harrigan and Son* (December 9), "The House of the Seven Gables" on *Shir-*

*ley Temple Theatre*, and "Miss Bertie" on ABC's *Rifleman* (December 27).

In 1961 she appeared in the Allied Artist mystery *Twenty Plus Two*, MGM's *Bachelor in Paradise*, "Aunt Harriet's Way" on CBS's *My Sister Eileen* (March 1), and "The Protectors" on the same series (March 29); in 1962, United Artists's *Jessica* and *Poor Mr. Campbell* pilot film (August 7); in 1963, MGM's *How the West Was Won*, Paramount's *Who's Minding the Store?*, and "Who Killed Beau Sparrow?" on ABC's *Burke's Law* (December 27); in 1964, "Freedom Is a Lovesome Thing" on ABC's

*Channing* (March 4), "This Train Doesn't Stop Till It Gets There" on ABC's *The Greatest Show on Earth* (April 14), and the May 1 episode of *Burke's Law*.

The success of Robert Aldrich's *What Ever Happened to Baby Jane?* led to another Aldrich Gothic-styled shocker, the 1964 *Hush . . . Hush, Sweet Charlotte* (titled *What Ever Happened to Cousin Charlotte?* before release). Moorehead joined the cast headed by Bette Davis.

Also in 1964 Moorehead began a series role that made her a well-known face to many youngsters unfamiliar with her credits of the preceding forty-five years. This was Endora, mother of the attractive witch Samantha (Elizabeth Montgomery) on ABC's *Bewitched*. Others in this highly successful series, which ran for many years, were Dick York and Alice Pearce. When *Bewitched* was in its fifth year, Moorehead stated, "I say that when you have a job you're lucky. But if I didn't do that, I'd go out and do something else. I'd pick up my grip and go teach a seminar or coach. I can't just sit around. I can't be bothered with that."

After a May 1, 1964, episode of *Burke's Law*, Moorehead appeared in the November 6, 1966, NBC special *Alice Through the Looking Glass*, adapted from the Lewis Carroll fantasy classic. Her last motion-picture credit was as Sister Cluny in *The Singing Nun* (1966). On February 10, 1967, she essayed a role in "Night of the Vicious Valentine" on CBS's *Wild, Wild West*, and she was seen December 13, 1967, in "Spirit Woman" on ABC's *Custer*.

In a January, 1969, interview with Robert Brandes Gratz, Agnes Moorehead talked about her 320-acre family farm in Ohio that was purchased by her grandfather when he arrived from Scotland. "My grandfather was from Edinburgh, and my grandmother was from London. My maternal grandfather was from Wales and grandmother from Dublin, and they settled in Pennsylvania. My mother is now still lively as a cricket and living in Wisconsin. She was always very musical, had a beautiful mezzo-soprano voice, and at 60 decided to take up the cello. She's very anxious for me to retire to the farm so she can come too. I'd love it. It's really the loneliest sort of

Robert Aldrich directs Olivia de Havilland, Bette Davis, and Agnes Moorehead on the set of *Hush . . . Hush, Sweet Charlotte* (1964).

life. Sure, it's terribly exciting, but when I'm making a film or traveling in stock, how long am I in one place to make good friends? I did become good friends with Debbie Reynolds when we made *How the West Was Won* and *The Singing Nun*. Mostly, it's just cold hotels. But that's the wandering minstrel life. I'd love to just stay home and be married again, to have someone take care of me, but I've never been that fortunate."

After a September 29, 1969, episode of ABC's *Love American Style* came the made-for-TV movie *The Ballad of Andy Crocker* (1969) and a September 24, 1970, episode of ABC's *Barefoot in the Park*.

With Dick York on *Bewitched*.

On December 30, 1970, she appeared in "Certain Shadows on the Walls" on Rod Serling's *Night Gallery*; on another *Night Gallery* (September 22, 1971) Moorehead and Ruth Buzzi teamed for a verse recitation of a witch's menu. After the TV movie *Marriage: Year One* (aired on NBC October 15, 1971), she appeared four days later in the follow-up titled *Suddenly Single*. On November 6, 1971, Moorehead was seen in "The Strange Monster of Strawberry Grove" on NBC's *World of Disney*, followed by an episode of *Marcus Welby* aired October 17, 1972.

After the expiration of *Bewitched*, she reappeared in her role of Dona Anna in a new revival of Shaw's *Don Juan in Hell*, co-starring with Edward Mulhare, Ricardo Montalban, and Paul Henreid. Following an extensive road engagement, it opened on Broadway January 15, 1973, in the Palace. Moorehead's notices were typically good, but overall critical reaction ranged from

Agnes Moorehead as Emma Valentine in her Emmy-winning TV role in the "Night of the Vicious Valentine" episode of *Wild, Wild West*, telecast December 13, 1967.

Agnes Moorehead as Endora on ABC-TV's *Bewitched*.

negative to moderate; the show shut down after a limited engagement. Before taking off on her cross-country tour of *Gigi*, she made two more TV movies late that year: NBC's *Frankenstein: The True Story* (as Mrs. Blair) and *Rolling Man* on ABC.

Though never having indulged in liquor or tobacco, Agnes Moorehead had undergone medical treatment for lung cancer, resulting in some examinations at the Mayo Clinic. On April 30, 1974, at the Methodist Hospital, Rochester, Minnesota, she died. No one, it seems, outside her immediate family knew how she suffered. Surviving her at the time were her adopted son, Sean, and her mother, Mrs. John Henderson Moorehead.

With Agnes Moorehead's passing the world lost another immortal. And, very sadly, we became also shockingly aware that most of the original Orson Welles family of Kane and Amberson had fallen victims to the terrible enemy, Time:

Ray Collins, Everett Sloane, Harry Shannon, Dorothy Comingore, Erskine Sanford, Philip Van Zandt, Gus Schilling, Richard Bennett, Fortunio Bonanova, and Tim Holt.

God bless them all.

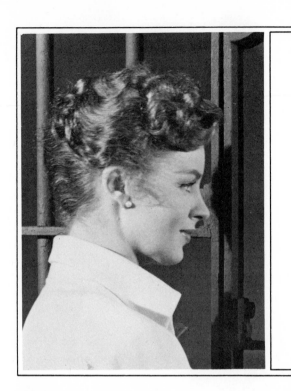

_T_itian-haired Helena Carter was dubbed The Atomic Beauty when she was filming the 1953 20th Century-Fox science-fiction fantasy, _Invaders from Mars_. She was born in New York City on August 24, 1926, and her real name was Helen Rickerts. She spent much of her childhood in Kerry, Ireland, but returned to New York in her teens. After attending Mount St. Vincent College, she received a bachelor's degree from Hunter College and did postgraduate work at Columbia University. During a visit to Radio City she attracted the attention of one of the world's leading beauty connoisseurs, Harry Conover, who convinced her to become a model. In a short time she had appeared on the covers of most of the leading fashion magazines, bringing her to the attention of Hollywood producers.

Her motion-picture debut was the 1947 _Time Out of Mind_ with Phyllis Calvert, Ella Raines, and Robert Hutton. After the Deanna Durbin comedy _Something in the Wind_ (1947), she was third-billed in the soldier-of-fortune drama _Intrigue_ (1948) with George Raft and June Havoc. Universal's _River Lady_ (1948) was followed by a role opposite Douglas Fairbanks, Jr., in _The Fighting O'Flynn_ (1949), the 1950 _South Sea Sinner_ (a remake of the 1935 _East of Java_), Warner's _Kiss Tomorrow Goodbye_ (1950) with Cagney, a co-starring role with Donald O'Connor in the pirate comedy _Double Crossbones_ (1951), _Fort Worth_ (1951), second-billing in the cavalry Western _Bugles in the Afternoon_ (1952) with Ray Milland, and _The Golden Hawk_ (1952), a swashbuckler adapted from the Frank Yerby novel. In 1953 she co-starred with George Montgomery in Columbia's _The Pathfinder_, based on the James Fenimore Cooper tale set in 1754.

_Invaders from Mars_ (1953) top-billed Helena Carter with Arthur Franz and eleven-year-old Jimmy Hunt. Released by 20th Century-Fox on the heels of _Destination Moon, Rocketship X-M, The Thing_, and _The Day the Earth Stood Still_, it was part of the early fifties boom in science-fiction movies and was one of the few science-fiction films of that period to be made in color. The director was William Cameron Menzies, known for his direction of the

225

1936 *Things to Come*, but equally famed for his art direction and production design on such films as *Gone with the Wind* (1939) and *Thief of Bagdad* (1924). During his lifetime (1896–1957), Menzies wrote, designed, directed or co-directed a number of fantasies and genre films: *The Spider* (1931), *Chandu the Magician* (1932) with Lugosi, *The Bat* (1926), *Alice in Wonderland* (1933), and the later remake of *Thief of Bagdad* (1940). In 1953, in England, he also directed the 3-D fantasy *The Maze*. Assisting Menzies on *Invaders from Mars* were two of the top technicians in films—Russian-born production designer Boris Leven (who won an Academy Award for *West Side Story*) and cameraman John Seitz (who photographed *Sunset Boulevard* and the 1951 *When Worlds Collide*, among many others).

*Invaders from Mars* was produced by Edward L. Alperson, who said at the time, "The advent for this unusual motion picture entertainment opens a vast market for such stories, because the subject matter dealing with the unknown creates great interest with young and old. Science fiction stories permit the use of new and entirely different plot structures in the dramatization of screenplays. Additionally, it permits the producer to capitalize on new discoveries and progress of the scientific world."

Horror films, by the early fifties, had degenerated into horror comedies such as *Abbott and Costello Meet Dr. Jekyll and Mr. Hyde* (1953), and the studios had a feeling that straight horror films had run their course. Anxious that *Invaders from Mars* not be taken as horror, Alperson stated, "One must keep in mind not to confuse the Dracula-Frankenstein type of film with the science-fiction photoplay, such as *Invaders from Mars*. The first is an out-and-out horror-mystery thriller based on the impossible. The science-fiction film is based on that which, while unknown, can be given credibility by the judicious use of scientific facts. Forgetting that almost every studio has at least one science-fiction story on its agenda, one need only check on the growing popularity of the science-fiction

David (Jimmy Hunt), having awakened in the middle of the night, tells his father, George Mc-Lean (Leif Erickson), about the *Invaders from Mars* (1953).

No one believes David's fantastic tales, but he soon finds a friend in city health-department physician Dr. Pat Blake (Helena Carter).

magazines to ascertain the ever-increasing demand for this type of reading. Ten years ago there were fourteen such magazines. Today there are fifty-two. Circulation of such literature is skyrocketing." In addition, science fiction was beginning to proliferate in both hardback and paperbacks, book clubs, radio, and also in comic books such as Bill Gaines' and Al Feldstein's *Weird Fantasy* and *Weird Science*.

*Invaders from Mars* was a calculated effort to capture this market of young, comic-book readers—with the experiences of an eleven-year-old a prominent thread in the plot. The Richard Blake screenplay also blends a consciousness of thirties pulp adventure with a basic idea reminiscent of H. G. Wells' *War of the Worlds* and the aftermath of the 1938 radio production of *War of the Worlds* by Orson Welles. David Mac-Lean (Hunt), a typical American youth whose hobby is astronomy, awakens one night to see what appears to be a spaceship magically disappearing underground in a field near his house. The boy's father, George MacLean (Leif Erickson), engaged in secret atomic missile work at a nearby

plant, goes out to investigate. When he returns, a small scar is apparent on the back of his neck, and a curious change has overtaken his personality. These scars are later discovered to be the result of radio receivers implanted by the aliens. It's not long before David's mother, Mary MacLean (Hillary Brooke), also falls victim. Young David then sees a neighbor's little girl (Janine Perreau) being swallowed up by the earth near the spot where the spaceship had landed. She later turns up safe—but acting oddly and carrying the same unusual scar. No one believes the boy's fantastic story—a theme that had earlier provided excellent suspense in Ted Tetzlaff's *The Window* (1949), based on Cornell Woolrich, when no one believed that Bobby Driscoll had witnessed a murder.

Increasing terror strikes David, with fear and concern for his parents. Finally, Dr. Pat Blake (Helena Carter), an attractive, young physician with the city health department, takes him to a mutual friend, Dr. Stuart Kelston (Arthur Franz). An astronomer, Kelston soon finds evidence to support the lad's discovery. After they look

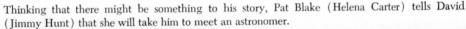

Thinking that there might be something to his story, Pat Blake (Helena Carter) tells David (Jimmy Hunt) that she will take him to meet an astronomer.

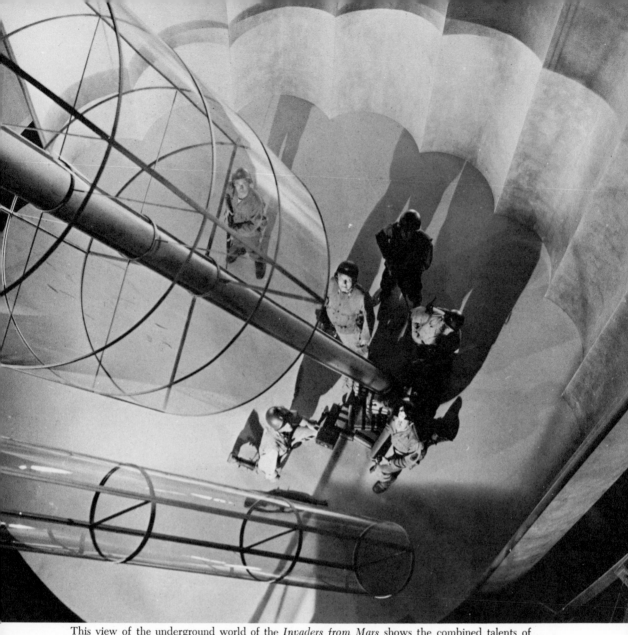

This view of the underground world of the *Invaders from Mars* shows the combined talents of director-designer William Cameron Menzies, designer Boris Leven, and cameraman John Seitz.

through the observatory's telescope and see the commanding general in charge of security (Morris Ankrum) being swallowed up by the earth, they instantly alert the Army. As demolition squads begin to blast down under the earth, Pat and young David are pulled underground. Eight-foot-tall humanoids force them through luminous passages to the underground spaceship. They encounter a tentacled Martian in a glass globe who is directing the operations of his synthetically created giants. At first the terrifying invaders, immune to bullets and armed with devastating weapons,

appear invincible. But, at the last moment, David manages to get control of one of the rayguns himself. He blasts the way to freedom only seconds before a demolition charge blows up the spaceship. In the closing scene, the experiences are all then explained as a dream fantasy of David's, a disappointing and cliché ending for a film that has quite a few imaginative visuals throughout. In prints shown in England, the dream climax was deleted. Special photographic effects were by Jack Cosgrove, and Raoul Krushaar composed the score. Also in the cast were Max Wagner and character actor Milburn Stone, who later became famous as Doc in the long-run *Gunsmoke* TV series.

The film was promoted with ad copy that read, "Out of the peaceful heavens comes a menace beyond all imagination! Natural or supernatural? Where did they come from? How did they get here? Will future invaders from Mars destroy us all?" Movie exhibitors were urged to promote the film by "arranging a small invasion of your own" with costumed space aliens parading the streets. The Fox publicity department also suggested that a "Miss Mars" or "Mars Girl" be locally selected through radio, newspapers, and television. Helena Carter figured in some of this ballyhoo via a four-page color promotional comic book synopsizing the film and featuring Carter with her orange-red hair in the drawings. But the color of the comic ran a poor second to the glowing color of the film that made a memorable appearance for Carter. At the time, she seemed to have a rising career ahead of her. All the more curious then that she chose this moment to retire and vanished from the screen.

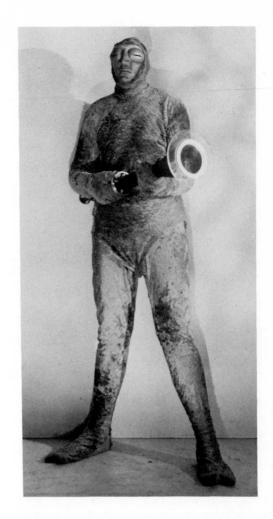

RIGHT: One of the aliens in *Invaders from Mars*.

# Katherine Victor

## by Barry Brown

*I*mmersed with popcorn and fear at the old Padre Theatre in San Jose, I saw every Roger Corman and Jerry Warren movie that hit town. Very little got past my young mind in those days, and no one could fool me. There were two evil women in the movies, and they weren't Gale Sondergaard or Agnes Moorehead but those two beautiful man-killers, Allison Hayes and Katherine Victor. Hayes was Corman's *femme fatale*; Victor was Warren's.

Times change. It's July of 1975. Allison's dropped out of pictures in 1967, suffering from serious internal damage sustained from medication mistakenly prescribed by an inept doctor. It led to her death in 1977. Katherine hasn't done a picture since 1970. With the aid of the Screen Actors Guild and the late actor Bruno VeSota, I was able to locate Miss Victor and arrange an interview, first at a restaurant and then, a week or so later, at her home.

She was on a diet the day we met for lunch at Diamond Jim's on Hollywood Boulevard. She's still quite attractive. The raven-dark hair no longer falls in tresses; now it's shorter, coiffed, more sedate and conservative. Being used to contrasts in offscreen and onscreen images, I wasn't thrown off in the least. What did knock me for a loop, however momentarily, was her friendliness. It taught me something about myself. A few years ago, I was doing an episode of *Ironside* when my mother asked me if Raymond Burr was really crippled. Then, I laughed at her; now, I understand her naïveté. I was somehow expecting Katherine to be a regal, haughty, and threatening woman, the character I'd seen her play in *Teenage Zombies*. But, excepting a certain dignity and caution, understandable under the circumstances, she actually seemed a bit shy and embarrassed to encounter an enthusiastic fan. However, having previously interviewed Bruno VeSota and having heard his own feelings about acting in Jerry Warren films, I was able to piece together in my mind the reasons for Katherine's surprise. Most of her more prominent parts were in Warren films. What she apparently didn't realize was that these films had an audience, primarily children, I suppose, who didn't have jaded views. They simply enjoyed escapist entertainment and were impressed by performances and plots, not by how well or badly a film is done. In retrospect, I see that Warren's films were abominable (in a different sense from, say, *Airport* or *The Towering Inferno*). Yet, when I was a kid watching *Curse of the Stone Hand*, all I knew was that I did not understand what was going on onscreen. But *The Incredible Petrified World* and *Teenage Zombies* (which I saw on a double bill) looked fine to this viewer, and so, at first, it unnerved me to see the notorious Dr. Sheila Myra of *Teenage Zombies* sitting with me and suddenly, no longer menacing, but vulnerable and open and feeling flattered. The shock is related directly to the elementary contrast between film life and real life. I was mistaken in thinking I was no longer susceptible to that shock. But by the end of the two-hour interview, we were both comfortable.

Katherine Victor was born Katena Ktenavea (pronounced Kuh-ten-uh-vay-uh) on August 18, 1928, at 350 West 42nd Street, near Eighth Avenue, in the section of New York City referred to as Hell's Kitchen. She was the younger of two daughters born to Greek immigrants, Stamatia and Valsios Ktenavea. In 1930, due in part to the stock market crash and to the ill health of her father and sister, the Ktenavea family moved to Los Angeles, where young Katena grew up. Vlasios Ktenavea was a lover of music and a frustrated violinist and so, in early life, both girls were led to an appreciation of music. Katena began taking violin lessons when she was four years old, and, while still a child, found herself performing at hotels and various social functions.

At the age of eight or nine, her devotion to classical music already firmly entrenched, Katena's affections began to shift from the violin to the instrument her father had planned for her elder sister to master—the piano. Vlasios, a stern man, disapproved and unsuccessfully sought to discourage the child's spontaneous expression, just as he openly frowned upon his daughter's participation in grade-school

dramatics. For, at this time, Katherine was, in her own words, a "ham"—at school, she wrote, produced, directed, made costumes, and/or acted in plays, a decidedly undignified mode of behavior for a young classical musician. Still, her father's opposition was no match for his daughter's bullheadedness. True to her astrological sign, Leo, she would have her way. After waging a relentless battle for several years, at the age of eleven, she made the move to the piano final, studying first at the Hollywood Conservatory, where previously she'd studied the violin. Her parents offered little moral support, and, to even things out, Katena remained just as set in her rebellion. She recounted one amusing incident in which she defied their orders not to participate in a performance of the local children's orchestra. She used her sister to cover for her while she sneaked out the bedroom window to play at the concert.

Katena's dedication to the piano proved not to be a whim. By the time she attended Hollywood High, she'd concentrated her energies solely on her beloved instrument. Her grade-school romance with acting became a thing of the past, dead and buried. During the last years of World War II, Katena, who had developed a natural aptitude for drawing, worked as a technical illustrator at Douglas Aircraft, a job that, once accepted, she was forbidden by the United States government to leave. Since this cut severely into her practice time at the piano, she made up a story concerning her doctor's "orders" that she not overwork herself, thus maneuvering her working hours around her practice schedule.

Throughout our meeting, Katherine was amiable, except when she spoke of that love for classical music and the piano. Of a sudden, she would become intense and her voice would rise as the speed of her speech increased until suddenly she would slam to a halt, groping for words and lulling in pauses as if she were reliving, in some visible acting metaphor, all the pain and the work and the energy, the sacrifice and the patience and the determination to play her music well. That all ended, abruptly, in

231

1946, with a very simple accident: she broke her finger.

Katherine, who calls herself a fatalist, grants that the accident may not have been wholly accidental. She had been preparing for a concert at the Wilshire Ebell Theatre and wasn't too happy about it. She was, in fact, partially relieved when she "accidentally" slammed the car door on her right index finger, smashing it so badly that it was a full year before the fingerprint whorls came back. Accident or not, she hadn't bargained for the consequences. The finger wasn't put back together well and even when it did heal it had a tendency to lock. Katherine took the setback severely and, in retrospect, she admits, a bit overdramatically: "My whole world was absolutely shattered. My whole life just crumbled." Justified or not, the young girl blew the impediment out of proportion. Instead of seeing the accident for what it was—a major, but by no means conclusive, setback—she allowed the dark side of her imagination to turn against her. The result: a lethargic, apathetic depression. Finally, it was a friend who pulled her out of it, counseling her to go to a modeling school, telling her she had to learn to see herself apart from music (and do something about her clothes, too). Incredibly, Katherine had thought of herself as being an ugly girl. Modeling school not only taught her the more-or-less mechanical aspects of poise and deportment, but also it instilled in her a quality that was heretofore lacking—an awareness of her beauty. As Katherine mildly puts it: "I found I was photogenic."

In 1947, rapidly regaining a self-respect that had suffered badly for a year, she embraced with new-found strength the glamour and unapologetic manner of the fashion model. Unconsciously or not, she turned in part against her former existence, resenting the sedentary routine the piano had imposed on her, in order to more fully enter into her new life. The quiet, determined pianist blossomed when once she knew her power. "It's loads of fun to walk down a staircase, especially with a flowing gown," she said.

Within a year of beginning modeling school, she began to work as a model, first in garment showrooms and later in live TV—a show co-hosted by Betty White and the late Al Jarvis that got her her first union card (AFTRA). She entered beauty contests. She even began to turn her artwork to use, designing clothing and jewelry.

In 1948, the hyperimaginative, newly established model had her astrological chart done. When she went to hear the results, the astrologer told her that she had the finest chart for an actress she'd ever seen. Although Katherine hadn't acted since grade school, the day after this advice was given, a friend of hers, Jack Hearn, a writer of historical articles, asked her to play the title role in a production of *Antigone* that he wanted to do in Beverly Hills. At first, she thought he was kidding. After reflecting on the astrologer's opinion, the fatalistic Katherine thought she had discovered her destiny, the justification and *raison d'etre* for the unfortunate accident of two years before. She decided to give her dead and forgotten love another try and resurrected it from the grave. She began again to act.

At the night on which a first reading of the play was to be held, Katena was nervous and apprehensive. "We sat down and as soon as my cue came, I delivered my lines as if I had been doing it all my life. It was a wonderful feeling." Though the production, for various reasons, never got off the ground, it gave Katherine a decided lift. She felt comfortable with acting, reexperiencing to a degree the same natural affinity she'd formerly felt for music. She received compliments and encouragements from those around her, particularly Jack Hearn, for whom she holds a special esteem, crediting him with giving her the confidence necessary to pursue an acting career. She made her last name into her professional name, Katena Vea, and embarked on a study program: voice placement and projection with Dr. David Hutton (husband of evangelist Aimee Semple MacPherson) and drama with actress Eugenie Leontovich. Appearances in Los Angeles's little theatres followed, along with acting in the early days of live TV. Her stage appearances of this period included *Troilus and Cressida*, *Salome*, *Fabulous Invalid*, *Wuthering Heights*, and the title role in *Hedda Gabler*, starring opposite the late Michael Mark of *Wasp Woman* fame. One of her favorite roles of her entire career was the role of Nina, the fallen woman with a touch of class in Alfred Hayes' play, *The Girl on the Via Flaminia*. One of her great career disappointments was losing the role in the movie version, *Act of Love*, to Barbara Laage.

Her first professional acting job came in 1948, when she did two characters in an episode of the radio show, *Tarzan*, that starred then-actor, now-director (*You'll Like My Mother, Lipstick, The Last American Hero*) Lamont Johnson as Burroughs's jungle hero. She began doing a lot of live television in Hollywood in the late forties and early fifties and remembers it as a wonderful and manic arena. She appeared on early shows such as *Lights, Camera, Action* and *Mystery House*. As well as putting up with a camera that would often be bobbing up and down, live TV actors had not only to act but, in those freedom-from-union-restriction days, also to help move props and furniture around.

As Katherine explained it, (and Bruno VeSota, a veteran of Chicago live TV, backed her up), when television began to catch on and more and more Eastern producers and entertainers began to accept the upstart medium, many of live TV's pioneer performers were shunted aside in favor of already established actors who had not had the desire to be associated with TV when it was struggling through its infancy. Thus, Katherine found herself, in the fifties, being passed over for New York talent, and she began looking for an excuse to transfer her base of operation to New York. That excuse came in 1952 when the parents of Leonard Sillman, producer of *New Faces*, suggested Katherine audition for him. In January of 1953, she arrived in New York, determined to build a strong launching pad for her career.

Before she made that exodus, however,

she appeared in her first film, *Lost Women* (also titled *The Mesa of Lost Women*). Filmed in 1952 and released the following year, the movie starred Jackie Coogan as a mad scientist who creates giant tarantulas and superwomen and featured Tandra Quinn as "The Tarantula Woman." Katherine, who worked one day on the project, foreshadowed in her speechless performance the character she was later to play to the hilt—the mysterious, dark-garbed, half-smiling villain, beautiful, elegant, and supremely menacing. Her bit is silent, appearing at the beginning of the picture. The footage was shot at Red Rock Canyon in Death Valley and shows an auto driving up to Coogan's abode. The car comes to a stop and Katherine emerges, along with an innocent scientist whom she escorts into the building.

The first thing Katherine did in New York was rent a piano. Then she auditioned for Sillman, who said there'd be a place for her in his next revue but that the show was a distance away from production at the moment. In April 1953, Katena Vea landed a part in the national road company of *School for Brides*, a farce by Frank Gill, Jr., and C. Carleton Brown. During the next three years, she did some runway fashion modeling; played in an off-Broadway production of *Everyman* at the Jan Hus Playhouse; toured New England and Canada as a torch singer in her own nightclub act; did bits in films such as *The Eddy Duchin Story* and *Sabrina*; played straightwoman to a comic in New Jersey and, at a particularly desperate time, even demonstrated the first Papermate pen in Macy's basement. Around 1954, Katena Vea became Katherine Victor when, one day, tired of explaining "Vea! V as in Victor" in interviews, she spouted out "Katherine Victor" for the sake of expediency and, from that time on, assumed the name. As a singer, when she played a dive, she used the name Kathy Victor; when she played Ciro's, she used Katherine. Later, in the late sixties, at the suggestion of a numerologist friend, she altered it to Kathrin Victor. By 1955, she had managed to make Earl Wilson's col-

233

Katherine Victor at the Artists and Models Ball in New York, circa 1955.

West Coast, realizing this would be a geographical wrenching that might cause temporary difficulty for her career, but hoping that her hard-earned New York background would finally help her out. Resettling in Hollywood, Katherine obtained a real-estate sales license and went to work for a broker. But in less than two months, she landed an acting job in a surprisingly casual way. To her, it was simply a pleasant opportunity that, hopefully, would lead to something else, and it was also her first starring role in a film, even if the movie were a low-budget independent. Little did she know that the movie, *Teenage Zombies*, an unpretentious little horror drama, would be her first major step toward a firm position in film history.

To fantasy-film buffs and historians alike, the names Jerry Warren and Katherine Victor are inextricably linked. She was the only prominent horror-film personality spawned by Warren's films. He misused Bruno VeSota, who, at any rate, was already established as a horror-film favorite through his perennial appearances in Corman films. John Carradine gave to a number of Warren films performances beyond the call of duty, but he couldn't save them. Other Warren regulars such as Chuck Niles and Lloyd Nelson just didn't have what it takes to make an impression—though Niles' zombie, Ivan, in *Teenage Zombies*, is memorable. In retrospect, I can think of only four positive aspects of Warren's entire output: (1) the laughs provided by his editing and dubbing work, (2) the few glimpses of Mexican horror-film art direction and lighting, (3) the money Warren made for himself (at the expense of the audience and the actors who labored for him for a song), and (4) the discovery and use of Katherine Victor.

Katherine is painfully aware of the dubious distinction of being a "star" creation of Warren's, but the fact is that her reputation was made from *Teenage Zombies*, *Creature of the Walking Dead*, *Curse of the Stone Hand*, and *The Cape Canaveral Monsters*, three of which are Warren releases.

umn, but the actual career progress was all on the surface. She looks back on her New York days with a sense of humor. While there, she did anything that was available —a Broadway show might be in the offing, but by the time it was ready to be cast, Katherine had accepted some less prestigious engagement. "You could say I'd separate the wheat from the chaff and take the chaff," she told me with a smile.

Each summer since she'd moved East, Katherine had commuted to Los Angeles for a few weeks to visit her ailing mother who, in 1957, took a turn for the worse. The hassle of traveling back and forth was too much, so she decided to move back to the

234

Jerry Warren came on the scene in 1956 with the release of *Manbeast*, an attempt to exploit the Abominable Snowman stories that were rife at the time. In the fall of 1957, he was preparing another project, *Teenage Zombies*, hoping to tap the youth market that had prompted producers to pair the topical rock 'n' roll culture with the more timeless appeal of the monstrous and the mysterious. It was a time that saw the release of *Teenage Caveman* (starring Robert Vaughn), *Teenage Monster*, *Teenagers from Outer Space*, *I Was a Teenage Werewolf* (starring Michael Landon), and *I Was a Teenage Frankenstein*. Unlike most of Warren's other efforts, *Teenage Zombies* was not the worst of its genre. A group of teenagers on a waterskiing party come upon an isolated island where a mysterious woman doctor is conducting experiments with a nerve gas that changes people into mindless slaves. She is aided not only by her zombielike servant Ivan (Chuck Niles, now a Los Angeles jazz-radio-station announcer) but by a crooked sheriff on the mainland. She also keeps a gorilla around for protection. The seventy-three-minute melodrama sees the teenagers, headed by Don Sullivan (also the star of *Giant Gila Monster*) captured and properly menaced before they escape.

Jerry Warren's films are notorious for their slipshod production values: uneven sound and atrociously expeditious editing that makes *Dragnet* look like a Bergman film. In *Curse of the Stone Hand*, a tavern filled with at least thirty obviously loud and boisterous people sounds like five or six embarrassed actors standing too far away from a microphone. Everything was done in one take, usually a master shot. Only rarely was a closeup included. Still, a few positive tones crept in quite accidentally—snatches here and there of a solitary, elegiac ambiance uncommon to horror films of any budget— yet this was quite by chance.

It was through luck that Warren ran into Victor. It so happened that the house he was using for Dr. Myra's dwelling belonged to an old friend of Jack Hearn's, and the old friend mentioned to Hearn that Warren had not yet cast his leading lady, the villainous Dr. Myra, even though the film was scheduled to begin in less than a week. Hurriedly, Hearn arranged a meeting between Warren and Katherine at the five-acre estate in Mandeville Canyon. They met and talked and without even hearing her read, Warren gave her the role.

With little more than an introduction and after nearly ten years of pursuing an acting career from California to New York, to be given the lead in a film, any film, was a shock to Katherine. She discounted the fact that Warren had told her to costume herself in her own gowns, without asking to see them beforehand. He trusted her, she must have surmised. When the filming began, she was a bit disturbed by the utter lack of direction (other than Warren's admonition to her to "Keep it simple"). "I thought at the time it would lead to other things," she later said. Warren lucked out when he hired Katherine. If Tor Johnson would have walked in that day, Jerry would have put a wig on him and cast him as Dr. Myra. An actress more cynical about the Warren operation and less intensely serious about her career and the part she was playing would have been a distinct liability to so tenuous a project. If the actress had been one of those naturalistic stammerers, afraid of the broad stroke and the overdone action, the movie would have been as disjointed in concept as its editing was in reality. What Katherine brought to the role was a flair for the melodramatic that raised the film from general dullness to a level where it could actually be enjoyed. There was no character description in the script Warren handed her. With her first film lead, Katherine was, more or less, on her own.

Dr. Myra, as Katherine plays her, is one of those imperious, ice-palace bitches, the kind described in movie publicity releases as beautiful but deadly. Five foot seven, weighing 135, with deep dark-brown eyes, she walks and talks like a queen. Every minute you expect her to give one of those irritating, self-satisfied smiles and say, oh so quietly, "Let them eat cake." When she isn't dressed in her white laboratory coat with its high-necked Mandarin collar, she flaunts her sex appeal in a sophisticated, form-fitting evening gown with two straps in front forming a seductive V at her neckline.

The film, completed in one week in October 1957, lay on the shelf for three years before being co-billed with *The Incredible Petrified World* and released in 1960. Warren got Katherine to attend the premiere at the World Theatre in Hollywood. Katherine hadn't seen the film before, and, though she may have had some idea she wouldn't care for it too much, she didn't quite expect it to be as bad as it was. "I cringed at the whole thing. I was very disappointed."

By the time *Zombies* saw release, Katherine had another horror film in the can, but the story was not much happier. In 1959, an actor-friend of hers, Billy M. Greene, called to tip her off about an independent science-fiction film he'd been cast in, *The Cape Canaveral Monsters*.

Phil Tucker had written the screenplay and was going to direct this tale of life forces from another world that take over the bodies of humans in order to sabotage the space program. Producer Richard Greer had arranged for healthy financing through the investments of a group of doctors. Katherine went in, met Tucker, and read for the part of Nadja, the cold and ruthless woman-puppet of the alien forces who, with her partner (Jason Johnson) is the prime menace to hero Scott Peters and heroine Linda Connell (daughter of cinematographer Merle Connell). She got the part.

"I had great hopes for that picture because everybody was so enthused," she said. Tucker knew what he wanted and didn't hesitate to fulfill his responsibilities as a director. This, plus a two-week shooting schedule, enough money to enable him to shoot several takes per shot if something went wrong, and the added attraction of color, all made the project seem promising. The color was the first thing to go. Last-minute budget cuts restricted it to black

Katherine Victor and Jason Johnson in *The Cape Canaveral Monsters* (1959), written and directed by Phil Tucker.

and white. Then, as the filming days went by, the cost of necessary special effects ate away at the money reserve and made it necessary to take shortcuts in the acting department. Scenes were shortened, changed, or compromised. When the film was finally screened, it proved a disappointment for everyone involved and was never released theatrically. It occasionally shows up on TV. A year went by before the actors received their salaries.

By 1963, Katherine had begun working often in television. She did as many as four episodes of *Day in Court*, five of *Night Court*, as well as guesting on now-defunct series such as *Shannon, Manhunt, Police Station, Slattery's People, The Andy Griffith Show, Space Cadet*, and others. She played a nurse in three episodes of *Ben Casey*. Every time she went into a theatrical venture, however, she had to pull out of her real-estate work, and, in 1960, when she suddenly found herself out of funds, she had to find another job, one with a more flexible schedule. It was that year that she first entered the animation business as an assistant production coordinator, working first with Bob Clampett on the *Beany and Cecil* cartoon show, later with Dale Robertson on the full-length animated *Man from Button Willow* (1965). In 1963 she accepted a position at Hanna-Barbera, where (with the exception of short stays with DePatie-Freleng, Kinney-Wolf and Filmation) she remained until 1970. Throughout those years, she was able to take two or three days off at a time to work an occasional acting job.

She hadn't heard from Jerry Warren for nearly three years, since the disastrous premiere of *Teenage Zombies*, when one day he called to ask her if she'd like to do another film for him. Against her better judgment, she accepted. "Why did I do it? It was just the call of the firehorse, I guess. It was just wanting to do something. It was just wanting to work, no matter how awful."

Her next film for Warren *was* awful, and Katherine's performance didn't help this one. *Curse of the Stone Hand* is a mess, even by Warren standards. Mexican film footage, interesting in itself, is spliced into poorly written expository scenes performed by American actors (John Carradine, Katherine, and Lloyd Nelson) with the whole package held together by a narrator (Bruno VeSota). Katherine appears in the second story, which concerns two brothers, one good, one evil, and the destruction they bring upon themselves over their love for the same woman. Playing a tavern girl whose own sister has been compromised and then cast off by the evil brother, her first scene in the film is embarrassing. In the Mexican footage, we see the evil brother walking in the street below her window. Suddenly, with no preparation for or understanding of who she is or where she came from, Warren cuts to a medium shot of Katherine, standing at a window looking down on the fellow, while tearfully and angrily shouting reprimands at him for his conduct toward her sister. The speech is hurried and emotionally unconvincing, the writing atrocious. Her calmer scenes occur with Carradine as she mulls over what she

intends to do to avenge her sister's honor. These scenes are counterpoised, however, with another puzzlingly bad confrontation scene that ends when Katherine, having upbraided the man for coming again to see her sister, suddenly freezes in horror and utters something to the effect of "What's the matter with you?" Then she renders a violent scream, apparently in response to the man's face. Cut to another scene. Later in the picture, Katherine is back again, plotting revenge. There is no clue whatsoever as to why she'd screamed before.

*Curse of the Stone Hand* has the only sympathetic character Katherine played in a film, and it did not suit her talents. "Since I started acting, I have looked the villain, and I have been selected to play the villain. I enjoyed these parts. For me, it was real escapism. I don't feel comfortable in sympathetic roles. I haven't been asked to do many, but whenever I have I've just felt very uncomfortable." If there was one positive aspect to Katherine's experience with *Curse of the Stone Hand*, it was that it enabled her to meet and work with John Carradine. "I enjoyed working with him. He always had humorous anecdotes. I remember asking him, 'Why are you doing this?' He said, 'The color of the money is the same.'"

Katherine's next for Warren, shortly after *Stone Hand*, was another Mexican-American hybrid: *Creature of the Walking Dead*. This time, however, the story made a little more sense, and Katherine, dressed in black, was again the woman with an air of mystery. As a conductor of séances whose maid has mysteriously disappeared, she enlists the aid of police inspector Bruno VeSota. That aid, of course, consists of a lot of Jerry Warren expository theorizing to clarify the Mexican footage—taken from a film called *La Marca del Muerto* about a doctor who experiments with immortality and brings his dead ancestor back to life. The séance scene was shot in one room above a go-go dance bar, while, in the adjoining room, the set for a scene from *Attack of the Mayan Mummy* (1963) was made ready for use the same night.

The actual chronology of Katherine's work in Warren films is difficult to determine. So many wild lines and nebulous scenes were being done at the same time and fitted, almost like replaceable parts, into any number of films that her recollections are understandably hazy. One recording session might include lines from three different films. Whatever the case may be, it seems certain that at least a year had passed since her last work for Warren when, again out of the blue, probably sometime in the mid-sixties, he called once again. This time his pitch was different— he wanted to do a film of his own again. No splicing job this time! And he wanted Katherine for the lead.

In the best Warren tradition, *The Wild World of Batwoman* was meant to cash in on a popular subject—the national enthusiasm over the debut of the *Batman* TV series. Instead, just prior to a thirty-theatre multiple run in Philadelphia, Warren found that labs were mysteriously stalling on print delivery. Obviously, someone feared that small-time producer Warren would somehow cut into their own fortunes (as if there weren't enough to go around). This failure to come through with booked prints foreshadowed the end of Warren's film career, even though, in the end, Warren won the case.

*Batwoman* is Katherine's least favorite film, and she asked me to soft-pedal my mention of it. Her own words describe it best: "This was absolutely going to be top grade! Color! I was going to have my props made, my batmobile, my boatmobile, everything was going to be top-dollar. Of course, I was flattered, naturally . . . so you always think it's going to be different, but then I saw it was going to be just the same old thing." The first thing to go, of course, for money reasons, was the color. Katherine worked one week on the film, which pitted Batwoman against an evil scientist, Dr. Neon (George Andre), who is interested in obtaining an atomic bomb. The film co-starred a tired-looking Steve Brodie, much changed from his days as a B-movie tough guy.

In early 1966, an injunction by National Periodicals, which had a tie-in with 20th-Fox re *Batman* licensing, stopped Warren from distributing *Wild World*. He filed a $12,000,000 anti-trust countersuit and successfully fought the case, but the months of legal wrangling left him weary and discouraged. After distributing the film under the absurd title *She Was a Hippie Vampire*, he withdrew it from circulation. It will never be shown on TV, he insists, and so, for all intents and purposes, is a lost film. Katherine could not be more pleased.

Her last film for Warren was also Warren's last film. In *House of the Black Death*, Katherine played the high priestess of a group of devil worshipers. The film starred Lon Chaney, Jr., John Carradine, and forties film stars Andrea King and Tom Drake. It was not released theatrically, but is occasionally given a television airing. Soon after its completion, Warren gave up filmmaking and is now an avocado grower somewhere in California,

Katherine didn't do another film until 1969. In that year, she got two small parts, back to back, and had to take two weeks off from her animation work. In the TV-movie, *Fear No Evil*, made at Universal for NBC and starring Louis Jourdan, Bradford Dillman, and Carroll O'Connor, Katherine appeared in a séance scene, dressed in a man's tuxedo, in one of the first overt TV characterizations of a lesbian. The part is so small, however, as to be easily missed. In *Justine*, a 1969 Fox release starring Anouk Aimee and Dirk Bogarde, she was a prostitute in a bordello and had one good closeup. With work so sparse, Katherine thought it best not to jeopardize her animation job, and so, after working in *Justine*, she decided not to accept any more insubstantial acting jobs. On April 19, 1970, she married for the first time. Her husband is a retired consultant whom she met at a Screen Directors Guild awards banquet in 1968. Finding it no longer necessary to work, she quit her job and moved with her husband to Sherman Oaks, a suburb some ten miles removed from Hollywood.

Katherine did one last film in 1970.

Thankfully, it is something she isn't ashamed of. *Captain Mom* is a fifteen-minute 16mm short, presently available for college and library use, made by two Filmation writers, Charles Menville and Len Janson. They met Katherine when she briefly worked for that company, interviewed her, and cast her as the girl who tames Captain Mom (co-producer Menville), a superhero who is lonely and out of sync with society. He meets Katherine through a computer-dating service, falls in love, breaks up, considers suicide but can't bring himself to do it, and ends by marrying the girl and flying off with a string of cans tied to his ankle while Katherine, with her knowing, self-satisfied Dr. Myra smile, rides the conquered hero's back. Shot in eleven or twelve days with a small crew ("They were all under three feet," Janson told me), *this* film *is* in color.

The disheartening blow she'd suffered so long ago in music had been followed by a lacklustre and often depressing acting career. However much enjoyment that career gave my generation, it did substantially little for Katherine. Her marriage having freed her of the necessity to work, she was free to travel extensively with her husband, which she did. She found, too, that her husband (who prefers his name not be used) enjoyed music. "He encouraged me to play, and he enjoyed listening to me." Her husband is one of those tough, plain-spoken men who worked hard to get what he got and isn't ashamed of the fact. He serves as the ample oak for the flitting, artistic vine that is Katherine. With his encouragement, in 1973 she auditioned for, and was accepted by, Sergei Tarnowsky, a distinguished pianist, then ninety years of age, a native of Kiev, Russia, who attended St. Petersburg Conservatory and taught at Kiev Conservatory (one of his students was Vladimir Horowitz). Katherine's praise for her instructor was unstinted. She didn't so much as order as she did imply in her offhand way that I'd best include a mention of her reverence for the inspiration he's given her. She referred to him as "the last of the masters."

TOP: *The Wild World of Batwoman* (1966), later retitled *She Was a Hippie Vampire* and withdrawn from circulation.

BELOW: *The Wild World of Batwoman.*

Sergei told Katherine what someone should have told her nearly thirty years ago: "Every pianist has had a broken finger. Just disregard it and don't favor it." She added, with a laugh, "which is what I have done, and it's behaved beautifully." A disciplinarian who knows the piano better than Katherine ever hopes to, he told her, more or less, that she'd been a fool to neglect her musical talent with such a poor excuse.

In the last two years, Katherine's been where she always wanted to be—doing

239

what she wants, able to work at her piano, with no fear of emotional or economical reprisal. "I don't have to do anything I don't want to do. I'm just enjoying myself, and I'm enjoying music. It's a real thrill that in the past two years my ability on the piano has come back, and it's improved so much. It's very possible I will play again professionally. . . . I'm not ready right now. Perhaps in a year or two I'll get a program together."

"If she does it, it's strictly because she feels the need," adds her husband.

"I'm not striving the way I used to," says Katherine. "I always had the urge to have to do something, to have to show everybody I could be the best. I don't have that urge anymore."

Indeed, she seems relaxed now— enough to speak of her acting career with some degree of objectivity. We spoke of her

favorite musical pieces, the melancholy first movement of Edward MacDowell's *Piano Concerto in D Minor* and Brahms' *G Minor Rhapsody*, and the similarity between the type of music she likes and the acting style she used. In music, she leaned toward the melancholy and the dramatic, the deepest, darkest feelings of her soul: the same feelings, in effect, of the characters in her most memorable film performances. Not feelings so simple as love and hate, but feelings of obsession and compulsion, truly more complex and foreboding than simple emotional reactions.

Katherine, even now, does not quite accept or understand the fact that there exists, somewhere apart from me, a growing number of Katherine Victor fans. Even Allison Hayes, whose popularity was considerably more widespread, expressed surprise in discovering there was an Allison

Katherine Victor astride Charles Menville in *Captain Mom* (1970). Menville was also the film's co-producer.

Captain Mom (Charles Menville) and his bride (Katherine Victor) fly off to their honeymoon in *Captain Mom*.

Hayes cult. To Katherine, Warren films meant little. To the "industry" (for which too many actors hold a pitifully ludicrous respect, even to the point of being afraid of their own agents) Warren films meant nothing. But to the kids (i.e., the money source), a thirty-foot image is a thirty-foot image and who the hell cares what Leota Lovely was being paid by what impressive rich person? I was watching the performance. It's not an exaggeration to say Katherine Victor was a bigger star in my mind than Lana Turner was in reality. My compatriots and I weren't sophisticated enough to take orders about what to like and what not to (in fact, most of us still aren't *that* sophisticated). It's not a charitable white lie to say the number of her fans is growing as her films are replayed.

"This is absolutely incredible to me. It really is incredible because as I said, I always wanted to have fans and to be in the movies, but to have it come out of such a poor list of credits! I really don't have any substantial credits. A couple of the stage things were excellent, but still they weren't big time, so it's just incredible to me that, shall we say, my dreams as an actress for fans and admiration would come about so indirectly through productions that, being given the chance again I certainly would not have done. It's a thrill to me to have my name even listed among the greats of horror."

Still, she'd like to do a truly "good" horror film. "I think it would be a fulfillment of my life if I could have a part in a fine horror film with proper effects and production values . . . a good Gothic horror film."

It seems doubtful whether anyone in the industry will be altruistic enough toward horror fans to feature Katherine in a decent horror film, and Katherine herself left no doubt that she does not intend to pursue the idea. But she's still an active member of Screen Actors Guild, and she did leak information that she might act again in a movie some acquaintances might do. One might assume one will see her on the screen again, but, for the nonce, it's music all the way.

As we came to the close of the interview, Katherine said, in reference to her performances in horror films, "My contribution is so dubious. But I'm grateful for this interview. This makes me, really, not be so ashamed of what I have done."

Her husband, a film buff, might be able to explain it to her. I couldn't do it adequately. Perhaps the interest of future film historians will make it clear. Most readers will already understand. When D. W. Griffith died in 1948, he died broke and obscure, but twenty-seven years later his face was on a United States postage stamp sold at the Knickerbocker Hotel in Hollywood, where the man had met his Maker. The example is not farfetched; it's applicable. Katherine can feel content knowing that she's been happily reunited with her first love, music, after so long a separation. But for her to feel her film career wasn't successful would be unrealistic. She can take or leave the facts that film historians accept—that's her human prerogative. But there is no denying them. Dr. Myra is forever in the clutches of her own creation, and those of us who intrepidly watch horror films of any year, country, or budget, can testify that Katherine is one of our Scream Queens.

# Diana Dors

*U*nlike many former screen sexpots, who either can't or don't want to change with the times, Diana Dors is among the several (such as Shelley Winters) who have intelligently made a successful transition in order to continue their careers. In Diana's case, the changeover from a one-time screen sex queen to Scream Queen has been somewhat more dramatic. Considering her status back in the fifties—in a category shared by Marilyn Monroe, Jayne Mansfield, Kim Novak, and other great beauties—Diana's transition is not only dramatic, but also visually mind-boggling.

Diana (nee Diana Fluck) was born in England in 1931. She gained experience by appearing in varied roles, before and even after emerging as a curvaceous sex symbol of the fifties.

One of her early films was *The Shop at Sly Corner* (1946), starring Oscar Homolka as a kindly antiques dealer. A deceitful clerk knows Homolka buys stolen goods on a few occasions, and blackmails him by degrees, losing his life by finally demanding too much. Diana is involved in this complex triangle. Another was *Oliver Twist* (1948).

Director David Lean's classical handling of Dickens's masterpiece added dark, sinister qualities even Dickens didn't emphasize. Diana is in a small supporting role.

*A Kid for Two Farthings* (1955) was one of the best. *Castle of Frankenstein* #12 gave this evaluation in one of its capsule reviews: "Top-drawer, offbeat, touching, often arty drama. Youngster from London slums finds one-horned baby goat and thinks it's a unicorn with magic powers." Director Carol Reed's natural, unpretentious style in capturing a less-familiar, humbler side of London makes this a visual story masterpiece. Diana plays a young wrestler's fiancée; former boxing champ Primo Carnera (in a rare screen role) hovers around ogrelike, menacing her boyfriend while lecherously ogling Diana.

And still another was *Man Bait* (British title: *The Last Page* (1952), directed by Terence Fisher. This is an atmospheric, competent blackmail thriller with highly subtle touches of evil. It was produced by Hammer at a period when they were still experimenting in mystery-horror, several years before taking the direct plunge that established them as England's House of Horror. Working as a clerk for well-to-do rare-book dealer George Brent, Diana Dors is influenced into blackmailing him by her insidious boyfriend (played with magnificent vileness by Peter Reynolds). Diana's performance is quite good as a girl torn by her own greed, manipulated by evil, Svengali-like Reynolds, but evincing gradual ambivalence and, finally, capitulating from remorse when she learns Brent's ailing wife has died.

On television she appeared in "The Lovely Place" on the *Rheingold Theatre* (December 8, 1954); on *The Phil Silvers Show* (January 23, 1959); in "The Sports Car Breed" on *Straightaway* (December 8, 1961); in "Run for Doom" on *Alfred Hitchcock Presents* (May 17, 1963); in "Who Killed Alex Debbs?" on *Burke's Law* (October 25, 1963); and in "87 Different Kinds of Love" on *Eleventh Hour* (February 19, 1964).

After skimming in and out of the genre Diana truly joined the ranks in 1972's *Theatre of Blood*, dominated by Vincent Price as Edward Lionhart, a deranged actor who, with his equally dotty daughter (Diana Rigg), plots to eliminate critics who denied him London's Best Acting Award. One of them is the jealous Jack Hawkins, whose

Diana Dors and George Brent in *Man Bait* (1952), originally titled *The Last Page*.

wife, Diana Dors, is a nice but narcissistic tease. Using incidents from Shakespeare's plays as inspiration for killing his victims, mad Vincent Price creates an Iago-like situation against Hawkins who, like Othello, winds up strangling his own Desdemona, Miss Dors.

Only a few months before *Theatre*, Diana formally announced her plans to specialize in character roles at the expense of her former blonde-bombshell image. Speaking seriously, she said, "I'm forty now, and can't go on playing good-time glamour girls and tarts forever. I want to play women of my own age, now—and in the future."

The same year, following *Theatre of Blood*, she appeared in *Nothing but the Night*, co-starring with Chris Lee and Peter Cushing: "In that one I play a triple murderess with a record of assault, larceny, and prostitution. I play a mother who fights to get her daughter back from an orphanage. I was hunted like a wild animal all over the moors. We spent three days filming the scene on Dartmoor with helicopters and police tracker dogs after me—the lot! Back at the Pinewood Studios I was having lunch in the restaurant one day and still wearing my film costume, when a lot of old friends failed to recognize me. I wore a red wig, my clothes were dirty and dishevelled, a million miles from my old image. Michael Caine was completely foxed, and Sid James and Kenny Williams, who were making a *Carry On* at the time, were puzzled at first. But I was really pleased that the others didn't know me. It proves that I must have looked like a totally different person to them.

"After that film I stayed on at Pinewood and went straight into *The Amazing Mr. Blunden*, which Lionel Jeffries directed. Lionel and I are old friends, as we've acted together in several films. *Blunden* is a Victorian ghost story, and I played the villainess of the piece—a sort of female Sweeney Todd. They tarted me up, padded me out, and had me looking like I was sixty, which was the age required for the part. They even blacked out my teeth; they

243

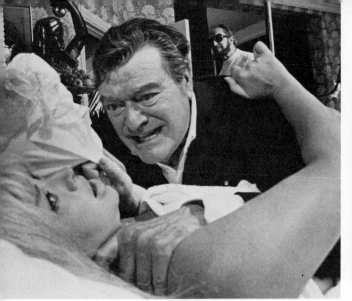

Diana Dors, Jack Hawkins, and Vincent Price in *Theatre of Blood* (1973).

Diana Dors in *Blonde Sinner*.

were actually painted over with Friar's Balsam! They also gave me a wig that made me look bald when someone snatched it off my head. As the final straw, they even put a big wart on my chin! That was so funny. It was really only a piece of Puffed Wheat glued to my chin. I really went over the top in that film, but I had myself a ball. I could storm and rave, and generally have a great time. There was none of the old me in that role. This was really a character part they handed me. Playing the gin-swigging, wicked housekeeper, Mrs. Wickens, gave me lots of good old-fashioned melodrama. There were a few cracks about me not needing much makeup for the part! In fact, I spent a lot of time in the makeup chair before I emerged as the old harridan Lionel wanted me to play."

Suffering the same problem affecting *numerous* fine productions, *The Amazing Mr. Blunden* has been undistributed in the United States and in other areas, a victim of the colossal blunders created by some men of narrow vision currently in charge of film distribution monopolies. This form of senselessness only begins bordering on madness in light of the fact that hundreds of theatres continued to be in increasingly severe distress (or forced to shut down) in 1976–77—not for *lack* of patrons but from a *shortage* of film product! It cannot be denied that many films (a majority of them actually tax-shelter rip-offs)

scarcely deserve to see the light of day: e.g., *Who?*, starring Trevor Howard and Elliot Gould, a semi-sci-fi monstrosity purchased by cable TV Home Box Office (perhaps for a song) and unloaded upon unsuspecting subscribers in the fall of 1976. But there are also many, such as the critically acclaimed *The Wicker Man* (starring Chris Lee and Ingrid Pitt)—winner of a Paris film festival award—which had been rotting in Warners' vaults since early 1973, although a minor distributor tried to resurrect it in 1978. The respected British film critic and historian David Pirie, author of the excellent *A Heritage of Horror: The English Gothic Cinema* (Equinox/Avon, 1973) has this to say in his book about *The Amazing Dr. Blunden*: "This remarkable and unexpectedly disturbing film is one of the very few serious cinematic attempts to re-create the world of the Victorian ghost story. The subtle performances of the children, the plot's complexity, and Lionel Jeffries' enormous talent for establishing atmosphere and period certainly place it among the most important supernatural movies ever made in England."

Astonishing audiences and the critics who had once imagined her purely as a "sex symbol," Diana Dors decided to take on a serious acting career with profound determination: "The first time I ever really let my looks go on the screen was for *Yield to the Night* back in the mid-fifties. That was one of my favorite films. I played a convicted murderess, based on the true-life case of Ruth Ellis, who was the last woman to be hanged in Britain before capital punishment was abolished. It was the first time I ever had a chance to play such a part. I was very thankful to Lee Thompson, the director for having faith in me. Until then everyone thought I was just a joke, and certainly not an actress to be taken seriously, even though I knew within myself I was capable of playing other roles. The big problem was trying to convince other people. *Yield to the Night* provided the breakthrough I had been waiting for."

She does not deny having lived it up while enjoying her lush, youthful years. She's the first to admit, "Those corny glamour movies helped to build up my image— and I collected plenty of headlines along the way. People said it was the only way to go about becoming a star; so I believed them and went along with what they told me."

Diana lived around Hollywood for more than five years while under contract to RKO; during this time she was married for the second time to British funnyman Dickie Dawson. Like any young star who achieves fame, "Everything I said or did was big news at that time. About 1960 I was paid £35,000 for my life story by one of England's top-circulation Sunday papers. That was only one thousand pounds less than the record sum they paid out to Errol Flynn for his memoirs. Some day soon I would like to write my own autobiography, just to put the record straight."

While the world may not be waiting with bated breath to hear all of Diana's side of the story, she's quick to indicate: "So many stories have been *ghosted* for me. There was, of course, a book called *Swinging Dors*, which was intended to cash in on my name, but it turned out to be a big flop. It was a catchy title, I'll admit, but nobody seemed to buy it. Now if I wrote a book today, telling things as they really happened, I think it would be very different. But at the time I needed the cash, and they paid me a quite staggering sum."

She revealed having earned lots of money over the years; but managers, publicists, and agents depleted all her funds— the heavy price that many celebrities pay to remain in the public eye. "You see, I was very young when I began in show business. The money just seemed to go. When you're young and your career is going strong, you simply do not think that it might all end some day. But I'm not complaining, and I've few regrets. I've enjoyed a full life, and I think the best years are still ahead. If I had my time over again, I would certainly make sure about safeguarding my finances; but I don't think I would change anything else. If I can be accepted as a serious actress, then I'll be very happy."

Sometimes a victim of her own self-effacement, Diana has actually seen most of her ambitions realized over the years. At age nine, she wrote in a school essay about her ambitions of becoming a major film star. In less than five years she was awarded two silver-and-bronze medals for elocution; she also won her first bathing-beauty contest. At fourteen she was named "the most promising screen actress of the year," etched on an Alexander Korda Award. She studied for the stage at the London Academy of Music and Dramatic Art. She made her film debut at fifteen in *The Shop at Sly Corner*, which resulted in a ten-year contract with the Rank Organization. What Marilyn Monroe was to the United States, Diana was to England—her hourglass figure resulted in endless pinup sessions. A girlie booklet, *Diana Dors in 3-D*, became the rage of the 3-D era in the early 1950s. Her initials, DD, became internationally famous.

Soon after her success in *Yield to the Night*, she took off in 1956 for Hollywood, where she starred in the 1956 George Gobel comedy *I Married a Woman*, followed by the 1957 *Unholy Wife* (with Rod Steiger), and *The Lady and the Prowler*. She then returned to Britain for featured roles in *The Long Haul* (1957), opposite Victor Mature; *Tread Softly, Stranger*, with Terence Morgan; and *Passport to Shame*, a story on prostitution, which was considered daring at the time. Her shrewd managers also

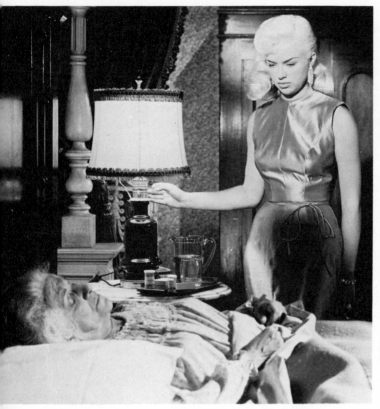

LEFT: *The Unholy Wife* (1956): Diana Dors and Beulah Bondi.

RIGHT: A tense moment from *Tread Softly, Stranger* (1958).

booked her successfully in the international cabaret circuit from Las Vegas to South Africa, the Far East, and European entertainment centers.

Some of Diana's top Hollywood films next included starring roles with Danny Kaye in *On the Double* (1961), opposite Jerry Lewis in *The Ladies Man* (1961), followed by *The Big Bankroll* with Stephen Boyd. She returned to Britain for other dramatic parts, including *Baby Love*, in which she played the alcoholic mother of a four-teen-year-old girl. This was all part of Diana's plan to seek acceptance and recognition as a serious screen actress.

In recent years, she acted in *There's a Girl in My Soup, Hammerhead, Hannie Caulder,* and the black poetry of Jerzy Skolimowski's overwhelming psychological study, *Deep End.*

Diana soon came up with a part in what turned out to be one of the best films of the last ten years, *The Pied Piper* (1972), under the fine hand of Jacques Demy, who had already attained an admirable reputation directing *The Umbrellas of Cherbourg* and *The Young Girls of Rochefort* and more recently, *Donkey Skin,* based on another children's fairy-tale classic. *Piper's* poetic quality made it a surprising and rare art-film entry in the usually commercial film market. It more or less touches on images and ideas set in similar period pieces, such as the notorious *Mark of the Devil* (publicized under the rating of "V" for "Violence") and Ken Russell's *The Devils.* The difference is that Demy's film is more artistically elevating and sounder in its resolution, whereas *Mark of the Devil* degrades and evokes revulsion, while Russell's *Devils* sacrifices poetic sensibility by thundering away horrifically at

Diana Dors in *The Pied Piper* (1971).

the injustice of bureaucratic and institutional criminality.

Demy's film is photographed with intense beauty—scenes seem to pop out like paintings by Holbein and Rubens coming to life. Delicate as *Piper's* structure seems, Demy invests in it strong portrayals of profound evil, of impending death, and the terrible destruction brought on by the Black Plague within an unobtrusive, unpreaching theme of sociological import: The Pied Piper (Donovan) is cheated out of his reward by the town fathers after he has rid Hamelin of a plague of rats (so ugly

and numerous they put those in *Willard* and *Ben* to shame); a Da Vinci-like Renaissance man, Melius the alchemist, is hated jealously for his wisdom, then persecuted, and finally burned at the stake for being a Jew and a "sorcerer." The Church is depicted in all of its abundant riches spending untold wealth on erecting a huge cathedral while the poor go hungry and the sick waste away. The piggish mayor's eleven-year-old daughter (played by Cathryn Harrison, daughter of Noel Harrison and granddaughter of Rex), is forced into a sick marriage of convenience, for monetary gain, to the Baron's evil son. Capping all of this "3-D" ambiance of decay, debauchery, and degeneration is an overweight, sassy Diana Dors, playing the self-indulgent wife of a corrupt local rich character—and herewith she proves to be not only the world's sexiest plump actress but also a matured and truly dedicated artist.

Fortunately, goodness wins out as Pied Piper Donovan (who also scored the film's superb music) leads all the innocent children away; their evil establishmentarian parents, neighbors, *et al.*, are soon properly rewarded as the Black Plague starts hitting them toward the close of the final reel.

Shamefully underrated in its initial release in the United States, and thrown away by Paramount in third-rate quickie neighborhood playoffs (double-billed with *Z.P.G.*), *Piper* suffered a fate shared increasingly by many productions in the last few years. Majors now shoot off all their big guns for one or two super-blockbusters —in this case Paramount was giddy over the bonanza brought in by the *The Godfather*, "so who gives a damn about *smaller* films," they probably questioned. (Answer: movie fans do!)

In Freddie Francis's *Craze* (1973) Diana played Dolly Newman; this Herman Cohen production concerned a murderer (Jack Palance) offering sacrifices to the African idol Chuka.

In the "An Act of Kindness" segment in *From Beyond the Grave* (1976), Diana's marriage to Ian Bannen is cut off abruptly when he befriends a weird street peddler, Donald Pleasance, who introduces him eventually to his even weirder daughter, Angela Pleasance. Diana plays a slatternly, apathetic sort who cares more for her hairdo and manicuring than running the house and caring for Ian. Weird Angela makes life more pleasant for Ian when she creates a wax image of Diana who, of course, dies once a pin stabs the doll. Soon Donald Pleasance is best man when his daughter and Ian marry. Ian dies horribly, though—blood gushes from his head as Angela's knife cuts through the little bridegroom figure on the wedding cake.

Proud of being a horror-film Scream Queen, Diana vows: "I've appeared in horror films before. I was also in *Berserk!* with Joan Crawford some years back. . . . I've worked with Vincent Price in *Theatre of Blood*, and he's marvelous. I've played my share of drunken sluts, good-time girls, and whores. Being bumped off is really no novelty for me. I've been shot, hanged, strangled, gassed, burned to death, and even pushed over a cliff. And, for a TV episode of *Alfred Hitchcock Presents* I was sawn in half by an electrical buzz saw."

Diana Dors with all the circus folk of *Berserk*.

# Patty
# McCormack

$T$he biggest Scream Queen of the late fifties wore pigtails—Patty McCormack as the child murderer Rhoda Penmark in *The Bad Seed* (1956), a role that brought her an Academy Award nomination. She was eleven years old then and had already been a working professional for eight years.

Patty was born in Brooklyn on August 21, 1945, and at the age of three won a baby contest that led to a modeling contract when she was four. Speech lessons got rid of her lisp, and, at six, her speech teacher presented her to an agent at a time when Elaine Perry was preparing the play *Touchstone* for Broadway. Patty played a child with an incurable illness who dies after her father refuses to allow her to enter a swimming pool that a boy (Josh White, Jr.) believes has healing waters.

She did much live television through 1953 and 1954: "The Party" on NBC's *Mirror Theatre* (August 18, 1953), "I Remem-

ber, I Remember" on NBC's *TV Soundstage* (January 15, 1954), "A Handful of Stars" on CBS's *The Web* (February 7, 1954), "The Golden Box" on *Soundstage* (February 12, 1954), NBC's *Armstrong Circle Theatre* (April 13 and September 14, 1954), and "Somebody Special" on NBC's *Philco Playhouse* (June 6, 1954). On September 3, 1954, she appeared on CBS's *Mama*, the TV series version of *I Remember Mama*, and she continued to appear as a *Mama* series regular for the next two years.

*The Bad Seed* is the best-known novel of William Edward March Campbell (1893–1954), who wrote under the name William March. The play version, dramatized by Maxwell Anderson, was staged by the Playwrights' Company and opened December 8, 1954, at the 46th Street Theatre in New York. Patty was eight and a half when she began appearing nightly as eight-year-old Rhoda Penmark, who kills her classmate Claude Daigle during a school picnic to get the penmanship medal she felt should have been awarded to her. Nancy

ABOVE: A posed publicity photograph of Patty McCormack assuming her famed *Bad Seed* characterization of Rhoda Penmark.

249

Kelly portrayed her mother, and Eileen Heckart was the near-hysterical mother of Claude. All three actresses, reprising their Broadway roles in the film, were nominated for Oscars, and all three missed out. "I remember the night of the Academy Awards," said Patty recently, "but I had no idea how important it was, so when I lost, I wasn't even upset." Both the novel and the play climax with Mrs. Penmark attempting suicide after believing she has also killed Rhoda. The story ends with Rhoda being saved while her mother, who had kept her suspicions secret, dies. In the fifties, audiences groaned at the *deus ex machina* that was concocted for the film version—her mother lives and Rhoda returns to the picnic area, where she is struck by lightning and dies. This was then followed by a

filmed "curtain call" (usually missing these days from TV prints) in which Patty, out of character, received a spanking from Nancy Kelly! Because of the weakened ending, the film is not today regarded as the classic it should have been, and one must return to the William March novel to get the full

OPPOSITE PAGE

TOP LEFT: Chris, after learning that her natural mother was the murderess Bessie Denker, questions Rhoda about Claude's medal that she found in Rhoda's jewelry box.

TOP RIGHT: Rhoda panics. She steals a handful of matches and sets fire to LeRoy's mattress, killing him.

BOTTOM: She sneaks out of the house and goes to the pier during a storm. Here she is struck by lightning. In the original ending of the book and play, Rhoda survived an overdose of sleeping pills given her by Chris, and Chris blew her own brains out.

BELOW: In the garden of the house, the half-witted LeRoy taunts Rhoda about Claude's death.

effect of this powerful story. The structure of the original ending, however, seems to have finally made it to film in the climax of 1976's *The Omen*, when the child Damien lives as his parents (Gregory Peck and Lee Remick) die with the knowledge of Damien's malevolence.

Patty returned to TV: "An Episode of Sparrows" on CBS's *Climax* (March 29, 1956), "Alien Angel" on CBS's *GE Theatre* (June 17, 1956), "The Miracle Worker" on CBS's *Playhouse 90* (February 7, 1957), "Dan Marshall's Brat" on ABC's *Dupont Theatre* (March 19, 1957), "We Won't Be Any Trouble" on NBC's *Matinee Theatre* (April 2, 1957), "Child of Trouble" on *Playhouse 90* (May 2, 1957), "Sing a Song" on NBC's *Kraft Theatre* (August 28, 1957), and "The Clouded Image" on *Playhouse 90* (November 7, 1957).

After the 1957 *All Mine to Give* (also titled *The Day They Gave Babies Away*), she was briefly under contract to Universal, where she starred in *Kathy O'* (1958) as a child actress who runs away. Meanwhile, she was still turning up everywhere on the tube: "The Spell of the Tigress" on *Kraft Theatre* (February 5, 1958), "The Devil's Violin" on *Matinee Theatre* (February 28, 1958), "The Dungeon" on *Playhouse 90* (April 17, 1958), "Chain and the River" on NBC's *Goodyear Playhouse* (September 19, 1958), and "The Mary Ellen Thomas Story" on NBC's *Wagon Train* (December 24, 1958).

While appearing in three different media during the fifties, Patty had still managed to get an education—progressing through the Willard Mace School for Professional Children in Queens, the St. Victor Parochial School in San Fernando, and Walter Reed Jr. High in Studio City, California. In 1959 she had her own TV series, *Peck's Bad Girl* on CBS, with Marsha Hunt and Wendell Corey portraying her parents. And she continued on other programs: "Project Immortality" on *Playhouse 90* (June 11, 1959), "Rachel's Summer" on CBS's *U.S. Steel Hour* (October 7, 1959), "Make Me Not a Witch" on ABC's *Alcoa Premiere* (December 22, 1959), "Summer

Hero" on NBC's *Mystery Show* (June 12, 1960), and "Black November" on CBS's *Route 66* (October 7, 1960).

She played a brat in MGM's *The Adventures of Huckleberry Finn* (1960), joining the cast of Eddie Hodges, Archie Moore, and Tony Randall. On TV she did "Sleep on Four Pillows" on *Route 66* (February 24, 1961), "Thousands and Thousands of Miles" on *New Breed* (April 17, 1962), and "Incident of the Wolves" on CBS's *Rawhide* (November 16, 1962). In *Jacktown* (1961), she played Margaret, a warden's daughter who befriends an inmate.

She co-starred with William Shatner in *The Explosive Generation* (1962) about high school sex education. Having outgrown child roles, she vanished temporarily from motion-picture screens during the sixties, but she could still be seen on TV: "Incident at Paradise" on *Rawhide* (October 24, 1963), "Cousin Helga Came to Dinner" on ABC's *Farmer's Daughter* (January 22, 1964), "Burning Bright" on *Play of the*

Week (October 19, 1966), and an episode of CBS's Wild, Wild West (January 26, 1968). She married in 1967 and has two children—Bobby and Daniel.

In 1968 she made three films for American-International—*The Young Runaways*, *The Miniskirt Mob*, and *Born Wild*. She toured in the play *Barefoot in the Park* and turned up in the TV soap operas *Young Dr. Malone*, *As the World Turns*, and *Best of Everything*. On February 4, 1972, she appeared in an episode of CBS's *O'Hara, U. S. Treasury*. Her marriage came to an end in 1974, and she moved back to the West Coast.

With William Castle's *Bug* (1975), for Paramount, she was finally seen in a for-real horror movie. Thomas Page and Castle did the screenplay from Page's novel *The Hephaestus Plague*. An earthquake hits a small Western town, setting loose strange three-inch-long insects from the bowels of the earth in an area near the Tacker farm. Gerald Metbaum (Richard Gilliland) dis-

covers that they are able to make fire. This intrigues his biology professor, James Parmiter (Bradford Dillman), and he begins experiments, learning that they feed on carbon. Norma Tacker (Jamie Smith Jackson) is injured by the bugs, and when Parmiter's wife Carrie (Joanna Miles) falls prey to the critters' arsonous activities and dies, Parmiter moves his lab to the Tacker place, where he mates a cockroach with one of the firebugs. Result? A new bug that not only causes fire but also eats raw meat—mainly Parmiter. Mark Ross (Alan Fudge) and his wife Sylvia (Patty McCormack) learn of Parmiter's obsessive experiments. Norma, Gerald, and Mark try to get Parmiter to leave the Tacker farm. Meanwhile, the bugs are beginning to communicate—by arranging themselves to spell out words somewhat like a half-time drill formation. Sylvia Ross comes to the farm and is attacked by the bugs. She dies. Now the insects can fly, and Parmiter is overwhelmed by them and dies. Another earthquake

Dan Duryea and Patty McCormack in *Kathy O'* (1958).

LEFT: Patty McCormack as she looked in *The Explosive Generation* (1962). The cast also included William Shatner, Lee Kinsolving, and Billy Gray (best known for his long-run role from 1954 to 1962 on the TV series *Father Knows Best*).

RIGHT: Patty is attacked by the mysterious three-inch insects from the bowels of the earth in William Castle's *Bug* (1975).

sends the bugs back below. Directed by Jeannot Szwarc (see Shelley Winters chapter), it seems to adhere to a more-outdated type of horror filmmaking. Jim Morrow, reviewing in *Cinefantastique*, viewed *Bug* as "a throwback to the kind of fifties science-fictioner in which heroic scientists unintentionally unleash a cataclysmic menace (dinosaur, giant insect, space monster) upon humanity and succeed in subduing it only at the eleventh hour. . . . But by the time *Bug* is 45 minutes underway, it becomes clear that Castle and his director are scrupulously avoiding these conventions. . . . It's all very well to reject tired old fifties conventions, so long as you come up with some tired new seventies conventions to replace them. But *Bug* has no conventions. It's never clear at any point where the story is going or why it isn't going there."

Richard Combs, in *Monthly Film Bulletin*, concurred: "The film is both too vacantly plotted, and too much of a carnival in its special effects, to score as an ecological fantasy on the lines of *The Birds* (although the ending makes a similar try for a note of unsettling enigma).

"Jeannot Szwarc displays an incongruous aptitude for directing actors, since so many scenes just play crudely on the audience's anticipation of the next incineration —a fate, moreover, which seems to befall only the female characters, whether as part and parcel (the screaming Fay Wray syndrome) of the film's generally old-fashioned orientation, or as a sly misogynist delight in a sexist species of bug." And, in fact, Patty McCormack, seventh-billed in the cast, seems to be present in the film for no other reason than to be a victim in the sense Combs refers to, having no real opportunity to display the kind of acting she's capable of executing. Nevertheless, audiences screamed their loudest during her final scene while she flails about as one of the critters crawls over her left eye. Rhoda Penmark, you realize, would never have stood for any of this nonsense. She would have set fire to the bugs *first*!

# Faith Domergue

Faith Domergue was born June 16, 1925, in New Orleans, Louisiana, of French and Spanish stock. At the age of six, she went with her family to California, where she was educated in the Los Angeles public school system. She was thrown into the windshield in an auto accident when she was sixteen, resulting in eighteen months of elaborate plastic surgery. While still in her teens she was married for a year to Acapulco nightclub owner Teddy Stauffer, a former bandleader who later married Hedy Lamarr. In 1946 she appeared in United Artists' *Young Widow*.

Howard Hughes spent $3,200,000 in an effort to launch Faith as a star in a 1946 vehicle called *Vendetta*, with much of the promotion for this RKO film comparing her to Hughes's earlier find, Jane Russell. After the acclaimed German director Max Ophüls came to this country in 1941, he was involved in many projects that led to nothing; finally, he began work with Preston Sturges on *Vendetta*, but Hughes did not like what he saw and dismissed Ophüls. Preston Sturges took over, only to be replaced by veteran director Stuart Heisler. As the money continued to pour down a bottomless funnel, it appeared that *Vendetta* was becoming the motion-picture industry's answer to the *Spruce Goose*, but it was finally completed by Mel Ferrer with uncredited directorial contributions by Hughes. Domergue played opposite Nigel Bruce in a W. R. Burnett screenplay based on *Columba* by Prosper Merimée. *Vendetta* was not released until 1950, and it was not very successful.

Meanwhile, in 1947, Faith had married the Argentinian writer-director Hugo Fregonese. After medical school in Buenos Aires, Fregonese had worked as a journalist before attending Columbia University in 1935. In 1938, he returned to Argentina, where he made short films and climbed up through the ranks as editor, assistant director, and director. In the late forties he labored as a Hollywood scripter before directing *Saddle Tramp* and *One Way Street* in 1950. Fregonese was later the uncredited codirector (with R. L. Jacks) of *Man in the Attic*, a 1953 Jack the Ripper tale starring

Jack Palance and Constance Smith. Faith and Fregonese, divorced in 1955, had two children, Daniel and Diana.

John Farrow's *Where Danger Lives* (1950) had Faith, Robert Mitchum, Claude Rains, and Maureen O'Sullivan in a story about a doctor romantically involved with a woman going insane. After *Duel at Silver Creek* (1952) with Audie Murphy and *The Great Sioux Uprising* (1953) with Jeff Chandler, she made *This Is My Love* (1954) with Dan Duryea. She also began working in television during this period, appearing in "Equal Justice" on the October 17, 1953 *Mirror Theatre* on CBS; "Retribution" on the March 23, 1954 *Fireside Theatre* on NBC; and "The Roman and the Renegade," an August 6, 1954 production of CBS's *Schlitz Playhouse of Stars*. On November 11, 1954, she was in "The Road Ahead" on NBC's *Ford Theatre*.

In 1954 Domergue was the female lead in director Joseph Newman's *This Island Earth*, a Universal release now considered one of the science-fiction classics of the fifties. Based on a Raymond F. Jones novel,

the story begins with a jet piloted by nuclear physicist Cal Meacham (Rex Reason) going out of control. Rescued by a weird green ray, he returns to his laboratory to find a catalog of apparatus completely foreign to him. Obtaining the parts for an interocitor, one of the devices in the catalog, he assembles them into a receiver that enables him to hear the voice of Exeter (Jeff Morrow), visitor to Earth from the planet Metaluna. Invited to Exeter's secluded workshop in Georgia, Cal meets a former college friend, Ruth Adams (Domergue), also an expert in nuclear fission. Exeter is seeking a new source for uranium, but both Cal and Ruth are suspicious of his motives. After an escape attempt, they are kidnapped in Exeter's spacecraft. Before leaving Earth, Exeter turns a red death ray on several aides fleeing the lab as it is destroyed.

Enroute to Metaluna, Meacham and Ruth find that the distant planet is fighting for its very existence, being under almost continual attack from enemy forces. New uranium sources are needed to power the

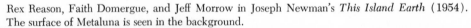

Rex Reason, Faith Domergue, and Jeff Morrow in Joseph Newman's *This Island Earth* (1954). The surface of Metaluna is seen in the background.

defense. Landing on Metaluna, they learn that they are too late. Only a few Metalunans are still alive. The Monitor (Douglas Spencer) in charge of the planet unfolds his plan for relocating on Earth. Ruth and Cal realize the danger to Earthlings of such a project. Exeter undergoes a change of heart and sides with them, and they seek to escape the planet in their spacecraft. In so doing, Exeter is savagely clawed by a Mutant—a half-human giant insect. The spaceship, with the three aboard, manages to take off minutes before Metaluna is destroyed. As they approach Earth's atmosphere, Ruth and Cal soar to safety in their plane, still stored within the craft. Exeter, his wounds fatal, dives into the sea. When filming was completed, Domergue commented, "If the space world materializes during my lifetime, I think I'll be more than ready for it."

Produced by William Alland (one of the original members of Orson Welles's Mercury Company), the screenplay of *This Island Earth* was written by Franklin Coen and Edward G. O'Callaghan. Others in the cast were Lance Fuller, Russell Johnson, Robert Nichols, Karl Lindt, and Regis Parton. Ed Parker portrayed the Mutant, a $24,000 creation of makeup man Bud Westmore. The head was five times the size of a human head, with the brain completely exposed and all the facial muscles on the surface. With each heartbeat the entire cranium would pulsate. Hands dangled to the ankles, and fingers were replaced with lobster-like claws. There were five tiers of interlocking mouths, one serving double use as a nose. A shell like an armadillo's covered the spine.

For Philip Strick, author of *Science Fiction Movies, This Island Earth* has "some of the best science-fiction images the cinema has ever seen—the matter-transmitters that transform their occupants to skeletons before beaming them through space, the giant observation room on the flying saucer, and the magnificent landscape of Metaluna itself, lurid with the destruction wrought by the neighboring world of Zahgon. Despite its lockjaw performances and

Rex and Faith struggle with Bud Westmore's $24,000 creation, The Mutant (Ed Parker).

A nuclear moment from *This Island Earth* as The Mutant has Ruth (Faith Domergue) not too firmly in his clutches.

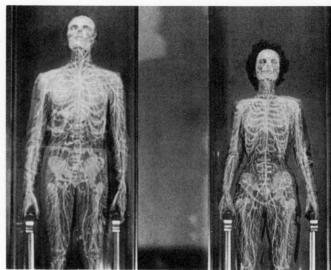

The climax of *This Island Earth*, resulting in Visible Man and Visible Woman.

ponderous dialogue, *This Island Earth* gradually draws us into an extraordinary intergalactic adventure that eradicates the bland self-confidence of the early sequences and justifies the film's title only too clearly —our planet is an offshore fragment, ignored by the politics of the universe, and there are some advantages to be gained by this detachment."

David Kyle in *A Pictorial History of Science Fiction* compares it to the original novel, calling it "outstanding sf, despite the contrivance of a banal mutant-monster and likewise changing most of the plot." John Baxter in *Science Fiction in the Cinema* liked the film but not Domergue: "Rex Reason, stolidly inappropriate to the part of a progressive young physicist, does well enough with the equally flat Faith Domergue, but special effects and colorful photography of ethereal settings engage our attention and divert it from the actors. . . . The shattered surface of Metaluna, the space landing and takeoff, the enemy boring in with captive meteors to drop on the planet—these are given lavish attention, in contrast to the flaccid direction of the actors."

Raymond Durgnat, in *Films and Feelings*, analyzed *This Island Earth* in terms of American social and political attitudes: "If we assume that the film responds to authentic currents of American thought, we could have deduced from it how deeply rooted in the American psyche were attitudes which would naturally try to emerge, on the political plane, as McCarthyism, McArthurism, or Goldwaterism. The old 'isolationism' turns to bellicosity. There is a haunting fear that a 'liberal' policy towards Communism is the policy of men who are, not exactly feminized, but neutered, castrated, by their scruples. Similarly, Margaret Mead and Geoffrey Gorer tell us that in America the woman rather than the man tends to possess the moral ascendency within the family; and it may be that this ascendency is subtly reinforced by the masculinization of woman imposed by an individualistic, and therefore competitive, society. Thus, femininity disappears on Metaluna, and Faith Domergue, the woman dressed like a man, has undergone a transmogrification analogous to the insect-slave's."

In Columbia's *It Came from Beneath the Sea* (1955), produced by Sam Katzman and Charles H. Schneer with special effects by Ray Harryhausen and Jack Erickson, Faith played opposite Kenneth Tobey, who had headed the cast of *The Thing* in 1951. The George W. Yates and Hal Smith screenplay from a story by Yates detailed how H-bomb testing drives a giant octopus to attack submarines and then begin laying waste to San Francisco before finally being destroyed by an electronic torpedo. Robert Gordon directed with Mischa Bakaleinikoff providing the music score. Others in the cast are Donald Curtis, Ian Keith, Harry Lauter, R. Peterson, Dean Maddox, Jr., and Del Courtney. Today, *It Came from Beneath the Sea* is not as fondly remembered as another fifties Harryhausen creature from the watery deeps—*The Beast from 20,000 Fathoms*, directed by Eugene Lourie and based on Ray Bradbury's short story, *The Fog Horn*.

Universal's *Cult of the Cobra* (1955) saves its snake-human transformation for the finale. The film begins with a group of Air Force men enjoying their pass. They pool $100, which gets them into a meeting of the Lamian snake cult, but the course of events results in the death of one member of the group, Nick (James Dobson). The snake cult priest (John Halloran) utters a curse, stating they will all die.

Some time later, back in New York, the peculiar but alluring Lisa (Faith Domergue) moves into an apartment across the hall from Tom (Marshall Thompson), who shows her the city. A series of deaths occur. First, Rico (David Janssen) is closing up his bowling alley when he is attacked by a cobra. Tom's roommate, Paul (Richard Long), explains to his actress-fiancée Julia (Kathleen Hughes) why he thinks the death isn't an accident: "Well, it started overseas. It was our last pass, and we spent it like a bunch of tourists. We got mixed up with a snake cultist who got us into a religious meeting—a cult that believed human beings could be changed into snakes. . . . What we saw there was pretty ugly."

Tom finds Lisa missing from her apartment at the time Carl (Jack Kelly) falls to his death. Pete (William Reynolds) sees Lisa outside the building. Returning to her apartment, Lisa finds Tom asleep there. "Do you know what it's like to believe in something all your life and then one day suddenly decide it's wrong?" she asks. "There are things I have to do . . . things I have no control over." Tom doesn't under-

A moment of cosmic significance. "If the space world materializes during my lifetime, I'll be more than ready for it," said Faith Domergue in 1954.

stand. She then confesses her love for him but suddenly turns venomous and orders him out of her apartment.

The next morning, Julia arrives while Tom and Paul are having breakfast. A call from the police informs them of Carl's death. After they leave for the police station, Julia remains behind and meets Lisa. Lisa discovers that Paul has been studying books on snake cults. Frightened of Lisa, Julia leaves.

At the police station, Tom falls under suspicion because of a fight he had with Carl. Paul tells the Inspector (Walter Coy) that he suspects Lisa. Meanwhile, Pete, who also suspects Lisa, goes to her apartment and confronts her. He, too, dies. Tom and Lisa go to the theater to attend Julia's

The Ray Harryhausen creature in *It Came from Beneath the Sea* (1955).

opening. When Paul and the Inspector discover Pete's body, they phone Tom at the theater. With the evidence that all of the men have died of snake venom, Tom finally is willing to admit the truth.

In her dressing room, Julia panics when a cobra slithers toward her. Tom enters the room, drops a cloth over the snake and then shoves it out the window and over the ledge to the street below. As Paul and the Inspector arrive, the cobra dies—making a glowing transformation into Lisa. Others in the cast are Myrna Hansen, Leonard Strong, Olan Soule, Helen Wallace, Mary Ann Hokinson, and the dance team of the Carlsens.

Patrick Agan, in the third volume of *Is That Who I Think It Is?*, says the role of Lisa brought Faith "a lasting distinction of sorts." The Cecil Maiden and Richard Collins screenplay from a Jerry Davis story was directed by Francis D. Lyon. The theme was later pursued in Sidney Furie's *The*

*Snake Woman* (1960) with Susan Travers, and Andrew Meyer's *Night of the Cobra Woman* (1972) with Joy Bang.

After *Santa Fe Passage* (1955), Domergue, on the heels of her divorce from Fregonese, left the United States to do films in England, playing opposite Gene Nelson in *The Atomic Man* (1956). Charles Eric Maine's screenplay from his own novel, *The Isotope Man*, detailed the problems in London resulting from a nuclear accident that gives a man a radioactive brain that jumps seven seconds ahead in time. Ken Hughes directed, and the music was by Richard Taylor. Others in the cast are Joseph Tomelty, Donald Gray, Vic Perry, and Peter Arne.

The British-made *Spin a Dark Web* (1956) starred Faith as an underworld queen, holding sway over London mobs. In her TV work of 1956, she made a March 17 appearance in the syndicated *Count of Monte Cristo* series.

In Universal's *Man in the Shadow* (1957) she appeared with Jeff Chandler and Orson Welles. After "No Boat for Four Months" on the January 31, 1958 *Schlitz Playhouse*, she made an April 28, 1959 appearance in "The Vultures" on ABC's *Sugarfoot*, had an October 12, 1959 role in "The Rebellion" on ABC's *Cheyenne*, and was seen November 2, 1959 in the "Girl in Trouble" episode of ABC's *Bourbon Street Beat*.

United Artists' *Escort West* (1959) was made in black-and-white Cinema-Scope. More TV work followed: "Breakthrough" on ABC's *Colt .45* (March 27, 1960), "La Rubia" on ABC's *Bronco* (May 17, 1960), "Beach Boy" on ABC's *Hawaiian Eye* (June 1, 1960), an October 25, 1960 episode of CBS's *Exclusive*, "The Jealous Man" on NBC's *Tales of Wells Fargo* (April 10, 1961), "The Case of the Guilty Clients" on CBS's *Perry Mason* (June 10, 1961), "The Lonely House" on NBC's *Bonanza* (October 15, 1961), "Concert in Hawaii" on *Hawaiian Eye* (December 27, 1961), and appearances in CBS's *Have Gun, Will Travel* on October 13, 1962 and April 13, 1963.

In American-International's *California* (1963), she appeared opposite Jock Mahoney in a story of Monterey in 1841. After "The Case of the Greek Goddess" on *Perry Mason* (April 18, 1963) and "The Compañeros" on *Bonanza* (April 19, 1964), she appeared in a December 20, 1966 *Combat* episode and the two-part "Plot to Kill" on *Garrison's Gorillas* (February 13 and 20, 1968). Another 1968 credit was the motion picture *Track of Thunder*.

Finally, in 1972, she stepped before cameras for a return to horror—*The House of the Seven Corpses*, a ninety-minute TCA production that was not released until 1974. Gayle (Domergue) is a temperamental actress who is slowing production of a film being made by producer-director Eric Hartmann (John Ireland), who is attempting to complete the film without going over the budget. Price (John Carradine), caretaker of the mansion where the filming is taking place, explains the history of the house and

Faith is overwhelmed by her captors in *The Atomic Man.*

the ghastly deaths that have taken place there. In the nearby cemetery are seven graves, but a mystery surrounds the unmarked eighth grave. For the final scenes of Hartmann's film, Gayle begins reading from the Tibetan *Book of the Dead*, and the mystical incantations cause the corpse in the eighth grave to stir and become ambulatory. When Price investigates, he is attacked.

Dan Scapperotti, reviewing in *Cinefantastique*, comments, "The idea of having a film revolve around the making of a movie has been used in horror pictures before, most notably in *Frankenstein 1970*, but never as well as in this low-budget entry. . . . The film boasts a genuine surprise ending even for those who have been able to decipher the cryptic message of the film's advertising, and it is only a failure to provide motivation for the climax that prevents this little film from being a low-budget gem." Produced by Paul Lewis and Paul Harrison, it was directed by Harrison from a screenplay by Thomas J. Kelly and Harrison. Others in the cast are Charles Macauley, Carol Wells, and Jerry Strickler.

In recent years, Faith Domergue, married to Italian film-producer Paolo Cossa, has made her home in Rome. Her credits have dwindled, but her fans, who have not forgotten her various forays into fantasy, horror, and science fiction, wish producers would cast her in still more Scream Queen epics. "Keep the Faith!" they chant.

# Carol Lynley

Carol Lynley was born Carol Jones in New York on February 13, 1942. She went to school in New York; Winthrop, Massachusetts; and Teaneck, New Jersey. She began ballet training at the age of seven and was modeling when she was ten. As a model she used the name Carolyn Lee, and one year her face was well known throughout the world as "The Coca-Cola Girl." Work as a TV extra led to an August 26, 1956 role in "Grow Up" on NBC's *Goodyear Playhouse*. Her stage debut was in the road company of *Anniversary Waltz*; at this time she discovered that another Carolyn Lee was registered with Actors' Equity, resulting in the name change to Carol Lynley. At fifteen, she played opposite Dame Sybil Thorndike on stage in *The Potting Shed*, but it was the stage version of *Blue Denim* that was the real steppingstone for her career.

She has rarely been absent from the TV screen, and much of her work in both films and TV has been in the area of horror, fantasy, science fiction, or thrillers, beginning with a December 1, 1957 *Alfred Hitchcock Presents* tale, "The Young One." A teenager (Lynley) imagines that her well-meaning aunt (Jeanette Nolan) is overprotective, ruining her chances for finding love and happiness. Her paranoia drives her to extremes. At the local teen hangout she deserts her conservative boyfriend and throws herself at a passerby (Vince Edwards). He likes her but is aware of her "strangeness." At home, late at night, she pretends she has been attacked by Vince. A neighborhood cop arrives and finds the girl's aunt dead. He is about to arrest Vince for the deed when it is revealed that the girl had killed her aunt much earlier.

After "Junior Miss" on CBS's *Dupont Show of the Month* (December 20, 1957), she appeared in "The Young and the Scared" on CBS's *GE Theatre* (May 18, 1958), "The Vengeance" on CBS's *Pursuit* October 22, 1958), and the classic fairy tale "Rapunzel" on NBC's *Shirley Temple's Story Book* (October 27, 1958).

Walt Disney saw some of her TV shows, and, when she was featured on the front cover of *Life* magazine, he signed her to a contract. She made her film debut in July 1958, as an indentured servant girl Shenandoe in Disney's *The Light in the Forest*, receiving credit "and introducing" credits in the main titles. Location footage was shot near Chattanooga in Tennessee by director Herschel Daugherty (also making his debut). Lynley's co-star was James Mac-Arthur, who was cast in several Disney features that followed. Despite her contract, she never made another film with Disney.

In February 1959, she received her high school diploma from New York's School for Young Professionals. *Holiday for Lovers* (1959) was a romantic comedy set in South America, and she also made two 1959 appearances on *GE Theatre* in "Deed of Mercy" (March 1) and "The Last Dance" (November 22). But it was her role as a pregnant teen that year in the film version of *Blue Denim* (also titled *Blue Jeans*), opposite Brandon de Wilde, that brought her real attention. Today, the film has a dated aspect, but the quality of Lynley's acting in it has not diminished.

As one of the teen queens of the fifties, Lynley had an influence on fashion and behavior. Marjorie Rosen in *Popcorn Venus* notes, "For adolescents, especially vulnerable, movies structured behavior and standardized values. Girls who learned the rules of flirtation and sexual conduct from Sandra Dee and her golden counterparts, Yvette Mimieux, Carol Lynley, and Tuesday Weld, also took their beauty cues from them. Rhinoplasty, or nose surgery, became an obsession with middle-class teenagers. . . ."

In 1960 Carol was seen with Fabian in *Hound Dog Man*. After *Return to Peyton Place* (1961) and *The Last Sunset* (1961), she turned up in "Final Vow" on NBC's *Laf Hit* (September 25, 1962), "Whatever Happened to Miss Illinois?" on ABC's *Alcoa Premiere* (November 22, 1962), "Man from the Sea" on NBC's *Virginian* (December 26, 1962), and "The Rage of Silence" on NBC's *Dick Powell Theatre* (January 29, 1963). Her films of 1963 were *The Stripper*, *Under the Yum Yum Tree*, and the role of Mona in Otto Preminger's

Carol Lynley with Clifton Webb on the South American *Holiday for Lovers* (1959), directed by Henry Levin.

Panavision *The Cardinal* for Columbia.

After *The Pleasure Seekers* (1964), she joined Stuart Whitman to repel the villainy of Lauren Bacall in Denis Sanders' *Shock Treatment* (1964). Two film biographies of Jean Harlow, both titled *Harlow*, were made in 1965. Lynley appeared as Harlow in the cheaper Electronovision version, and Carroll Baker starred in the Joseph E. Levine bigger-budgeted production (which opened in Los Angeles on the day before the Watts riots). Neither one is memorable. Lynley was also seen that year in "The Fliers" on NBC's *Bob Hope Chrysler Theatre* (February 5).

She was cast again by Preminger in his psychological mystery-thriller *Bunny Lake Is Missing* (1965), prompting *Cinema* magazine to note, "With a face like that of a fallen angel, Carol Lynley has beauty that is often awe inspiring. She is now back in

263

the hands of Otto Preminger for his mystery *Bunny Lake Is Missing*. And, from the looks of it, Otto is well aware of the quality of that with which he is dealing." The story followed the arrival of a young woman (Lynley) and her brother (Keir Dullea) in England. She places her child Bunny in a day-care nursery. Later, when she goes to pick up Bunny, not only is the child miss-

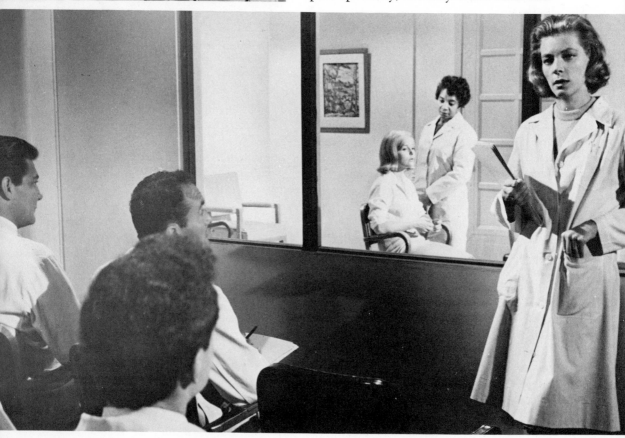

ing, but also no one at the nursery recalls ever seeing her. Adding to the young woman's problems is a police inspector who doesn't believe her story. She becomes increasingly hysterical, convinced that her daughter is in genuine danger wherever she is. In the obvious climax, events reveal that Bunny has been kidnapped by Lynley's own brother in an aberrant effort to keep his sister all for himself.

The Columbia release garnered little praise from critics. *Castle of Frankenstein* magazine commented: " 'Bunny is the face in the misty light . . . footsteps that you hear down the hall. . . .' Maybe that should be the theme of this Otto Preminger suspenser about missing child; many macabre and skillfully directed moments, but Keir Dullea's inept, clumsy performance reveals ending far too early. The Preminger of *Laura* and *Whirlpool* has returned. Based on novel by Evelyn (*The Nanny*) Piper. Exciting opening title designed by Saul Bass. Carol Lynley, Laurence Olivier, Noel Coward, Martita Hunt, Victor (*Blood of the Vampire*) Maddern, Finlay Currie, Megs Jenkins."

Harlan Ellison, reviewing in *Cinema*, found the film a "cheat" because the derangement of the brother was altered to create the punch ending. "Had Preminger wished to make the film honestly," stated Ellison, "he would have carried the psychotic nature of the brother through the film, but obviously that would not have been dramatic enough, and the shock ending would have been pre-revealed." To prove his point, Ellison contacted Dr. Eugene A. Levitt, clinical psychologist of the Peterson-Guedel Family Center in Beverly Hills for Levitt's professional opinion: "Given a deviant personality structure as grossly pathological as that of the brother in *Bunny Lake*, it would seem highly improbable that it would be manifested solely in the area of his *feelings about* his sister. One would certainly expect to see signs of deviancy in his behavior *toward* the sister; not just at the dramatic moment when it best suits the purposes of the plotmakers of the film, but *consistently*, throughout."

With Oliver Reed in David Greene's *The Shuttered Room* (1966), adapted from the story by H. P. Lovecraft and August Derleth.

Lynley's television appearances of 1966 were "In Search of April" on NBC's *Run for Your Life* (February 14) and "Runaway Boy" on the *Bob Hope Chrysler Theatre* (May 25). *The Shuttered Room* (1966), starring Lynley and Gig Young, was a Troy-Schenck Production for Seven Arts. The screenplay by D. B. Leaderman and Nathaniel Tanchuck was based on *The Shuttered Room* by H. P. Lovecraft and August Derleth (published in 1959 by Derleth's Arkham House in *The Shuttered Room and Other Pieces*). The film story told of a hideous chain-rattling *thing* finally revealed to be the maddened twin of Susannah Whately (Lynley). During the course of the production, the British *Films and Filming* magazine reported, "Quite the most scandalous thing of recent months has been the quiet, almost unpublicized burning down of a bit of Britain for an American-financed movie. The film, *The Shuttered Room*. The bit of Britain that went was an old flour mill by a stream, at Hardingham in Norfolk. It appears that the film company purchased the mill, then destroyed it. The property laws in France and other civilized countries would make such disgusting antisocial behavior impossible. I would not be surprised if the Church Commissioners sold St. Paul's at a price and we saw that burnt down for another American epic. (And perhaps after the way we have allowed the City of London to be rebuilt with tasteless expediency it would be just as well). Back to the caves."

Directed by David Greene, *The Shuttered Room* is a scary affair, aided by the edgy anxiety acted by Lynley. Ivan Butler in *Horror in the Cinema* raved, "A really believable and terrifying 'thing in the attic' raises this conventionally shaped thriller well into the region of superior horror, despite some gratuitous violence. The introductory sequence is a masterly exposition of terror. Carol Lynley looks unnervingly vulnerable, and Flora Robson grandly eccentric." Others in the cast were Oliver Reed, William Devlin, Bernard Kay, Judith Arthy, Robert Cawdron, and Celia Hewitt. Basil Kirchin provided the music score.

Although this is easily the best of the Lovecraft film adaptations (the others include the 1963 *Haunted Palace*, the 1965 *Die, Monster, Die!*, the 1969 *Dunwich Horror*, and episodes of *Night Gallery*) it is not necessarily the most faithful to the original story. To make matters worse, the screenplay was *rewritten into a new novel* (a sad fate that also, unbelievably, happened to Kipling's *The Man Who Would Be King*). Derleth commented on the matter in the Summer 1967 issue of Arkham House's news magazine and house organ, *The Arkham Collector*: "A few patrons of Arkham House have recently become irate about the appearance on newsstands of *The Shuttered Room* by one Julia Withers. 'A shattering story of Gothic romance and terror—now an unforgettable motion picture. She was beautiful, young and damned by the echoes of an unspoken curse'—the typical Hollywood claptrap that is a far cry from *The Shuttered Room* familiar to collectors of Arkham House books. But the setting is Dunwich, the action takes place in an old

mill, the Whately family is the focus of the story, and the plot is generally the same. . . . We hasten to assure our patrons that the whole distasteful thing is perfectly legal. When Arkham House sold *The Shuttered Room* for filming, the contract contained a 'tie-in' clause permitting the producers to farm out their script and have it 'novelized' for paperback reproduction. Julia Withers's version is pretty dreadful stuff, but she had no alternative but to follow the screen script in which the protagonist is not Abner Whately, but one Susannah Whately, no less, and encumbered by her husband, Mike Kelton. . . . Once a story has been sold for filming, the author loses control over what happens to it. August Derleth keeps his sense of humor and reflects that the fees paid for such films help defray the cost of publishing the letters of H. P. Lovecraft."

After the 1967 *Danger Route* (also titled *Escape Route*), Lynley was seen in the two-part "Prince of Darkness Affair" on NBC's *The Man from U.N.C.L.E.* (October 2 and 9, 1967) and a December 5, 1967 episode of ABC's science-fiction series *The Invaders* about architect David Vincent (Roy Thinnes), who has discovered the arrival of aliens on Earth. On September 26, 1968, Lynley guest-starred in "Eve," the debut episode of ABC's science-fantasy anthology series *Journey to the Unknown*.

In the science-fiction TV-movie *Shadow on the Land*, which premiered on ABC on December 4, 1968, Lynley appeared with Jackie Cooper, John Forsythe, Janice Rule, Gene Hackman, Marc Strange, and Myron Healey. The Nedrick Young

OPPOSITE PAGE

ABOVE: Carol Lynley with Dennis Waterman in "Eve" on ABC's *Journey to the Unknown*. Lynley plays a department-store mannequin who comes to life in this debut episode on September 26, 1968.

BELOW: Dan Rowan (*center*), Dick Martin, and Carol Lynley prepare to operate in MGM's *The Maltese Bippy* (1969). There's not much hope for the patient (Jerry Mann), a corpse they found in the dumbwaiter, but successful surgery could lead the trio to the world's largest diamond.

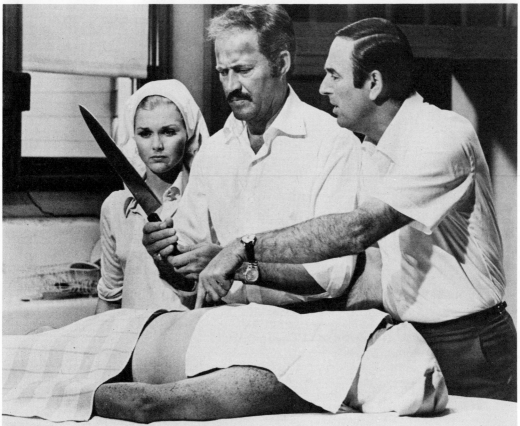

The trouble Rowan and Martin had with their "Laugh-In" TV cohorts was mild compared to *The Maltese Bippy* gang. Starting at eleven o'clock and moving clockwise: Broadway star Fritz Weaver, with clenched fists, as a part-time werewolf and full-time con man; European star Eddra Gale, caught in the midst of delicate surgery; Carol Lynley as a student who carries a human skull; Pamela Rogers as an under-age, overambitious movie starlet; Mildred Natwick as Rowan and Martin's housekeeper who almost talks herself to death; and, at left, Julie Newmar as a 300-year-old werewolf hip to American men.

screenplay, from an idea by Sidney Sheldon, told of a fascist organization controlling the United States in the very near future. Sol Kaplan scored, and Richard C. Sarafian directed. Lynley followed this with a role in the NBC TV-movie *The Smugglers* (1968). She began 1969 with "Boom at the Top," a February 25 episode of ABC's *It Takes a Thief*. MGM's *The Maltese Bippy* (1969) featured Lynley cavorting with Dan Rowan, Dick Martin, Julie Newmar, Mildred Natwick, Fritz Weaver, Robert Reed, and Dana Elcar in a horror-comedy spoof on *Dracula* and *The Wolf Man*. Without *Laugh-In*, this Norman Panama picture would never have been filmed.

Robert Specht's screenplay for the ABC TV-movie *The Immortal* (1969) was based on a novel by science-fictioneer James Gunn. Directed by Joseph Sargent, the story began with racing-car driver Ben Richards (Christopher George) donating blood to save his millionaire employer Jordan Braddock (Barry Sullivan). When Braddock makes a too-quick recovery, doctors conclude that Richards's blood contains immunity antibodies that can halt aging. Braddock then imprisons Richards so he will always be available for transfusions. The escape of Richards is engineered by Braddock's wife (Jessica Walters), who wants to see her husband die. He then sets out to find his long-lost brother, who may also have blood with similar properties. Lynley appeared in the role of Richards' fiancée. Caught in a dangerous spot because of her closeness to Richards, she reveals his secret as a way of saving her own skin. Critic Robert L. Jerome found her character "sensibly enacted." The seventy-four-minute feature was produced by Lou Morheim. Dominic Frontiere scored, and the cast also featured Ralph Bellamy. When *The Immortal* began as an hour-long series in the fall of 1970, Lynley turned up again in an early episode (October 24), but the private detectives and millionaire's minions were still in pursuit (à la *The Fugitive*) so Richards bid farewell to his lady, entrusting her to Glenn Corbett. The series was cancelled shortly afterwards.

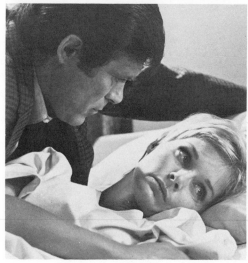

ABOVE: Carol Lynley and Christopher George on the run (à la "The Fugitive") in this exterior from the 1969 ABC TV-movie *The Immortal*, aired September 30 of that year prior to the beginning of the TV series. Ben Richards (George) is a man whose blood contains antibodies that make him immune to all known diseases, including the aging process.

BELOW: In *The Immortal* Carol Lynley portrayed a woman near death, and Chris George was the man who saves her—by donating his blood with its miraculous curative antibodies.

After the feature *Norwood* (1970) and *Once You've Kissed a Stranger* (a 1970 remake of Hitchcock's *Strangers on a Train*), Lynley was seen in "Giants Never Kneel" on NBC's *Bold Ones* (October 25, 1970) and "Who Killed Kindness" on ABC's *Most Deadly Game* (November 7, 1970). *Weekend of Terror* was a made-for-TV fright feature that preemed December 8, 1970, on ABC. Then came the February 20, 1971 "Voice in the Dark" episode of *Mannix* and the TV-movie *The Cable Car Mystery* (November 19, 1971) on CBS.

In the TV-movie *The Night Stalker*, first aired on ABC January 11, 1972, Lynley portrayed Gail Foster, girlfriend of Carl Kolchak (Darren McGavin). Seeking a story that will put him on top of the heap, Kolchak encounters a modern-day Las Vegas vampire, Janos Skorzeny (Barry Atwater). John Llewellan Moxey directed,

Shaken by the news that her girlfriend has been the victim of a horrible murder, Carol Lynley, as a Las Vegal change girl, is consoled by a somber Darren McGavin, a crack newspaper reporter in ABC's TV-movie *The Night Stalker* (1969).

with many scenes shot on location. Richard Matheson scripted from Jeff Rice's previously unpublished novel, *The Kolchak Papers*. Produced by Dan Curtis, who is responsible for *Dark Shadows* and other genre creations, *The Night Stalker* was scored by Robert Cobert, also of *Dark Shadows*. Others in the cast were Simon Oakland as Kolchak's editor, Claude Akins as the police commissioner, and Ralph Meeker as Bernie Meeks. But Atwater provided most of the suspenseful impact of the film with his leering, leaping, and violent superhuman acts—turning the once-cliché image of the vampire into something contemporary and frightening, brilliantly contrasted with McGavin's underplayed reporter. Perhaps these elements were overlooked when *The Night Stalker* became a series—with McGavin turned into something of a comic figure pitted against a different kind of ghoul or harpy each week. While the feature remains one of the very best of the *Movie of the Week* productions, the series died quietly after only a handful of episodes put viewers to sleep.

On January 26, 1972, Lynley guest-starred in "Last Rites for a Dead Druid" on Rod Serling's *Night Gallery*, still quite evident in syndication. This was followed by an appearance in ABC's short-lived *Sixth Sense* series on February 5, 1972. In Irwin Allen's *The Poseidon Adventure* (1972) she portrayed rock singer Monnie Parry, who goes into a state of shock after she loses her brother when the ocean liner capsizes; *Variety* called her performance "specially effective."

Early in 1977 Lynley appeared in the cast of a TV-movie on ABC called *Fantasy Island*, which later became a series. Ricardo Montalban portrayed the sadistic host of Fantasy Island, a sort of amalgam of *Westworld*, *The Millionaire*, and TV game shows. For a huge fee Montalban stages whatever fantasy a client requests. Exactly how he pulls off these theatrics is never made clear, weakening the structure of the film, which concentrates more on how Montalban double-crosses not only his clients but also the actors he has hired for the realization of the fantasies. One woman (Eleanor Parker) wants to witness her own funeral to find out if her relatives are conspiring against her, so Montalban flies in the relatives— one of whom is Lynley. Sure enough, Lynley is running the dirty tricks department, but by the climax of this pic the audience has gone to sleep.

In 1978, scheduled to appear in a Richard Gordon remake of *The Cat and the Canary*, she seemed to be ready to tackle many Scream Queen roles to come.

Carol Lynley, as vocalist Nonnie, reaches out desperately when the ocean liner capsizes in *The Poseidon Adventure* (1972).

# 𝒱ampira

Vampira, the West Coast counterpart of Zacherley, rose to fame during the fifties as the horror hostess of fright films on Channel 7 in Hollywood. Her real name is Maila Nurmi, but her highly popular characterization of Vampira was so well conceived that when she turned to film acting it was as the Vampira her fans knew and loved.

She was born in Petsamo, Finland, on December 11, 1921, and was brought to the United States at a very early age by her father, a writer who toured, giving lectures. When she appeared in *Spook Scandals,* a Mike Todd horror stage production, she made a strong impression on Howard Hawks. Hawks, who had directed Lauren Bacall in *To Have and Have Not* (1944) and *The Big Sleep* (1946), was struck by Maila's curious resemblance to Bacall, and he brought her to Hollywood. However, a projected film version of *Dreadful Hollow,* with Maila Nurmi and a William Faulkner screenplay, never quite got under way. In-

ABOVE: Vampira as she emerges from her graveyard domain in *Plan 9 from Outer Space* (1958).

stead, she worked as a dancer and married writer-actor-director Dean Riesner. It was an appropriate mating. Riesner, in 1947, wrote and directed one of the strangest feature-length dramatic films ever made— Republic's sixty-one-minute *Bill and Coo.* It might have proved one of Hollywood's greatest scandals—the performers were actually paid in *birdseed*—except that all of them were trained birds (finches and parakeets), performing on miniature sets and enacting a tale about a mean crow who threatens their idyllic existence.

The Vampira shtick began at a costume ball. Maila, with her seventeen-inch waist, wore a torn black dress with bloody scratches on her bosom. She was seen by producer Hunt Stromberg Jr., and the debut of her TV series of movies and funny horror bits created just the kind of word-of-mouth publicity Stromberg had hoped for —leading to coverage by *Life* and guest appearances on other shows. Later, she added an *outré* element to Liberace's Las Vegas club act. She made many personal appearances and pulled off such stunts as becoming an entrant in the Miss Rheingold contest. But she was not the only person of note in her family; her uncle, Paavo Nurmi, was a champion Olympic runner.

Maila hung out at Googie's Restaurant —and she was often there when James Dean came roaring down Sunset Strip on his motorcycle to join her and others in a vigil they called "The Night Watch." Dean's former roommate, screenwriter Bill Bast, recalled, "Jimmy was always a night person, and Googie's and Barney's Beanery were the only places in town that were open after twelve o'clock. You start out by talking to someone because they're kooky or interesting and you wind up getting to know them. I think he was interested in these people because they were not bourgeois, mundane, ordinary people." And Maila was the *least* mundane of any of the Googie gang.

Maila and Jimmy Dean became friends. The fanmag writers couldn't have been more delighted—here were Hollywood's two biggest eccentrics *together*! So much copy poured out of typewriters about the "romance" between Dean and Vampira that the truth is lost in the misty past of the Sunset Strip dawns—and the ghosts of Googie's aren't talking. In fact, Googie's is gone, replaced by Stake & Stein—a name that almost reverberates with echoes of Maila and Dean's long-ago laughter.

Writer Logan Smiley saw it as "a Halloween thing that stayed around for a while. Everybody didn't take down their decorations right away if you know what I mean. It was kooky, and it was fun. Everyone was getting into pills too. She was from Europe, and she was pushy. It was a very sure way for her to break into the business, but I don't think she and Jimmy were as close as her 'planters' made it out."

Both Maila and Dean started giving out statements to counteract the fanmag-fabricated affair. Soon, Maila refused to talk to reporters about Dean. "He is very weird when it comes to publicity," she said. "He doesn't want to be talked about, and I have to respect that. I don't want him to be angry with me."

Dean told Hedda Hopper: "I don't go out with witches, and I dig dating cartoons even less. I have never taken Vampira *out*, and I should like to clear this up. I have fairly adequate knowledge of satanic forces, and I was interested to find out if this girl was obsessed by such a force. She was a subject about which I wanted to learn. I met her and engaged her in conversation. She knew absolutely nothing! She uses her inane characterization as an excuse for the most infantile expression you can imagine."

A 1956 publication, *James Dean Album*, tried to clear up the contradictions: "A good deal older than Jim, Vampira first attracted him with her eccentric charms. . . . Knowing firsthand the lonely climb up the ladder to success, she befriended him in the same way she'd befriended Marlon Brando a few years earlier. He'd go to her apartment for advice, professional and romantic —nothing more. Contrary to an article in a recent scandal magazine, which tried to paint a sordid picture of their dates, the only relationship they had was on a platonic basis."

"We have the same neuroses," was Maila's explanation for the relationship. Bill Bast saw that Maila and Dean had something in common. In his now legendary out-of-print 1956 paperback biography, *James Dean*, he wrote, "Maila, an interesting offbeat personality, is a compassionate girl who understood his esotericism, a claim few could make, and she quickly penetrated the protective fortress that surrounded him." Further, both had a "macabre sense of humor," prompting ghoulish gags. Dean, in high school, played Frankenstein in a play called *Goon with the Wind*, and he had hoped to make a horror movie. When he died on September 30, 1955, he and Bast had been at work on their own screenplay adaptation of *Dr. Jekyll and Mr. Hyde*. Had Dean lived to portray Jekyll-Hyde, he undoubtedly would have capitalized on his gift for executing striking changes of mood on screen, and it would have been regarded as one of the finest acting performances ever seen in the horror genre. Yet another loss is that Dean had no opportunity to display his comedic talents in a feature-length comedy film.

Maila recalled her first meeting with Dean when they were introduced by actor Jack Simmons at Googie's: "Jimmy acknowledged the introduction and I got right to the nitty-gritty. Instead of saying, 'How do you do?' I said, 'Where is she?' Psychically, I knew him before I even met him, so I didn't waste words: 'Where is she?' He said, 'Who?' And I said, 'Your mother'; and he made a whooshing sound, reddened and threw his arms over his head. And so then immediately, he said, 'I want you to come to my apartment. I want to read a poem to you.' And it was actually a Ray Bradbury short story about a boy who hanged himself, a boy who had a close relationship with his mother. So he read the story to me. He was on Sunset Plaza Drive then, the little place above a garage that he described as a wastebasket with walls. . . . Intellectually, he knew that she had died, but emotionally, he felt that she had abandoned him. So then he told me the circumstances of his mother's death and how he had been orphaned at nine."

As Maila remembers "The Night Watch," "We'd coffee-klatsch about Googie's, Schwab's, Barney's Beanery, the little coffee shops. It was chatter. I guess we wanted to share the experiences we'd had during the course of the day, as you do when you like someone, feel close to someone. I think it was rather adolescent. And Jack Simmons was always with us. We were never alone. . . . And the three of us would drive around. We didn't go far. We had Jack's little car, an old car that shimmied a lot in the back. We'd go to drive-ins maybe, to Tiny Naylor's. It was very like when I was in high school and going to the local drugstore, except that I was with someone with whom I could see the world in unison. I mean, I had someone who understood how I was seeing the world."

In the summer following James Dean's death, Maila Nurmi traveled by train to Indiana to visit his grave. In the dining car she stared at a shining metal sugar bowl on the table in front of her. A feeling came over her that she should steal the sugar bowl although she could not understand why. She picked it up and put it in her purse. Later that day, she learned that the nine-year-old James Dean, while accompanying his mother's body from California to Indiana in 1940, had stolen a sugar bowl from the train.

Another of Maila's actor friends from the fifties recently confirmed Bast's impression of her as a warm human being rather than just a costumed publicity-grabber: "Maila dyed her blonde hair black and wore half-inch fingernails. She used to smoke with a foot-long holder. But under all of that, she was goodhearted and very real."

Only a few months after Dean's death, Maila (still billed as Vampira) made a horror film, the infamous *Plan 9 from Outer Space*, which had the original release title of *Grave Robbers from Outer Space* at its premiere. She had the female lead, second-billed after Bela Lugosi, and the cast also included Lyle Talbot, Tor Johnson, Tom Keene, Gregory Walcott, Mona McKinnon, and Duke Moore. However, a case could be made that Vampira is the true "star" of this film inasmuch as Lugosi is seen only in a fragment of footage filmed at the doorway of his actual residence, and in about sixty seconds of film showing him going to a mausoleum and returning. Other scenes in the film purporting to show Lugosi are of a stand-in holding a cape in front of his face. Lugosi died August 16, 1956, and his scenes in *Plan 9 from Outer Space* were originally shot for another film that was not completed. In truth, Lugosi was virtually not in *Plan 9 from Outer Space* at all! Produced by J. Edward Reynolds for DCA, *Plan 9* was written, directed, and edited by Edward D. Wood, Jr., who had previously directed Lugosi in *Glen or Glenda?* (1952) and *Bride of the Monster* (1954). The story concerned aliens who have failed in several previous attempts to conquer Earth; then, realizing that the old "living dead" gimmick is always cheaper than special effects, they animate a few corpses to stalk Earthlings. Or something like that. It seems that no one

Alien-directed Tor Johnson menaces innocent bystander in *Plan 9 from Outer Space.*

who has seen *Plan 9 from Outer Space* has ever agreed with anyone else on just what the plot is all about. Even in the late fifties it was so baffling that release was delayed until 1958 while Ed Wood, Jr., himself tried to figure it out.

Joe Dante, reviewing retrospectively in *Castle of Frankenstein*, commented, "From the hammy intro by Criswell to the hammy afterword by Criswell, this grade Z 1956 home movie masquerading as a theatrical film is an unalloyed delight, raising rank amateurishness to the level of high comic art. Residents of San Fernando, California, are terrified by UFOs in the shape of thermos plugs that revive the dead, if not the audience, in one of the chinziest graveyard sets ever seen. Among the disinterred is the actually dead Bela Lugosi, via silent film clips that look like test footage for a remake of *Scared to Death* and lend an appropri-

ately morbid tone. Tor Johnson's game line readings make this his greatest role (no small accomplishment, considering), and perfectly incompetent support is provided by Vampira, Mona McKinnon, Lyle Talbot, Tom Keene, and others too humorous to mention. Screenplay, production, and direction by Edward D. Wood, Jr., a name to conjure with. Wow."

In 1959 Maila began work in a string of Alfred Zugsmith low-budget productions, beginning with *The Big Operator*, which starred Mickey Rooney as a crooked union boss, with Vampira in the role of Gina. *The Beat Generation* (1959) had nothing to do with the "beatific" founding principles of Jack Kerouac's Beat Generation; instead, it featured Ray Danton as a psycho assaulting California housewives. Vampira and Venice, California, were simply tossed in for atmosphere. One of

Hard times for the aliens—their hideout has been discovered! The camp classic, *Plan 9 from Outer Space.*

Maila's biggest fans was Orson Welles, who also worked with Zugsmith in the late fifties, directing *Touch of Evil* (1958).

In Zugsmith's *Sex Kittens Go to College* (1960), Vampira was eleventh-billed in the cast of Mamie Van Doren, Tuesday Weld, Mijanou Bardot, Mickey Shaughnessy, Louis Nye, Pamela Mason, Martin Milner, Jackie Coogan, John Carradine, Norman Grabowski, Charles Chaplin, Jr., Harold Lloyd, Jr., and Conway Twitty.

Zugsmith changed the original title, *Teacher Was a Sexpot*, to *Sexpot Goes to College* before finally settling on the title *Sex Kittens Go to College*. However, all three of these titles were considered too racy for television where the film was re-titled *Beauty and the Robot*. In the story Dr. Mathilda West (Van Doren), a brainy ex-stripper, is chosen, sight unseen, by THINKO, a humanoid electronic robot, to head the Collins College science department. West's arrival on campus causes a furor, stirring up jealousy and envy. Football captain Woo Woo Grabowski (playing

himself) faints whenever he's in her presence. This bugs Woo Woo's girlfriend, Jody (Weld). Two gangsters (Mickey Shaughnessy and Allan Drake) arrive to rub out THINKO, who has been picking racehorse winners and causing heavy losses for the Big Boss. They believe the robot is a rival racketeer. Eventually, the gunsels expose Dr. West as Tassels Monclair, the Tallahassee Tassel Tosser. Angered, she goes into a wild provocative dance and then confesses that her attempt to realize her childhood dream to be a teacher was folly. The film ends with her accepting a proposal of marriage from Barton (Marty Milner), the public-relations director of the college. Maila, under the billing of Vampira, played a character called Etta Toodie.

The Vampira makeup and costuming seem to derive from the cartoons of Charles Addams. David Dalton, in his book *James Dean, The Mutant King*, refers to "the Charles Addams character on which she had modeled herself." According to Richard Lamparski, Maila "believes that she is still a

Cast regulars of ABC-TV's "The Addams Family" (*left to right*): John Astin as Gomez, Ted Cassidy as Lurch, Lisa Loring as Wednesday, Carolyn Jones as Morticia, and Ken Weatherwax as Pugsley.

victim of an unspoken blacklist within the television industry." Could such be possible? One could speculate that the 1966 *authorized* adaptation of Charles Addams' cartoons into the TV series *The Addams Family*, with Carolyn Jones as Morticia looking almost exactly like Vampira, is somehow responsible, either intentionally or unintentionally, for the banishment of Vampira from her video throne. *The Addams Family* was so successful a show that it continues to play in syndication, viewed by youngsters who were not even born when Vampira was popular. Although the character of Vampira was truly Maila Nurmi's original creation (no matter the re-

semblance to Addams' cartoon character), her Vampira image was entirely supplanted by the network promotion of Morticia in the mid-sixties.

In 1969 a black-and-white comic magazine character named Vampirella (Vampi for short) was conceived by Forrest J. Ackerman and publisher James Warren, and shaped up by writer Archie Goodwin and artists Tom Sutton, Trina Robbins, and Frank Frazetta. This character seemed inspired by equal portions of Vampira, Dracula, and Jean-Claude Forest's *Barbarella*. There was a facial resemblance between Vampirella and Vampira, and, instead of bloody scratches, Vampirella (as revealed

ABOVE: A family portrait of "The Munsters" (*left to right*): Yvonne De Carlo as Lily, Al Lewis as Grandpa, Beverly Owen as Marilyn, Butch Patrick as Eddie, and Fred Gwynn as Herman. Like Morticia, Lily Munster is yet another TV-character creation inspired by Vampira.

LEFT: Vampira's East Coast counterpart— John Zacherley, New York City's monster master of ceremonies par excellence, circa 1960.

in the first 1969 story) has a batlike birthmark on her breast.

In the summer of 1973 producer Jack Wiener announced a film titled *Vampirella* to star David Niven as Count Dracula. Immediately encountering problems with this title duplicating that of the comic-magazine character, Wiener changed the name of the film to *Vampira*. However, it sat on the shelf and was not released until 1976, when it was given yet another title— *Old Dracula*, intended to hit a vein in the same lode Mel Brooks had mined with *Young Frankenstein*.

Today, Maila Nurmi, having been through two marriages, continues to live in

A Vampira lookalike in a scene from AIP's *The Ghost in the Invisible Bikini* (1966).

Hollywood in an apartment where various stray animals in the neighborhood have learned they will be well treated. Through her many friendships and contacts, Maila has become a wholesale dealer in movie memorabilia. However, one can't be certain that she will not make a television comeback. On a December 1976 *Tomorrow* show, a chortling Zacherley (now a disc jockey in New York City on WPLJ) re-created his well-remembered cauliflower brain routine, demonstrating that he is still frightfully fit for the job of East Coast horror host. In recent years, horror-movie fans have been entertained on TV late shows by the talented "Simon" (in syndication), the Lugosi-like Gore De Vol (in Washington, D.C.), M.T. Graves (in Florida), Dr. Shock (in Philadelphia), and many others around the country. But, for a large contingent of viewers, there is only one—the original, the genuine—Vampira and her pet spider Rollo. Bring her back, they chant!

Liz Torres as Morticia in a scene with Jim Nabors from ABC-TV's "The Addams Family Fun House" (1974).

# *Hazel Court*

*R*anking among the several most impressive film beauties of the sixties—along with amply endowed British scream goddesses such as Barbara Shelley, Honor Blackman, and Barbara Steele—regal-looking Hazel Court has been denied the recognition due to her. She first started her intermittent career in 1944, age eighteen, in *Champagne Charlie*. Several years later, in a good supporting part in her first macabre film, she appeared opposite Eric Portman, Dennis Price, and Greta Gynt in *Dear Murderer* (1947); it was one of the many smaller-budget but excellent, stylish British thrillers that came out in the forties and fifties but, alas, are now rarely evident.

A victim of circumstances, perhaps poor press and management—whatever the cause, the talented and very personable Hazel Court is an actress whose natural ability for classical-styled suspense and horror has been overlooked by too many, and only exploited intelligently by such directors as Roger Corman, Sidney J. Furie, and Terence Fisher.

ABOVE: Hazel Court in *The Masque of the Red Death*.

Her first major genre film was *Ghost Ship* (1952), written, produced, and directed by Vernon Sewell. In the story, Hazel Court and her husband, Dermot Walsh, decide on buying the yacht *Cyclops*, planning to make it their floating home. While painting the ship, they occasionally smell the cigar smoke that has inspired a local rumor that the ship is haunted. Hazel is terrified after members of the crew quit, claiming that they saw a ghost aboard. She calls in a medium, who relates the tale of the murders that once took place on the yacht. It had been found derelict on the Mediterranean with its owner, his wife, and her lover all missing. Dermot, who refuses to believe in ghosts, reveals the murderer—who was also responsible for faking spiritual manifestations. Much of the film was shot aboard director-writer Sewell's own yacht, the *Gelert*. Others in the cast included Hugh Latimer, Joan Carol, Hugh Burdon, John Robinson, Jack Stewart, and Joss Ambler.

Three of her finest British chillers have been *The Curse of Frankenstein* (1957), *The Man Who Could Cheat Death* (1959),

and *Dr. Blood's Coffin* (1961). In each film
Hazel was consistently cast to portray the
Inviolate Goddess of classical tradition.
Horror-film scholar and writer Paul Roen
observes that "in each frame of this
tryptych, however, her voluptuous body
also serves as a passive impediment to the
nefarious aims of her leading man."

Although Hammer Films was founded
in 1935, it is generally recognized that *The
Curse of Frankenstein* was their milestone,
launching as well the film careers of two
comparatively unknown actors, Christopher
Lee and Peter Cushing, and advancing director Terence Fisher's status after ten
years and twenty-five films (he had already
achieved considerable recognition in England for quality programmers and several
outstanding efforts such as *So Long at the
Fair*). However, *Curse*'s success also stereo-
typed Hazel Court's acting position for the
next few years.

Playing Elizabeth, Dr. Frankenstein's
(Peter Cushing) doting mistress and
housekeeper in *Curse*, Hazel's loyal presence is perhaps the strange scientist's greatest hindrance, blocking the successful at-
tainment of his "unnatural" experiments.
Ingratitude proving to be sharper than the
proverbial fang, even after Cushing saves
her from certain death, Hazel calmly
watches Cushing being marched off at the
climax to the guillotine—she then jogs
away happily with her new companion,
Robert Urquhart, Cushing's former mentor.
Roen notes that Hazel herewith ". . . demonstrates just a soupçon of the emotional
poison that was later to characterize her
performances in American films."

*The Man Who Could Cheat Death*—
also directed by Fisher—displays the
unique and excellent villainy of Anton Diffring, a magnificent heavy who has been
shamefully neglected by filmmakers. He
portrays a scientist who has extended his

TOP RIGHT: Robert Urquhart and Hazel Court in
*Curse of Frankenstein* (1957).

BELOW RIGHT: Hazel takes a peek at her husband's
handiwork in *Curse of Frankenstein* (1957).

existence for 104 years through gland transplants; unfortunately, the transplants have been selected from hapless victims. Hazel is a beautiful model, who is the tender concern of Drs. Diffring and Chris Lee. Diffring's life-prolonging dreams go awry, however, when an old scientist and friend (who preferred old age to being involved) refuses to offer vitally needed assistance and is killed by Diffring. Diffring then goes to Dr. Chris Lee, forcing him to perform a rejuvenation operation by revealing that he has kidnapped Hazel, but he won't disclose her whereabouts till the gland has been successfully transplanted. Dr. Lee very wisely fakes the operation, sensing treachery. Meanwhile, Hazel has been incarcerated a whole day as an unsuspecting hostage in Diffring's hidden, private mad lab . . . together with one of his unfortunate female victims, a pathetic, disfigured creature delightfully enough crazed to create the right atmosphere. Thinking the operation on him has succeeded, Diffring, burning with love, rushes to the imprisoned Hazel and confesses he wishes to have her share his eternal youth via the usual heinous means. She cringes and screams properly, finding the prospect appalling. Old age suddenly, rapidly overtakes Diffring; and if that weren't bad enough, his crazed victim tosses a flaming oil lamp on him . . . cooking his goose. Chris Lee arrives just in time with the gendarmes, as Hazel runs screaming into his warm non-Draculaian embrace.

On the heels of director Sidney J. Furie's *The Snake Woman* came his fourth film, *Dr. Blood's Coffin*, starring Hazel as a nurse who has a libidinous effect on another crazed doctor, Kieron Moore. Just as Lee unexpectedly reversed his usual monster-villain image in *The Man Who Could Cheat Death*, Moore shifts from his usual "good guy" image. He demonstrates extreme irritation on learning that Hazel still clings lovingly to her dead husband's memory. To jolt her from her annoying reveries, Moore reanimates her husband's corpse. Hazel once more runs screaming to safety while her two former lovers are burned in the traditional horror-film holocaust.

By now Hazel Court's screen personality had taken firm root: in all three of the preceding films she depicts the outwardly pleasant but potentially sinister household liability whose presence helps undermine the men in her life. Continuing in this filmic capacity, she appeared in a Hitchcock-directed segment of *Alfred Hitchcock Presents* titled "Arthur," starring Laurence Harvey as a conscienceless Australian farmer in the title role. Her unwanted romantic overtures disrupt his agrarian tranquillity; he reacts by strangling her, then grinding up her corpse, and finally feeding the pieces to his chickens, who thrive so well on this unusual diet that they win first prize at the county fair.

While reflecting on her career during an interview some years ago, she was asked how could one as attractive as she become so identified with horror roles: "I frankly don't know. Maybe it stems from my parts in *The Curse of Frankenstein* and *The Man Who Could Cheat Death*. Whatever the reason, I suppose I'd better watch it before I'm offered only horror roles."

She had also appeared in macabre films such as *The Tell-Tale Heart* and *Mania*. Did she mind being so much in the genre? "Not really, I suppose. The public likes this type of film and it's great fun making them, although it might not look so from a theatre seat."

WE DARE YOU TO LOOK INTO "DOCTOR BLOOD'S COFFIN" in *gori-est* Eastman COLOR

Can you stand the terror . . . the awful secret it contains?

starring
KIERON MOORE
HAZEL COURT • IAN HUNTER
Released thru UNITED UA ARTISTS

THEATRE

What did she mean by *fun* . . . ? "Well, there's usually more dramatic potential for an actress in a horror film than in, say a situation comedy. Moreover, only the nicest people make horror movies. Roger Corman, for example. You couldn't have a nicer or more helpful director. . . . Having worked with him on *The Premature Burial* and *The Raven*, I think he has a genuine feeling for the mood of Edgar Allan Poe and a tremendous enthusiasm."

Many film scholars and historians meanwhile agree that the very colorful, mass-market orientation of most Corman films belies their complex structure. *The Masque of the Red Death* seems at first

RIGHT: In *Dr. Blood's Coffin* (1961) the corpse of Steve Parker (Paul Stockman) is disinterred.

BELOW: Hazel Court screams in the dream sequence of Roger Corman's *The Masque of the Red Death* (1964).

glance a finely made but simply essayed horror film with a moral ending. Closer study shows it to be, however, anything but simplistic moralizing. This same ambiguity highlights Hazel's characterizations in both *Masque* and *The Premature Burial*. In *Masque*, despite appearing to be a devout satanist deeply enamored of her diabolical lover Prince Prospero (Vincent Price), Hazel is not altogether unregenerate but more of a romantic, hapless pawn.

In *The Premature Burial*, her personality is, if anything, more clear-cut and variegated. Superficially, the tale seems to be another Poe-type, macabre adventure of decadence and hyperparanoia, with Hazel getting her just desserts for attempting to murder her husband, Ray Milland. The story begins with medical student Milland —he is still suffering from a severe trauma while witnessing the exhumation of a corpse that showed evidence of having

been buried alive. Milland's professor, Alan Napier, and another student, Richard Ney, attempt to ease his mind. Milland is obsessed by the notion that his own father had also been buried alive in the family crypt and fears that he, too, will have a similar fate. He builds a tomb containing every possible means of escape and survival. In the meantime, the professor's daughter, Hazel Court, marries Milland and offers to help him. Her several attempts are rebuffed each time; Milland wallows so deeply in self-pity he cannot sense loving concern, and unconsciously sows the seeds of his own destruction. It is Ney who seems to succeed in talking Milland out of his nightmarish frenzy. No sooner does Milland destroy the tomb than he falls into a cataleptic coma, is declared dead, and has a premature burial. Napier hires grave robbers to recover the body, and when Milland is freed he kills the violators. He next kills Napier, and starts stalking Hazel, whom he discovers trying to seduce Ney, who despises her

Hazel Court in *The Premature Burial* (1962).

conduct. Milland carries away the screaming Hazel to his grave, binds her, and buries her alive. When Ney tries to intervene, they struggle, and Milland's sister (Heather Angel) shows up with a gun, killing Milland. She informs Ney that she has learned that Hazel was responsible for the tricks that were used to drive Milland out of his mind.

Regardless how wretchedly unconscionable Hazel's character may seem at the climax, every indication early in the story shows that she had come into Milland's life with noble intentions. It is rather Milland's contrariness, if not lack of proper intelligence, that acts as a catalyst to turn her to evil. Paul Roen notes that "Women's liberationists in the audience should surely empathize when she throws up her hands in despair and, with poetic irony, contrives that he should meet with the very doom he so ardently deserves."

Proving her dexterity also in a frothier and more whimsical vein in *The Raven*, Roen observes, "If Hazel succeeded in humanizing the Fatal Women in *Masque of the Red Death* and in *Premature Burial*, then it's also true that in *The Raven* she effectively parodies this character. In this film, the broad comic overstatements of Vincent Price and Peter Lorre are pleasantly contrasted with the subtle, witty sadism depicted by Miss Court and Boris Karloff. Occasionally these conflicting styles of performance make *Raven* seem a rather schizoid film. In any case, though the character Hazel portrays is guilty of several attempted homicides, she nevertheless strikes us basically as a saucy, flirtatious, charming minx."

Born in Sutton Coldfield, England, in 1926, Hazel had been (until *The Raven*), primarily established in British-based productions until she had settled down permanently in Hollywood with her husband, Hollywood director Don Taylor (*Jack of*

Ray Milland with Court in *The Premature Burial*.

*Diamonds, Escape from the Planet of the Apes*). During filming of *Masque of the Red Death,* she explained also her reason for frequently commuting to England at other times: "My thirteen-year-old daughter, Sally, is at school here, and it is because of her that I come over regularly. I had to turn down the chance to appear on Broadway—the best stage offer I ever had—but acceptance would have kept me from England for a long time."

One might be quick to assume that this was a blow to her career: "Not at all," Hazel answered promptly. "My private life has always come before my career. I'd feel lost without my work, but my domestic affairs still come first. I've never been able to pass on my responsibilities to someone else—to allow my daughter to be brought up by a nanny, for example. I need a happy home background with my family around me. That's why I settle for a *middle-height* career. I just haven't the necessary dedication for the dizzy heights of top stardom."

The reason for Hazel's more than ten-year semiretirement is thus clarified to a certain extent: A fine, striking actress at all times—but, a dedicated wife and mother *first*.

Jack Nicholson, Olive Sturgess, Hazel Court, and Vincent Price in Roger Corman's *The Raven* (1963), a satiric adaptation from Poe by screenwriter Richard Matheson.

# Yvette Vickers

Yvette Vickers was born August 26, 1936, the daughter of Mr. and Mrs. Charles Vedder of Kansas City, Missouri. At the age of 16 she entered UCLA, where she majored in motion picture and theatre arts for three years. She began appearing locally in little theatre productions such as *That's Life, Ring Around the Ring, Strictly Informal,* and the leprechaun musical fantasy *Finian's Rainbow.* Standing 5' 3", with blue eyes and honey blonde hair, she became a familiar face to televiewers after a trip to New York in the mid-fifties resulted in her being cast as the "White Rain Girl." She danced with raincoat and umbrella in what might almost be interpreted as a commercial spin-off of Gene Kelly's famed *Singin' in the Rain* number of 1952. Yvette returned to the West Coast to do both live and filmed television roles.

Her motion-picture debut came in *Short Cut to Hell* (1957), a remake of *This Gun for Hire* (1942). The story of a hit

ABOVE: The scheming "other" woman, fifties-style: Yvette Vickers as Honey in *Attack of the 50 Ft. Woman* (1958).

man who gets double-crossed, *Short Cut to Hell* was also the directorial debut of James Cagney. After *Sad Sack* (1957), Yvette Vickers was seen in *Reform School Girl* (1958) and *The Saga of Hemp Brown* (1958).

In 1958 she was third-billed as Honey Parker in producer Bernard Woolner's *Attack of the 50-Foot Woman.* Mark Hanna wrote this story about a huge alien from a UFO who causes Nancy Archer (Allison Hayes) to become a giant. Dr. Cushing (Roy Gordon) and Dr. Von Loeb (Otto Waldis) chain her. Her husband, Harry (William Hudson) plots with Honey (Vickers) to kill his now-immense wife. Breaking loose from the chains, Nancy kills Honey and squeezes Harry to a pulp before she is shot by Sheriff Dubbitt (George Douglas). Jacques Marquette was both executive producer and cameraman. Nathan Hertz directed.

After *I, Mobster* (1959) Vickers co-starred with Ken Clark in the 1959 Gene and Roger Corman production of *The Giant Leeches* (also known as *Attack of the Giant Leeches*). Bernard L. Kowalski di-

rected the sixty-two-minute picture by American International. Leo Gordon's screenplay begins with poacher Lem Sawyer (George Cisar) traveling through the Florida Everglades, where he encounters a weird water creature that he kills. Florida State Fish and Game Warden Steve Benton (Clark), while searching for poachers with his fiancée Nan Greyson (Jan Shepard), hears a scream. Liz Sawyer (Vickers) has found the body of Lem, who has been brutally attacked. The following day, Steve finds Sheriff Kovis (Gene Roth) uncooperative. Later that night, Dave Walker (Bruno VeSota) encounters his wife Liz locked in

an embrace with the lecherous Cal Moulton (Michael Emmet). He pushes the two to their feet and forces them, at gunpoint, through the dismal swamp. Both Liz and Cal are carried off by the leech monsters. When Dave protests his innocence and no one believes him, he commits suicide. Meanwhile, Nan and her father, Doctor Greyson (Tyler McVey), dynamite the swamp pool, knowing of the game warden's disapproval. When Steve arrives at the swamp, he sees the explosion along with three human bodies floating on the surface of the water. Seeing the caverns of the monster leeches through the water, Steve and his companions decide to dynamite the pool again, ridding the swamp of the leeches forever. In 1975, a year before his death, Bruno VeSota reminisced about *The Giant Leeches* and Yvette Vickers in an interview held by actor Barry Brown. Their conversation went like this:

VESOTA: *The Giant Leeches* as a picture wasn't bad at all. The only thing I found

OPPOSITE PAGE

TOP: Enjoying life for the moment, Honey entertains Harry Archer and customers at the local watering hole. A scene from *Attack of the 50 Ft. Woman.*

BOTTOM: Oblivious to his wife's discovery, Harry Archer (William Hudson) enjoys a romantic interlude with Honey.

BELOW: Just desserts for the faithless husband: William Hudson in the hands of the fifty-foot woman.

fault with was the monsters. One of the things that separates the men from the boys in this business is knowing that if you're making a monster picture you'd better make a perfect monster, or as near perfect as possible. A producer cannot allow himself to get trapped in a financial situation where he lets the zippers on the monster suits show! Know what I mean? So it came to pass with *The Giant Leeches*. Ed Nelson, who was going to be in the picture, was delegated to make the monster suits. As he started to make them, he was hired for another movie and had to relinquish the making of the suits to someone else. So when the monster suits were finally made and put on the swimmers, who were wearing airtanks—these suits were rubber-looking things with octopus-like suction cups all over to make them look like monsters—the suits didn't fit over the airtanks. They split and had to be pinned together with paperclips and sewn with needle and thread. And they looked so bad and so phony that, in the final cutting of it, as in *The Brain Eaters*, you can only take a six-frame or a twelve-frame cut. WHAM! Show the monsters and cut away to show somebody running away from them.

If you took one close look, you'd laugh your head off. You see airtanks sticking out of the monster suits, you know? It's the same thing as *Attack of the Crab Monster*. You see this giant monster moving towards you with human feet underneath it. (*Laughs.*) And that was *The Leeches*. If you get a man who doesn't have a track record of making monster suits, you're taking a great chance.

BROWN: You could at least put some money into monster suits!

VESOTA: Whatever it takes! Everything else comes after that! Whatever it takes to make a monster suit, the monster is your star! Whatever it takes to make a suit, spend it, 'cause that's your star!

BROWN: There was one other amusing story regarding *Leeches* I wanted you to tell. The story about the water breaking.

VESOTA: During the shooting of the underground cave where the leeches bring their victims, we were standing around watching the leeches, their crummy suits coming apart, hauling up their victims and trying to pretend they're so strong they can lift Yvette Vickers up on this level. They had a watertank loaded with several tons of water and because of the pressure of the four or five people that were in it, the tank gave. It was a canvas tank held up by wood, and it gave. Tons of water came pouring toward the viewers, and a friend of mine visiting the set, G. J. Mitchell, had to scamper out of the way. The crab dolly almost ran Mitchell over.

BROWN: Where did this take place?

VESOTA: I believe it was in the Producer's Studio.

BROWN: Did you go on location at all for *Leeches*?

VESOTA: Yes. Somewhere near the Santa Anita racetrack. It's supposed to take place in the bayou in the South. This was some type of jungle gardens or whatever, where some of the Tarzan movies were shot. They had these high palm trees, and it looked very much like a jungle. We shot almost all the outdoor stuff there.

BROWN: How did you like Yvette Vickers? I met her once about two years ago at a party.

VESOTA: I loved Yvette Vickers. I think Yvette Vickers was a better sex symbol than ten Marilyn Monroes put together. She was most certainly a fine actress.

After her appearance as Lilly Peters in Paramount's *Hud* (1963), directed by Martin Ritt from Larry McMurtry's novel *Horseman, Pass By*, Yvette Vickers' career began to taper off abruptly. Outside of a few TV appearances, such as in *One Step Beyond*— in a supernatural story involving a highwire act—her last known credit was in a supporting role in the Shelley Winters–Debbie Reynolds vehicle, *What's the Matter with Helen?* (1971).

# Barbara Steele

*"Do you know the Draculas, by any chance?"*
—BARBARA STEELE in *The She-Beast*

**B**arbara Steele's emergence in the sixties brought not only glamour to the horror film but also a grand style that was allied with a return to the origins of the genre. Even though this was followed by several long absences from the horror field (and, at times, from films of any type), her initial impact and prolific output were such that she must be considered as the actress most closely identified with horror. How appropriate, then, that she would marry a writer named Poe—scriptwriter James Poe. However, she says, "I hate graves and all those things. I began with too many horror films. This is dangerous. Horror films are made for directors, not for actors. One never thinks of the character of the people or their psychology. One always follows the same dramatic pattern. That's what I object to about nearly all these films—they always exploit the same fears." Even so, she admits, "I love witchcraft, the supernatural. All that's intuitive. I don't like people who are too rational."

Her roles have ranged from witches and vampires to prostitutes and character parts, and she is equally outspoken about the rise of eroticism in films: "So often, eroticism and pornography are confused. Personally, I think that modesty is a form of hypocrisy. Unfortunately, eroticism is very often used solely for commercial ends. I think that eroticism should be related to a dramatic necessity. And also, cinema is much less free than the other arts. Why? Possibly because the performance is too direct. That frightens people. They're a little afraid to see these things on the screen."

The facts of Barbara Steele's birth are as shrouded as some of the characters she has portrayed. "I was born in Ireland. It's a humid and green country. Not at all like Rome. I was born on the same day as Fellini . . . but not the same year. I'm, therefore, a Capricorn." According to J. Arthur Rank publicity, she was born in England near Liverpool at Birkenhead on December 29, 1937. American-International Pictures press releases had it that she was born on a ship headed for Liverpool. ("The tall, slender, green-eyed brunette got off to a dra-

Two publicity shots from the early sixties.

matic start in life being born abroad a ship halfway into port at Liverpool, enroute from Ireland to England.") The 1964 *Film-lexicon degli Autori e delle Opere*, published in Rome, gave her birthdate as December 29, 1938, and the place as Trenton Wirrall, Cheshire. Elsewhere, the date has been given as January 29, 1938. As Jean-Claude Romer, co-editor of *Midi-Minuit Fantastique*, succinctly put it, "Who can we believe?"

One fact, however, is certain—as the top-ranking actress in the area of horror-fantasy, there is no one to equal her, in either quantity of films, horrific imagery, or physical appearance. Even in still photographs, her chiseled features and demonic beauty have a magnetic and haunting appeal. Measuring 35–22–34, with raven tresses framing her bone-china complexion and liquid-green eyes, she is Horror Chic personified. John Brosman in *The Horror People* calls her "the Queen of Horror." As the international *femme fantastique*, she has no competitors.

Steele is multilingual (English, Italian, Spanish, and French), although she states, "I don't speak Italian very well. I have an accent." On her off-hours, she enjoys horseback riding, swimming, and decorating. "It's easy to know my mood," she says. "I'm thin when I'm happy, but, during all the seasons, my eyes are green, my hands too big, and my legs too long." Once, when a journalist asked her, "What are your plans?" she answered, "I want to fuck the whole world!" She hates "Doris Day and other professional virgins, being alone, and imagining myself in prison." She loves to walk alone at night, but adds, "unfortunately, there are too many dangers in the big cities." She also likes to "lie on the ground and paint, look at the sky while relaxing in the hay, and drink red wine in the bathtub." She executed the latter, with spectacular élan followed by grisly horror, in the 1974 Canadian film *They Came from Within* (also titled *Shivers* and *The Parasite Murders*).

Her introduction to fantasy drama came at the age of seven when she made her stage debut as Snow White in *Snow White and the Seven Dwarfs*—and hungrily ate the prop apple. Her father was an Irish exporter who traveled with a maritime company on the Mersey River. "My family is a family of frustrated Irish actors. My grandmother built in the barn a kind of small theatre for me and my cousins. We would amuse ourselves by putting on plays for neighbors. I never thought that I would be doing anything other than acting."

When Barbara was eleven years old, her father enrolled her in a progressive school. "We didn't have any locked doors," she recalled. "Our study program was not regular, and there were no punishments...." Her education continued at Birkenhead High School, at The Cotswolds, the Coeducational Mobile School of Beltane, Wiltshire, and the King Alfred School of Hampstead. She then embarked on an esthetic roller coaster—studying dance, theatre, and painting (at the Chelsea Art School in London and the Sorbonne in Paris). But her passion for theatre dominated. "I really love to feel that the audience is interested in me," she said in an interview with *Midi-Minuit Fantastique*. "I love to attract attention. I must be a bit of an exhibitionist. What's most depressing for me is indifference. I took courses in dramatic art in an English school called Summerhill, founded by A. S. Neill. It's a course that leaves much freedom to the students. The teachers believed enormously in improvisation." She also studied at the London School of Dramatic Art.

Her professional stage debut came in a comedy with Robert Morley. On the opening night she provided unexpected laughter with an unscheduled bit of business: overturning an entire tray of boiling hot tea on the stage. Next she appeared in Shaw's *Arms and the Man*. At Stroud, in 1954, she appeared with the Amberley Players in the title role of Oscar Wilde's *Salome*, followed by repertory parts in Brighton. At the Citizen's Theatre of Glasgow, her performance in John Van Druten's *Bell, Book, and Candle* was seen by Olive Dodds, who signed her to a long-term contract with J. Arthur Rank. "When the Rank Organisation signed Barbara Steele," wrote Raymond Durgnat, "they saw in her (one presumes) a cross between Jean Simmons and Belinda Lee, two earlier fugitives from the chain-gang charm school." Durgnat described her as possessing "an art-school face, with something wild and regional, possibly even Mary Webb-ish, a round-square face which chops and changes its character as the lights carve at its neat, stark cheekbones, high forehead. In monochrome, her immense, green eyes photograph a liquid Italian-black. She is the only girl in films whose eyelids can snarl. In this clime of dim discretion, English film actresses (and actors, too, mostly) do little more than quiver their voices, hoping that the one-tenth above the surface will imply the nine-tenths below. It sometimes does, but we have a very close and special place in our critical heart for those rare ladies who, like Diana Wynyard, in Thorold Dickinson's *Gaslight*, can depict the excess, the self-forgetfulness, the heedless ecstasy of unrestrained emotion. Barbara Steele is one of the few to have a vibrato as well as a tremolo. She comes from rep and isn't afraid of old-fashioned ham, in the highest (or Donald Wolfit) tradition."

Durgnat's Jean Simmons-Belinda Lee comparison was later supplanted by other similar descriptions. In the "Cine de Terror" special issue of *Film Ideal*, Ramon Moix called her "the illegitimate daughter of Chris Lee and Cyd Charisse," and Gerard Legrand in *Positif* #53 said that she "is to Juliet Prowse what Juliet Prowse is to Leslie Caron,"

Her first Rank Picture, *Bachelor of Hearts* (1958), concerned with comedic preparations for a student May Ball, had Barbara in the role of Fione. According to her it was *really* rank: "It wasn't important at all. In England one can do nothing of interest." Hardy Kruger headed the cast of Sylvia Syms, Ronald Lewis, Peter Myers, and Miles Malleson.

Next came *The 39 Steps* (1959), a color remake of the 1935 Alfred Hitchcock classic. This version was directed by Ralph

Thomas and starred Kenneth More and Taina Elg. That was *39 Steps* for Rank and one giant leap for Barbara, for it put her solidly in the suspense-thriller genre, only a hop, skip, and jump away from the horror roles that were to focus attention on her. *Upstairs and Downstairs* (1959), predating the popular TV series of the seventies with a similar title, was a comedy about a couple seeking the right servant girl.

Then came *Your Money or Your Wife* (1960) and her role as Roslyn in *Sapphire* (1960), also seen under the title *Operation Scotland Yard*. This was directed by Basil Dearden, one of the directors responsible for the memorable 1945 British anthology-fantasy classic *Dead of Night*. The socially conscious theme of *Sapphire* is revealed as Scotland Yard investigates the murder of a girl, discovering that she was passing for white. Described by one critic as "the mystery of who done it being the mystery of human responses," the film explored the undercurrents of the racial situation in London. The Rank Organization made the Eastmancolor *Sapphire* not long after explosive British conflicts with black immigrants from the West Indies surfaced in the press. At a time when American films still shied away from the reality of this subject, *Sapphire* pulled no punches and stands as the first powerful filmic document of the Civil Rights sixties. However, as noted by Daniel J. Leab in *From Sambo to Superspade,* "*Sapphire* is not without flaws; somehow most of the blacks in it contrive to spend their time drinking, dancing, and gambling. Indeed, the black manager of one dive tells the police that 'no matter what the color of their skin, you can always tell them when the bongo drums start beating.' Moreover, the film is glib, self-satisfied, and somewhat preachy." Also in the cast are Nigel Patrick, Yvonne Mitchell, Michael Craig, Bernard Miles, and Paul Massie (who appeared that same year as the lead in *The Two Faces of Dr. Jekyll*). *Sapphire* was Barbara Steele's last film for the Rank Organization, who sold her contract to Fox. She lived in Hollywood for two years. Later she said her time was mostly spent sitting on the beach waiting for phone calls. During an actor's strike she decided to go where the work was and left for Italy.

With *Black Sunday* (1960) Steele began her horror career, making a strong impression on audiences in the dual roles of Asa and Katia. "It was a very attractive film, very well made," she said, "but it is always the same. These are the films where one is the victim of a predictable situation. The events are the appearances of the characters. I find that it's more interesting being the victim of a man rather than of a situation. I would say right away that these are directors' films, but there are those for whom I have great admiration: Fellini, Truffaut or Kazan, for example." Her director on *Black Sunday* was Mario Bava, making his directorial debut after having previously served as cinematographer for Riccardo Freda on *Caltiki, the Immortal Monster* (1959) and *The Devil's Commandments* (1956). Bava "had seen one of my films," said Steele. "I don't know which. It must have been an English film, I think. In any case, it was after *Black Sunday* that I was classified as a witch or vampire or whatever you wish."

The Italian-made *Black Sunday* was originally titled *La Maschera de Demonio* (*The Mask of the Demon*). It has also been seen under the titles *Revenge of the Vampire* and *House of Fright*. Bava worked with screenwriters Ennio de Concini, Marcella Coscia, and Mario Serandre in adapting Nikolai Gogol's folktale, "The Vij." (In 1967 the story was filmed in Russia under the original Gogol title.)

Carlos Clarens, in *An Illustrated History of the Horror Film*, noted that *Black Sunday* served to introduce "the extraordinary Barbara Steele, eventually to become Freda's favorite interpreter," adding, "As might have been expected, the quality of the visual narrative was superb—the best black-and-white photography to enhance a horror film in the past two decades." Steele commented, however, "In ten days Mario Bava had not been able to work the lighting as he had planned it. As an old chief cam-

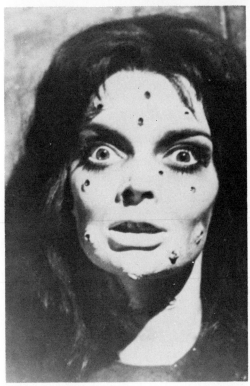

TOP: Barbara as the prospective lodger, Juliet, in the seldom-seen British comedy of manners, *Your Money or Your Wife* (1960), shown here with Donald Sinden.

BELOW LEFT: Barbara Steele as Princess Asa, complete with the wounds from the Inquisition's demon mask, in Mario Bava's *Black Sunday* (1960).

BELOW RIGHT: Asa awaits her sentence.

Asa about to meet the fate of the Inquisition in
*Black Sunday*'s first terrifying sequence.

The film's introduction of Asa's normal descendant,
Princess Katia.

era operator, he attached much importance
to the image. I find that, in our time, the
cinema is less and less a visual art. It was
much more beautiful in the 1930s, for example. One finds less and less imagination
concerning the visual planning. Love scenes
are filmed in a mechanical and cold fashion.
One doesn't embrace this way in life. It
would be necessary, on the contrary, to suggest this by imagery—a detail, the curve of
a shoulder . . . I don't know . . . I never go
to see supernatural films. Not my own.
There is, perhaps, some good in them." Audiences, though, flocked to see *Black Sunday*,
making it a popular hit in both Europe and
the United States. American-International
handled the United States release in 1961,
with music by Les Baxter replacing the
original score by Roberto Nicolosi. In some
locations it was double-billed with Roger
Corman's 1960 *Little Shop of Horrors*.

Ivan Butler, in *Horror in the Cinema*,
wrote that *Black Sunday* "appears to combine horror, beauty, and the ludicrous in
about equal proportions." Jean-Andre
Fieschi, in *Notebooks of the Cinema*
#166–167, described Steele as "all at the

same time, a fairy with claws like the drawings of Charles Addams and the Vera of the
count of Villiers." Her appearance in *Black
Sunday* inspired Fieschi to write, "An apparition, in short, the most beautiful, the
most pure, and the most moving, who sus-
pends the beating of the heart and time,
this real, young girl, living and dead at the
same time but real and terrifying, dark and
darkly dressed against a background of a
stormy sky, among the ruins, holding on
leash two dogs of a tall race and whose eyes
don't blink, don't shine, but are open, in an
irresistible invitation to Terror." *Castle of
Frankenstein* #4, in its "Special Vampire
Issue," devoted a full article to *Black Sunday*, offering this detailed description of the
story: "An eerie procession of black-robed
figures, members of the Inquisition, dread
religious order of the seventeenth-century
Balkan country of Moldavia, are carrying
out a sentence of execution. The victim is a
lovely young black-haired girl, Princess Asa
(Steele) of the House of Vaida. She and
her lover, Javuto (Arturo Dominici), have
been accused of worshiping Satan, of prac-
ticing witchcraft and black magic. Both

296

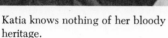
Katia knows nothing of her bloody heritage.

Gorobec (John Richardson) and Jovuto struggle in Asa's crypt in *Black Sunday*.

must die. The Grand Inquisitor, who has passed sentence upon the Princess, is her own brother. Mercilessly, he watches as she is held, helpless, as the mask of Satan is placed upon her. This hideous bronze face is lined inside with sharp spikes. Before she dies, the witch curses her brother, vowing vengeance on his descendants. Then, screaming horribly, she meets her awful fate.

"Two centuries later, in 1830, old Dr. Choma (Andrea Checchi) and his young assistant, Dr. Gorobec (John Richardson), are driving through a dark forest on their way to a nearby medical congress. As they take a shortcut, the axle of their coach breaks, and they are forced to halt near an old, half-ruined castle. While their driver makes repairs, the two men venture further into the dark wood, idly exploring the castle's vicinity. They come upon an old chapel and a burial vault. There, a single coffin reposes. Through a window in the lid they see an ugly mask with features distorted in a horrible smile. Dr. Gorobec feels strangely impelled to remove it. He does so, revealing an uncannily preserved face, still beautiful. Does he imagine it or does it seem to

be alive, pulsing with some evil half-life? There is a peal of thunder, and a storm breaks. The two men leave the crypt.

"Outside, they see a startling sight: apparently the same woman buried in the crypt stands there, dressed in flowing black garments. She has two huge dogs on a leash. However, she is not the witch, but her great-granddaughter, Princess Katia (Steele). The resemblance is uncanny. As they continue their journey, the two men set off for the nearby village, where they plan to spend the night. Behind them, in the crypt, the dead woman stirs. Her eyes open. She has become a vampire, having remained in an undead state within the coffin for two hundred years. The removal of the mask and of a cross placed upon the coffin have freed her. Still unable to move, she can give only mental commands. In a nearby graveyard, the corpse of her lover, Javuto, also stirs. At her order, the mound of earth above his grave begins to heave. Slowly but inexorably, the body emerges, still wearing the terrible mask. Javuto heaves himself upright, walks forward and removes the mask. Then he vanishes into the shadows.

"At the Vaida castle the old Prince, Katia's father, suddenly falls ill. A servant is sent for Dr. Choma. But it is Javuto who knocks upon the doctor's door. Offering to take him to the castle, he leads Choma to a sombre coach. Their journey ends at the Vaida tomb, where the vampire is waiting. Eyes blazing, she places Dr. Choma under her spell. He is now her slave, carrying out all her hellish commands. Choma comes to the castle, pretending to treat the old Prince. Instead, he draws out his life blood to provide sustenance for the evil sorceress.

"Dr. Gorobec visits the castle, finding it under a dark shadow. The dogs howl, sensing some malign presence. Doors open, curtains move. An evil force is everywhere: striking at an old servant (who is found hanged) and at Katia's brother, Constantine (slain by Javuto). To add to the mystery, there is the strange behavior of Dr. Gorobec's older colleague. Puzzled, Dr. Gorobec consults the village priest. The old man deciphers writing found on Princess Asa's coffin and tells Gorobec the truth: she is of the undead and must be destroyed. By the ancient methods, the vampire must be returned to the grave that it has unlawfully left. But it is nearly too late. The witch's plans are almost complete. She has drawn Katia to her through a hidden passageway leading to her tomb. From Katia's body, she begins stealing her life and youth, transferring it to her own body. Thus, she shall walk the earth again, assuming the identity of her descendant. Katia's body will be left in the tomb so that it will be taken for that of the sorceress. Gorobec arrives at the castle and discovers the passageway. He finds the tomb—and the two women. One is young and beautiful, the other old and haggard. He assumes the young one to be Katia and the other one to be the vampire. As he prepares to slay the wrong one, the villagers and the priest arrive. The young-looking vampire is revealed in her true guise and seized by the crowd, tied to a ladder, and consigned to a flaming pyre. As she finally gives up the life that should have ended two centuries before, the real Katia awakes, youthful as before. The nightmare has ended." But for Barbara Steele it was only the beginning of a career of nightmares—for no one who saw *Black Sunday* could forget her vampiric persona.

In realizing her role with such dynamic intensity, had she unwittingly doomed herself? If producers were to see her only as a horror actress, critics did not, as evident in Raymond Durgnat's early sixties projection of her possibilities: "We feel there's a moral somewhere in her progress from *Snow White* to *Black Sunday*. But it would be a pity if her eloquence as a victim-monster typed her to horror roles. As Katia, the demon's innocent double, she displayed a heavy, puzzled sadness, a pure and blessedly unsultry sensuality. Surely vast tracts of virgin territory lie unexplored in a screen personality situated, perhaps awkwardly, but how fascinatedly, somewhere in the regions between a Celtic feminine occultism and a devil-may-care energy." Later, in *Films and Feeling*, Durgnat continued: "Everybody has nightmares, and every well-appointed harem has its witch-bitch, for the same reason that fairy stories have them. Fellini's 8½ has a sort of Laurel-and-Hardy pair, the fat one, La Saraghina, and the thin one, Barbara. With her lean and hungry look, she is nervous, insomniac, masochistic, and addicted to philosophy and father-figures; she's wryly observant of the Frenchwoman with the healing hands and she's terrified of the telepathic clown who smiles like death and truth, and who is to 8½ as Anton Walbrook is to *La Ronde*. What Barbara is here is everything that fascinates and frightens Fellini about secular *thought*. . . . It's fitting perhaps that Barbara Steele reciprocally plays the harem game, and is putting the finishing touches to a novel about a girl who has to have three lovers, each for a different aspect of her character."

A near-necrophiliac enthusiasm was expressed by Jean-Paul Torok re Steele in *Black Sunday*: "When aesthetic admiration is absolutely fused with desire and terror, it 'blacks out' . . . Where are your vaunted intelligence and your cultivated taste when everything in you freezes and is fascinated before the revelations of the utmost horror? Beneath the flowing robe of this young woman with so beautiful a countenance there appear, distinctly, the tatters of a skeleton. *Is she any the less desirable?*"

When *Black Sunday* was released in England eight years after it was made, the *Monthly Film Bulletin* of the British Film Institute observed, "Released at long last from the censor's ban, *Revenge of the Vampire* (better known as either *Black Sunday* or *The Mask of the Demon*) is still one of Bava's best films, with a fluid visual style and a narrative grip that weakens only towards the end. Some chilling moments of both beauty and terror, he has never surpassed: the great hammer blow which nails the spiked mask to the witch's face in the prologue; two eyes surfacing like poached eggs to drive the insects from the witch's skull as she slowly returns to life; the first sight of Katia, black-robed and flanked by huge dogs as she stands silhouetted in the doorway of the ruined chapel. . . . In general the atmosphere, beautifully managed with its swirling ground fogs, stunted trees, lowering mansions and ruined crypts, is much closer to what one might call Gothic Transylvanian than is usual with Bava; and there are a number of appropriate reminiscences, notably of Whale and of Murnau. . . . About three-quarters of the way through, unfortunately, Bava's restlessly prowling camera suddenly gives up; after that the precarious atmosphere of unease is dissolved in a series of shock cuts and much rushing to and fro as all the loose ends are tidied neatly away as quickly as possible." The review was credited to "T.M."

In the same year she was seen December 12, 1960, in the "Daughter of Illusion" episode of ABC-TV's *Adventures in Paradise.* Other Steele TV work includes *I Spy, Alfred Hitchcock Presents,* and a 1965 Peter Yates-directed episode of *Secret Agent,* "The Man on the Beach."

As revealed in a later interview with Michel Caen, she had hoped to get more work in the United States and move out of genre roles: "I love the small problems of

Asa's fiery end in *Black Sunday.*

life. It's this that is important. I would love to make a beautiful love film. It's been a long time since I've seen a beautiful love film. Myself, I adore love. Perhaps the French directors are too preoccupied with these problems. It's not like that here [in Italy] or in the USA. In the United States, I had a contract with Fox. It was a very unhappy period in my life. Finally, I never made a film for them. I was paid. I was bored and suffering a lot not being able to work. The only film I shot in America was *The Pit and the Pendulum* [1961] for AIP. My contract with Fox was dreadful. Rank, with whom I was under contract, didn't know very well how to use me. Then, they sold my contract to Fox. In the USA they wanted to change me completely. I was too big. I should be a brunette or a blonde. And, then, life there is so artificial. I arrived without much but left with nothing. I was completely demoralized."

She played Elizabeth Barnard Medina in *The Pit and the Pendulum,* the second in Roger Corman's series of Edgar Allan Poe adaptations, and she was third-billed in a cast that included Vincent Price, John Kerr, Luana Anders, Anthony Carbone, Patrick Westwood, and Lynne Bernay. Fantasy-and-science-fiction author Richard Matheson provided the screenplay, and the score,

Steele as Elizabeth Medina in Roger Corman's adaptation of Edgar Allan Poe's *The Pit and the Pendulum*.

The lovers, Dr. Leon (Anthony Carbone) and Elizabeth, enjoy a moment together in *The Pit and the Pendulum*, knowing their plan is working.

once again, was by Les Baxter. *Castle of Frankenstein* #1 offered this review: "AIP's movies do well in most departments: top special effects, excellent color and camera techniques, but for one constant weakness —the supporting cast. This was evident in *House of Usher*, where the young hero resembled more of a matinee rock 'n' growl idol. At times it was sheer punishment in *The Pit*; of course, thank God for Vincent Price, the Crown Prince of Horror. Barbara Steele was outstanding from every dramatic and physical standpoint—what little was actually seen of her. But there had to be John Kerr, who, at least, could have cooperated if only he had pretended he didn't hate his job. Since his is the largest part next to Price, the effect is appalling. Fortunately, Vince's priceless personality dominates enough of the production so that defects like Kerr, Luana Anders, and Carbone are quite easily forgotten. The trouble with the last two is miscasting. The original tale actually being too brief for full movie treatment, *The Pit* is mostly Matheson's spookdracular concoction of other Poe themes neatly wrapped together: a pinch of *The Black Cat* and, at times, something like a sequel to *Usher*." (*Usher* and *Pit* were, in

fact, later double-billed.) Similarly, critic Ivan Butler wrote, "Once again performances did little to help, although there was the advantage of the presence of Barbara Steele, arch-heroine of horror, and, of course, Vincent Price," while Bruce Hallenbeck, in a *Cinefantastique* letter column, noted that "Barbara Steele was sinister and chilling as his wife, while at the same time, as in all her films, retaining a strange kind of sexuality about her."

Steele later contrasted her own approach to acting with that of Price: "I find that it's very difficult, when one is a young actress, to make this type of film. When one is no longer young, one calls oneself Vincent Price. He can be successful through those very melodramatic effects. For an actress like me, it's terrible because the director always demands some of that 'to add

OPPOSITE PAGE

TOP: Elizabeth, risen from the dead, pushes the unstable Nicholas (Vincent Price) over the brink.

BELOW LEFT: Elizabeth with one of Sebastian's many instruments of torture.

BELOW RIGHT: Cynthia (Barbara Steele) in *The Horrible Dr. Hichcock*.

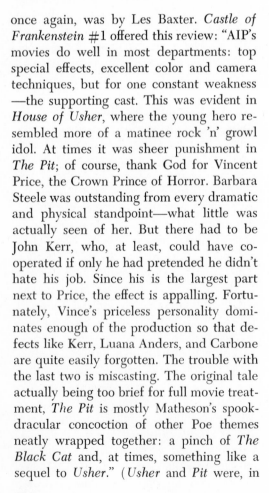

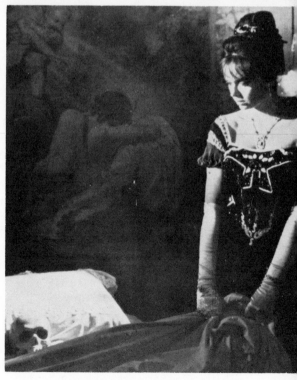

more.' He's not looking for shock effects. It's not these roles that suit me the most. It's not that it's more difficult. There are no easy roles and difficult roles. Myself, I prefer 'honest' roles."

In Riccardo Freda's *The Horrible Dr. Hichcock* (1962), Steele played Cynthia, the second wife of the insane Dr. Hichcock (Robert Fleming). Set in 1895, the film concerns Dr. Hichcock, well known for his blood chemistry experiments, who attempts to satisfy his hyperactive sexual mania with his wife, Margaretha (Teresa Fitzgerald). After she dies of a drug overdose he has administered, he leaves London grief-stricken. He returns twelve years later with his youthful second wife, Cynthia (Steele). Margaretha's ghost seems to stalk the house. Cynthia, however, refuses to believe she is subject to hallucinations and nightmares, even when Dr. Curd Lowe (Montgomery Glenn), Hichcock's young assistant who is attracted to her, comes to believe Hichcock's explanation. On the night of a storm, Hichcock learns the truth: Margaretha herself, aged and withered after having been buried alive, is haunting the house. Once again under the influence of his insane and macabre mania, Hichcock determines to restore Margaretha's early beauty—by a transfusion of Cynthia's blood. Hichcock gives Cynthia a glass of milk, but instead of drinking it, she takes the milk to Curd. Discovering poison in the milk, Curd rushes to the villa in time to save Cynthia from torture and death. A fight ensues, with a fire erupting in Hichcock's secret mortuary chamber. Hichcock and Margaretha perish in the blaze. Cynthia and Curd, injured but safe, leave for a new life.

*Castle of Frankenstein* #10 commented, "Originally titled *The Horrible Secret of Dr. Hichcock*. Frenetic, tongue-in-cheek Italian horror film about a young girl imprisoned in her scientist-husband's gloomy mansion. Ghosts, madness, burial alive and hints of necrophilia make it all quite entertaining, but 12 minutes were removed for USA release. Dubbed." Produced in scope and color by Panda/Sigma III, the film has also been seen under the titles *Raptus* and *The Terror of Dr. Hitchcock*. Steele was second-billed in a cast that also included Harriet White, Maria Teresa Vianello, and Montgomery Glenn. Julyan Perry did the screenplay, and the score was by Roman Vlad. The Eastmancolor photography was by Raffaele Masciocchi, whose name was changed in the credits to Donald Green. In an apparent attempt to hoax ticket-buyers, this ridiculous notion (perpetuated in countless foreign language films destined for English-language release) disguised several in the cast and production staff: actress Vianello became Teresa Fitzgerald, editor Ornella Micheli became Donna Christie, art director Franco Fumagalli became Frank Smokecocks, producer Ermano Donati became Louis Mann, and director Freda was billed as Robert Hampton. But, as Carlos Clarens notes, "the films themselves belie this imposture. They are strictly Continental affairs and most successful where their Anglo-Saxon counterparts fail: in the evocation of mood through color and decor and in a visual sophistication that reveals the director's earlier occupation as an art critic. On the other hand, Freda's direction of actors is without method and haphazard, while his pacing, at least by American standards, lags once too often. In spite of Freda's avowed preference for the genre, his horror movies are marked by a denial of the fantastic—they are in substance melodramas of jealousy and machinations, usually directed against the sanity, or the life, of the heroine. Freda's center is invariably the woman, either as victim or victimizer, and logically his work is subtle, unathletic, and velvet soft."

Steele continued with Freda that same year in a sequel to *Horrible Dr. Hichcock* titled *Lo Spettro de Dr. Hichcock* (*The Spectre of Dr. Hichcock*) and retitled *The Ghost* in its 1965 American release. "I shot the first in eight days and the second, *Lo Spettro de Dr. Hichcock*, in six days," said Steele. In *The Ghost*, playing the role of Margaret, Steele was top-billed in a cast that also included Peter Baldwin, Elio Jotta (whose name was Americanized as Leonard G. Elliott), Harriet White, and Um-

Peter Baldwin and Barbara Steele as the lovers in
*The Ghost.*

berto Raho. The screenplay was by Freda
and Oreste Biancoli (hiding behind the
name Robert Davidson). Roman Vlad
again did the music, this time along with
Ennio Morricone and Franco Mannino
(who was called Frank Wallace). The in-
consequential story concerned the ghost of
a murdered man haunting his unfaithful
wife. The name "Dr. Hichcock" was now
spelled "Hitchcock"—undoubtedly a ploy
to bring forth subliminal associations with
Alfred Hitchcock.

In Scotland in 1910, Dr. Hitchcock
(Leonard G. Elliot) lives with his wife
Margaret (Barbara Steele) and their
housekeeper Catherine (Harriet White).
Once an able physician, Hitchcock is paralyzed and no longer practices, devoting
himself instead to scientific research and
spiritualistic sessions with Catherine as the
medium. Using curare, Hitchcock tests an
anti-paralysis formula on himself with the
assistance of Dr. Livingstone (Peter Baldwin). Catherine, speaking in Sanskrit during a séance attended by Margaret, Hitchcock, Livingstone, the notary Fisher
(Reginald Price Anderson), and the police
superintendent (Charles Kechler), predicts
that there will be a death in the house.

Having become romantically involved
with Livingstone, Margaret incites him to
rid her of her crippled husband. On the following night, while Fisher and the police
superintendent are guests, Livingstone gives
Hitchcock a lethal dose of the drug he has
been concocting. Later, the lovers pretend
to be concerned by his absence, and, with
the visitors, they go up to his room, where
they find him apparently dead. Margaret
soon learns that only a small part of Hitchcock's wealth has been willed to her, on the
condition that she retain the services of
Catherine, whom she hates. Strange voices
and happenings bring the "widowed" Margaret to despair.

Margaret and Livingstone, who want
to withhold some jewels from the estate,
learn that the key to the safe is in a pocket
of the suit Hitchcock was buried in. They
open the coffin and take the key, but find
the safe empty. Livingstone answers a call
from the hospital, and Margaret, alone in
the room, sees Hitchcock's ghost. She fires a
gun at it. Hearing the shots, Livingstone
returns to the room, and, as the two lovers
embrace, blood leaks from the ceiling to the
bed. Livingstone rushes to the attic.
Through the open door he sees the hanging
corpse of Hitchcock. The door closes, and
when he finally opens it, there is no trace
of the body.

Margaret then learns from Catherine,
in a trance, that the jewelry is hidden in
Hitchcock's coffin. She hurries to the crypt
and uncovers the coffin, but there are no
jewels. Returning to the house, she becomes
suspicious of Livingstone, goes to his room,
finds the jewels in his suitcase, attacks him
with a razor, and drags his body into the
cellar and burns it. The film ends with police leading Margaret, a raving lunatic,
from the house.

Carlos Clarens felt that "what Freda
obviously needs, and what we should look
forward to, is a solid literary source for his
talents: Wilkie Collins or maybe even Charlotte Brontë. (There are echoes of both
*Jane Eyre* and *The Woman in White* in
*Raptus* and *Lo Spettro*.)" Both films, says
Clarens, are "lovingly wrought miniatures."

In Federico Fellini's critically acclaimed *8½* (1962), Steele played the part of Gloria Morin, but one of her important scenes was cut. She explained, "When I act, I often love what I'm doing. In general, I love acting. Afterward, I hate all that, and I'm in a hurry to forget it. On the other hand, I love the little trick in the Fellini film *8½*. It's a small role, but it was very likable. Fellini had cut a rather long scene that I played. It was a scene where I danced the evening in a nightclub with candlelight and all that. I liked that scene very much. It was a little dance parody of Monica Vitti in *Eclipse*. Fellini used the candles in a very symbolic way. At the end of the dance, I took the candles as if sex were involved. The sequence was cut, but not because of this. Fellini's friends when they saw the rushes told him 'You shouldn't keep this passage. The reference to *Eclipse* is too visible. The critics will hold it against you.' And, finally, he himself decided to cut." In a "Guide de la Conversation Contemporaine" in *Candide* #277 it was stated, "Her astonishing body (large, thin, very feminine) has allowed her to remarkably interpret the roles of witches, the wife-victim of a magician husband, etc. She is the only reason to love Fellini's *8½*."

In 1963 she played Flotiana in *Il Capitano di Ferro*, a Taurisano production made in Italy. Directed by Sergio Griego, the Cinemascope film was distributed by Les Films Marbeuf. The cast also featured Gustavo Rojo and Maria Petri. In *Un Tentavio Sentimental* (1963) she portrayed Silvia in a cast that also included Francoise Prevost and Jean-Marc Bery. The Italian-French co-production was made by Franca Film and France Cinema Productions. Pasquale Festa Campanile and Massimo Franciosa co-directed. Referring to *Un Tentavio Sentimental*, *Positif* #56 asked, "Must one see a very bad film for the sole pleasure of seeing Barbara Steele in it with short hair?" and immediately answered the question: "Undoubtably."

*Castle of Blood* (1963) practically has more titles than cast members. Originally titled *La Danza Macabre*, it's also been shown as *Terrore* (*Terror*), *La Lunga Notte del Terrore* (*The Long Night of Ter-*

As Gloria Morin in a scene from Fellini's *8½*.

ror), *Tombs of Horror*, and *Coffin of Terror*. On television look for it as *Castle of Terror*. Steele plays Elizabeth Blackwood in this story of a man who spends a terrifying night in a castle haunted by blood-sucking ghosts. Antonio Margheriti directed—with his name changed to Anthony Dawson. Steele commented, "The one with Margheriti, *La Danse Macabre*, I shot in ten days with television technique—three cameras and all that. It's very difficult for the lighting. And then it's exhausting—it meant sometimes working eighteen hours a day! When you make big plans, after fourteen hours of shooting, you see that this leaves little to give. The producers say, 'You're working for a week, and you will be paid for a month.' That's also tiring."

The story begins as *London Times* reporter Alan Foster interviews Edgar Allan Poe at a roadside tavern. Death, says Poe, is not the end of life but merely a resting place from which the spirit still roams the earth. Foster is unconvinced. Another man sitting silently at the table now introduces himself as Sir Thomas Blackwood. He wagers with Foster that the young man cannot spend a single night in Blackwood's castle, from which no man or woman has ever returned. They happen to be speaking on the Night of the Dead—a night during which each person who has ever disappeared into the castle will enact the last violent five minutes of his life. The wager complete, they leave immediately for the castle.

Left alone in the castle, Foster prowls around and becomes increasingly aware that strange forces are hovering nearby, yet remaining beyond his ken. Suddenly a beautiful young woman, Elizabeth Blackwood (Barbara Steele), arrives. She is the sister of Thomas Blackwood—who thinks that she is dead. Strongly attracted to each other, they are just getting acquainted when they are interrupted by another attractive woman, Elizabeth's cousin Julia. The two women argue over Foster, and then leave him in the bedroom which had been prepared for his visit.

When Elizabeth returns to Foster's room, the two realize they have fallen in love. Foster discovers, to his horror, that Elizabeth has no heartbeat. She tells him that they live in different worlds—that she has been dead for ten years. Outside the room, Julia seethes with jealousy. Accosted by Elizabeth's husband, William, she announces that she will get revenge on Elizabeth. She summons Herbert, a menacing gardener who loves Elizabeth. Herbert bursts into Foster's room, and, in a jealous rage, he plunges a knife into Elizabeth. Foster pursues him through the haunted corridors, finally overtakes him, and shoots him.

But Herbert's body disappears. When Foster returns to his room, he discovers that Elizabeth is gone as well. A mysterious Dr. Carmus appears. Long ago he rented the castle to prove his theory that if life is torn from a living thing in an act of violence, its existence is sustained by its senses. He demonstrates his theory with a snake which threatens to attack even though it has been mutilated. This, the doctor explains, is what happened to Elizabeth and the others in the castle: they died violently and therefore they still exist. Foster is then shown how each had died, beginning with a scene of dancing and music years ago. Elizabeth's husband, returning from a distant country, interrupted her idyll with Herbert. Later, when Elizabeth was alone with her husband, Herbert had jealously murdered William. Then, as he was turning to assault Elizabeth, Julia had arrived and killed Herbert. Distraught because of Herbert's death, Elizabeth killed Julia. Suddenly, all of them disappear. Foster, who can't stand reruns, seeks an exit from the castle, but no such luck. Doctor Carmus appears again, from another time dimension. As Foster watches, the doctor descends to the catacombs, releasing the fleshless, yet living, forms of those who died in the castle. Foster learns that their only means of returning on the Night of the Dead is by drinking the warm blood of the castle guests. Foster flees, and, with Elizabeth's help, he manages to elude them. He tries to take Elizabeth with him, but outside in the half light of dawn, she withers into the horrible remains of a long-dead human. Foster succeeds in leaving the castle grounds as the sun comes up, but as the gate swings shut behind him, he is impaled on one of the iron barbs and dies.

Poe and Lord Blackwood return. Blackwood collects his wager from the dead man and promises a decent burial. Poe knows that he will have a difficult time convincing the world of the truth of this story he is about to write.

The *Monthly Film Bulletin* reviewed: ". . . The effectiveness of Riccardo Pallottini's camerawork is vitiated—partly by Ortolani's cliché-ridden score which makes every surprise twist predictable, partly by the heroine's ludicrous Charles Addams make-up, partly by the wooden quality of the dubbed dialogue ('I'm very attracted to you, my dear.'). Essentially, though, the film's weakness lies in its plot; Poe chose to leave this story unpublished during his lifetime, and one can't help feeling that his choice was a sensible one."

The film was produced by Marco Vicario (renamed Frank Belty) and Leo Lax (who was called Walter Sarch). Cinematographer Riccardo Pallotini was disguised as Richard Kramer, and editor Otello Colangeli was dubbed Otel Langhel. Jean Grimaud and Gordon Wilson, Jr., based their screenplay on Poe's "Dance Macabre." Riz Ortolani did the music. Complicating the name-change confusion is the fact that there is a *real* Anthony Dawson employed in films, the respected British character actor of *Dial M for Murder* and many other British and American films dating back to the mid-forties.

Discussing *Castle of Blood* with Michel Caen, Steele mentioned one scene in the film that she thought was "terrible." As she explained it, "My partner, Margaret Robsham, didn't want to embrace me. You see, she's the wife of Ugo Tognazzi. She argued with the filmwriter. He wanted her to play the scene, but she said that she just couldn't kiss a woman. Margheriti was angry. He said, 'You have only to imagine that it's Ugo you're embracing and not Barbara.' However, I don't resemble him

very much, eh? I don't know whether this scene was used. I haven't seen the film."

Nor did she bother to see herself as Thelma in the Jean-Francois Hauduroy-directed sequence of *Les Baisers* (1963), explaining, "I would love to live in Paris. I love French cinema—what one calls the *Nouvelle Vague*. But it's a little old already, the New Wave, isn't it? Myself, I played in a New Wave film—*Les Baisers*. But, that one was horrible . . . the film, I don't know. I haven't seen the film, and I have no desire to see or speak of it. I rarely go see the films in which I play. I don't like to see myself on the screen."

Also in 1963, she appeared in *White Voices* (Julia), once again under the direction of Campanile and Franciosa. This was followed by Luciano Salce's *The Hours of Love* (1963) as Leila. In *Le Monocle Rit Jaune* (1964), directed by Georges Lautner, she played Valerie in a cast that included Paul Meurisse (of *Les Diaboliques* fame) and Marcel Dalio. "The film was made solely for Meurisse to exploit the 'Monocle' series. I was cast there in as much good as bad." In *Amore Facile* (1964) she appeared in the sequence, "Divorzio Italo-Americano," directed by Gianni Puccini.

Barbara Steele also made her second film for director Antonio Margheriti in 1964, playing Mary in the Italian production *I Lunghi Capelli della Morte* (*The Long Hair of Death*). Felice Testa Gay produced for Cinegai SPA, and Steele was top-billed in the cast of Giorgio Ardisson, Halina Zalewska, Robert Rains, and Jean Rafferty. Riccardo Pallottini had a new pseudonym this time—Richard Thierry. Robert Bohr's screenplay has Lizabeth (Halina Zalewska) witnessing the burning of her mother, Adele Karnestein, who has been accused of witchcraft and is suspected of murdering Franz, the brother of Count Humboldt (Jean Rafferty). Adele delivers a curse on the count and all his descendants. The count hurls Adele's sister, Helen, to her death. Years later, the curse brings a plague. The count becomes aware that his son Kurt (Giorgio Ardisson), who intends to marry Lizabeth, is the real murderer of

Franz. After seeing Mary (Barbara Steele) lost in a storm and mistaking her for the ghost of Helen, the count dies of terror. Falling in love with Mary, Kurt seeks her help in murdering Lizabeth. Mary reveals that she is actually the resurrected Helen, and, bringing the curse full circle, she traps the now insane Kurt inside an effigy. During a ceremony celebrating the end of the plague, he is burned at the stake.

*Castle of Frankenstein* #15, commenting on *I Lunghi Capelli della Morte*, referred to Steele as the "acknowledged queen of some of the finest unworldly, eerie films for nearly a decade," and Ivan Butler felt the film was "noteworthy, as always, for Barbara Steele." The *Monthly Film Bulletin* reviewed, "The *clou* of the film is, of course, Barbara Steele's return from the grave; freed by a bolt of lightning which splits her tombstone in two, she shakes off earth and worms to make a well-timed apparition, somewhat disheveled but little the worse for wear, in chapel reading from the Apocalypse ('And on the Day of Judgment, the dead shall return to life'). If Antonio Margheriti hasn't quite the same gift as Bava for this sort of thing, he acquits himself very creditably; Barbara Steele is her usual extraordinary self (though a trifle muted); and there is a nice performance of injured innocence by Halina Zalewska."

For *Midi-Minuit Fantastique* she had the following anecdote on her work with *I Lunghi Capelli della Morte*: "One is obliged to give right away that which comes. It's always been necessary to be available. It's the sympathetic aspect of the system. Freda adored working like that—on the nerves, against the clock. It's very interesting for action scenes, but sometimes there are all the scenes that demand little thought. It's necessary to be able to repeat very calmly. *I Lunghi Capelli della Morte* went very well. The filming began with the 'psychological sequences.' I would arrive for the shooting at seven o'clock in the morning, and I would have to play a love scene with someone whom I had never seen before. I arrive, and, like that, he must embrace me and all that. And I wouldn't know his name! I would like to know, at least, the name of my partner."

In the February 1964, issue of *Cinema* magazine, Steele was profiled in a piece titled "The Elegant Macabre," accompanied by photos showing her in gowns from the Italian fashion house Valentino.

Two scenes show Barbara as the vengeful ghost of *I Lunghi Capelli della Morte* (1964).

*Cinema* commented, "Barbara Steele's appearance on the screen frolics between a high-fashioned intellectualism and a voluptuous sadism. She glides about with the elegance and eroticism of a black patent-leather high-heel. . . . The Irish-born Barbara found Hollywood to be more of a mortuary for her talent than a home and even before she played the affectionate, exotic mistress in Fellini's 8½ she discovered that the Roman moon gave her a glow that no California sun ever could. . . . Barbara has often forgotten to stop acting. She innocently admits to a time when she was in love with three different men simultaneously, each of whom 'filled a different need for a lascivious voluptuousness, a childish care, and a sadistic sensuality.' . . . Barbara is a mystery to many of those producers and directors who seek to employ her talent, but in her case it is the mystery they seek. She seems to be part of that individual female movement that mocks marriage and established mores, and courts the primitive mysteries of the female. This contemporary attitude has created striking screen stars in the characters of Jeanne Moreau and Romy Schneider and may put Barbara Steele on her own high-heeled, porcelain-skinned, vamp-eyed way to stardom as a modern Theda Bara."

The European press was equally ecstatic. *Stop* #54, in a piece titled "Miss Dracula," stated, "For some years, there hasn't been a horror film of quality without the participation of Barbara Steele who embodies with an exceptional talent the victims of vampires and the damned soul of the monster. She who entices the innocents and the young in a world cursed with the living dead. . . ." Leo Vidal, in *Noir et Blanc* #1119, wrote, "Some actors like Boris Karloff or Bela Lugosi have acquired a sulphurous reputation. Today, it's Barbara Steele or Christopher Lee that connoisseurs talk to you about with respect."

*Terror-Creatures from the Grave* (1965) was originally titled *Cinque Tombe per un Medium* (*Five Graves for a Medium*). At the turn of the century, a young lawyer, Kovaks (Walter Brandi, American-

ized to Walter Brandt), arrives at a secluded villa in a small village in Central Europe. Cleo Hauff (Barbara Steele) and her stepdaughter Corinne (Marilyn Mitchell) live there. Kovaks, whose law partner is Morgan (Riccardo Garrone, Americanized as Richard Garrett), Cleo's secret lover, has come in answer to a letter from Cleo's husband, Dr. Hauff, who has stated that he wishes to review his will. Kovaks learns that Hauff has been dead for a year, and, investigating the mystery of the letter, he finds that the death came about through mysterious circumstances. Furthermore, the body has disappeared from its grave. He also learns that Hauff had dabbled in the occult with special references to twelfth-century "scourge-spreaders," buried in the grounds of the villa. Meanwhile, several unexpected and horrible deaths occur in the neighborhood, and it becomes apparent that each victim had been a friend of Hauff. Eventually the truth comes to light: they had conspired with Cleo to murder her husband. Dying, Hauff had invoked the Terror-Creatures to rise from their graves and avenge his death. Kovaks is told about

In 1965 Barbara portrayed the scheming, evil wife Cleo Hauff in *Terror-Creatures from the Grave*.

the "corpse-collectors." As each death is about to take place, the creaking wheels of the approaching coffin carts can be heard. When the fifth murderer and last intended victim, Morgan, arrives at the villa, the ghost of Hauff follows him through the house, summoning the Terror-Creatures to inflict their curse on Cleo and Morgan. Kovaks and Corinne are saved by a downpour of rain—the only means, according to an old legend, of washing away the evil curse.

"Fortunately," said the *Monthly Film Bulletin*, "in what is otherwise a rather routine and stilted exercise in horror, more grisly fare is provided in the form of a collection of mummified limbs on permanent exhibition at the sinister villa, in which the ever-dependable Barbara Steele seems comfortably at home."

The MBS Cinematografica production was directed by Massimo Pupillo (with his name changed to Ralph Zucker) and written by Roberto Natale and Romano Migliorini. Five minutes were cut from the ninety-minute film for its 1967 release in the United States.

*Nightmare Castle* (1965), originally titled *Amanti d'Oltretomba* (*Lovers Beyond the Tomb*), has also been seen as *The Faceless Monster* (its British title) and *Night of the Doomed*. Steele played the dual role of Jenny and Muriel Arrowsmith in the Fabio de Agostino/Mario Caiano screenplay about an insane scientist who kills his wife and her lover. Stephen Arrowsmith (Paul Muller, Americanized as Paul Miller), a brilliant but demented scientist, is conducting secret experiments in the regeneration of human blood through electrical impulses. Married to Muriel, he works in his lab with his assistant Solange (Helga Line). Finding Muriel with the gardener, David (Rik Battaglia), Arrowsmith disfigures him with a poker and then uses electrical discharges to kill both David and Muriel. By injecting Muriel's blood into Helga, he transforms the elderly crone into a youthful beauty. After stabbing the hearts of the two corpses with a dagger, he hides the hearts in an urn at the base of a statue. Learning that Muriel's will has been changed to disinherit him in favor of her

As Muriel Arrowsmith, with her scientist-husband (Paul Miller), in *Nightmare Castle* (1965).

The lovers, David (Rik Battaglia) and Muriel, at the hands of the deranged Dr. Arrowsmith in *Nightmare Castle*.

sister Jenny, a former mental patient, Arrowsmith marries Jenny and then attempts to drive her insane. Jenny hears Muriel's voice urging her to kill her husband, but although she attempts this twice while in a trance state, she fails.

Derek Joyce (Lawrence Clift), Jenny's former doctor, is curious about her insanity, and Arrowsmith tries to eliminate him, but kills the butler by mistake. Returning to the castle later, Dr. Joyce discovers the two hidden hearts. When he pulls the dagger from the united hearts, the lovers come back to life and begin their revenge. The ghost of Muriel burns Arrowsmith alive, and the ghost of the gardener sucks the blood of Solange, who is transformed into a

Barbara gets the whip in Mario Monicelli's *L'Armata Brancaleone*.

grinning skeleton. Cured forever of her nightmares, Jenny leaves the castle with Dr. Joyce, while the loud and sinister beating of two hearts can be heard.

Mario Caiano (under the altered name of Allan Grunewald) directed, and the popular Ennio Morricone provided the music score. Carlo Caiano produced the film for Emerci-SRL. For its American release, there were cuts adding up to about fifteen minutes. Steele was top-billed in the cast, which included Giuseppe Addobbati (changed to John McDouglas) as well as those identified previously.

Frederic Vitoux, in *Midi-Minuit Fantastique* #15–16, commented that Steele in this film was "fascinating and macabre, alarming and mysterious, equally provocative, violent and silent. . . . The beginning doesn't spare us a progressive introduction into the universe of Horror (the entrance of the heroine into cursed places, chateaus and forbidden manors, for example) but immediately culminates in a violent dream. There is a very beautiful love scene in a conservatory at night, where the white dress of Barbara Steele is soiled. There are the episodes of torture and sadism. . . . One will dream of a meditation about the Actress and the Woman, a restrained sensuality and a violent eroticism—immovable, obscure, cinematographic."

*Once upon a Tractor* (1965) was made for the United Nations Telsun Foundation, Inc., as an hour-long television drama. Argentinian director Leopoldo Torre Nilsson, who made the mysterious *Hand in the Trap* (1960), the haunting *Summer Skin* (1961), and other memorable melodramas, directed the *Tractor* cast of Steele, Alan Bates, Diane Cilento, Albert Dekker, and Melvyn Douglas. *I Soldi* (1965), was co-directed in Italy by Gianni Puccini and G. Cavedon; joining Steele were Enrico Maria Salerno and Silva Koscina. *Un Angelo per Satana* (1965), a Discobolo Cinematografica production, was directed by Camillo Mastrocinque. In this film, a two-hundred-year-old statue is brought up from a lake at the end of the nineteenth century. Young sculptor Roberto Morigi (Antonio De Teffe, under the name Anthony Steffens) is commissioned by Count Salvoni (Claudio Gora) to restore it. The statue resembles Harriet De Montebruno (Barbara Steele), who has just arrived on her vacation. Harriet's ability to change into the Angel of Death is unknown to Roberto, and they fall in love. She brings to an end the love affair of her maid, Rita (Ursula Davis), and schoolmaster Dario (Aldo Berti), and Dario hangs himself. Next, she prompts the village idiot to rape a girl and then causes a woodcutter to murder his family. Suspecting Harriet of witchcraft, the villagers also feel the statue is to blame. Roberto, however, discovers that the count has been hypnotizing Harriet. The count claims he has been under the influence of his housekeeper, Illa (Marina Berti), who shoots him. Illa then runs toward the statue, which falls off its pedestal and causes her to be thrown into the lake. The *Monthly Film Bulletin* had no praise for this one, adding, "apart from a few moments of imperious whip-cracking, even Barbara Steele is diminished."

*L'Armata Bracaleone* (1965) was a French-Italian-Spanish co-production. Mario Monicelli, better known in the United States as one of the *Boccaccio '70* directors, wrote and directed for Fair Film, Les Films Marceau, and Vertice Film. Steele portrayed Teodora in this widescreen Technicolor drama. Vittorio Gassman, Catherine Spaak, and Maria-Graccia Buccela were also in the cast. Michel Perrot, covering the 1966 Cannes Festival for *Midi-Minuit Fantastique* #15–16, felt that Barbara had "a veritable triumph in the role of the sado-masochistic Byzantine princess during a brief but astonishing scene in *L'Armata Brancaleone*, a film by Mario Monicelli. The action takes place in the era of invasions. Vittorio Gassman plays Brancaleone, who could be a synthesis of Don Quixote and Matamore. Accompanying a troupe of four or five odd people, he lives out many adventures during the course of the expedition. Their end is a little explicit and was made only as a pretext for the unusual and agitating battles. We are not about to forget the extraordinary flogging scene between Barbara Steele and Vittorio Gassman and the extraordinary cohort of beggars and poor following a sort of prophet-Christ. The interest in this film lies chiefly in the parts made deliberately in bad taste and perhaps even as a provocation; there are coarse jokes and rough situations. Evidently, Monicelli isn't Rabelais, but the tone is often risqué. By its sincerity and self-confidence, *L'Armata Brancaleone* is no less of a very sympathetic enterprise than *Alfie* or other intended satires."

*The She-Beast* (1965), originally titled *La Sorella di Satana* (*The Sister of Satan*), has also been seen, in England, under the title *Revenge of the Blood Beast*. Steele starred as Veronica, a tourist possessed by the spirit of a two hundred-year-old witch, Vardella. Veronica and Philip (Ian Ogilvy) are vacationing when they are bothered by a voyeuristic innkeeper at Vaubrac in Transylvania. The next day an auto accident sends their car into a lake. Veronica is apparently dead, but Philip catches a ride back to the inn from Count von Helsing (John Karlsen), who is transporting the body of Vardella for a planned exorcism. Vardella is revived, but before the exorcism can take place, the witch goes on a murderous rampage throughout the village. When Vardella is thrown back into the lake, Veronica reappears, seemingly okay. But the film ends with the suggestion that Vardella is now possessing Veronica. The British Film Institute review in the *Monthly Film Bulletin* took note of the continuing practice of Americanized names, noting that it was not the case this time: "An engaging horror film made, not by a pseudonymous Italian, but by a young English director. Although the beginning is a trifle comatose with its self-consciously stylish slow tracks and compositions (black-cloaked figures silhouetted against the sky-line), it gradually gathers momentum while developing a nice line in comic grotesquerie with its furtively lecherous innkeeper, an amiably incompetent police force, and a pustule-covered witch placed for safekeeping among the vegetables in the kitchen icebox. The jokes about Transylvania now being an Iron Curtain police state are rather tediously drawn out, but do lead to one splendid gag when Vardella, after hacking the innkeeper to bits with a sickle, throws it away to land emblematically across a stray hammer. Barbara Steele gets little chance to display the grand manner in her comparatively brief role, but the acting in general is sound (enormously helped by the fact that the leading players would appear to have dubbed their own dialogue, though the innkeeper speaks with what sounds suspiciously like Akim Tamiroff's voice)."

Paul M. Maslansky produced the Italian-Yugoslavian co-production for Leith (Europix-Consolidated), and Michael Reeves directed. The screenplay is by Reeves under the pseudonym of Michael Byron. Ralph Ferraro scored. The cast also included Jay Riley, Richard Watson, and Mel Welles (a pseudonym for Ernst von Theumer, who directed the 1966 *Island of the Doomed*). In *Horror of the Cinema* Ivan Butler summed up both Steele and the picture in two sentences: "An Italian-made vampire film that achieves the rarely successful task of laughing at itself without altogether losing the sense of horror. Barbara Steele is, as usual, splendiferous, though in a comparatively small role."

In *Cinema 65* (#97), a critic hiding behind the Stoker-inspired pseudonym of "Jonathan Harker" wrote, "But, finally, here come Barbara Steele and her retinue of spirits! One step closer. Looking at the cutting mouth and the angular nose of Barbara Steele, we are moved!"

David Pirie devotes an entire chapter to Michael Reeves ("A Renaissance of Themes and Ideas?") in his book *A Heritage of Horror*. As Pirie sees it, the three and a half films Reeves made between 1964 and 1969 introduced "a new and revolutionary approach to the entire genre." Reeves was a *cineaste* who knocked on the door of his idol, Don Siegel, and was immediately given a job as a dialogue director by Siegel. While working in England for Irving Allen on *The Long Ships* and *Genghis Khan*, he was invited to Italy by Paul Maslansky to work as assistant director on *Castle of the Living Dead*. Maslansky was so impressed he offered Reeves a screenplay and an eighteen-day shooting schedule. According to Pirie, "Reeves was so desperate to direct that he was prepared to put up a large amount of his own money to finance the film." With the script completely rewritten by Reeves, the final result was *The She-Beast*. Pirie feels it "tentatively indicates some of the themes that run through all Reeves's three films, for the evil of the indestructible witch, Vardella, has a force that derives clearly and directly from the evil in the other characters, including the hero. When the innkeeper is about to rape a girl, for example, Reeves cuts to Vardella's putrefying features, and when a boy is eagerly enjoying the savagery of a cockfight below his window, he is savagely attacked by Vardella. From moments like these it can already be seen that the world Reeves sets out to create is diametrically opposed to the dualistic universe elaborated by [Terence] Fisher. In Reeves' characters, evil is inextricably intertwined with good, and their violence is circular and ambiguous."

A projected production of *The Doctor and the Devils* in 1965, which would have had Nicholas Ray directing Steele, Laurence Harvey, and Geraldine Chaplin, was dropped from the schedules. Another abandoned project was a 1965 production of *La Diabolika Lady*, which would have given audiences the long-anticipated opportunity of seeing Steele opposite Christopher Lee.

This incredible onslaught of early sixties films, in which critics often agreed that Barbara Steele was sometimes the main reason for seeing certain films, brought her an award before the decade was half over. During the June 4 to 12, 1965 Retrospective du Film Fantastique and the XIII Festival International du Cinema de San Sebastian, she was given the Prix Special d'Interpretation by the French film magazine, *Midi-Minuit Fantastique*. Steele accepted, but stated, "I understand your enthusiasm on the subject of supernatural films. The supernatural attracts me, but not the films in which I play. I try to avoid these roles." That same year she was featured on the cover of *Midi-Minuit* (#10–11) and interviewed in its pages by Michel Caen (#12). In addition to discussing her films, she also talked about her novel: "I have already started over three times, and I don't find it very good. It's called *London Is a Town Called Liza*, but it's as autobiographical as one might wish to say. It's the history of a young girl who has three lovers. Each one represents one of the facets of her own personality but also in some sort of counterpoint. Finally, it's a terribly demystifying book. It's about a small girl who grows up and doesn't succeed in finding a home with one ideal man . . . that she had imagined. It's a book that is a little sad, a book of deceptions, but it's without doubt that I am unhappily a romantic. A dreamer. What do I desire? A huge house, all white, the sun, Mexico, and all the people that I love in this house. I would also love to write a film." In its June 1967, issue (#17), the publication, in its then-new large format, once again featured her on the front cover, and presented a complete Steele dossier, devoting thirty pages to a biography, a filmography, a synthesis of reviews, and a gallery of forty-five photographs (many full pagers) from almost all of her films. Included was a feature, "Who Are You, Barbara Steele?" This question was mainly answered with a listing of a few of her favorite things: "Favorite author—Dylan Thomas. Favorite composer—Bela Bartok. Favorite singers—Ray Charles, Bob Dylan. Favorite dance—depends on the partner. Favorite drink—condensed milk. Favorite city—Mexico City. Favorite actors—Oskar Werner, Jean-Paul Belmondo. Favorite directors—Fritz Lang, Federico Fellini, Jean-Luc Godard." Michel Caen introduced the whole package by writing, "It is necessary to resign oneself to not understanding her. Luckily, we add. Changeable and multifaceted, she is as moral as she is physical. Her character is capable of a total metamorphosis in a space of fifteen days. Her enthusiasm is unpredictable, her sincerity

disarming. Fascinating and mad, but then this sweet madness is, after all, only the most lucid art of living."

In *Young Törless* (1966), originally titled *Der Junge Törless*, Steele had the female lead but was billed fifth in the cast. Franz Seitz was the producer of the West German-French co-production, distributed by CFDC in Europe. Volker Schlöndorff directed. Made by Seitz-Film of Munich and Nouvelles Editions de Films of Paris, the credit of "artistic supervisor" was given to Louis Malle, the New Wave director responsible for tripping the light *fantastique* with the imaginative *Zazie* (1961) and later with the surreal *Black Moon* (1975).

Schlöndorff did his own screen adaptation of Robert Musil's *Die Verwirrungen des Zoglings Törless*, a novel that delved into the beginnings of Nazism. Törless (Mathieu Carrière) is a student at a boarding school on the Eastern frontier of the Austro-Hungarian Empire. He and his friends Reiting (Alfred Deitz) and Beineberg (Bernd Tischer) are headed for school, stopping at a cafe in the village. Törless and Beineberg later visit the teasing Bozena (Barbara Steele), well known to the students for her provocations. One day, Reiting finds that his classmate Basini (Marian Seidowsky) has taken money from his locker. Basini denies this. Later, he confesses he needed the money to pay a debt. Reiting devises a unique punishment—making Basini his "slave." This soon degenerates into torture, however, with Reiting and Beineberg humiliating Basini by stringing him up by his heels in front of all his classmates. Törless, who had no role other than interested spectator, is found guilty by association, despite his explanations, and is removed from the school. Originally written in 1906, the ending of *Törless* is quite similar to a now-forgotten (but excellent) American college novel of the 1950s titled *Entry E*, by Richard Frede. The hero of *Entry E* is also unable to take a position or intervene—during a frat gangbang—and the novel ends with his dismissal along with the real culprits. In *Positif* #79, "R.B."

313

ABOVE: Boys' night out: Torless (Mathieu Carrière) and fellow student Beineberg (Bernd Tischer) pay a visit to Bozena in *Young Torless.*

RIGHT: Mathieu Carrière and Barbara take direction from filmmaker Volker Schloendorff.

commented, "In this climate of latent homosexuality, it's up to Barbara Steele, sublime as always, to show the most direct desire." In the *Monthly Film Bulletin* "D.W." commented on the attitude of Törless in the Barbara Steele scenes: ". . . he can only stand by and look on bewildered as Beineberg plays cat and mouse with the village prostitute in her dingy, mysterious room at the back of the inn. And in the torture room itself, Törless remains a fascinated, perplexed observer, horrified by what he sees and yet unable to withdraw until he can satisfy himself that there is a rational explanation for Basini's willingness to submit to such degradation. This detachment is the key to the film; and by sustaining it Schlondorff has captured the essence of Musil's novel."

In the next ten years, Barbara Steele was seen in so few films (compared to her output between 1960 and 1965) that horror filmgoers began to wonder what had happened. The explanation, perhaps, might be found in this statement in a 1965 interview: "In America, one shoots in a studio, and it's not at all impressive. In Italy, the shooting was done in authentic manors, in real crypts . . . and then, I was, no doubt, a bit superstitious. Each time when I had to lie down in a tomb, I said to myself, 'This time, Barbara, it's the very last.' And then . . . I would like horror films very much if they had been made differently. I would like to make a very calm horror film. It's ridiculous. It's always necessary to come out of a tomb, very shriveled, convulsing. I hate that. I find, on the contrary, that it's necessary to make horror films very cool—like *Les Yeux Sans Visage* [*The Horror Chamber of Dr. Faustus,* 1959]. It's very diabolical. But people are only interested in the superficial aspect. They want to see daggers and murders. They want sadism. They didn't come to see cartoons. There's nothing more sadistic than animation."

Despite her *8½* and *Young Törless* roles, Steele encountered difficulty in obtaining parts in which she did not wander out of crypts. "It's the producers," she told *Midi-Minuit.* "They have a completely false image of me, I think. Once and for all,

314

Three scenes depicting the Devil worshipers of *The Crimson Cult* (1968).

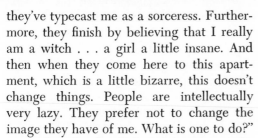

they've typecast me as a sorceress. Furthermore, they finish by believing that I really am a witch . . . a girl a little insane. And then when they come here to this apartment, which is a little bizarre, this doesn't change things. People are intellectually very lazy. They prefer not to change the image they have of me. What is one to do?"

What she decided to do was to make films globally, leaving Rome to make films in England, Canada, and the United States. In 1968 she co-starred with Boris Karloff in one of his last films. Originally titled *The Curse of the Crimson Altar* (and sometimes called, simply, *The Crimson Altar*), it was known as *The Reincarnation* in an early working title. The picture brought her together, finally, with Christopher Lee and also had the distinction of being filmed in Grimsdike Manor, the mansion of dramatist and librettist Sir William Schwenck Sullivan. Vernon Sewell directed the Tigon pro-

duction, released in the United States by American-International Pictures in 1970 under the title *The Crimson Cult*. Steele was fourth billed (as Lavinia) along with a cast that also included Mark Eden, Michael Gough, Rupert Davies, Virginia Wetherell, and Rosemarie Reede. This was the film in which Karloff caught the chest cold that led to his death. Ivan Butler states, "the promise of a combination of Lee, Karloff, and Barbara Steele is not fulfilled in this surprisingly tame witch story." In the 1971 issue of *Castle of Frankenstein* (#17), Joe Dante (the director of New World Pictures' *Hollywood Boulevard*) commented, "While several more Karloff films still await release, this was one of his last, and an excruciatingly bad, vapid one it is. Lugubrious nonsense about devil cult activity has Chris Lee standing stiffly around, Barbara Steele painted green, and wheelchair-bound Karloff giving his all to exit lines like, 'I always knew he had a split mind.' Though very weak tea, things perk up a bit when Boris is onscreen." Fred Clarke, in his debut issue of *Cinefantastique*, observed, "Unfortunately, the film's virtue is also its greatest fault; as a loosely constructed vehicle for Karloff, and the talents of Christopher Lee and Barbara Steele, it makes no sense. . . . With a little more attention to script detail, the mixture of stars could have been quite satisfying." The *Monthly Film Bulletin* agreed: "In spite of a deliciously bilious opening promising all manner of evil delights with Miss Steele in green-painted

315

face, scarlet lips and golden ram headpiece trailing peacock feathers, absolutely nothing materializes." Science-fantasy anthologist Michel Parry (*Strange Ecstacies*) notes that an early draft of the screenplay was based on H. P. Lovecraft's "Dreams in the Witch-House," which AIP had been considering for production as early as 1964. Parry, in the *Cinefantastique* letter column, described *The Crimson Cult* as "a terrible waste of talent (Lee, Barbara Steele, Michael Gough, etc.)," adding, "It was considered to be one of AIP's most ambitious European projects at the time." However, David Pirie, in *A Heritage of Horror*, states, "Though Lovecraft was not finally credited, it remains the closest that anyone has got to capturing the feeling of his work on the screen."

Mass-media attention was directed at Barbara Steele's films at this point in her career, when she, Roman Polanski, and *Midi-Minuit Fantastique* co-editor Michel Caen appeared on a March 28, 1968, French television program disucssing fantasy films. Included were clips from *The Horror Chamber of Dr. Faustus* and *The Horrible Dr. Hichcock.*

In 1970 she said, "The horrors are the only films one hears about, which is a drag. I always used to think they'd end up only in Sicily. It's not so. They end up at the Marble Arch Odeon in London while the things you did for love and nothing end up in late-night showings at the Tokyo Film Festival."

In 1974, after a long absence from the screen, Steele broke out of the tombs for an American exploitation film with something of a radical feminist slant. This was *Caged Heat!*, a Renegade Women Company Production for the Artists Entertainment Complex. Steele played McQueen, a sadistic crippled warden of the Connorville Women's Prison, where behavior modification is practiced with experimental brain surgery (referred to as "Corrective Physical Therapy"). A new inmate, Jacqueline Wilson (Erica Gavin), repelled by the way McQueen, Pinter (Toby Carr Rafelson), and Dr. Randolph (Warren Miller) run Connorville, escapes successfully with Maggie Cromwell (Juanita Brown). Then, teaming with Crazy Annie (Lynda Gold), they rob three male bank robbers wearing Walt Disney character masks, saving themselves the effort of pulling off the bank job. They return to Connorville to rescue Belle Tyson (Roberta Collins) and manage this by taking McQueen and Randolph hostage. In the gunfire that follows, the girls get away but McQueen and Randolph are killed.

The screenplay was written by Jonathan Demme—who also made his feature film directorial debut. *Monthly Film Bulletin* critic Tony Rayns found it "a genuine step forward for the Corman tradition in American independent production" and noted that the "casting plays merry hell with audience preoccupations: Russ Mey-

Barbara's *Caged Heat!* comeback.

Held at bay by former inmate Wilson (Erica Gavin) in *Caged Heat!*

er's perennial, knowing innocent Erica Gavin is presented as an ingenue who matures into a fearless radical, and Barbara Steele (making a long overdue return to the screen) as an ultra-repressed cripple, confined to a wheelchair." Rayns compared *Caged Heat!*'s feminist ideas to the political films of Rainer Werner Fassbinder: "Where someone like Fassbinder approaches melodrama from the outside, as one of any number of options open to him, Demme is, of course, fighting from the inside. It's a measure of his promise that he's managed to revive the 'girl gang' genre as much as retain a subversively feminist perspective." Michael Goodwin, reviewing in *Take One*, stated that Jonathan Demme "directs with a weird, nightmare continuity that makes the film oddly powerful, despite its essential shallowness," also taking note of "an outrageous supporting performance by Barbara Steele."

*Caged Heat!* was produced by Evelyn Purcell, the wife of director Demme. Erica Gavin commented on the working relationship of the couple: "Her relationship with Jonathan I found delightful. They're really nice to be around. Maybe they're getting a divorce—that's a joke—but to me they seemed like a beautiful couple, both respecting the other for what they do. They had a way about them that made everybody in the cast really want the film to work, not for the money, but for them. Evelyn did an incredible job. She had to give orders to a male crew and deal with the people at New World, who were male. She didn't come on heavy like, 'I'm a woman and you're a male and you'll have to take my orders whether you like it or not.' There was nothing male-female involved. And everything ran smoothly. Everything worked." During the filming Evelyn Purcell and Barbara became friends.

Erica Gavin also had some interesting observations on Barbara's professionalism: "Barbara Steele was sort of divorced from the rest of the cast. I don't know if that was intentional on her part or because the rest of us were in awe of her because she's a name star. . . . . Barbara is a real profes-

sional. I watched her get into character by applying makeup. She was very careful with every eyelash. She was very meticulous about what her makeup should be and what she should hold, thinking whether or not she should have a cane and how long the line over her eye should extend. She worked it through as she slowly applied the makeup. It was very interesting watching her. I think she's really good."

The 1974 *They Came from Within* received a United States release in the summer of 1976. Steele played Betts, who luxuriates in her high-rise apartment until she becomes one of the "parasite" victims. With scenes seemingly inspired by George Romero's *Night of the Living Dead*, these parasites dwell in the stomach, turning their hosts into zombielike sex maniacs. The story begins with the deaths of a strange doctor, Emil Hobbes (Fred Doederlein), and his mistress Annabelle (Cathy Graham) in one of the rooms of the Starliner Hotel, a luxury apartment building isolated on an island near Montreal. Hobbes' associate, Rollo Linsky (Joe Silver), tells the Starliner doctor, Roger St. Luc (Paul Hampton) about Hobbes' curious experiments: correcting imbalances in the body by implanting parasites. Meanwhile, throughout the Starliner, people are beginning to complain of stomach pains. Janine Tudor (Susan Petrie) is concerned about her husband, Nicholas (Allan Migicovsky), who has pains and coughing fits before exhibiting odd and violent sexual behavior. As parasites are coughed up around the hotel, they head for other victims. While Betts (Steele) is bathing, one parasite comes up through the drain, crawls between her legs and enters her. She then joins the horde of sex maniacs prowling the corridors, seeking others to join them. Forsythe (Lynn Lowry) and St. Luc escape to the basement. Nicholas Tudo attacks and kills Linsky. Discovering that Forsythe has a parasite, St. Luc leaves her but is soon pursued by the entire horde of fiends. They trap him in the hotel swimming pool. Betts leers at him from the pool. There is no escape, and he becomes one of them. With the entire hotel infected, they set out for Montreal (and perhaps the world).

Frank Jackson, in *Cinefantastique*, commented, "Parasites, which also function as aphrodisiacs, attack the residents of a modern apartment complex. The results are extremely gross and graphic. One of the bloodiest films ever made—and the audience thought it was funny!"

Written and directed by David Cronenberg, who had previously filmed the sf-oriented *Stereo* and *Crimes of the Future*, this horror *hommage* (which also has hints of *Invasion of the Body Snatchers*) was produced by Alfred Pariser and Ivan Reitman for Cinepix with the assistance of the Canadian Film Development Corporation. Others in the cast are Ronald Mlodzik, Barry Boldero, Camil Ducharme, and Hanka Posnanska.

Richard Combs, in the *Monthly Film Bulletin*, critiqued, "The expected conflicts are somewhat nullified by the way the film illustrates the spread of the parasites, from individual to individual through the hotel, underlining the peculiarly physical nature of its assault in each case and seemingly not only to justify mad scientist Emil Hobbes' belief that man has lost contact with his own body, but to demonstrate that he has lost contact with his fellows in this plushly anomic world. 'The true nature of horror films,' Cronenberg has stated, 'is death and anticipation of death, and that leads to the question of man as body as opposed to man as spirit.' Generally, he had a more inventive and rewarding time toying with the possible permutations of the physical nature of man in the science-fiction contexts of his two previous films; here the question is worked out largely in terms of some graphically gory special effects. But *The Parasite Murders* [British release title of *They Came from Within*] remains a fresh

and diverting variation on a hoary entertainment formula, recently (and much more tediously) embodied in *The Towering Inferno*."

In 1978 Barbara joined Keith Carradine, Susan Sarandon, and Brooke Shields for a strong supporting role in Louis Malle's controversial *Pretty Baby*. She then appeared in *Piranha* under the aegis of *Castle of Frankenstein* contributors Joe Dante, Jr., and Jon Davison, who respectively directed and produced. Others in the cast of this New World-United Artists release are Barry Brown, Kevin McCarthy, Keenan Wynn, Bradford Dillman, Heather Menzies, Dick Miller, and Richard Deacon. The story begins during the Vietnamese conflict: military scientist Kevin McCarthy creates piranha mutations in a plot to ruin the Communists' North Viet environment, and mines their river system. The river beds explode, scattering the nightmarish creatures, which eventually wind up in the United States, spreading horror throughout American waterways. The screenplay is by John Sayles, winner of the O. Henry Best Short Story Award and author of the novel *Union Dues*.

What lies ahead for Barbara Steele? *They Came from Within* saw her dramatizing a situation (drinking wine in the bathtub) that she herself had outlined during the period she was trapped in the tombs as something that appealed to her. *Caged Heat!* produced by Evelyn Purcell, was a document with hidden messages from the rising feminist cinema. So perhaps the answer lies in the implicit meaning of the words "A Renegade Women Production." After years of confrontations with producers who saw her only in the same role in picture after picture, Barbara Steele now seems to be finding her own directions.

# Hope Summers

*T*he Hollywood career of Hope Summers began in 1956 with roles on *Alfred Hitchcock Presents.* More recently, in 1978, she was a cast regular on the short-lived CBS-TV series, *Another Day.* Although she has appeared in only a few fantasy films, she has gained a reputation based on her ability to shriek and scream better than most actresses. During the thirties she toured her one-woman show, *Backstage of Broadway,* while also appearing in stock. After her Hitchcock appearances, she made California her home, and was shortly seen in *Storm Fear* (1956), followed by *Zero Hour!* (1957).

Her first horror film was Paul Landres's *Return of Dracula* (1957), a black-and-white film with color sequences, which is sometimes seen on television under the title *Curse of Dracula.* Pat Fielder's screenplay updates the Dracula legend to the fifties and shows him stalking the residents of Southern California. Francis Lederer played Dracula, and others in the cast were Norma Eberhardt, Ray Stricklyn, Jimmie Baird, Greta Granstedt, and John Wengraf.

She next appeared in *I Want to Live!*

(1958), *Hound Dog Man* (1959), and *Inherit the Wind* (1960). Her screaming trademark began with William Castle's *Homicidal* (1961), a variant of *Psycho* (1960), in which a psychotic murderess attempts to gain an inheritance through various transvestite activities. Playing the part of a woman who witnesses the stabbing of her husband, Hope screamed at length, waiting for a signal to stop from Castle. "I kept screaming this wild horrible scream at the top of my lungs, and he just looked and grinned, and I kept screaming and screaming." Others in the cast were Glenn Corbett, Patricia Breslin, Jean Arless, Eugenie Leontovich, Alan Bunce, Richard Rust, and James Westerfield.

After *Parrish* (1961), *Claudelle Inglish* (1961), and *The Children's Hour* (1962), she was cast in Owen Crump's *The Couch* (1962) as a woman running a boardinghouse. Robert Bloch's screenplay concerned a psychotic committing murders in Los Angeles between visits to his shrink. Others in the cast were Grant Williams, Shirley Knight, Onslow Stevens, William Leslie, Anne Helm, and Simon Scott.

319

Although Hope is best known for her TV series roles in *The Rifleman, The Andy Griffith Show*, and *Mayberry R.F.D.*, she was seen throughout the sixties in *Rome Adventure* (1962), *Spencer's Mountain* (1963), *On Man's Way* (1964), *The Hallelujah Trail* (1965), *The Shakiest Gun in the West* (1967), and *The Learning Tree* (1969).

She played Susanna Blush in *The Ghost and Mr. Chicken* (1965), directed by Alan Rafkin for Universal. The comedy told of typesetter Luther Heggs's (Don Knotts) small-town newspaper article about a mansion where murders were committed twenty years earlier. This leads to a follow-up article about Luther's terrifying experiences spending a night in the house, believed to be haunted. A haint there ain't, but when the truth comes out, Luther is hailed as the hero of the day. Others in the cast were Joan Staley, Liam Redmond, Dick Sargent, Skip Homeier, Reta Shaw, Lurene Tuttle, Philip Ober, Harry Hickox, George Chandler, Charles Lane, James Begg, J. Edward McKinley, Eddie Quillan, and Hal Smith.

William Castle had not forgotten Hope's wild screaming in *Homicidal*, and he made her part of the witch coven in his production of *Rosemary's Baby* (1968), directed by Roman Polanski. Hope found the film "fascinating, morbid, and horrible." After *Where Does It Hurt?* (1972) and *Ace Eli and Roger of the Sky* (1972), she appeared with Tommy Smothers and Orson Welles in Brian De Palma's contemporary

Hope Summers in *Rosemary's Baby* observes Roman Castavet (Sidney Blackmer) and Rosemary (Mia Farrow).

fairy tale, *Get to Know Your Rabbit* (1972) the story of a businessman who drops out of his dull life to become a tap-dancing magician and the successful head of the Tap Dancing Magician Corporation. De Palma described the original climax of the film: "I had a much more complex ending. Originally I showed Donald, the dropout, ending up on the Johnny Carson show doing his routine, and talking about how 'fresh' and 'spontaneous' he has become. Gradually, it dawns on him he's being exploited all over again. So he does his magic trick, sawing his rabbit in half, but seems to be *really* sawing it in half by mistake. The audience screams, Johnny loses his cool, and Donald flees. But it *was* only a trick, the rabbit is OK, and at last Donald is free

of everything. Nobody wants him after he saws a rabbit in half on television. This is much better than the studio ending, which simply shows Donald disappearing from his brand-new office for no reason at all." Others in the cast were John Astin, Katharine Ross, Suzanne Zenor, Samantha Jones, Allen Garfield, Charles Lane, Robert Ball, Larry D. Mann, and King Moody. Hope played the part of Mrs. Beeman.

For *Five Card Stud* Hope Summers was requested to travel all the way to Mexico for the filming of one scream and a single line of dialogue. Director Henry Hathaway proclaimed, "We wanted the best screamer from Hollywood, and we got her!"

*Rosemary's Baby* (1968). The coven gather round the still-unsuspecting Rosemary to await the birth of Satan's child. *Left to right*: Charlotte Boerner, Bruno Sidar, Hope Summers, Patricia O'Neal, Robert Osterloh, Ralph Bellamy, Walter Baldwin, John Cassavetes, and (in foreground) Mia Farrow.

# Martine Beswick

Martine Beswick is a sharp contrast to the cooler, fairer-looking movie adventuresses personified by Kim Novak, Janet Leigh, Tippi Hedren, and other golden-tressed screen sirens who arrived during the fifties and sixties. Sultry, tall, and willowy, the raven-haired beauty actually had no intention of embarking on an acting acreer at all.

"I was born in Kingston, Jamaica [in 1941], and had only one ambition as long as I could remember," Martine admitted. "I wanted to grow up and go to live in Britain and have fun! It seems odd, I know, because all the British people I've met have had an ambition to live in Jamaica."

Still in her teens, Martine achieved her goal and left Jamaica, bound for England. "I came to London with my mother and younger sister Laurellie when I had won a beauty contest awarding me a brand new car as first prize. I then sold the car to pay our way. It turned out to be a shrewd investment."

Martine's unusual good looks and outstanding personality soon opened the doors of many London agencies. "At first I just wanted to do a little modeling to earn enough money to live and have fun."

Pretty soon, though, film company executives were discovering her. She made her film debut in 1962 as a barmaid, speaking the line, "Time, gentlemen, please" in Robert Hartford-Davies' *Saturday Night Out.* "Eventually I began getting small parts in films, and it fired my ambition to be an actress. The part of one of the fighting gypsies in the Bond film *From Russia with Love* helped me the most. It led to small parts in lots of films and gave me confidence."

*From Russia with Love* (1963) was the second James Bond film, after *Dr. No* (1962). Like the first in the series, it was directed by Terence Young. Buried in the listing of twenty-five cast members was Beswick, receiving fourteenth billing. She played a character called Zora, and her bit was so outstanding that of the fifteen *From Russia with Love* stills printed in John Brosnan's *James Bond in the Cinema*, a photograph of Beswick's sequence is included. Ian Fleming's *From Russia with Love* was one of John F. Kennedy's favorite books, but exactly what Kennedy thought of Martine Beswick's sizzling performance has never been recorded for posterity.

The death of Bond (Sean Connery) is planned by Blofeld, Rosa Klebb (Lotte Lenya), and Kronsteen (Vladek Sheybal) of SPECTRE. Klebb goes to SPECTRE Island in the Mediterranean, where she picks Donovan Grant (Robert Shaw) to carry out the plan. In Istanbul, Bond meets the British agent Kerim Bey (Pedro Armendariz) and, after Bey's room is blown to bits, they spy on the Russian embassy with a periscope. Fearing another murder attempt, they decide to spend the night at a gypsy camp, where they are entertained—first by a belly dancer and then by a cat-fight between two women. One of the battlers is Martine Beswick and the other is Aliza Gur (portraying Vida). The fight is executed with much shrieking and hair-pulling. John Brosnan, who refers to this sequence as the gypsies' "way of settling a disagreement," compares it with the same scene from the novel: "Even Kingsley Amis, Bond's most prestigious defender, regarded this episode in Fleming's novel as blatantly sadistic. But the film tones down the fight considerably." It develops that the catfight is only a minor prelude to a gun battle between the gypsies and the Bulgars. This shootout, which almost results in Bond's death, is the first of many narrow escapes before Bond floats safely down a Venice canal at the climax.

Highly impressed by Martine's presence in the Bond hit, Saltzman and Broccoli cast her in *Thunderball* (1963)—"because of her sexy and tigerish quality," they claimed. It was this kind of appeal that made her, in the mid-sixties, the only young actress to appear in different roles in more than one Bond production. *Thunderball* is the fifth film in the Bond series. Martine had a larger role and seventh billing in a cast of twenty-one. Once again, Terence Young directed, this time with a budget seven times that of *Dr. No*. SPECTRE plans to ransom the world by hijacking a NATO bomber carrying nuclear bombs. At Shrublands, a health clinic outside London,

Bond (Connery) encounters SPECTRE agent Lippe (Guy Doleman), who tries to kill him. Rescued by Patricia Fearing (Molly Peters), Bond makes sure Lippe is sealed—in a steam cabinet—and heads for London. Lippe follows but is killed by a rocket-firing cyclist, Fiona (Luciana Paluzzi), head of the SPECTRE executive division. Bond then goes to Nassau, where he frees Domino (Claudine Auger), trapped underwater with her foot caught in coral. Helping Bond in Nassau is Paula (Martine Beswick), who is piloting his boat. After rescuing Domino, Bond goes back to his boat and Paula, but engine trouble forces him to return to shore with Domino. That night he sees Domino again at the Cafe Martinique and meets Largo (Adolfo Celi). The next day, Bond and Felix Leiter (Rik Van Nutter) check out Largo's yacht, the *Disco Volante*. That night, Bond, after donning a scuba outfit to investigate the *Disco Volante* underwater, survives a frogman fight. Leaving, he gets a lift from Fiona, and the next day he visits Palmyra, Largo's residence, where he meets the weird Vargas (Philip Locke).

Martine Beswick returns to the film at this point. She waits alone for Bond in his hotel room, hears a knock at the door, opens it—and falls into the clutches of Vargas, Fiona, and Quist, who drug her with chloroform. Leiter informs Bond that Paula is missing, and Bond immediately leaves Domino to head for Palmyra after asking the authorities of the island to cut the power in Largo's area. He finds Paula—but she has taken poison after Vargas has tortured her. So—Beswick's contribution to *Thunderball* is cut short well before the film's spectacular underwater sci-fi scenes, and the script effectively squelched any possibility of her appearing in any future Bond films as this character.

In the Hammer Films/7 Arts co-production, *One Million Years B.C.* (1966), Beswick, portraying Nupondi, was fifth-billed in the cast of John Richardson, Raquel Welch, Percy Herbert, Robert Brown, Jean Wladon, Lisa Thomas, Malya Nappi, William Lyon Brown, Richard James,

The beginning of the end for one of James Bond's fellow agents. Martine Beswick versus The Opposition in *Thunderball*.

A storm-swept confrontation between Martine Beswick and John Richardson in *One Million Years B.C.*

Frank Hayden, Terence Maidment, Micky de Rauch, and Yvonne Horner. *Castle of Frankenstein* commented, "Has all the same basic plot as the 1940 original—and all the drawbacks—but enhanced by use of color, Raquel Welch's bouncy talent, and especially by Ray Harryhausen's animation effects. Original's action and suspense superior compared with Don Chaffey's uneven, often torpid direction." The Michael Carreras screenplay, from a story by Mickell Novak, George Baker, and Joseph Frickert, was based on the previous 1940 film.

Granted that both *B.C.*'s were badly flawed, the vicissitudes they shared were in almost opposite areas: the 1940 original had embellishments indicating an investment of affection sorely lacking in Hammer's version; ironically, Harryhausen's acclaimed animation techniques, while artistically impressive, did hardly anything to mitigate the remake's assembly-line patina.

Though Martine's role in *B.C.* was comparatively short, there are many who share this writer's impression that she displayed better inherent dramatic talent than most of the leads. Hammer also thought so and asked her to star in *Prehistoric Women*. The occasion may have been historical; unfortunately, through no fault of hers, the production results were almost hysterical.

Hammer/7 Arts' quality of publicity concerning Martine's image was about one level above 42nd Street porn flicks, generating the impression that she was most adept cracking a cruel whip over her slaves and victims. In return, she rebutted: "I'm not mean. I'm not even sexy and tigerish ever. I'm afraid I'm quite shy and inhibited."

However, filmic evidence refuting such statements seemed incontrovertible. Martine went on to say: "But I don't mind people saying I have an animal quality. It helped me get the part of Nupondi in another Hammer film, *One Million Years B.C.*, and that led to my starring in *Prehistoric Women*. Michael Carreras produced both pictures, and I was overwhelmed when I was pulled from the sidelines to play Raquel Welch's romantic competition in *One Million*."

Thrilled by the star status she had won in her first major role, but tired and emotionally overcome by this sudden responsibility, she admitted: "It is all very exciting, but I'm really terrified by the whole movie business. I really can't wait to get back to my London flat to be with my sister and mother."

In the ninety-five-minute *Prehistoric Women* (1966), another Hammer/7 Arts co-production, Martine was top-billed, portraying Kari, and presiding over a cast of

Kari (Martine Beswick) in her luxurious, if primitive, boudoir in *Prehistoric Women*.

Kari (Beswick) is furious when her captive, David Marchant (Michael Latimer), refuses to make love to her. *Prehistoric Women* was filmed at the Elstree Studios in Herts, England.

Edina Ronay, Michael Latimer, Stephanie Randall, Carol White, Alexandra Stevenson, Yvonne Horner, Sydney Bromley, Frank Hayden, Robert Raglan, Mary Hignett, Louis Mahoney, Bari Jonson, Danny Daniels, and Steven Berkoff. Michael Carreras produced and directed the Henry Younger screenplay, and Carlo Mantelli scored. Robert Stewart, reviewing in *Castle of Frankenstein* after a film foray on 42nd Street, seemed to find Beswick the picture's only asset: "Martine Beswick gives commanding performance which transcends amusing nonsense about jungle women subjugating men, wretched clichés, trite plot twists, and heavy-handed phallic symbolism. Martine wades through this mess, completely in control and determined to prove she's got more going for her than script and director (a feat often executed in past by Lee Remick)."

In 1974, *Castle of Frankenstein* re-reviewed *Prehistoric Women* in its "Frankenstein TV Movieguide" section: "One of the most incredible Hammer projects ever (from its lackluster 7 Arts days) has the stupendous Martine Beswick as the leader of a bunch of bosomy jungle girls who subjugate men in a lost African kingdom where time has stopped. Plenty of seminude British starlets can't keep Martine from stealing what there is of the pic to steal, coming through as sexy and imperious as ever. Pic

is so unbelievably bad it wasn't released in England until two years after completion in a seventy-four-minute version titled *Slave Girls*." *Prehistoric Women* was the turning point; Beswick's electric qualities transformed what would have been another forgettable motion picture into her own showcase; it is, obviously, *her* film, despite the directorial credit given to Carreras.

In *The Penthouse* (1967), a ninety-seven-minute British production, written and directed by Peter Collinson for producer Harry Fine and executive producers Michael Klinger and Guido Coen, Martine Beswick is fifth-billed as one of three terrorists menacing a young couple. Based on C. Scott Forbes' play, *The Meter Man*, the theme was better served in Stanley Kubrick's later *Clockwork Orange* (1971). Others in the cast were Suzy Kendall, Terence Morgan, Tony Beckley, and Norman Rodway. John Hawksworth furnished the score.

In Roy Ward Baker's ninety-seven-minute *Dr. Jekyll and Sister Hyde* (1971), a Technicolor Hammer Film distributed by EMI and American-International, Beswick co-starred as Sister Hyde. Brian Clemens' screenplay was based on the original Robert Louis Stevenson characters (making it one of the more than fifty films on the Jekyll-Hyde theme). Jekyll (Ralph Bates)

Martine Beswick, Tony Beckley, and Norman Rodway as the three terrorists in Paramount's *The Penthouse* (1967).

Ralph Bates and Martine Beswick as *Dr. Jekyll and Sister Hyde* (1971).

is convinced, after experiments on a fly, that prolongation of life can be induced with a special secret serum consisting of female hormones. His experimental fly has lived several times its normal lifespan, but it has also turned female. After weeks of further reclusive hours in the lab, Bates finally becomes the attractive Sister Hyde, a switch on the traditional hirsute Hyde of previous films. This proved to be a welcome relief to the audience, which knew what was going to happen all along, having entered the theater past posters that read, "Warning! The sexual transformation of a man into a woman will actually take place before your very eyes!" Hyde then sets out to find female victims who can furnish him with the hormones necessary for his research, and the Jekyll-Hyde story becomes interwoven with the Jack the Ripper murders. Since resurrectionists Burke (Ivor Dean) and Hare (Tony Calvin) have been dispatched by a group of angry citizens, Bates forages alone. This goes on quite frequently, but it doesn't suffer from repetition due to adroit direction by Baker and humorous vignettes alleviating the gory stalkings. The highlight of the script's humor is the sexual triptych: the male Jekyll appeals to the young woman next door, and the female Hyde to her brother, but when Jekyll gets his personae mixed up, he makes a pass for the brother! This violation of Victorian manners so stuns the brother that he tells his sis never to see Jekyll again.

Eventually, Hyde becomes the domi-

nant side of the good doctor—who now wants out. But, too late, he's discovered and takes his drag routine to the rooftops. Eaves dropping, he/she falls to his/her death, changing back to the non-snide side of Hyde.

*Variety* critic *Jock* found the film "highly imaginative" and stated, "Ralph Bates and Martine Beswick, strong, attractive personalities, bear a strange resemblance to each other, making the transitions entirely believable. They are admirable." Joining the duo in the cast were Gerald Sim, Lewis Flander, Dorothy Alison, and Neil Wilson.

*Seizure* (1974), written by Edward Mann and Oliver Stone from Stone's story, was filmed in Quebec. Directed by Stone, a twenty-eight-year-old graduate of Yale, it was his debut in directing commercial feature films. Top-billed was Jonathan Frid of *Dark Shadows* fame, and second-billed was Martine Beswick as the Queen of Evil, her best opportunity yet to display her talent for portraying dark dominance. Horror-mystery writer Edmund Blackstone (Frid), who lives in Joliette, Quebec, with his wife (Christina Pickles) and two sons, has a series of disturbing dreams that he decides to develop into story material. Starring in his nightmares is Martine Beswick—with a supporting cast of Henry Baker, as Jackal, The Giant, an executioner with half a face, and Herve Villechaize (later a regular on ABC-TV's *Fantasy Island*), as The Spider, a plump dwarf driven by strange sadistic

impulses. This trio is a living nightmare—
for when Blackstone has some guests over
for the weekend the evil threesome step
into reality to crash the party. The guests
are pseudohip middle-aged millionaire
Charlie (Joe Sirola), his wife Mikki (Mary
Woronov), the cultivated Serge (Roger De
Koven), his wife Eunice (Anne Meacham),
and swinger Troy Donahue. Of this group
of nine, so say the intruders, only one will
survive. Most dangerous games follow, beginning with an opportunity to escape. The
Spider, however, announces, "Only the
young and the fit will survive. The old will
perish at our hands." As the nightmare un-
ravels, there is a duel with knives, an execution with an ax, the hanging of a dog, a
strangulation, a crushed head, and two sui-
cides. Blackstone, finally, is given a choice
—save his own skin by watching his son
burned alive. Choosing to live, Blackstone
screams—and awakens. Was it all a dream?
He stumbles into the bathroom to find a
past-tense farewell from his wife: "I loved
you." He goes back to the bedroom and, to
his horror, the woman in his bed is not his
wife but the Queen of Evil. Blackstone's
unending nightmare has now entered a new
realm—the cyclic maze of Borges.

In opposing critical stances, *Variety*
critic Mack found *Seizure* "a stylish but
overindulgent directing debut for Oliver
Stone" with "half-baked intellectual preten-
sions" and had no words for Beswick other
than to call her "spooky." On the other
hand, Tim Lucas, in the pages of *Cinefantastique*, exulted that "*Seizure* is the most
remarkable horror film to appear since William Friedkin's *The Exorcist*," and commented, "the fact that *Seizure* is, as literally
in its own right as is a film like *Last Year at
Marienbad* (1961), a cinematic exercise,
does not subtract any of its hazy realism. It
instead imposes overwhelming, consuming
mystery over the entire picture. . . . The
horror of *Seizure* is one of severe, curt irra-
tionality; a sense of fear made unrealistic
through the eyes of hysteria." Lucas also
found Beswick's abilities in full flourish:
"Martine Beswick, a very good actress who
is just as wasted as Barbara Steele, is at last
used to good advantage as the Queen of
Evil."

Relocating in California, she began to
do TV work. In 1975 she turned up in the
cast of the ABC Sunday Night Movie
*Strange New World*, directed by Robert
Butler. This 100-minute Robert Larson production for Warner Brothers Television
tells of a trio (John Saxon, Kathleen Miller,
and Keene Curtis) who spend 180 years in
suspended animation, awakening to find
odd new societies on earth—a concept or-
iginated by *Star Trek*'s Gene Roddenberry
in his *Planet Earth* (also with Saxon) and

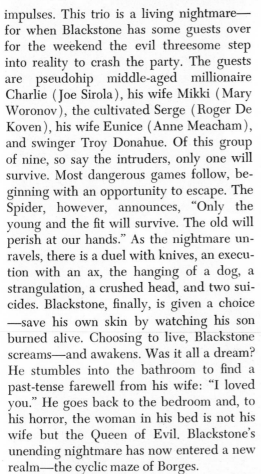

*Genesis II.* Setting forth, the intrepid adventurers enter Eterna, a place about as utopian as it can get. They find a few flaws while touring about, and the high point of the expedition is definitely their encounter with Martine Beswick. The script was by Walon Green, Ronald F. Graham, and Al Ramrus. Others in the cast were James Olson and Gerrit Graham. Her TV credits in recent years have been highlighted by a notable guest appearance on *Baretta.*

Martine Beswick is indeed the Queen of Evil, and her casting as such in *Seizure* only confirmed what fantasy-filmgoers of the sixties knew all along—that the genre had finally found a forceful actress with the rare gift of hypnotizing audiences into submission.

Queen of Evil Beswick holds court from her throne during the terrifying night of death and torture in Cinerama's *Seizure.*

# Stephanie Rothman

**D**irector and screenwriter Stephanie Rothman, who has worked in both horror and science fiction, was the first woman ever awarded a fellowship by the Directors Guild of America. With seven feature films behind her, she stands out as the one American female director dealing with low budgets and genre material in the Roger Corman tradition. With her husband, the writer-producer Charles Swartz, Rothman headed her own production and distribution outfit, Dimension Pictures. Although most of Rothman's films have vanished into the maw of drive-ins and third-run theatres, she deserves attention for her ability to function within the Hollywood system as a working writer-director—concentrating on commercial films with hidden feminist messages rather than the overt feminist stance taken by many women filmmakers. Sharon Smith in *Women Who Make Movies* comments, "While Elaine May is the best-

known woman director of Hollywood features, the distinction of having made the most features belongs to Stephanie Rothman. . . ."

In 1957 Rothman was graduated as a sociology major from Berkeley. From 1960 to 1963 she studied filmmaking at the University of Southern California's Department of Cinema, receiving her Director's Guild fellowship during her last year there. She went immediately into film fantasy as an associate producer on Curtis Harrington's *Queen of Blood*, which plays on television today under the title *Planet of Blood*. Harrington incorporated footage from a Russian science-fiction film, an addition that was a bonus to the slim production values. He explained, "Roger Corman had acquired the rights to some spectacular Russian footage of spaceships. I saw the footage and wrote a screenplay around it. We shot the film in seven and a half days at a cost of $65,000. Pretty fast, considering the Russian footage occupied only 20 percent of the finished film."

*Castle of Frankenstein* #9 carried a brief review by Robert Stewart: "*Queen of Blood* (81 min—AIP—1966). This

ABOVE: Florence Marly as the mysterious space creature who, unbeknownst to her human companions, is a vampire. A scene from *Queen of Blood*. Stephanie Rothman was associate producer on this film.

sf-horror, written and directed by former experimental filmmaker Curtis Harrington, comes as something of a disappointment after Harrington's brilliant Val Lewton-styled *Night Tide*. Vampire (superbly delineated by actress Florence Marly in a beautifully *outré* green makeup) feeds on space crew taking her to Earth. Flavor of illustrator Frank R. Paul is neatly captured in several early scenes, and Forrest J. Ackerman puts in a nice cameo appearance (which isn't as clever as his bit in *Time Travelers*). Near-psychedelic paintings by John Cline give this pic the best opening title credits of any film we've seen in the past few years. John Saxon, Basil Rathbone, Dennis Hopper (who starred in *Night Tide*), Judi Meredith. Color." Joe Dante, Jr., also in the pages of *Castle of Frankenstein*, concurred: "Flat, cheaply made space opera has green alien woman from wrecked spaceship draining blood from Earthling astronauts who rescued her. Director Curtis Harrington is surprisingly disappointing, bringing no discernible style or talent whatever to this assembly-line affair, the only imaginative portions of which are special-effects sequence lifted from a Soviet space movie."

Screenwriter Robert Mundy, in *Cinema*, offered a retrospect review in 1974: "An engaging blend of science-fiction and horror, in which a Martian lady, a queen on her own planet, is rescued from a crash in space by astronauts Hopper and Saxon. Beautifully and wordlessly played by Florence Marly, the queen is literally green, lays eggs in aspic, thrives on human blood, and has iridescent eyes (like the children in *Village of the Damned*). The astronauts take turns in donating their blood to keep her alive as they return to Earth, but the queen gets greedy. Harrington inventively integrates the Soviet footage, cutting from a long-shot of a Russian scientist making a speech to a closeup of Basil Rathbone. Hardly imperceptible, but more than one would expect from such intractable resources. The script has touches of humor: one of the astronauts remarks that the queen can't be expected to conform to

human standards of behavior, and, after all, there's not much difference between drinking blood and eating a rare beefsteak. Clearly the work of a vegetarian." Vilis Lapeniks handled the Pathecolor cinematography, and the film was scored by Leonard Morand. Also in the cast were Robert Boon, Don Eitner, Virgil Frye, Robert Porter, and Terry Lee.

Rothman was also involved in another splice job as associate producer with Curtis Harrington on *Voyage to the Prehistoric Planet* (1966), almost 90 percent of which was composed of footage from the Soviet science-fiction film *Planeta Bura* (1962). The original film told of an expedition to Venus finding prehistoric life and the remains of a once-great civilization there but no surviving intelligent beings. In the final shots the spaceship leaves as the camera focuses on the reflection in a pool of the Venusian they never encountered. Directed by Pavel Klushantsev, the original cast members were Kyunna Ignatova, Gennadi Vernov, Vladimir Yemelianov, Georgi Zhonov, and Yurie Sarantsev. With an added cast of Basil Rathbone, Faith Domergue, Marc Shannon, Christopher Brand, John Bix, Lewis Keane, and Robert Chanta, Harrington's new storyline had the explorers stranded on the planet while maintaining contact with a female crew member in orbit up above. Although the Russian film had become pretty familiar by the middle of the decade, there was still more to come —Peter Bogdanovich's *Voyage to the Planet of the Prehistoric Women* (1968) with Mamie Van Doren, Mary Mark, and Paige Lee in a revamp in which the spacemen are threatened by the telepathic abilities of the planet's women inhabitants.

Rothman would prefer to forget she ever had anything to do with *Blood Bath* (1966), her directorial debut. She came into the project when Corman fired Jack Hill (who later went on to direct the 1973 *Coffy* and the 1974 *Foxy Brown*). There's also footage in *Blood Bath* from an earlier source—in this case, half an hour from a Yugoslavian vampire film. Robert Stewart's capsule review in the November 1966 *Cas-*

Florence Marly's other horror film credit is the featured role of Tana in Eddie Saeta's *Doctor Death: Seeker of Souls* (1972). Here, Tana and Fred (Barry Coe) lift a toast to a time when the dead will be brought back to life.

A masquerader selects his next victim in this scene from Stephanie Rothman's first directorial assignment, AIP's *Blood Bath* (1966).

*tle of Frankenstein* stated, "Mediocre beatnik-vampire tale features, oddly, occasional flashes of Bava-like brilliance—but good moments are few and far between due mainly to hackneyed script by Jack Hill and Stephanie Rothman, who also co-directed. Vampire-artist murders his models (an idea already overdone in sexploitation films) while carrying on a fairly normal relationship with another girl (an idea executed with skill in *Peeping Tom* and *The Cat People*). William Campbell, Linda Saunders, Marissa Mathes, Sandra Knight."

The film deserves comparison with Corman's satirical classic *Bucket of Blood* (1959), set in Venice, California, with an artist unable to gain favor with his beatnik friends until he hits on the idea of encasing living animals and humans inside his sculpture. Similarly, in the original Hill footage for *Blood Bath*, the insane painter (Campbell) is also seen in opposition with the beatniks of Venice and also needs beautiful women as an ingredient to produce his portraits. To link Hill's beatniks with the Yugoslavian vampire (on the face of it, a curious

and difficult task), Rothman added a new character, portrayed by Sandra Knight, and shot a final chase sequence in Venice. Terry Curtis Fox, in *Film Comment*, noted, "Despite her wish to disown the film, Rothman's sequences do show a remarkable feeling for atmosphere and architecture. Faced with an incongruent picture, Rothman increased the sense of displacement. There is one marvelous shot in which the camera pans down an ancient-looking building to a parked car in which the vampire is destroying a victim: passers-by assume that the couple in the car are making love. Both time and action are pulled out of joint: at the same time that Rothman makes a comic point about street perceptions, she expresses the horrific atemporal nature of a vampire's existence. *Blood Bath* is sometimes seen on television under the title *Track of the Vampire*.

Rothman's first feature in which she had sole director credit, the eighty-six-minute *It's a Bikini World* (1966), shot in 35mm Colorscope for Trans-American Films, is also her only film in scope. Rothman did away with the typical passive girls of beach pictures by having Deborah Walley's character challenge Tommy Kirk's male ego in athletic competition. Since most of the bikini-and-music films were created to exploit a youth market, Rothman satirized this by introducing a character called "Daddy," a manufacturer of products aimed at exploiting the youth market. "I became very depressed after making *It's a Bikini World*," said Rothman. "I had very ambivalent feelings about continuing to be a director if that was all I was going to be able to do. So I literally went into a kind of retirement for several years until more than anything in the world, I wanted to make films."

She then resurfaced with *The Student Nurses* (1970), which Verina Glaessner in a 1974 issue of *Monthly Film Bulletin* called "probably her best-known feature." The Rothman-Swartz story, produced by Swartz for Roger Corman's New World Pictures, followed the individual paths taken by four different nurses as they embark on diverging lifestyles. One, a political activist, shoots a policeman. Swartz stated, "When we saw the film with a very middle-class audience in the San Fernando Valley, there was a gasp of tragedy that this had gone so far. They seemed to be taken with the reality of this particular killing much more than they would be in a film in which the killing was more common."

In *The Velvet Vampire* (1971) Rothman performed a switch on the usual vampire clichés by centering the film around a sympathetic vampire, Diane (Celeste Yarnall), who defends herself in the opening scene against a biker brandishing a knife. By mounting the camera on a scaffolding outside a cathedral, Rothman succeeded in getting an unusual dissolve from day to night for the beginning shot. The day portion shows a zoom down to Wilshire Boulevard. Despite winds of forty miles an hour, Rothman returned to the scaffolding at night, and, with the camera still locked in position, completed the shot.

At the opening of an art gallery, the vampire Diane seeks out her victims, Susan Ritter (Sherry Miles) and Lee Ritter (Michael Blodgett), who are introduced to Diane by the art gallery owner (Gene Shane). Also present at the art gallery is bluesman Johnny Shines. Rothman explained, "The writer who worked with us, Maurice Jules, felt that it would be quite surreal if people were looking not only at pieces of sculpture but also at a live musician who was there and treated as another object. Everything in the picture is very American, and what is more indigenously American than a blues singer—not one whose style has been modified in order to make it acceptable for some pop record market, but rather somebody who was a purist."

Diane invites Susan and Lee to spend the weekend at her home in the Mojave Desert, where she serves the couple steak tartare. Meanwhile, Diane feasts on raw hearts and liver. Later in bed, the couple hears a scream. Diane has claimed a victim —a garage mechanic whom she called to repair her dune buggy. In the next twenty-four hours she satisfies her thirst for blood with both her Indian servant and the mechanic's girlfriend. Lee wants to leave, but Susan, having seen Lee and Diane making love, is fascinated with the idea of being with Diane herself. Susan and Lee have erotic dreams that give them a prophetic glimpse of their eventual fate in Diane's house. Lee dies as a result of the delay in leaving. At the film's climax, Diane's vampiric charms prove no match in an encounter with a freaky California cult gang. Susan is consoled by gallery owner Shane. Terry Curtis Fox calls *The Velvet Vampire* a "horror film of manners" and opines that while it "does not have quite the thematic and narrative complexity of *The Student Nurses*, its stylistic and directorial authority mark the movie as Rothman's first complete success." *Boxoffice* magazine noted that "strict vampire lore is not adhered to since Miss Yarnall spends quite a bit of time in the sun (always protected by a large black hat) and, instead of winging her way around the sandy slopes, she travels by dune buggy." Also in 1971, Rothman wrote but did not direct *Sweet Sugar*.

Dimension Pictures was then formed

by Rothman, Swartz, and Larry Wollman (who had been the sales manager at Corman's New World). In 1972, Dimension released *Group Marriage*, directed by Rothman and written by her with Swartz and Richard Walter. The film is a comedy with the *ménage-à-quatre* getting involved in a test case after their togetherness lifestyle is reported on a newscast—leading to an outraged establishment reaction. Heading the cast is the voluptuous Victoria Vetri, veteran of several Hammer Film fantasies, and Rothman manages to use this to her own advantage—showing Vetri in a satiric reference to Hammer. Throughout there is light satire on traditional male-female societal roles and, as Verina Glaessner puts it, "the conscious deflation of stereotypes." Rothman explained, "I'm very tired of the whole tradition in Western art in which women are always presented nude and men aren't. I'm not going to dress women and undress men—that would be a form of tortured vengeance. But I certainly am going to undress men, and the result is probably a more healthy environment, because one group of people presenting another in a vulnerable, weaker, more servile position is always distorted."

Another Dimension Pictures release of 1972 was the fantasy *Beyond Atlantis*, written by Rothman but directed by Eddie Romero, who also directed the women's prison drama *Black Mama, White Mama* that same year. As if this were her cue, Rothman set out to make her own tough prison action movie, *Terminal Island* (1973), which she wrote in collaboration with Swartz and Jim Barnett. With its ideas on prison reform and future utopian societies, it has a sociological science-fiction aspect (but no connection with J. G. Ballard's surreal *Terminal Beach*). A TV program prologue tells of Terminal Island, a penal colony, without guards, located off the coast of California, where convicted murderers, male and female, are permanently exiled. Carmen Sims (Ena Hartmann) arrives at Terminal Island, discovering it is ruled by the psychotic Bobby Farr (Sean David Kenney) and his cohort

William Campbell in the process of disposing of another of his *Blood Bath* victims.

Trapped with one of the vampire-artist's corpses in *Blood Bath*.

Sherry Miles, Michael Blodgett, and Celeste Yarnall in *The Velvet Vampire*: a poisonous snake bite provides Diane (Yarnall) the perfect opportunity to display more of her mysterious powers.

Monk. Carmen finds that Joy Land (Phyllis Davis), Lee Phillips (Marta Kristen), and mute Bunny Campbell (Barbara Leigh) are slaves to the males of Terminal Island. But A. J. Thomas (Don Marshall), and Cornell (Ford Clay) believe in equality, and a rebel group is formed, led by Carmen. The rebels launch several attacks, finally winning out, with Bobby getting killed in the process. Bunny regains her speech. The film ends with another new prisoner arriving—only this time to a peaceful community. Things are so rosy that the mercy killer, Dr. Milford (Tom Selleck), turns down an opportunity to

leave the island for a retrial. A new society has been formed.

During the location filming, lead actress Hartmann pulled a tendon that resulted in the rewriting of certain sections of the script minus the all-important unifying character of Carmen. In addition, Rothman seemed uncomfortable with a plotline in which the depiction of violence was required, stating, "I do not like to think that I may be showing people how to perform violent acts, or suggesting that one can perform them without creating serious and often tragic consequences for oneself, and yet I've just made a violent film."

*The Working Girls* (1974) is ironically titled, since the story actually concerns unemployed women exploring the options open to them for survival. Filmed on a low budget, it was Rothman's last film for Dimension Pictures. She and Swartz then took to writing scripts (the 1978 *Starhops*), and the Dimension company was dissolved. This turn of affairs prompted Terry Curtis Fox to write, "The most bitter irony of Stephanie Rothman's career is that the one woman filmmaker of the seventies with a consistent and solid body of work—a body of work that expresses the possibilities of American society—seems to have a better future as a cause than as a director." However, there have been some directing offers that Rothman has turned down and some projects under way that need money to set a starting date. One can only hope that Rothman might someday choose to bring to the screen some project such as Philip Wylie's *The Disappearance* (long on George Pal's production schedule), which recounts the problems faced by women in running the world after all men vanish. Nor should *Picnic on Paradise* and *The Female Man* by Joanna Russ be overlooked. But whatever the choice of material, as interest in Rothman's films increases, chances are strong that she will be back on the set in the near future.

# Bibliography

Aaronson, Charles S. *1961 International Motion Picture Almanac*. New York: Quigley Publications, 1960.

Abel, Bob. "Roberta Findlay: She's No Angel." *Film International* (May 1975).

Ackerman, Forrest J., and Sutton, Tom. "Vampirella of Drakulon." *Vampirella* (September 1969).

Adler, Renata. *A Year in the Dark*. New York: Berkley, 1971.

Agan, Patrick. *Is That Who I Think It Is?* Vol. 1. New York: Ace, 1975.

———. *Is That Who I Think It Is?* Vol. 3. New York: Ace, 1976.

Aldiss, Brian W. *Billion Year Spree*. New York: Schocken Books, 1974.

Amory, Cleveland, ed. *International Celebrity Register*. New York: Celebrity Register Ltd., 1959.

Balshofer, Fred J., and Miller, Arthur C. *One Reel a Week*. Berkeley and Los Angeles: University of California Press, 1967.

Bartholomew, David. "The Poseidon Adventure." *Cinefantastique* (Winter 1976).

———. "The Tenant." *Cinefantastique* (Fall 1976).

———. "Who Ever Slew Auntie Roo?" *Cinefantastique* (Winter 1973).

Bast, William. *James Dean*. New York: Ballantine, 1956.

Baxter, John. *Hollywood in the Thirties*. New York: Paperback Library, 1970.

———. *Science Fiction in the Cinema*. New York: Paperback Library, 1970.

Beale, Kenneth. "Black Sunday." *Castle of Frankenstein*, no. 4 (May 1964).

———. "Freaks." *Castle of Frankenstein*, no. 4 (May 1964).

———. "Freak and Other Mutations." *Castle of Frankenstein*, no. 24 (Fall 1974).

———. "Karloff." *Journal of Frankenstein* (Summer 1959).

Beck, Calvin Thomas. "Dr. Jekyll and Sister Hyde." *Castle of Frankenstein*, no. 19 (January 1973).

———. "Frankenstein TV Movieguide." *Castle of Frankenstein*, no. 21 (Spring 1974).

———. *Heroes of the Horrors*. New York: Macmillan, 1975.

———. "Psyche It to Me!" *Castle of Frankenstein*, no. 15 (Summer 1970).

———. "The Pit and the Pendulum." *Castle of Frankenstein*, no. 1 (February 1961).

———. "Vampira." *Castle of Frankenstein* (Spring 1974).

Behlmer, Rudy, ed. *Memo from David O. Selznick*. New York: Avon, 1973.

Belton, John. *The Hollywood Professionals*. Vol. 3. London: Tantivy Press, 1974.

Benét, William Rose. *The Reader's Encyclopedia*. New York: Thomas Y. Crowell, 1965.

Benson, Eric. "Black Sunday." *Castle of Frankenstein*, no. 9 (November 1966).

Benson, John. "Movie Reviews." *Castle of Frankenstein*, no. 5 (Fall 1964).

Berle, Milton, with Frankel, Haskel. *Milton Berle*. New York: Dell, 1975.

Best, Marc. *Those Enduring Young Charms*. South Brunswick, N.J. and New York: A. S. Barnes, 1971.

Betancourt, Jeanne. *Women in Focus*. Dayton, O.: Pflaum/Standard, 1974.

Bridgewater, William, and Sherwood, Elizabeth J., eds. *The Columbia Encyclopedia*. 2d ed. New York: Columbia University Press, 1952.

Brosnan, John. *James Bond in the Cinema*. London: Tantivy Press, 1972.

———. *Movie Magic*. New York: St. Martin's Press, 1974.

Brown, Barry. *Interview with Bruno VeSota*. Unpublished, 1975.

Butler, Ivan. *Horror in the Cinema*. New York: Paperback Library, 1971.

Buxton, Frank, and Owen, Bill. *The Big Broadcast*. New York: Viking, 1972.

Caen, Michel. "Barbara et l'Exégèse." *Midi-Minuit Fantastique* (June 1967).

———. "Entretien avec Barbara Steele." *Midi-Minuit Fantastique* (May 1965).

335

———. "Un Million d'Années Avant Jesus Christ." *Midi-Minuit Fantastique* (June 1967).

Cameron, Ian and Elisabeth. *Dames.* New York: Praeger, 1967.

Canby, Vincent. "M is for the Mothers That She Gave Us." *New York Times* (July 7, 1968).

Capra, Frank. *The Name Above the Title.* New York: Bantam, 1972.

Chierichetti, David. "Hope Summers," in Leonard Maltin, ed. *The Real Stars.* New York: Curtis Books, 1973.

"Cineguide." *Midi-Minuit Fantastique* (December 1967/January 1968).

Clarens, Carlos. *An Illustrated History of the Horror Film.* New York: G. P. Putnam's, 1967.

Curtiss, Thomas Quinn. *Von Stroheim.* New York: Farrar, Strauss and Giroux, 1971.

D. W. "Junge Torless, Der." *Monthly Film Bulletin* (July 1968).

Dalton, David. *James Dean, the Mutant King.* San Francisco: Straight Arrow, 1974.

Dante, Joe. "Frankenstein TV Movieguide." *Castle of Frankenstein,* no. 22 (Summer 1974).

Davidson, Bill. "To Find Shelley Winters, Even at Several Hundred Paces, You Don't Need Radar." *TV Guide* (January 6, 1973).

Durgnat, Raymond. *Films and Feelings.* Cambridge, Mass.: MIT Press, 1971.

"Elegant Macabre, The." *Cinema* (February/March 1964).

Ellis, Royston. *Rebel.* London: Consul Books, 1962.

Ellison, Harlan. "3 Faces of Fear." *Cinema* (March 1966).

Everson, William K. *The Bad Guys.* Secaucus, N.J.: Citadel, 1974.

Fernett, Gene. *Hollywood's Poverty Row.* Satellite Beach, Fla.: Coral Reef Publications, 1973.

Finley, Charles. "The Girl Next Door." *Movie Classics* (October 1973).

Fliegelman, Avra, ed. *Serials, Series & Packages.* New York: Broadcast Information Bureau, 1972.

———. *TV Feature Film Source Book.*

New York: Broadcast Information Bureau, 1967.

Fox, Marion, and Dante, Joe. "Theatre of Blood." *Castle of Frankenstein* (Summer 1973).

Fox, Terry Curtis. "Fully Female." *Film Comment.* (November/December, 1976).

"Ghost and Mr. Chicken, The." *Monthly Film Bulletin* (June 1966).

Goodwin, Michael. "Caged Heat." *Take One* (March 1975).

Goodwin, Nat C. *Nat Goodwin's Book.* Boston: Gorham Press, 1914.

Gottesman, Ronald, ed. *Focus on Citizen Kane,* Englewood Cliffs, N.J.: Prentice-Hall, 1971.

Gow, Gordon. *Suspense in the Cinema.* New York: Paperback Library, 1971.

Guy, Rory. "Horror, the Browning Version." *Cinema* (June/July 1962).

Halliwell, Leslie. *The Filmgoer's Companion.* 3d ed. New York: Avon, 1970.

Helpern, David. "At Sea with Steven Spielberg." *Take One* (June 1975).

Hennessee, Judith Adler. "The Dirty Little Open Secret of Book Publishing." *More* (December 1976).

Herman, Hal. *How I Broke into the Movies,* 1931.

Herndon, Venable. *James Dean, a Short Life.* New York: Doubleday, 1974.

Higham, Charles. "My Films Come Out of My Nightmares." *New York Times* (October 28, 1973).

———. "Robert Aldrich." *Action* (November/December 1964).

———, and Greenberg, Joel. *Hollywood in the Forties.* New York: Paperback Library, 1970.

Jerome, Robert L. "Short Notices." *Cinefantastique* (Spring 1972).

Jock. "Dr. Jekyll & Sister Hyde." *Variety* (October 27, 1971).

"John Warner Weds Elizabeth Taylor." *New York Times* (December 5, 1976).

Kael, Pauline. *Going Steady.* New York: Bantam, 1971.

———. *The Citizen Kane Book.* Boston: Little, Brown, 1971.

Knight, Arthur. *The Liveliest Art.* New

York: Macmillan, 1959.

Knight, Chris. "Vampira." *Cinefantastique* (Spring 1974).

Kyle, David. *A Pictorial History of Science Fiction*. New York and London: Hamlyn, 1976.

Lacassin, Francis. "Out of Oblivion: Alice Guy Blaché." *Sight and Sound* (Summer 1971).

Lake, Veronica. *Veronica*. New York: Bantam, 1972.

Lambert, Virginia. "Shelley Blossoms in 'Marigolds' Role." *Bergen Record* (1973).

———. "Shelley the Star." *Bergen Record* (April 12, 1973).

Lamparski, Richard. *Lamparski's Whatever Became Of . . . ?* New York: Bantam, 1976.

———. *Whatever Became Of . . . ?* New York: Crown, 1967.

———. *Whatever Became Of . . . ?* Vols. 2, 3. New York: Ace, 1970, 1971.

———. *Whatever Became Of . . . ?* 4th & 5th series. New York: Bantam, 1975, 1976.

Larue, Kalton C. *Continued Next Week*. Norman: University of Oklahoma Press, 1964.

———. *Ladies in Distress*. Cranbury, N.J.: A. S. Barnes and Co., 1971.

Leab, Daniel J. *From Sambo to Superspade*. Boston: Houghton Mifflin, 1975.

Lee, Walt. *Reference Guide to Fantastic Films*. Vols. 1, 2, 3. Los Angeles: Chelsea-Lee Books, 1973.

Lucas, Tim. "Seizure." *Cinefantastique* (Summer 1975).

McBride, Joseph. *Orson Welles*. New York: Viking, 1972.

McCarthy, Todd, and Flynn, Charles, eds. *Kings of the Bs*. New York: E. P. Dutton, 1975.

Mack. "Seizure." *Variety* (November 20, 1974).

Maltin, Leonard. *The Disney Films*. New York: Bonanza, 1973.

———. "The Hildegarde Withers Mysteries." *Film Fan Monthly* (July/August 1974).

———, ed. *The Real Stars*. New York: Curtis, 1973.

Mamber, Steve. "The Television Films of Alfred Hitchcock." *Cinema* (Fall 1971).

Martinetti, Ronald. *The James Dean Story*. New York: Pinnacle Books, 1975.

Michael, Paul, ed. *The American Movies Reference Book*. Englewood Cliffs, N.J.: Prentice-Hall, 1969.

Millar, Sylvia. "Blume in Love." *Monthly Film Bulletin* (May 1974).

Milne, Tom. "Le Locataire." *Monthly Film Bulletin* (September 1976).

———. "Maschera del Demonio, La." *Monthly Film Bulletin* (July 1968).

———. "Retrospective." *Monthly Film Bulletin* (November 1976).

Mosk. "Le Locataire." *Variety* (June 2, 1976).

*Motion Picture, 1894–1969*. Washington, D.C.: Library of Congress, 1951, 1953, 1960, 1971.

Mundy, Robert. "Curtis Harrington." *Cinema*, no. 34. (1974).

Murf. "Next Stop, Greenwich Village." *Variety* (February 4, 1976).

———. "What's the Matter with Helen?" *Variety* (June 9, 1971).

"News." *Cinema* (November/December 1963).

"News." *Cinema* (August 1965).

*New York Times Directory of the Film, The*. New York: Arno Press/Random House, 1971.

Norton, Haywood P. "Birth of Frankenstein." *Castle of Frankenstein*, no. 3 (Summer 1963).

O'Leary, Liam. *The Silent Cinema*. London: Studio Vista, 1965.

Parish, James Robert. *Actors' Television Credits—1950–1972*. Metuchen, N.J.: Scarecrow Press, 1973.

———. *The Fox Girls*. New Rochelle, N.Y.: Arlington, 1971.

Pirie, David. "Theatre of Blood." *Monthly Film Bulletin* (June 1973).

Pratt, George C. *Spellbound in Darkness*. Greenwich, Conn.: New York Graphic Society, 1973.

Probst, Leonard. *Off Camera*. New York: Stein and Day, 1975.

"Qui Etes-Vous Barbara Steele?" *Midi-Minuit Fantastique* (June 1967).

Robinson, David. *Hollywood in the Twenties*. New York: Paperback Library, 1970.

Romer, Jean-Claude. "Biographie." *Midi-Minuit Fantastique* (June 1967).

———. "Filmographie." *Midi-Minuit Fantastique* (June 1967).

Rosen, Marjorie. *Popcorn Venus*. New York: Coward, McCann and Geohegan, 1973.

Roud, Richard. *Max Ophuls, an Index*. London: British Film Institute, 1958.

Scapperotti, Dan. "Short Notices." *Cinefantastique* (Spring 1976).

Scheuer, Steven H., ed. *TV Key Movie Guide*. New York: Bantam, 1966.

Shearer, Lloyd. "Shelley Winters at 50." *Parade* (June 11, 1972).

Shipman, David. *The Great Movie Stars*. New York: Crown, 1970.

Silke, James R. "Hollywood . . . Still an Empty Tomb." *Cinema*. Vol. 1, no. 3 (1962).

Smith, John M., and Cawkwell, Tim. *The World Encyclopedia of the Film*. New York: World, 1972.

Smith, Sharon. *Women Who Make Movies*. New York: Hopkinson and Blake, 1975.

"Sorella di Satana, La." *Monthly Film Bulletin* (July 1966).

Stein, Elliott. "Journals." *Film Comment* (November/December, 1976).

Stewart, Robert. "Frankenstein TV Movieguide." *Castle of Frankenstein*, no. 7 (Summer 1965).

———. "Frankenstein TV Movieguide." *Castle of Frankenstein*, no. 8 (Spring 1966).

———. "Frankenstein TV Movieguide." *Castle of Frankenstein*, no. 9 (November 1966).

———. "Frankenstein Mini-Reviews." *Castle of Frankenstein*, no. 12 (Summer 1968).

Stine, Whitney. *Mother Goddam*. New York: Hawthorn, 1974.

Strick, Philip. *Science Fiction Movies*. London: Octopus Books, 1976.

Thomas, Bob. *King Cohn*. New York: Bantam, 1968.

———. *Selznick*. New York: Pocket Book, 1972.

———. *Thalberg*. New York: Bantam, 1970.

Thomas, D. B. *The Origins of the Motion Pictures*. London: Her Majesty's Stationery Office, 1964.

Thomson, David. *A Biographical Dictionary of Film*. New York: William Morrow, 1976.

Valenti, Michael. "Look, It's Fay! And Kong's Got Her Again!" *Nostalgia Illustrated* (July 1975).

Von Stroheim special issue. *Film Culture*. (April 1958).

Weaver, J. *Forty Years of Screen Credits*. Metuchen, N.J.: Scarecrow Press, 1970.

Weiss, Ken, and Goodgold, Ed. *To Be Continued. . . .* New York: Crown, 1972.

Wenden, D. J. *The Birth of the Movies*. New York: E. P. Dutton, 1975.

"What Ever Happened to Baby Jane?" *Cinema*. Vol. 1, no. 3 (1962).

Whit. "The Poseidon Adventure." *Variety* (December 13, 1972).

———. "Who Slew Auntie Roo?" *Variety* (December 22, 1972).

Winogura, Dale. "Harrington." *Cinefantastique* (Fall 1974).

Winters, Shelley. "I Wish They'd Lose the Negative!" *Cinema* (June/July 1962).

———. Studio Biography, American International Pictures.

Woodmansee, H. A. *How "Wicked" Is Hollywood?* Girard, Kan.: Haldeman-Julius Publications, N.d., but probably published in mid-thirties.

Zierold, Norman. *The Moguls*. New York: Avon, 1972.

# Index

340

## About the Contributors

CALVIN BECK is the author of *Heroes of the Horrors*, a companion volume to *Scream Queens*, and the editor of *The Frankenstein Reader*, a collection of Gothic horror tales. From 1959 to 1975 he edited and published *Castle of Frankenstein*, a film magazine devoted to all aspects of fantasy and science fiction. His late night talk show, "Radio Odyssey," was aired in the early seventies to listeners in the New York area.

ROBERT (BHOB) STEWART is the author of *Henry, Jane and Peter*, a biography of the Fonda family, and the editor of *EC Horror Comics of the 1950's*. His film criticism and articles have appeared in *TV Guide, Nostalgia Illustrated, International Times, Fantastic Films, Cinefantastique*, and Boston's *Real Paper*. He currently edits *Ophemera*, a popular arts journal.

BARRY BROWN contributed several outstanding articles to *Castle of Frankenstein*. As an actor, he received critical attention for his lead roles in Robert Benton's *Bad Company* (1972) and Peter Bogdanovich's *Daisy Miller* (1974). He died on June 25, 1978, at the age of twenty-seven, as this book was in its final stages of production.